Internet Audio
Sourcebook

Lee Purcell
Jordan Hemphill

WILEY COMPUTER PUBLISHING

John Wiley & Sons, Inc.
New York • Chichester • Weinheim • Brisbane • Singapore • Toronto

Publisher: Robert Ipsen
Editor: Robert Elliott
Managing Editor: Micheline Frederick
Electronic Products, Associate Editor: Mike Green
Text Design & Composition: Benchmark Productions

Designations used by companies to distinguish their products are often claimed as trademarks. In all instances where John Wiley & Sons, Inc., is aware of a claim, the product names appear in initial capital or ALL CAPITAL LETTERS. Readers, however, should contract the appropriate companies for more complete information regarding trademarks and registration.

This text is printed on acid-free paper.

This publication is designed to provide accurate and authoritative information in regard to the subject matter covered. It is sold with the understanding that the publisher is not engaged in rendering legal, accounting, or other professional service. If legal advice or other expert assistance is required, the services of a competent professional person should be sought.

Library of Congress Cataloging-in-Publication Data:
ISBN: 0471–19150–7

Printed in the United States of America

10 9 8 7 6 5 4 3 2 1

Dedication

To Vagelia, who brought her own music into the world.

Contents

Chapter 5: More HTML Audio Techniques

Introduction

We hear long before we can see. From the womb, embryonic ears hear and respond to sounds—voices and music and car horns and barking dogs. Sound is a deep and fundamental part of our existence, even before birth, and the influence of sound is pervasive and inescapable. The effect of sound on human emotions is primal in its intensity; you can use it to shock, soothe, awaken, stimulate, frighten, or mesmerize a listener. Through vocal patterns and cadences, through sound effects in film and video, through the powerful emotions generated by music; music composers, politicians, advertisers, educators, newscasters, and religious leaders all learn to master the subtle nuances and effects of sound on an audience. Sound communicates to us on many levels.

We've learned how to capture approximations of the sound waves that we hear in nature, first in scratchy reproductions on wax cylinders, later on shellac and then vinyl records, and most recently on compact discs using vastly superior optical storage techniques. Techniques for storing sound as digital audio have brought the computer into the sound studio and made it easy to manipulate and transfer audio material. Digital audio has created a renaissance in sound processing and delivery and the benefits of this technology are inexpensively available not only to well-heeled studio moguls, but to anyone who can afford a computer.

What Does This Book Cover?

This is a book about digital audio and different ways to move it about the Internet. Through techniques available to you using the tools discussed in this book, you can present digital audio in a variety of formats over the Internet. You can provide compressed audio files in MPEG, Shockwave, or QuickTime formats for downloading and playback. You can provide streaming audio to worldwide audiences—the Internet equivalent to real-time radio broadcasting. You can use telephony techniques to converse long distance over the Internet—at local phone rates. Businesses can use the same telephony techniques, in a form following the model of some groupware applications, to conduct teleconferences around the world. You can very simply enhance a Web site with music and sound effects, using a combination of MIDI playback, JavaScript, and Java. You can use the built-in sound support features in Netscape Navigator and Internet Explorer to add the dimension of sound to even simple Web presentations. If you get tired of reading text on screen, you can activate a text-to-speech plug-in and have the words read to you in a clearly intelligible (though obviously mechanical) voice. You can compose musical works interactively with other musicians using the Internet as the communication medium. All of these kinds of applications have been elevated from peripheral roles in Internet communication to mainstream, fundamental methods of communication. The World Wide Web has sprouted vocal cords, gained a voice, and begun to *sing*.

If you have developed any kind of Web material for Internet distribution, you know of the omnipresent issues associated with the limited bandwidth of the Net. Simple text and hyperlinks can be navigated at respectable speeds, but large files composed of graphics or video or sound inevitably slow things down. While everyone craves multimedia content, few want to spend the time waiting for that content to download over 28.8K or 33.6K modems. Delivering audio material over the Internet presents challenges similar to those for presenting graphics, animation, Java applets, video, or other data-intensive content. And, as with these other forms of multimedia, the goal is similar: You try to compress the information as much as possible while minimizing the loss of fidelity. This can be a challenge and we've spent a good deal of time and energy exploring the tradeoffs and different approaches for dealing with this problem.

If you want to make your Web pages talk or sing or reverberate with orchestral brilliance, this book will explain how to do it. It's easier than you might suspect and a satisfying way to communicate beyond the silent world of text and images.

How Is the Book Organized?

This book contains three main parts plus a set of appendices.

- **Part One: Creating, Processing, and Storing Audio**
  Presents the basic principles of audio recording, particularly as they apply to the digital audio world. Also provides a discussion of the different methods of working with digital audio, explaining how to use the available computer-based tools to shape audio content for the Internet.

- **Part Two: Presenting Audio on the Internet**
  Covers the fundamental techniques used to deliver audio content on the World

Wide Web, including the basic HTML coding used to access different types of audio files. Also explains the techniques for integrating Java applets, JavaScript code, and VBScript code into your HTML documents for presenting audio content.

- **Part Three: Pushing the Envelope**
  Covers a number of emerging technologies, including streaming audio, MIDI applications on the Web, voice synthesis and recognition, and Internet telephony. Part Three concludes with a discussion of push technologies as they apply to audio and the future impact of this new method for distributing information on the Internet.

- **Appendices**
  Provides reference material for your use, including a summary of HTML 3.2 with a primer for beginning coders, a resource appendix for exploring audio-related sites on the Web, and a full glossary of terms specific to both audio and Internet technologies.

Webmaster, Musician, or Newbie?

Given the broad appeal of audio content on the Internet, we can't be sure of the precise background of our audience or its level of knowledge. Nonetheless, we're assuming that our readers will fall into some general categories and we've tried to provide specific material for each of these groups.

For Webmasters

We suspect there will be a fair number of experienced Webmasters who know the tools and techniques for developing HTML documents, but who may have never stepped foot in a recording studio. While the jargon of the Web may have been fully assimilated to the point where it's a second language, the unique terminology of audio technology with its own vocabulary—terms such as decibels, impedance, frequency modulation, and quantization values—will take some getting used to. Chapter 2, *Compact Sound for the Web: MIDI* and Chapter 3, *The Digital Sound Studio* should be helpful in introducing the fundamentals of creating and processing digital audio.

For Musicians and Audio Enthusiasts

Likewise, for musicians and audio enthusiasts who feel that the Web offers a new dynamic medium for reaching and attracting listeners, the language of the sound studio may ring familiar, but the terms that are second nature to Webmasters may sound like the gibbering of confused chimpanzees. The fundamental techniques for embedding audio files in HTML documents as described in Chapter 4, *Basic HTML Audio Techniques*, should be useful for becoming familiar with the essential concepts in this area. Appendix A, *HTML 3.2 Primer*, serves as a simple introduction to the most recently standardized version of HTML.

For Newbies

The pathway may be steep for Newbies, who are attracted to the idea of using the audio possibilities offered by the Web to reach an audience, but who may not have done any HTML coding or audio recording. Wherever possible, we've tried to provide suggestions for additional references to bridge any gaps in knowledge. Many excellent books and Web sites can provide the fundamental knowledge required to learn HTML coding, JavaScript, Java programming, or to gain proficiency in music theory, MIDI techniques, audio recording technology, and so on. While you can't become an expert in any of these subjects overnight, you should still be able to learn a great deal from this book and to supplement your understanding, where necessary, with other references. Putting audio on the Internet requires some interdisciplinary knowledge, the confidence to try to grasp a wildly spinning technology that is changing day by day, and—last, but not least—a good ear. We can help you master the two former requirements, but you'll need to train yourself to recognize the differences in the characteristics of audio material. The material and tools provided on the CD-ROM included with this book should be helpful in that regard.

TIP For all these audiences, we've tried to provide the necessary path to gaining at least a fundamental understanding of those areas that to you may represent a completely new technology—regardless of your perspective or background. We strongly encourage you to skip over those chapters dealing with fundamentals with which you are already familiar (whether we're discussing audio fundamentals or simple HTML coding) and dwell a little longer in those chapters that enter unfamiliar terrain.

What Browser Do You Need?

While there are many different ways to move files around the Internet, the World Wide Web has become the favorite in many circles, so—in most cases—our discussions of audio file access and playback will be centered around the capabilities offered through browsers. Since the vast majority of users are either running Netscape Navigator or Microsoft Internet Explorer, we'll spend the most time on those particular browsers—particularly version 3.0 of each and Netscape Navigator 4.0, although newer versions may be available at the time this book is released. Where possible, we'll provide highlights and details of those sound-oriented features that are slated for release in the next versions of Internet Explorer and Navigator, and how upcoming features may affect your strategies for delivering audio for browser consumption.

Built-In Audio Features

Both Internet Explorer and Navigator feature significant built-in support for certain kinds of sound files. Both can also be enhanced and extended through the use of plug-in technologies, that provide modules that operate through the browser to add specialized features and capabilities. Internet Explorer also provides additional possibilities through its ActiveX technology, which can provide online activation of many Windows applications within the familiar browser environment, including applications dealing with audio processing. As you're considering the various ways to present audio information on the Internet, these various technologies can either broaden your audience or cut you off from potential listeners.

For example, while Microsoft's ActiveX technology has some appealing characteristics, it does not yet have cross-platform support, so using ActiveX audio components in an HTML document could potentially cut off Macintosh and Unix users. Other users might resist the notion of having to download and install plug-ins to be able to listen to audio, ruling out specialized MIDI plug-ins or any of the streaming audio plug-ins. However, if you limit yourself to the built-in sound support of Internet Explorer and Navigator, you restrict yourself to very simple and basic audio applications. There are some ways around this problem, such as using JavaScript to detect the operating environment of the browser, interpreting the HTML document, and then dynamically link to appropriate pages containing the type of audio (or no audio) that is best suited to the listener's environment. The more transparent the delivery of high-end audio features over the Web, the more appreciative your audience will be. On the other end, if the audio experience turns into a buggy, failure-prone debacle or a download nightmare, you'll lose your audience faster than they can click the channel changer on a TV remote control.

What Techniques Are Covered?

We're trying to cover a lot of ground with the material in this book and we suspect that some users will be more interested in certain approaches than others. To provide a sense of the terrain that will be covered—and the corresponding chapters—the following subsections summarize the subject areas.

Understanding the Potential of Internet Audio

Digital audio and the Internet are two rapidly converging technologies that are evolving in many surprising and potentially revolutionary ways. Chapter 1, *A Concise Audio Primer*, provides the broad view of how these technologies have developed and how they are appearing on the Internet.

MIDI: Compact and Accessible

For many years, computer game producers have relied on MIDI sound files to provide background music to fast-moving games. MIDI has gained increased prominence recently as an attractive vehicle for adding music to Web sites, since the file sizes are so compact. MIDI manages to remain compact by capturing the essential characteristics of a piece of music in a shorthand format. During playback, the MIDI information is decoded in real time, including details such as what instrument voices are playing what notes for what duration. This type of information takes up much less file space than an elaborate mapping of the actual waveform of the music (which typically requires 10 Megabytes of storage per minute of stereo CD-quality sound). MIDI files, whether processed by a Wintel, MacOS, or Unix machine, are played back through some type of synthesizer either resident on an installed sound board or an external tone generator. The sound quality can be modest on inexpensive sound boards (you might call it crude, if you were feeling less polite), but excitingly realistic on high-quality synthesizers using high-quality wavetables and sampled sounds based on recordings of real instruments. You might never be able to lay your hands on a 17-century Stradivarius violin, but you can play one through MIDI using actual sound samples.

The nature of MIDI also provides a level of programmability that offers some very interesting opportunities for creating Web pages designed for music training, online jamming, configurable sound environments, or other flexible music options. The same characteristics that make MIDI attractive to game producers make MIDI a valuable tool for Webmasters looking for low-bandwidth techniques to add rich music to a site. Although some observers scorn the notion that MIDI will ever offer anything of value to the Web, we point to a number of different sites that are already using MIDI in highly imaginative ways—without long download times and without complex playback strategies. We suspect this whole area will become one of the most vital and energized techniques for composing, sharing, and delivering music over the Web.

MIDI is discussed in Chapter 2, *Compact Sound for the Web: MIDI*, and in Chapter 8, *MIDI on the Web*.

Working with Computer Sound Processing

From reading the magazine ads, you might think you can plug a microphone into your 16-bit CD-quality PC sound board and start instantly recording high-quality audio for use on the Internet. If only it was that simple. In truth, if you just plug that $10 microphone included with your Sound Cadet sound board into the microphone jack and start recording, the first thing you'll hear is the woefully loud fan noise from your computer. You'll probably realize that the typical sound-card microphone maybe really isn't pro-audio quality and reduces your resonant broadcast voice to a timbre closer to that of a scuba diver gurgling through his mask. The circuitry in most mass-market sound boards—even though they are touted as being capable of CD-quality sound—is nowhere near what you can call CD-quality when you are recording incoming sounds. To make matters worst, the PC itself is a hotbed of stray and intrusive electromagnetic interference that can inject unwanted noise and grisly audio artifacts into what you hoped would be a pristine recording.

We've devoted Chapter 3, *The Digital Sound Studio*, to describing the tools and techniques for constructing a reasonably inexpensive desktop audio studio and getting the highest quality sound when recording or processing sound for Internet distribution. Once again, the CD-ROM included with this book has several top-notch audio applications that you can use to try out different effects and processes, and to preview some of the actual procedures that you might follow in creating audio files for use on the Web. While these tools and our coverage of them won't turn you into a sound engineer overnight, you'll certainly learn enough of the important sound editing techniques to support many types of Internet applications.

Choosing the Right Sound Format

One of the biggest decisions you'll face in planning to deliver digital audio over the Internet is what sound format to use. There are tradeoffs in each of the different approaches. For example, MIDI offers a compact, flexible format that can play back audio interactively, but the quality of the playback is dependent on the equipment on the user's desktop—accordingly, the resulting MIDI music quality can range from magnificent to barely tolerable. Compressed audio formats, such as Shockwave, QuickTime, and MPEG, help solve the bandwidth dilemma, but require that special software be installed through the browser to provide support. Native browser sound formats, such as WAV and AIF, sound good, but take a long time to transfer, so they don't typically offer the best audio bang for your buck. Each of these formats makes sense in certain situations; we'll clarify which situations are most appropriate for which formats as you explore the chapters of this book. Chapter 1, *A Concise Audio Primer*, and Chapter 3, *The Digital Sound Studio*, explain the fundamentals of the different formats.

Built-In Sound File Support

Without resorting to plug-ins or helper applications, you can automatically recognize and play back a number of different sound file formats from within Navigator. Netscape's pre-eminent browser supports these formats: WAV, AIFC, AIFF, AIF, SND, and AU. In other words, if you provide links to these type of files from within an HTML document, Navigator can automatically play the sound files through an installed sound board and speakers. These file formats are essentially digital representation of sound waveforms and they can range in size depending on the sampling rate used to capture and produce the waveform from its analog source. While the quality can be quite satisfying and realistic, these sound files tend to be fairly large in size and downloading them can try the patience of Job. Chapter 4, *Basic HTML Audio Techniques*, explains the fundamentals of working with these supported formats. Chapter 5, *Advanced HTML Audio Techniques*, expands on the topic and offers additional techniques for distributing sound.

JavaScript and Java Control of Audio

JavaScript, because of its direct and logical control of all of the elements within an HTML document, provides an extremely useful tool for working with Internet audio. We provide a number of different examples of JavaScript in action within this book. However, because of space considerations, we can't provide a full primer on JavaScript (which is at least another book's worth of material); the JavaScript examples provided will necessarily be fairly simple. JavaScript 1.1 is fully supported by both Microsoft Internet Explorer 3 and Netscape Navigator 3 (although Microsoft call their interpretation of the language "JScript," probably just to be obstinate). Although both browser interpreters are supposed to support all constructs of JavaScript equally well, you'll undoubtedly encounter some quirks and differences in the way certain JavaScript code is handled—in Navigator as well as Internet Explorer. The technology is still young, and is not yet fully polished.

Likewise, Java presents some extremely promising possibilities, but it's not something you can easily start working with overnight if you don't have a strong programming background. We'll touch on some Java applications, and explore some applets that have been constructed for audio use, but Java programming is too big a subject to deal with effectively in a book of this scope. The recommendations and guidelines provided in these pages should help you get a sense of what would be required to construct a Java applet for a special-purpose audio application; we'll also provide some pointers to useful references and training materials if you decide to pursue the course of obtaining Java proficiency. Chapter 6, *Scripting Techniques for Handling Audio*, describes the JavaScript and Java approaches to sound.

Streaming Audio on the Web

Another rapidly rising phenomena has been the birth of streaming audio on the Web, a technique by which compressed audio information is rapidly downloaded, cached, decompressed, and played back through the user's sound board and speakers. The technology has improved to the point where many radio stations and other broadcasters have set up real-time broadcasts (or slightly delayed broadcasts), which can be accessed on demand by simply "tuning in" to the appropriate site address. The technique has improved to the point where someone with a 28.8Kbps modem can play back audio broadcasts that have near-CD quality. While audio files can be created in a format that can be streamed by a number of different sound editing packages, setting up a server to deliver the files on demand requires some additional software and setup. If you're interested in the opportunities available for setting up your own Web broadcast site or music preview center, we've devoted a chapter to this technology explaining the procedure. Two leading contenders in this area are RealAudio and Liquid Audio, and each of these companies provides some strong features and options. Never has it been so inexpensive to enter the realm of broadcasting—with a potential international audience—a fact which may help usher in a whole new generation of college, alternative, or special-interest Web broadcast sites. Chapter 7, *Streaming Audio on the Web*, covers this topic.

Talking on the Web

To the perpetual chagrin of Microsoft and other companies, Apple Computer remains the predominant development platform for many multimedia technologies, including the authoring of CD-ROM titles, digital audio production, and desktop video production. Apple has teamed up with Netscape to devise standards-based application and development tools that will provide platform-independent delivery of real-time audio and video conferencing across the Internet. Apple's QuickTime standard has been a strong contender in the struggle to bring audio/video materials to the Internet, and Apple's long-term direction includes refinements to their evolving QuickTime Media Layer, an architecture that Apple hopes will carry their developer loyalty into a Web-oriented future.

For business teleconferencing and other forms of creative collaboration, the potential of being able to easily (and inexpensively) link a project time that has members spread out around the world has radical implications. Telecommuting, already an increasingly important factor in the employment picture worldwide, will become even more effective when a group of people will be able to communicate using the Internet as the medium. Beyond simple voice communication, the Apple/Netscape approach also includes support for real-time video (smile at the camera, Jane) and computer whiteboard applications (our team members in Germany can see the cache lines hook to the processor where I've drawn this arrow).

A number of other third-party applications offer interesting telephony support, including Netscape's bundled CoolTalk—an integral part of Navigator 3. We devote a chapter to the implications and the implementations of telephony and teleconferencing. These technologies are booming and may change the way many companies do business. Chapter 10, *Live Conversations on the Internet*, discusses teleconferencing and telephony.

Another means of voice communication aided by computer techniques are the related fields of voice synthesis and voice recognition. You can escape the perils of carpal-tunnel syndrome by tossing your keyboard and controlling your computer by voice commands. Equally effective for navigating the Web through a voice-controlled browser or composing an HTML document by spoken dictation, voice recognition is here. Voice synthesis has also made sweeping strides in recent months. Why generate eyestrain reading the contents of a Web page when you can have your computer read it to you? Chapter 9, *Voice Synthesis, Recognition, and Other Applications*, covers these two topics and other related topics as well.

Pushing Audio Content

In a paradigm shift that is surging through Web communities like a tsunami, push technologies have arisen on the scene almost overnight. As vendors scramble to create the models by which information can be selectively funneled to Web viewers, some practitioners are moving beyond pushing banners and stock quotes to adding audio content to the push arena. Others, however, are skeptical of this approach to Web information dispersal. Chapter 11, *Push Technology: the Promise of Things to Come*, covers this important subject.

Special Elements and Icons

To highlight certain types of information that appears throughout this book, we've used special elements and icons in the following manner.

 Reference material and pointers to company and personal Web sites are indicated with the compass icon. The URL generally follows these kinds of references, as shown:

www.anywhere.net

Tips offer the benefit of the authors' experience in avoiding pitfalls and solving task-oriented problems. These often deal with hardware and software issues, as well as techniques for obtaining the best results during sound processing.

Sidebars

Sidebars offer peripheral information about a topic, including technical details, the evolution of certain technologies, and issues involving industry figures and trends.

 Software that appears on the CD-ROM included with this book is highlighted using the CD icon. You can also refer to a summary of the disc contents in Appendix E or open up the appropriate HTML file on the CD-ROM: pc_cd.htm for PC users and mac_cd.html for Macintosh users.

Giving a Voice to the Web

Computers are often characterized as being cold and distancing people from each other. As a communication tool, however, the computer has the ability to extend human expressiveness and creativity to entirely new levels. Given the nature of audio, you can counter this characterization of coldness and give the Web a more human voice. In fact, you could use your own voice to greet new users to your site and to provide instructions as to how to navigate to key areas. You can interweave content with musical accompaniments that set a mood or a tone to a site visit. For example, if you're constructing a museum site that showcases eighteenth-century artifacts from Scotland, you could play a Celtic background piece stored as a MIDI file to create the appropriate atmosphere. If your site includes literary material— maybe poetry—you could provide a audio reading of your favorite Emily Dickinson work or a stirring version of your own original piece. You could devise a Java applet to show a young music student how to play a pentatonic scale on the fretboard of an electric guitar and how to improvise against a common chord pattern. You could offer viewers of your Web pages an option to activate text-to-speech playback so they could lean back and relax while simultaneously reducing eyestrain.

The human voice and music are two very powerful forms of communication. We'll show you how to bring both of these to the Internet and add the dimension of sound to the Web. The voice you give to the Web may be your own.

Acknowledgments

Thanks to the many individuals who contributed their insights and knowledge about audio on the Internet. Thanks also to agent Chris Van Buren and the dedicated, professional staff at John Wiley & Sons, Inc,

Special thanks go to Gail Koffman for contributing Chapter 11 on Push technology.

Part One

Creating, Processing, and Storing Audio

1

A Concise
Audio Primer

This chapter charts the history of sound recording, from the very earliest efforts of Berliner and Edison, to the current desktop computer approaches. The latter part of this chapter discusses the techniques by which sound files have migrated to the Internet and the different file formats that have evolved along the way. Examples are provided showing the different ways by which sound is presented on the Web.

We're a species that likes to capture things and we're fond of marking our presence on this planet by tracking and recording all of the most important moments of our existence. Communication has slipped beyond the bonds of the present and gained the added dimensions offered by focused windows into the past, through video, film, sound recordings, and—more recently—combinations of all of these on multimedia CD-ROMs. You can listen to the flat, yet moving recordings of Robert Johnson playing his unique style of blues on guitar in front of a single microphone in a cold hotel room, and you've caught a glimpse (or an earful) of an important slice of music history. You can watch a film of Adolph Hitler rallying the German people toward mass insanity, view photographs of the Civil War dead covering the fields in Gettysburg, or listen to recordings of Franklin D. Roosevelt talking to America on the radio during difficult times. You can also see the Neil Armstrong step onto the moon, watch stop-action photography accelerate the growth of a sunflower into seconds rather than weeks, or listen to voices from long-dead people captured during the birth of sound recording. Unique light and sound patterns recorded on tape, film, and other media freeze moments of our history in permanent (or semi-permanent) form.

The twentieth century has been marked by a progression of more and more sophisticated recording devices that can capture images, sounds, ideas, and—some would even say—thoughts. We play back these stored segments of time and space for amusement, recreation, education, and commerce. From the energy spectrums that surround us, we've learned to capture light on film and to convert sounds to data patterns. Audio storage techniques, in particular, have a long history dating back to the days of Thomas Edison and Alexander Graham Bell. After more than 100 years of evolution, audio storage technologies have moved from the analog to the digital realm. And now, to the Internet.

Moving to the Digital Realm

Digital works—whether music, still images, or video—are portable and malleable in their digitized form. The great benefit—as well as the risk—in all digital representations of our analog world is that the content can be reproduced without loss an infinite number of times. If you make a copy of something that exists in analog format—such as a continuous image photograph—the photographic copy loses some of the clarity and sharpness of the original photograph. Each subsequent copy exhibits more loss. In comparison, digital reproductions consist of a multitude of ones and zeroes that represent an exact duplicate of the original source. You can make 10,000 copies of a PCM file (the most basic digital sound format) containing the complex waveforms captured during a recording of Beethoven's Fifth Symphony performed by the London Symphony Orchestra and the 10,000th copy will have every bit of the fidelity of the original recording. As long as the transfers of the sound file don't introduce any errors at the bit level, the same digital information can be transferred across the Internet or pressed onto an audio CD or exchanged on a magnetic tape without ever suffering from the signal loss that undermines data transfers on analog media.

The film industry has relied heavily on computer technology to convert the archives of film prints stored on perishable and highly flammable cellulose nitrate (used prior to the 1940s) to digitally stored representations. The image quality of films on cellulose nitrate was exceptional, but the lifespan of this media was very short (and shorter still if the prints caught fire). In digital form, the original materials can be archived and copied without loss, offering a permanent record of this period in filmmaking history. Film content can be easily manipulated when in digital form, much to the chagrin of purists who were appalled by Turner Broadcasting using computer techniques to colorize black-and-white movies. Although the aesthetic improvements offered by colorization are controversial, few people will argue with the clear advantages of preserving an important era in film history on computer-based media. Similar techniques have been used with sound to capture and digitally process audio masters from records and tapes, material that without this form of preservation would be lost in a matter of years. Digital forms of storage offer a far more permanent method for preserving information than anything else the human race has devised.

The precision with which digital materials can be copied represents a serious problem if you're concerned about piracy, which, of course, is a major concern of the video, film, and record industries. With applications available that let you pull the digital content from an audio CD and copy it directly to a file or a recordable CD, the opportunities for wide-scale theft and redistribution of intellectual property are easily available. Materials placed on the Internet are especially susceptible to widespread illegal duplication; a digital copy of your carefully crafted musical masterpiece could in a matter of seconds be copied and played in China, Taiwan, Mexico, and India. Played back after this worldwide journey, the copies would sound every bit as good as the original. If some enterprising music pirate in Bangkok decided to release your work on an audio CD collection of fast-rising American artists, he or she would have the source material right at hand to do this. A number of companies concerned with this form of illegal duplication have developed techniques for tracking digital sound files and tracing illegal copies. More about this in subsequent chapters.

The malleability of digital information is also a major benefit. Once in digital form, stored as a sound file, the data representing sound waves can be processed and reshaped mathematically within computer-based sound editing applications. Effects can be previewed and discarded if they don't work. Computer-based equivalents of sound equipment costing tens of thousands of dollars in standalone studio boxes can be incorporated in a program no more expensive than a word processor or photo-retouching software. The sophistication with which these new computer-based tools work generates results that are indistinguishable from results accomplished with high-end studio equipment. In fact, in some ways they are superior to the conventional studio approach to sound editing because of the unique ability to perform nondestructive editing—editing where the effects applied to the sound can be applied, listened to, and—if inappropriate—rejected (often with several levels of undo). This capacity for rapidly trying out different effects until a desired result is achieved gives the computer-based audio producer a marked advantage over sound editors limited to sequential devices, whether analog or digital tape recorders.

Depending on the storage format, digital audio files can range from compact to voluminous. As is the case with storing graphics files, the digital replications of analog phenomena can be compressed to a fraction of their original sampled size. Compression takes the extraneous information—whether a block of unchanging red in the middle of a graphic or a four-second sequence of silence in a piece of music—and encodes it in a shorthand format. Some compression formats do this without altering the original content—these are called lossless compression schemes. Other compression schemes provide some degree of compromise to fidelity when the compressed format is decompressed—these are called lossy compression schemes. The degree of loss can range from subtle to unacceptable. Internet sound distribution requires a careful tradeoff between reducing the bandwidth of transferred sound and maintaining a high degree of signal quality. Making decisions as to how to best handle this issue will become one of your major concerns as you're processing sound to put it on the Internet.

The Nature of Sound

However sophisticated our analog and digital audio processing becomes, we need to remember that sound at its most essential level is nothing more than pressure waves in the air. The recording process takes the sound waves out of the air and puts them into a storable format, some means of capturing the shape and intensity of the pressure wave. On one side, we use microphones to capture the pressure waves and convert them to an electronic signal, which can be stored and manipulated. On the other side, we use speakers that rely on vibrating cones to turn the stored signals back into pressure waves once again.

The human ear responds to these vibrations in the air and interprets them as what we know as sound—the audible range for most people is between 30 and 20,000 cycles per second (Hertz). If you've been spending too many hours listening to Metallica with your stereo volume too high, your hearing range may be closer to 400 to 8000 Hertz. If you're a Rottweiler, those vibrations in the air will continue to be heard up to 30,000 Hertz. If you're a fruit bat cruising the air over the Bonin Islands, your pointy ears will continue to pick up and hear vibrations as high as 100,000 Hertz.

Measuring Frequency with Hertz

The term Hertz, usually abbreviated as Hz, is applied to the measurement of frequency in remembrance of Heinrich Rudolph Hertz, a German scientist and researcher who is credited with demonstrating the existence of radio waves and calculating their velocity as equal to the speed of light. One Hertz is equal to 1 cycle per second. As you read discussions about audio phenomena, you'll often see Hertz used in combination with the prefix kilo (kiloHertz or KHz), which represents 1000 cycles per second.

An individual sound can be analyzed as having three fundamental components: pitch, intensity, and timbre. The first two components are fairly simple to analyze and capture. Timbre, however, is a much more complex component.

What we perceive as the pitch of a sound—how high or low the audible wave appears to us—depends on the frequency of the sound wave. Low-pitched sounds, such as the output from an electric bass, have much lower frequencies than high-pitched sounds, such as the output from a soprano saxophone. If you stand in front of the speaker of a bass amplifier and play the low-E string a couple of times, you can literally feel the air from the speaker pulsing as the cone expands and compresses, recreating sound waves in the air. If you put a microphone in front of the soprano sax and play it into the same amplifier (while the bass player is still playing) the resulting sound wave becomes much more complex, consisting of a mix of the lower pitched waves from the bass combined with the higher pitched waves from the sax.

The waveform becomes more complex still when you realize that each instrument—besides generating a single fundamental frequency for each note being played—also produces harmonics, overtones, partials, and other elements. Harmonics are additional vibrations, or waveforms, based on physical properties of the instrument. You might think of them as a byproduct of the process of creating a basic note or a series of notes on the instrument. Harmonics are what give a particular instrument its characteristic sound. One set of harmonics is generated by the characteristics of a vibrating nickel-steel string passing back and forth over a magnetic guitar pickup. Another set of harmonics is produced by the action of air passing through the reed of a saxophone mouthpiece and being channeled through the body of the instrument. The fundamental and its accompanying harmonics combine to produce what is generally referred to as the timbre of an instrument, which is a complex construction involving the properties of all of the different materials composing the instrument, the temperature, the resonance of the instrument, the way in which the instrument is played, and so on. While it is simple to measure and reproduce the pitch and intensity of a sound wave (essentially the fundamental frequency of a sound wave and its relative volume), capturing the timbre becomes more difficult because of the complexities of the actual sound wave characteristics.

Similarly, if you're going to attempt to generate sound synthetically (which, of course, is what computer synthesizers and keyboard synthesizers do), you need to go beyond simply generating the pitch and intensity of a sound. You can produce a waveform of a single frequency using a single oscillator, and if you play that frequency back through speakers, you'll hear a thin, unvarying tone, something akin to the dial tone of a telephone. If you start from this initial waveform and start producing more complex sounds—by modifying the initial oscillator output with additional oscillators, by applying filtering, by emphasizing or de-emphasizing the harmonic content of the signal, by delaying portions of the waveform and feeding them back into the original—pretty soon you start generating waveforms that can provide fairly good replications of existing instruments and sounds. This is essentially what the early analog synthesizers did, and the types of sounds they can produce are unique. A new generation of analog synthesizers, some combining digital storage technologies with their analog roots, has found ongoing life in recording studios and with musicians who not only want to simulate real-world instruments but want to create sounds that may have never before been heard.

Digital synthesizers rely on samples of real-world sounds that are captured and stored in digital formats. In comparison with analog synthesizers, the stored samples can be incredibly precise and realistic. These stored sounds can be played back on demand—by pressing a key on a synthesizer keyboard or by sending a stream of MIDI data to a tone generator. A short sample of Middle C played on a Steinburg grand piano can be used to generate a waveform that will sound astonishingly similar to the original instrument. Through MIDI notation and applied digital processing effects, the waveform can be further manipulated—adding reverb to simulate a large hall, or changing the attack to simulate a key being struck sharply. Digital synthesis can be accessed through sound boards that contain samples of sounds, through wavetable techniques where the computer processor simulates the waveforms through its own processor using tables of stored sound samples, or through external tone generators or standalone synthesizers. These sounds become an audio palette that you can use to create and distribute MIDI files authored for Web playback.

Sound waves can also be stored as a digital replication of their actual analog form. This injects a two-stage conversion into the process of reproducing the pressure waves representing sounds traveling through the air. The original sound is still captured through a microphone (or electronic pickup), but the sound wave is then converted into a digital format using Analog-to-Digital (A-D) Converters. In a digital file format, the stored waveform can be enhanced using effects processing, compressed to remove extraneous data, transferred to a variety of other media, or downloaded through a link in an HTML document. The digital waveform then has to be converted back into an analog signal using Digital-to-Analog (D-A) Converters. The final stage in the process is to drive speakers to recreate the pressure waves that we hear as sound. Later in this chapter we discuss sampling techniques and digital storage in greater detail.

In preparing sounds for Internet distribution, you have two basic choices: You can use synthesized sounds—as incorporated in MIDI technology and text-to-speech techniques—or you can use any of a number of sound file formats that transfer reproductions of waveforms. There are drawbacks and advantages to each of these approaches, and, in some cases, you may even want to use combinations of the two (for example, MOD files combine MIDI formats with digital sound streams). In certain situations, you may be recording your own source material, such as when you may be creating voice-overs for a Web presentation, but you may also draw on libraries of prerecorded materials, such as MIDI sound files purchased from a distributor, recorded samples and sound effects, clip audio files (the sound equivalent to clip art), and similar sources. There are also some fairly simple techniques that allow you to take traditional sheet music from pre-copyright days and use computer techniques to bring it on line. We'll cover examples of each of these approaches in the book.

The Evolution of Sound Recording

To realize what advantages have been gained through using digital audio sound recording techniques, we only need to look back at previous methods of recording. The history of recording sound stretches back to 1857 when Leon Scott, intent on obtaining a picture of what sound waves looked like, devised a method for recording the vibrations in the air. His device, later patented as the Phonoautograph, used a large parabolic horn to channel incoming sound waves to a membrane covering the narrow end of the horn. A bristle attached to the membrane by a lever traced a path in a revolving cylinder coated with lamp-black. As the membrane vibrated in response to sound waves, the bristle etched a pattern in the lamp-black that corresponded to the frequency of the sound. Although this was useful for gaining a view of what different sound waves looked like, the device could only record incoming waves—there was no provision for playing back the sound wave traces.

After studying the Phonoautograph, Thomas Edison modified the basic design in 1877 so that it would be capable of playing back sounds. While the sound quality was rather pitiful, the fact that this feat could actually be accomplished encouraged others to continue development. Edison's device utilized a grooved metal cylinder encased in tinfoil. A horn concentrated the sound waves when someone spoke into it. At the apex of the horn, a thin membrane attached to a needle transmitted the vibrations—the resulting waves were scored into the tinfoil as the needle moved up and down, creating a path of varying depth. As can be seen in Figure 1.1, the cylinder in this device was rotated by means of a hand crank. Once the sound was recorded, the needle was returned to the beginning of the groove. Turning the hand crank caused the vibrations captured in tinfoil to travel from the needle to the diaphragm and a crude replica of the human voice emerged from the horn.

Alexander Graham Bell took this invention a step further by replacing the foil-covered cylinder with one coated with wax. The needle cut a pattern that varied in depth onto the wax surface. For recording, Bell relied on a very sharp stylus and firm membrane. During playback, he switched to a dull stylus and a looser membrane so as not to destroy the original impressions. To reuse the cylinder, the wax could be shaved and smoothed. For the first time, sound recording could be accomplished on removable and reusable media. The process was further improved with the addition of an electric motor to replace the hand crank, so that recording and playback took place at uniform speeds. Recorded cylinders were then metal-plated to create a mold so that a number of copies of the original could be produced.

The technology spawned a mini-industry. Phonograph parlors sprang up around the country in the late 1800s where amazed visitors paid a nickel to hear voices muttering from these primitive playback devices.

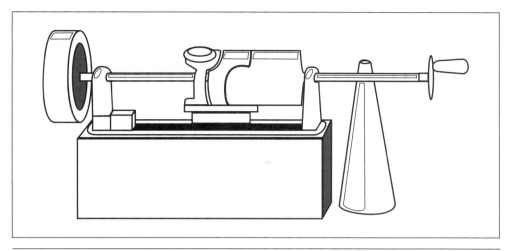

Figure 1.1 Edison's sound recording and playback device.

The recording cylinder was replaced by a disc in 1888 when Emile Berliner devised a variation of this basic recording technique. Berliner's gramophone, shown in Figure 1.2, used a stylus traveling within a spiral groove on a flat disc. Sound waves caused the stylus to cut a pattern side to side within the groove. The pattern on the disc could then be reproduced using a metal mold and hundreds of recorded discs could be manufactured inexpensively from each mold. The disc itself was fashioned of metal covered with wax. After the stylus cut the pattern, removing the wax from its path, acid was used to etch the resulting waveform into the metal subsurface.

While the sound quality wasn't up to par with that of the cylinders, the recording method was better suited to mass production. By the year 1910, discs and spring-wound players were being sold all over the world featuring recordings by some of the most popular singers of that era. Development of the vacuum tube amplifier in 1912 by Lee de Forest spurred efforts to combine the phonograph and gramophone with amplified playback, a process which took several more years.

During the same period that Edison, Bell, and Berliner were working on their sound recording devices, others were working on developing methods of magnetic recording of sound waves. The pattern of sound waves, instead of being imprinted on a disc or cylinder, is translated into a series of magnetic domains that can be

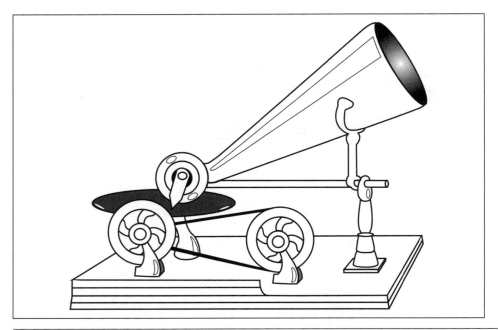

Figure 1.2 Berliner's gramophone captured sound on a disc.

stored on a variety of media. The first patent for such a device was claimed by Oberlin Smith in 1888. Later, a man by the name of Poulson created a magnetic sound recorder that used steel tape as the recording medium. He exhibited his invention at the Paris Exhibition in 1900, calling his device a Telegraphone.

The radio broadcast industry was very interested in equipment that could store sound and immediately play it back, since it enabled them to repeat some broadcast material—such as newscasts—whenever required. The tape could also be easily erased and reused—another major benefit. Work by DeStille in 1924 resulted in the Blattnerphone, which impressed the British Broadcasting Company enough to draw them into the development process. The Marconi Wireless Telegraph Company also jumped into the development effort, using steel-based magnetic tape that was initially biased to saturation. Rudimentary magnetic recorders were produced, although the early versions required literally miles of steel tape to accommodate 20 or 30 minutes of recorded sound.

Cumbersome steel-based tapes gave way to plastic-based magnetic tape. The magnetic oxides coating plastic-based tape can be formulated differently to change their recording and sound-storage properties. Undesirable characteristics such as print-through (the tendency of magnetic signals to leach through one layer of tape and affect adjacent layers) can be minimized through a choice of magnetic oxide.

Magnetic methods of recording are still widely used in cassette recorders and reel-to-reel decks, and improvements in electronics, recording media, magnetic recording heads, and noise-reduction techniques have maintained the viability of this recording method. However, this method of recording is subject to certain limitations that have been largely overcome by digital recording techniques. Signal-to-noise ratios of recorded sounds, among other factors, have been greatly improved by digital storage methods.

Modern Recording Equipment

After many years of development, digital recording gear has largely surpassed analog, reel-to-reel, and magnetic tape recorders. Digital recording machines—such as the DAT, ADAT, RDAT, recordable mini-disc, portable studios with removable hard disk drive storage, and home computers—have changed our perception of "high-fidelity" audio to startlingly clearer levels. In the digital realm, the signal-to-noise ratio is greatly improved over analog equipment, meaning the dynamic representation of the music is greatly improved. The familiar hiss and tape noise common to analog recording is conspicuously absent in digital recordings. This particular improvement in recording techniques ensures that the softest passages in a recorded musical work or speech will be as free of noise as the loudest levels of recorded audio. The recordist has a greater dynamic range to work with when using digital recording techniques, and fewer processing "tricks" are required to guarantee an effective sound recording.

The next generation of digital recorders provides storage directly to Flash RAM. Cassette recorders of the future will have no moving parts, unless you consider the movement of the electrons in the logic circuitry. Already, personal message savers using these types of storage techniques are inexpensively available. Not much larger than a credit card, they allow you to store and play back a series of messages. Most of them offer two to five minutes of total recording time, but improvements in memory chips should raise this limit considerably.

Beyond recording techniques that rely on digitizing analog sound, binary sound files are also used to synthesize music playback. MIDI (Musical Instrument Digital Interface) files contain binary information that tells MIDI synthesizer hardware (present on most sound boards, as well as through external tone generators and synthesizer keyboards) to play instrument and percussive sounds. The MIDI files handle the score or composition information and the hardware produces the sounds. MIDI techniques are explored further in Part Two of this book.

Combining the best of both worlds, a number of computer recording applications allow MIDI and digitized analog recordings to be sequenced together and recorded in multitrack fashion. Both the MIDI and digital recordings can be combined and used during mixdowns, effects processing, rate compression, and other processing operations, all within the confines of a single desktop computer. While several manufacturers have produced standalone hard disk recorders (which don't require a desktop computer for operation), the convenience of doing your sound recording and editing from a single computer makes sense for many Web page developers who are accustomed to the computer being the central design tool for text, imagery, video, effects programming, animation, and scripting, in addition to audio recording. Most of our attention in this book will be focused on techniques that can be employed using computer-based applications. However, where there are interesting standalone devices that may handle special-purpose audio requirements, we'll bring these to your attention.

Desktop Recording

While professional sound recording gear has made a steady transition from the analog to the digital medium, another transition has been the introduction of a new generation of sophisticated audio tools for personal computers. Sound recording has moved out of the studio and now can be easily and professionally accomplished with a desktop computer. Music recorded on desktop computers is either analog sound that has been converted to the digital domain, or score and note information like MIDI, which instructs synthesizer hardware or computer software on what to play, when to play, and how.

When converting analog sound to the digital domain, sample rate and sample resolution must be considered. The Nyquist theorem states that a minimum of two samples is necessary to represent any sound wave. This is why 44.1KHz (44,100 samples per second) was chosen for the audio CD standard, because humans can't hear sounds above 20KHz. This form of analog-to-digital recording is most commonly referred to as Pulse Code Modulation (PCM) recording. The instantaneous voltage of the analog waveform being recorded is stored as the binary number representing the voltage threshold that most closely corresponds. These snapshots of the instantaneous input voltage are recorded (and later played back) like frames of a movie. However, high-fidelity sound recording requires much faster sampling rates than the frames in a movie (44,100 samples per second for sound as compared with 30 frames per second for film or video).

Computer Processing of Sound

Computer processing of sound files has given us the revolutionary ability to edit, mix, add special effects, compress, normalize, equalize, and in other ways process any displayed, digitized waveform. You can zoom in, precisely select a portion of the waveform (by highlighting it with the mouse), and use conventional copy, cut, and paste techniques—much in the same way you might cut and paste text or portions of a bitmapped image. This ability lets you easily correct problems or glitches in a sound recording. Since many effects are created by the crafty mixing of delayed versions of the recorded signal in certain phase relationships, many sound processing applications can perform a list of special effects that would require dozens of specialized pieces of standalone equipment in a conventional recording studio.

Figure 1.3 shows the sound wave representing running water in a creek as displayed in Sound Forge 4.0. Using a variety of tools, you can process this sound wave to reshape it, combine it with other sounds, add a voice-over, downsample the digital waveform so that it takes up less disk space, or mutate it in ways that would make it unrecognizable (but that might make a nice sound effect in a science fiction movie).

 We've included demo versions of a number of leading sound editing and processing applications on the CD-ROM bundled with this book (including Sound Forge). These demos give you the opportunity to try out many of the more sophisticated sound processing techniques that can be applied to creating audio files for distribution on the Web.

Introduction to Sound on the Web

If you're running Netscape Navigator or Microsoft Internet Explorer, simple sound support is built right into your browser. In the case of Navigator, this support is referred to as NetSound. As you open different sites devoted to music on the Web, you'll quickly notice that people are delivering sound in a wide variety of formats and utilizing several common online players. If internal support is not provided for

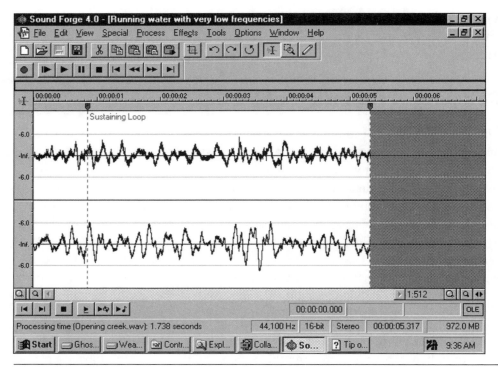

Figure 1.3 Sound wave produced by running water as shown in Sound Forge.

a particular sound format, you can generally download the appropriate plug-in to equip your browser for playback. In the case of Navigator 4, included as part of the Netscape Communicator package, the browser has the built-in intelligence to seek out and download any missing plug-ins as needed (with your permission), so you don't have to worry about managing the assortment of plug-ins required yourself. Likewise, if you place certain types of sound files in HTML documents that you develop, you can do so with confidence that the browser will take care of acquiring the necessary plug-ins for anyone who may be viewing your Web pages.

Sound File Downloading

Even if you're running an ancient, slow computer, you should be able to download sound files onto your hard disk drive and play them offline on the audio/media player of your choice. This method represents the most fundamental technique for delivering sound files to an Internet audience, and it can also be used for file distribution through FTP sites and electronic mail, as well as the World Wide Web. It has the advantage that the sound file is available for later playback, but the disadvantage that you can't start listening to the sound file until it has completely loaded.

For large files that haven't been processed for streaming audio playback, this technique will be the primary means that Web site visitors have for accessing files that you place within an HTML document. The disadvantage to this technique, of course, is the wait for the download to complete—not too many Web visitors are willing to put up with delayed gratification unless the content really justifies the wait. On the other hand, for users whose systems (whether the speed of their modem link or computer processor speed) aren't up to the performance demands of streaming audio playback, file downloading may be the only way they can acquire sound files from the Web. The ability to be able to play the file back any number of times once the Web link has been shut down can be useful, however. For example, if the sound file is a 30-second audio clip from a new album release that you have produced and you want as many people to listen to it as possible, you'll do whatever you can to have that sound file propagating its way across the Internet. The Listening Post at Music Blvd. (a Web-based music CD outlet) provides clips of albums for download in different sample resolutions, as shown in Figure 1.4.

MPEG-2 isn't an internally supported sound file type for either Internet Explorer or Navigator, so unless you've installed an MPEG-2 player and registered it within your browser, you can only download the file. If you do have an MPEG-2 player installed and registered, the file will begin playing as soon as the download is complete.

For the typical user running Netscape Navigator, initiating the download of a sound file is simple. From the hypermedia link connecting to the sound file, a right-click of the mouse brings up a drop-down menu with the option **Save This Link As...** If you select this option, it brings up the Save As dialog box so that you can specify a storage location for the sound file and select a different name for it, if necessary. Once saved as a file, you can play it inside your browser while off line (if the file type is recognized) or, alternatively, through any other media player you have on your system that can handle the sound file format.

Navigator also offers you the option to download and immediately play back those sound files that it supports internally. If you click with the left mouse button on the hypermedia link representing the sound file, Navigator pops up a secondary window that displays a gray "N" while the file is loading (as shown in Figure 1.5). Since the file is initially loaded into the Navigator cache, you may see some activity shown

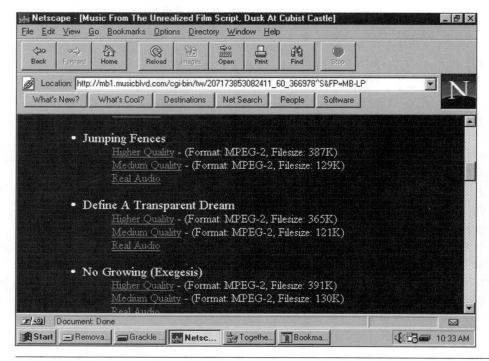

Figure 1.4 Downloadable MPEG-2 files from Music Blvd.

in the status bar as Navigator cleans out the contents of the cache in preparation for the file storage. As soon as the file download is complete, an audio player control replaces the "N" in the secondary window (as shown in Figure 1.6). Using the available controls, you can start, pause, rewind, or exit from the sound file playback.

While there is a definite role for supporting sound file downloads of this type, many of the streaming audio techniques will be more appealing to Web site listeners. Streaming audio plug-ins have been introduced by RealAudio, Xing, Liquid Audio, and other companies. Streaming techniques are also built into plug-ins such as Apple's QuickTime and Macromedia's ShockWave plug-ins, which not only let you produce animation and movies, but also distribute audio content.

Until the Web is faster, however, and the mainstream computers are up to the task, sound file downloading will be a slow, but necessary, ingredient in the toolkit of any Web developer who wants to distribute audio. With that fact in mind, we've provided a number of different examples throughout this book of how to prepare files for downloads and how to embed these types of files within an HTML document.

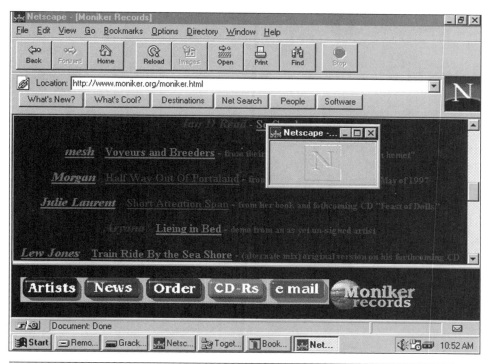

Figure 1.5 A blank Netscape window appears while the sound file downloads.

T I P Providing files for simple sound file downloading is one of the simpler tasks for a Webmaster. You only need to obtain or record the source sound files and save them in one of the appropriate formats. The file can then be referenced from an HTML document using a hypermedia link. MPEG-2 is frequently used for the quality of its sound output, but it requires somewhat higher performance machines for playback and requires the use of an MPEG player, since this file type is not directly supported. Other commonly used formats are AIFF for Macintosh users, WAV files for PC users, and AU files for Unix users. Playback is not necessarily limited to these platforms, since there are sound applications for Windows, Unix, and the MacOS that can play all three types. These sound file formats, however, are more commonly associated with specific platforms.

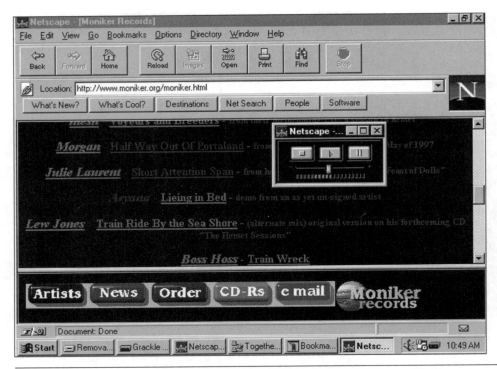

Figure 1.6 As playback begins, an audio player appears to let you control playback.

> The major consideration in delivering sound files of this type is maintaining the highest possible quality sound in the smallest possible file size. We'll provide a number of techniques for accomplishing this in later chapters.

Streaming Audio

The most promising Web audio technology to emerge recently has been streaming audio, a technique by which sound files can be played back as they are being downloaded. With the long waits for file downloading eliminated, your Web audience is more likely to tune in and sample your audio offerings in this format. Modems at 14.4Kbps can achieve AM quality sound during streaming. Modems at 28Kbps come up to stereo FM quality. Those with ISDN links can achieve near-CD quality using some of the newer products.

Streaming audio files are presented as both previously recorded segments and live broadcasts. Previously recorded segments are basically a playback-on-demand approach. You select a show or song, the streaming audio control panel installed on your system appears, and playback begins until you cancel it or select another. Live broadcasts are becoming more common as well, with many radio stations and news organizations providing streaming audio to the Web on a continuous basis. Streaming audio formats such as RealAudio and Liquid Audio have also become popular methods for musicians wanting to showcase their original songs, and for CD retail outlets that provide the ability to sample audio material before buying. For example, Smithsonian Folkways Recording, a well-known source for recordings from traditional American musical artists, presents RealAudio streams at their Web site.

The impetus for using the Web as a programmable information source (using filters or agents or similar technologies) has also been well supported by streaming audio techniques. Using Progressive Networks' Timecast site, you can choose from a wide variety of RealAudio broadcast sources and select material for a daily briefing. You also set up a login identifier, which is automatically recorded so that the next time you tap into the site you're automatically recognized through a cookie file stored on your hard drive. The Timecast site prepares your daily briefing based on your prior selections, which can include such items as highlights from the Pacifica Headline News (an alternative news service), CNET Radio News (for the latest announcements in computer technology), and audio columns, such as Jim Hightower's most recent essay broadcast from his Webactive site. The Timecast page is shown in Figure 1.7.

One example of a streaming audio playback device is the RealAudio Player Plus controller, shown in Figure 1.8. The title of the selection currently playing appears on screen, as well as the artist or announcer in the selection. You can select from several established sites using the Sites drop-down menu or use a set of programmable presets to set up your own favorite broadcast sites, much as you would set up the pushbuttons on your car radio to access favorite music or news stations. The RealAudio Player Plus panel also has a Scan function that seeks RealAudio broadcasts from around the Web. You can get a great sense of the depth and variety of streaming audio activity going on over the Web just by spending a half hour using the Scan button to sample random broadcasts. While growing up, it used to be great fun getting together with one of my cousins during summer visits and tuning in international stations over an old radio that handled every conceivable radio bandwidth. The surprise and fun of reaching an English station or a Spanish station

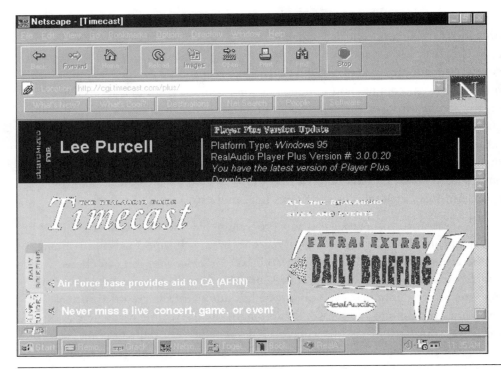

Figure 1.7 Timecast allows you to prepare a daily briefing from your personal selections.

or some station broadcast in a language so unfamiliar that it sounded like Venusian to us is the kind of fun you can have scanning the Web for live broadcasts. You're much more likely to find special-interest broadcast sites, alternative music, diverse viewpoints, and interesting perspectives than you would typically discover on your local commercial sites. Radio may be reborn in a fresh and new form given the capabilities of the World Wide Web.

There are still several companies vying for the honors of top streaming audio provider. Until a winner emerges, your streaming audio development will probably best be directed toward using one of the top three or four available tools for this purpose. Streaming audio support is built into Netscape's native environment using Netscape's own format, but so far, support for this format has been fairly minor compared to other formats.

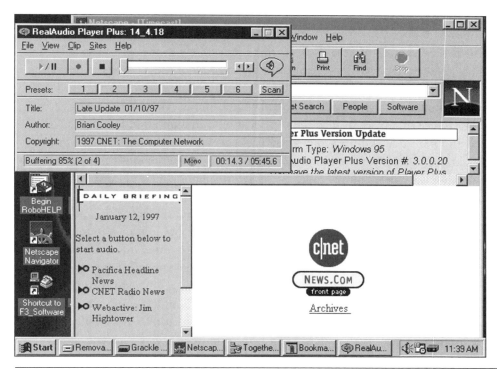

Figure 1.8 RealAudio Player Plus control panel.

WARNING The delivery of streaming audio files requires either a dedicated server or special arrangements with your Internet Service Provider to support the file formats and necessary software. Most of the streaming audio software producers offer special developer packages to simplify and streamline the setup and delivery of audio files for this format. More and more sound editing packages are including the ability to save sound files in streaming audio formats. Sound Forge 4.0, for example, offers this option. Most packages, however, have a server and a client component. The plug-in that provides the client access to the streaming audio formats is usually inexpensive or initially free. The server software will cost significantly more and will require some time and attention to master.

Of all the available sound delivery techniques, streaming audio is probably the most demanding for Webmasters, but also the most rewarding. With a fairly minor investment, you can be set up with a personalized broadcast station that can reach an international audience without ever looking at a transmission tower.

MIDI Techniques

The next time you log on to a Web site and immediately hear music playing, you've probably encountered MIDI—the most compact of all of the methods of delivering sound across the Internet. MIDI files no larger than 10 or 20Kb can play back two or three minutes of fairly intricate musical compositions. MIDI does this by recording the essence of a piece of music and presenting it in a notation that can be interpreted and played back by a synthesizer. The waveform of the music itself isn't stored in the MIDI file; instead, the notation breaks down the musical progression into component parts. For example, the MIDI file might contain information that identifies one instrument voice as an oboe. The oboe begins playing a harmony line starting at A below Middle C, and each note it plays and the note's duration and any variations in the note, such as a quaver, appear in notation form in the MIDI file. Each instrument voice has a similar progression of notated information, and this stream of information is directed to a synthesizer for playback. Other instrument voices are interwoven into this mix up to the level of polyphony supported by the MIDI playback device—the number of voices that can simultaneously be played by the device. Most inexpensive synthesizers can handle at least 16-voice polyphony. More elaborate devices can manage 32 voices or more at a given instant.

Here lies the rub. While MIDI notation is compact, the MIDI music composer has no control over the synthesizer that is used for playback. And synthesizers vary greatly in their ability to replicate the sounds of different musical instruments. Computer musicians have generally standardized on a convention referred to as General MIDI, which ensures that the musical voices identified for playback will map to a standard series of numbers. If all composers stick to General MIDI conventions when producing MIDI sound files, an oboe will sound like an oboe on Harvey's computer sound board as well as on Mary's tone generator as well as on Mick's Yamaha synthesizer keyboard. The music begins to sound very strange if the composer mixes the ID for a glockenspiel for that of an oboe and a timpani plays the notes that were intended for the piano. While most synthesizers have the ability to map different sound samples to different IDs, sound intended for computer playback general sticks to General MIDI.

Most modern sound boards and computers have built-in provision for MIDI sound support. Earlier sound boards use a technique known as FM synthesis, where the sounds of individual instruments are replicated by mathematically manipulating a waveform to create a model similar to what a particular instrument would generate.

Generally, FM synthesizers do not sound very realistic but provide at least a semblance of music when used for MIDI playback. Another synthesizer technique called wavetable synthesis relies on actual digital sound samples of actual instruments that are stored in the synthesizer and played back on demand (the duration, velocity, pitch, and other characteristics of the voice modified electronically during playback). Some synthesizer techniques referred to as software synthesis use the computer's own processor and a selected range of samples stored on hard disk to recreate musical sequences. Software synthesis requires a higher-performance computer than does synthesis that relies on a wavetable sound board or external synthesizer.

Escaping the MIDI Playback Trap

You can avoid the problem of unknown MIDI playback devices in your Web audience by creating files designed for playback using a plug-in such as Headspace's Beatnik. The Beatnik plug-in includes its own compact, fine-sounding software synthesizer, so that files played back through this plug-in sound consistent and reasonably close in quality to dedicated wavetable sound boards. The only catch in this instance is convincing your audience to download and install the Beatnik plug-in— Web users tend to resist installing plug-ins that they aren't familiar with. Once they sample MIDI playback through the Beatnik software synthesizer, however, many users will choose this approach over other options.

Netscape Navigator 3 and beyond includes built-in playback support for MIDI sound files. You can also extend MIDI playback capabilities with a number of plug-ins that generally provide enhancements to the MIDI support. For example, Yamaha's MIDplug supports the MIDI-XG standard, including support for a much greater range of instruments and greater expressiveness within a musical selection. The more complex notation system still supports General MIDI but allows much more realistic sounding capture of wind instruments and stringed instruments, as well as a richer, more elaborate set of instruments with which to work. Of course, a MIDI file created using the MIDI-XG extensions won't sound that good unless it is played back on a device that supports MIDI-XG. For Web playback, plug-ins are available from Yamaha that support both sound board synthesizers and Yamaha's own software synthesizer (you'll need a Pentium or PowerPC processor for reasonable playback). The results are worth the effort—MIDI-XG is a significant improvement over plain vanilla MIDI.

The playback of a MIDI file can be initiated using JavaScript or other methods from within an HTML document. In this manner, the MIDI music can begin the moment an HTML document is loaded, which can be a nice effect if you want to add a particular ambience to a site visit. Depending on the contents of the site, the music can range from quiet classical piano to hard-driving rock and roll. Yamaha chose the latter for their site, shown in Figure 1.9. The control panel shown in the figure provides control over the musical selection. You can pause, halt, or replay the current piece of music, or, if a number of songs are specified, scan through a list of titles for playback. Otherwise, the MIDI music can simply play in the background while someone browses the site. You may hear a brief skip or stutter in the music when the computer processor does something particularly demanding but, generally, MIDI playback is quite seamless.

MIDI sites abound on the Web. The great advantage of this format is that you can use it in a programmable manner, unlike the simple playback of a WAV or AIFF file. Songs composed in MIDI can be transposed to a different key, the tempo can

Figure 1.9 MIDI control panel playing rock at the Yamaha Web site.

be changed dynamically, instruments can be dropped in or out of the mix to show a comparison between musical effects (such as a harmony line being added to a melody line), or one instrument can be changed to another voice (perhaps to compare a saxophone lead line against a clarinet). This flexibility in handling the music construction and playback makes MIDI attractive for online instruction in music concepts, providing accompaniment to presentations and demos (altering the playback to match a course through a presentation), or to help budding musicians develop compositional skills.

The Ancient Future Web site provides several innovative uses of MIDI, including a section that explains polyrhythms and lets you listen to examples of two different rhythm patterns melded together. You can first listen to each individual pattern and then play the patterns back in combined form. This type of presentation is much more effective than trying to explain the same concept verbally or through graphics. Figure 1.10 shows a screen from the Ancient Future site.

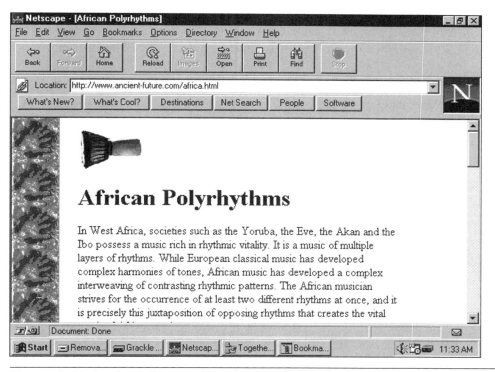

Figure 1.10 Ancient Future discussion of polyrhythms.

Controlling MIDI Playback

The use of JavaScript to control MIDI playback is particularly attractive to Webmasters. JavaScript, if you haven't yet encountered it, provides a robust event-driven programming language that provides interaction with all of the typical objects contained in an HTML document: forms, buttons, text boxes, and so on. JavaScript can also interact with Java applets and plug-ins (including MIDI plug-ins), so with a little imagination and some programming skills, you can handle sound playback interactively. Techniques for accomplishing this are provided in Chapter 8.

The creation or use of MIDI files can be simple or complex, depending on the level of involvement a Webmaster wants to have with these files. It is well within the realm of possibility for a Webmaster who is a non-musician to create music for playback by entering the notes from a piece of sheet music into a sequencer program and assigning instrument voices staff by staff. There is a vast library of sheet music dating back before copyright laws took effect and all of this music is accessible to you if you have the patience to enter and work with it a bit.

For example, if you are creating a Web site that deals with Civil War history, you could accompany the site viewing with MIDI music keyed in from sheet music from Civil War days. A simple banjo and guitar piece could effectively provide the musical backdrop you need (look at what Ken Burns did in his PBS Civil War documentary using minimal instruments that were hauntingly effective as accompaniment to the photos and diary readings in this series). Some techniques for accomplishing this and entering music in this manner are provided in Chapter 2.

MIDI composition can also be very complex. Those who come to this book from a musician's background know that the study and use of MIDI as a compositional tool can be an ongoing process taking many years to master. Quality MIDI music can have all of the characteristics that give expressiveness to live music, but handled improperly, MIDI can be as mechanical as a wind-up tin drum. Good musicians learn how to skirt the limitations of the genre, while taking advantage of the benefits.

Because of the compactness of the sound files, MIDI can be a high-powered tool in the hands of a Webmaster and one of the easiest ways to enhance a site with music. Chapter 2 goes into basic MIDI processes in more detail.

Other Types of Sound

This chapter has covered three of the major possibilities to consider when choosing to embed sound in an HTML document: sound file downloading, streaming audio, and MIDI. There are more, and we deal with some of the other techniques throughout this book, but the methods mentioned are those that are currently predominant and likely to retain their position for some time to come.

Another rising contender in the music arena is the MOD file. MOD practitioners are wildly enthusiastic about the potential of this medium, which combines some of the advantages of MIDI sample techniques and some of the clarity of WAV file playback and creates a compact format for storage and music playback. MOD stands for module. MOD files consist of a collection of sound samples and a sequence of instructions that dictate how to play back the musical selection. This format is rapidly evolving, and a number of different compositional tools have originated to handle file creation. Playback can be accomplished over the Web through plug-ins called trackers. MOD files have a major advantage over MIDI in that they can also handle vocals, and since the sounds contained in the file are sample based, you don't have to worry about what synthesizer is out there to handle the playback. A MOD file sounds pretty much the way the composer intended it to sound when it is played back.

Sound can also move in other ways across the Internet. Teleconferencing and telephony applications are gaining prominence rapidly. We devote a chapter to their evolution and current use. Tools such as Shockwave and QuickTime also have applications other than providing video playback or animation over the Web—they can be used for sound storage and playback as well, and we cover these types of applications in later chapters.

Sound is becoming commonplace on the Web. Your mastery of the techniques for capturing and presenting it will become a valuable asset in your repertoire of Web communication skills.

A Stern Warning

It's easy to get lost in the "one-more-piece-of-equipment" syndrome. Anyone who has ever owned a computer has faced this dilemma. "If I just had this one extra piece of software, I could train my computer to read Balinese poetry and recite it to me in Cindy Lauper's voice. Or, with just a small extra piece of hardware, I could set up my computer to sample my moods using galvanic skin response and then use an aromatherapy module to fill the room with appropriate smells." There is an endless array of tools, gadgets, and software available that can quickly drain the bank accounts of anyone less prosperous than Bill Gates.

The audio technology world is filled with similar temptations. The range and number of MIDI devices alone can fill many pages of a music catalog. There are similar assortments of equipment to fill up home studio recording racks, ranging from digital effects boxes to power amplifier modules, all of which can give you more capabilities, but you can quickly get caught up in the spiral of thinking you need just one more device to get everything exactly right.

We've written this book primarily for those Web enthusiasts who favor simplicity. Most of the audio recording discussed in these pages can be accomplished with a modest home studio including a basic mixer and a reasonable quality computer sound board. Techniques for boosting audio quality using accessible recording gear, such as a DAT recorder, are covered, but not required. Most of the sound processing can be accomplished using mainstream sound editing applications (rather than external gear), but anyone who has rack-mounted sound processing equipment could certainly perform the same types of tasks described in some of the procedures discussed.

The range of sound processing tasks that can be accomplished within the boundaries of modern digital sound editing software is incredible. Tools such as Hohner Midia's Samplitude Studio and Red Roaster, Sonic Foundry's Sound Forge, Macromedia's SoundEdit 16, Emagic's Logic Audio, and others can provide audio output that rivals anything that can be done in a professional studio. Digital sound processing is quite different from analog sound processing in that you can achieve extremely high-quality audio with inexpensive tools. With analog gear, the equipment to keep down noise levels and achieve professional results can easily require tens of thousands of dollars of investment. With a thousand-dollar computer, a four-hundred dollar sound board, and a top-notch sound editing application you can produce audio material of the highest possible caliber.

The other part of this stern warning is: Have some fun with all these digital tools. Working with computers tends to be a very mechanical, methodical thing. You can write music in a MIDI sequencer by tapping on computer keys and never touching an instrument and it can be very fine music. But it's also good to tap into the physical side and the emotion of music and speech. Howl into a microphone or read a poem with as much feeling as you can muster. Turn up the saturation on your guitar amplifier and play some wild '60s Stones' rock, beat on a drum, or even on a set of MIDI drum pads, or dance around the room and sing. Audio carries emotion and feeling as well as it conveys thoughts and ideas—these two areas can be linked in ways that are more effective than many other ways of reaching or communicating with people. As it says on the package of the RealAudio Player Plus software, "I listened and the Web roared." Take advantage of the best that audio has to offer and weave this philosophy into your Web audio productions.

Is that stern enough? Don't make us have to repeat this message again.

A Performance Stage for Anyone

Perhaps the most hopeful phenomenon of this decade is the mass acceptance and use of the Internet. In a simple and forthright manner, the Internet brings a healthy measure of equality to communication. No longer does a small group of multimillion-dollar broadcast corporations have exclusive access to the public airwaves. The Internet is open to all—anyone can put up his or her creations, opinions, mumblings, musings, or brilliant solutions to world problems, and maybe be rewarded or recognized for their efforts. It's a reassuring thought that a common person or young kid can have an easily accessible forum and platform for success. Likewise, as you develop audio files for Internet distribution, your aspirations have a worldwide media stage on which to develop, perform, and improve.

Internet audio is a medium for creative expression. It's now more available to anyone than anything that has ever existed before in our media-saturated society. This book is not written exclusively for Web-conscious musicians or recording enthusiasts. Rather, it is written for those Web page designers who recognize the cultural significance of music, and those who want to open up their Web audio capabilities. In the chapters that follow, we will approach all the Web audio possibilities, including Internet telephony, text-to-speech browser plug-ins, desktop broadcasting (multicasting), interactive audio hookups, and some fantasy daydreams for the future of Internet audio (such as collaborative music composition over the Internet).

With apologies to Shakespeare, "All the Web is a stage..."

Compact Sound for
the Web: MIDI

If you're new to MIDI (Musical Instrument Digital Interface), this chapter offers a basic primer in MIDI recording and editing techniques, including a summary of the different ways that you can create and work with MIDI files. A number of different programs that can work with the MIDI sound format are described, including products that can interweave MIDI tracks with digital audio material. MIDI is a complex subject, deserving book-length treatment. If your interest is in obtaining proficiency in this area, this primer should give you enough understanding of the processes involved in creating MIDI files to enable you to incorporate this sound format into your HTML documents. While not appropriate for every application, MIDI can deliver fine quality music with minimal bandwidth requirements.

Among the many techniques for putting sound on the Web, MIDI offers one of the most compact and flexible audio storage formats available. Native support for the MIDI file format in both Netscape Navigator and Microsoft Internet Explorer browsers ensures that most listeners in your Internet audience will be able to listen to MIDI sequences without problems. The major requirement is that their computer includes MIDI playback capability—either through a sound board with wavetable or FM synthesis or through software synthesis, such as is included in Macintosh computers in the form of the QuickTime Musical Instruments.

Musical Expression in the Digital Medium

Like a modern art movement, this digital musique era is catching our attention, weaving sound samples into patterned sequences like nothing heard before. Music is the virtual flower of culture, and we nonwilting earthlings are capable of some mighty awe-inspiring displays of sentimental amusement. In this and the following chapter we want to encourage you to use your computer as a digital recorder, to compose, edit, and process sound files (in other words, to do simple sound-file production). Even if your music training and background are minimal, you can present nicely sequenced and edited sound streams through your Web site. Digital music production tools encourage originality and experimentation, and these new technologies can help boost and enhance your own musical expressiveness and creativity. Even if you haven't spent years at Julliard studying music, you can craft music on the computer that is unique and expressive.

If someone drops into your Web site and hears "never-been-heard-before" original music, the flash of originality can cut through the endless mediocrity of the typical Web landscape. The unfamiliar refrain, the evocative melody, the tempo of the rhythm coerces him or her to linger. At this point in history, most people still find the Internet responding slowly. Getting some sign of life to your Web site visitor (as quickly as possible) is important to maintain interest and a sense of excitement. Properly engineered sound can captivate the visitor during those disturbingly long intervals while images are downloading. A recorded sequence of sound events interspersed with the warmth of a human voice can be good entertainment. Why not get crafty and follow your Web site visitor's info-selections with vocal or musical responses, prompting his or her next screen selection? In this and the following chapter we would like to suggest some simple but effective sound-file generation and processing techniques that you can use for final preparation of the audio for Web delivery. Before we go off blaming the Internet Web audio tools for being less than perfect, let's examine some sound-sample production and enhancement techniques. The quality of sound on the Web is improving. Let's be sure to have some cleanly prepared, sonically enhanced, righteous musical offerings to give the visitors. Catch their interest and they will probably come back more than once.

MIDI Vocabulary Lesson

Like many technologies of the twentieth century, MIDI has its share of acronyms (including the term MIDI itself), which can make it difficult for novices to penetrate the jargon and understand the underlying concepts. This section defines some of the more common MIDI terminology. If you're well versed in MIDI, you may want to skip ahead to a later section.

Aftertouch: The degree of pressure continuously applied to one or more keys (on a music keyboard) after the initial stroke and while the key is being held down. This value can be factored into the response of the MIDI voice that is played back for various effects.

Channel voice message: A message consisting of performance data that is transmitted via a channel between MIDI devices.

Digital Signal Processor (abbreviated as DSP): A special-purpose integrated circuit that performs high-speed processing of various types of digital signals, particularly audio waveforms. DSP chips are found on many quality sound boards and as components on the motherboards of modern, well-equipped computer systems. DSP chips make it much easier to process certain audio effects and to sample incoming audio waveforms at high rates.

Filter: A MIDI filter (usually implemented as a dialog box) permits the user to disable certain types of MIDI events, like modulation wheel data, aftertouch data, control or program change data, from being recorded. It can also be used to disable the record functionality of specific channels.

General MIDI (abbreviated as GM): A standardized means of referring to MIDI instrument voices through a series of numbers, called program assignments, ranging from 0 through 127. GM-compliant synthesizers can play MIDI data files created on other devices without scrambling the voices.

Musical Instrument Digital Interface (abbreviated to MIDI): An internationally respected standard designed to support communication between various types of electronic musical instruments.

MIDI channel: The ability to assign each part in a piece of music its own voice is accomplished using MIDI channels. It also provides a method of transmitting messages in MIDI format to separate MIDI devices (keyboards or sound modules) for layered or non-simultaneous playback.

MIDI device: A piece of equipment containing sound synthesis hardware and designed to support the MIDI standard for sending, playing, and receiving MIDI event commands and data.

Modulation wheel: A control wheel often located on the left side of a MIDI keyboard controller used to generate control modulation data for pitch bend, filter cutoff frequency modulation, vibrato depth, and so on, including whatever modulation control capabilities the keyboard has that can be assigned to modulation wheel control.

Multi-timbral: The capability of a MIDI device to generate multiple sounds at an instant in time.

Note off: A time-based MIDI message that denotes when and what key on the keyboard is released. Some keyboards issue a Note on event with an amplitude of 0 to generate note off instead of using the Note off event.

Note on: A time-based MIDI message that denotes when and what key on the keyboard has been pressed.

Patch: A physical or software linkage that maps a MIDI instrument voice to an ID.

Polyphony: The total number of notes that can be simultaneously played by a MIDI device. Common MIDI equipment will support between 16 and 32 voices.

Program Change message: A message transmitted via a MIDI channel that indicates that a different voice should be assigned to the specified part.

Release rate: The speed at which a note decays to the point at which it can no longer be heard.

Sample: A digitally recorded audio file packaged for a particular use. Short samples that include loop points serve as instrument voices that can be assigned to a MIDI channel. These are sometimes distributed on CDs from which they can be downloaded to memory in a synthesizer system and played as a voice. Longer samples might be pieced together to form music progressions using a program such as Hohner Midia's Samplitude Studio. In general, though, a sample can refer to any sound or series of sounds captured in digital format.

Sequencer: In its most common use, a sequencer is a software application that stores MIDI data, provides a means for editing and modifying the data, and plays back a datastream through some type of synthesizer. Sequencer programs such as Cakewalk Pro and Voyetra's Digital Orchestrator Plus provide a variety of means for viewing and changing the data, including standard musical notation, event lists in text form, and symbols representing the duration of notes and their pitch. Past-generation sequencers existed in hardware form where you could store a musical progression in a standalone box and play it back when needed, but this product use has faded with the proliferation of computer-based sequencing software applications.

Synthesizer (also called sound synthesizer): A synthesizer is a type of electronic musical instrument that has the ability to generate, combine, and shape waveforms to produce sounds and music in a variety of ways. Keyboard synthesizers often include internal modules featuring wavetables that simulate musical instruments, such as pianos, cellos, and trombones. Analog synthesizers can be used to physically shape waveforms using oscillators and filters to produce sounds unlike those of any other musical instrument. Many sound boards also contain ICs that perform synthesis either from wavetables of sounds or through FM synthesis (a less satisfactory way of reproducing sounds). Some type of digital synthesizer is required to play back sound files stored in MIDI format.

System Exclusive messages: A MIDI message custom-tailored to a specific MIDI device. These messages support features that are unique to an individual piece of equipment as defined by the manufacturer. Individual products tend to have different feature sets and respond to different SysEx strings.

Tone module (sometimes called a tone generator): An electronic device equipped with a collection of digital samples designed to interface with a MIDI sequencer for playback of MIDI data files. High-end tone modules can be expanded with libraries of digitally recorded sounds; for example, Kurzweil markets a module containing carefully constructed piano samples. Other tone modules, such as Yamaha's MU-80, support extensions to the MIDI standard—XG MIDI, in the case of Yamaha. Tone modules can be used either with computer MIDI interfaces or connected to the MIDI out of a keyboard controller for live performances.

Velocity-sensitive keys: When applied to a MIDI keyboard, this term indicates that the keys respond to the speed at which they are struck. The relative velocity is recorded as a MIDI value, and this value can be applied to a mathematical curve that indicates the amplitude of the note that is played in response to a given velocity. This feature allows the dynamics of a keyboard performance to be accurately captured and recorded (as opposed to recording every keyboard stroke at the same velocity, which can result in wooden, mechanical-sounding playback). Most MIDI sequencer programs also let you manually edit the velocity values stored for individual notes.

A Capsule History of MIDI

The Musical Instrument Digital Interface (MIDI) is a serial communications standard used specifically with MIDI-equipped hardware for electronic synthesis of musical sound. A number of sequencer programs have emerged with their own enhancements and file format extensions; however, the .mid file extension has become the trading-card standard for cross-platform MIDI file dissemination. Any piece of MIDI-equipped hardware can usually be recognized by the 5-pin DIN connector or connectors. Unfortunately, most sound cards for internal installation in the computer require a disgusting cable adapter that connects MIDI cables to a joystick port (D-Sub connector) on the card edge.

In the early 1980s, manufacturers started delivering MIDI-equipped products. This permitted synthesizers and drum machines to be synchronized and allowed keyboard players to cable together numerous music synthesizers (from different manufacturers) to create multipatch, layered, bliss-endowed sound. A keyboardist playing one music keyboard electronically commanded all the connected MIDI-equipped synthesizers (set to receive the transmitted MIDI channel) to play.

Soon people began to realize that MIDI-equipped musical instruments were nicely suited for use with computers. Using a MIDI sequencer program, you can record tracks from your MIDI music keyboard, MIDI-equipped guitar, or MIDI what-have-you. The recorded MIDI tracks are assigned to channels; each channel can be assigned a unique instrument voice (which can be changed as the track progresses through time). To eliminate the confusion over what patch corresponds to what voice (resulting in MIDI-mapping nightmares when trying to play back a file created by one system on another system), the General MIDI (GM) standard was adopted. GM standardizes the instrument voice program numbers. If you send program change command #26 it causes a nylon-string guitar voice to be set on any GM MIDI-compliant synthesizer, sound module, or sound card. Channel number 10 is reserved for percussion sounds. There are a few exceptions, like the rare piece of gear that uses channel 16 for percussion, but it's not difficult to change the channel number set for a specific track in the MIDI sequencer program. The point is that, in most cases, you don't have to. MIDI files following General MIDI conventions have become far more portable. This portability is one reason that you can successfully exchange MIDI files on the World Wide Web with reasonable assurance they will play back using the same instrument voices from system to system.

While MIDI dates back to the early 1980s it really is not terribly antiquated. The serial transmission of MIDI codes occurs asynchronously at a baud rate of 31.25Kbps This is a relatively fast serial transfer rate. Many computer modems use a serial transfer rate of 28.8 or 33.6Kbps. Faster MIDI serial transmission would require a more expensive hardware implementation on each piece of MIDI gear, and design engineers feared this cost increase would inhibit the mass acceptance of the MIDI protocol. Music keyboards that connect directly to one of the computer's serial ports are also now available. This arrangement does not require connection to a MIDI interface card. It does, however, require that a driver be installed to manage the device. Windows95 includes rudimentary MIDI handling capabilities, but for many types of keyboards or other devices—such as tone generators—you will most likely have to install software provided by the manufacturer for handling the equipment through the serial port.

The MIDI commands are transferred serially as multibyte commands. They always start with a status byte that defines the type of transmission, and then specifier bytes of immediate data values follow. The quickest way to examine MIDI commands in action is to open the events editor of a MIDI sequencer while playing back a MIDI file. Choose a track for viewing that has recorded events and watch each time-stamped MIDI command be highlighted by the display as it is performed. The MIDI events editor is an excellent way to examine and edit your favorite musical passages. You can see the actual MIDI commands that are issued, the notes, the patch changes, the pitch bends, and the filter modulations.

So what are the drawbacks of MIDI? It only generates synthesized sound or plays back wavetable samples. It will not handle speech or song vocals unless you go to the bother of making wave samples for each word and link each sample to a MIDI note number (a rather painstaking way to sing a song). However, MIDI is far from a dead language. It's quite useful for arranging rhythmic music and can be carried to artistic extravagance. Specifications for downloadable wavetable samples have been appended to the MIDI specification. In the future, the actual instrument sound samples, as well as the music, timing, voicing, and auxiliary information that is MIDI coding as we know it, will all be transmitted much like a MOD file. To utilize the downloadable sample feature of MIDI requires that you have wavetable RAM (Sample Store) on your sound hardware, or a computer fast enough to perform software waveform synthesis. Keep your consumer senses alert and choose your next computer and sound module wisely. Some computer manufacturers have already embedded sound support and DSP hardware on the computer mainboard.

T IP Don't think of composing in MIDI as making synthetic music. Perhaps the name synthesizer is a bit cruel to apply to musical instruments. Think of it as emusic; you are a composer of musical data, speaking a powerful language of coded abbreviations that can orchestrate sound from a MIDI synthesizer (like your sound board, sound module, or MIDI-equipped music keyboard).

Using MIDI, you can specify musical temperaments, alter tunings, change the current musical key, perform playback-rate compression without affecting the pitch, modulate time on record or playback, and enter new realms of perceptual paradigm. With the musical control and flexibility offered by MIDI, you'll soon be amazing yourself (if you aren't already) and others as well.

Ways for Creating MIDI Files

You have a number of interesting paths available to you—creative options for generating sound files for delivery on your Web site—based on several different MIDI utilities. Even if you don't have the musical ability to play complex music on a keyboard in real time, there are MIDI software applications that let you transcribe standard music notation into a form that can be saved as a MIDI file and played back through a synthesizer. Some of these programs that express MIDI data in coded form can initially be a bit daunting, but they offer control and flexibility even beyond what you can get in most sequencer software. Other programs make music entry and playback as simple as dragging notes onto a musical staff and assigning an instrument voice to the musical line.

Pick those methods that appeal to you and use them interchangeably to achieve your goal. Remember that many of the digital multitrack programs now will simultaneously track MIDI, so you can add voice, vocals, or conventional instrument lines recorded by microphone. These approaches are discussed in more detail in later sections of this chapter.

Score Some Notes

One of the most direct ways of creating a MIDI data file is to enter a musical composition using your mouse and computer keyboard. A number of programs let you place notes and music notation symbols onto displayed music staves and have the computer convert your input data to a MIDI file. Figure 2.1 illustrates this process.

Programs that let you create MIDI in this manner include NoteWorthy Composer (NoteWorthy ArtWare), Power Tracks Pro (by PG Music), and Digital Orchestrator Plus (Voyetra).

Scan Some Sheet Music

Entering music notation manually can be tedious. One way around this problem is to use a software application that lets you work from scanned image files of music. You can create a .tiff image from a page of sheet music and then have the computer translate it into a MIDI file. Figure 2.2 illustrates this process.

A program that lets you create MIDI in this manner is MIDISCAN for Windows by Musitek. This program can work with even fairly rough scans resulting from less-than-perfect sheet music.

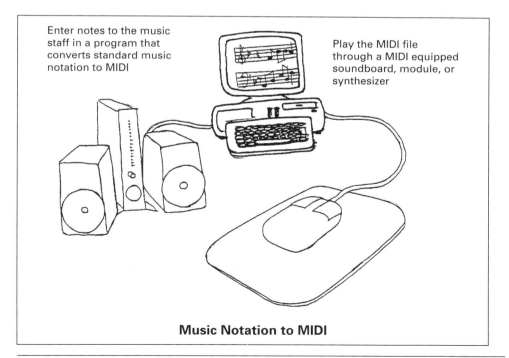

Figure 2.1 Entering a music composition by notation.

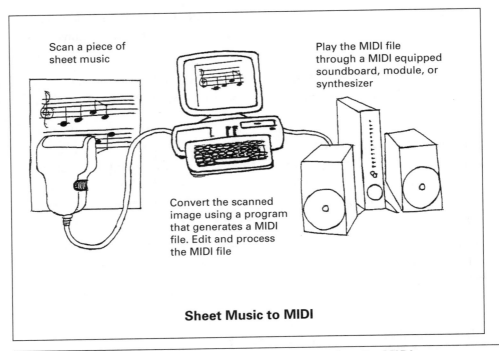

Figure 2.2 Scanning in sheet music for conversion to MIDI.

Record MIDI Tracks

If you're musically inclined or you have friends or colleagues who play instruments, you can record live performances as MIDI files. To enter the musical data, you can play a MIDI-equipped music keyboard, drum pads, or MIDI-equipped guitar and record the MIDI events into your computer's MIDI sequencer or multitrack waveform recording software that has MIDI record capability. Figure 2.3 shows this process.

Many different MIDI sequencer programs support this approach. Instruments can be recorded either one at a time, with performers listening to the previously recorded tracks as they lay down new tracks, or simultaneously, if you have the hardware to support the recording of multiple MIDI devices at the same time. Programs that record to MIDI include a large number of sequencer applications, including Digital Orchestrator Plus (by Voyetra), Cubase (by Steinberg), and Musicator Audio.

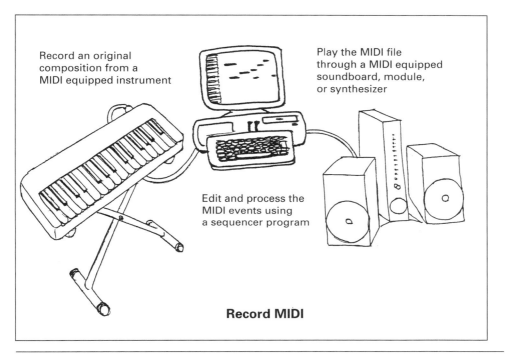

Record an original composition from a MIDI equipped instrument

Play the MIDI file through a MIDI equipped soundboard, module, or synthesizer

Edit and process the MIDI events using a sequencer program

Record MIDI

Figure 2.3 Recording to MIDI from instruments.

Compute an Arrangement

Some MIDI-capable applications allow you to compose an entire musical composition based on selected chord progressions, musical styles, and so on. To compose a MIDI file with this type of program, you enter the musical chord progressions using one of several different notation systems. For example, one program, Band-in-a-Box, lets you use a common chord formula notation (Gm7 stands for G minor seventh) or a system based on the chord's position in the diatonic scale with roman numerals representing the position (V7 represents a G dominant seventh chord in the key of C). There are other systems as well to suit your individual preference. You can also indicate tempo rates, specify the desired accompaniment style, and generate solos based on interpretations of different artists' soloing techniques (for example, you could generate a guitar solo over a particular chord pattern based on Wes Montgomery's technique). Once you're done with the composition, you can save it as a standard MIDI format file. Musical compositions of this sort can effectively capture the essence of certain periods in musical history and different musical genres.

Figure 2.4 shows the main application window for Band-in-a-Box, demonstrating how a chord sequence can be constructed while you are composing.

Although it is useful for some applications, you need to take care with this type of approach to avoid generating musical pieces that sound unduly mechanical. Some of the styles and effects work better than others, and as a Web author generating files for MIDI playback in a browser you should exercise discrimination in the choices.

Compose by Keystrokes

For the ultimate control over the MIDI datastream, learn a MIDI shorthand language and assemble MIDI code sequences from the textual strings entered via your computer keyboard. While this approach requires more skill and mastery of the underlying MIDI architecture, it also offers you a degree of control and precision that you are unlikely to find in a conventional MIDI sequencer program. Figure 2.5 illustrates one possible application, constructing the raw elements of a MIDI

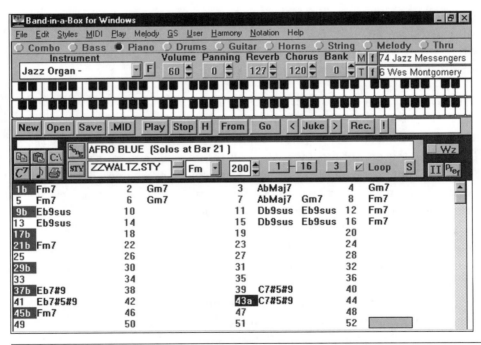

Figure 2.4 Constructing a chord sequence in Band-in-a-Box.

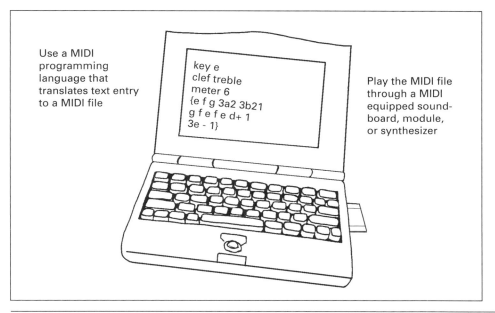

key e
clef treble
meter 6
{e f g 3a2 3b21
g f e f e d+ 1
3e - 1}

Use a MIDI programming language that translates text entry to a MIDI file

Play the MIDI file through a MIDI equipped sound-board, module, or synthesizer

Figure 2.5 Entering precise MIDI events.

datastream on a laptop for conversion into a MIDI data file. The program being represented that uses this approach is called MidiText (by Metsan Corporation). Extremely intricate and expressive MIDI sequences can be devised using this approach, but mastery of the program for accomplishing this task requires commitment and patience.

Open Mic to MIDI

Sometimes called Pitch-to-MIDI, this approach lets you sing (or hum) into a microphone and have the computer convert the input to MIDI data. You can also play a monophonic musical instrument into a microphone (like a flute or recorder) and have MIDI event code generated in real time. Singing or humming can be a useful means for entering melody lines for a person who may not play a musical instrument but who has a good pitch sense and can sing well. Figure 2.6 illustrates this process.

Each of these approaches has its own tradeoffs. The requirements of a particular project will probably suggest the approach that makes the most sense. In some cases, you may be able to combine several of these techniques to finalize a MIDI file.

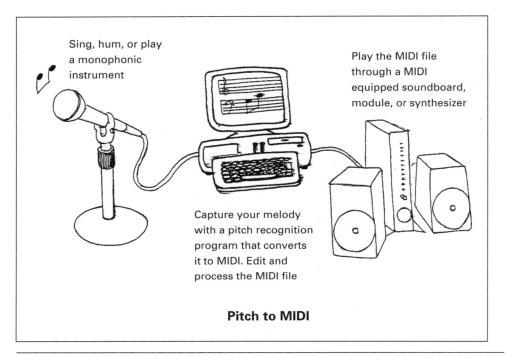

Figure 2.6 Using a microphone to go from pitch to MIDI.

Sources of MIDI Material

Anything musical (and some things completely nonmusical) can be expressed in MIDI notation. If your goal is to acquire or create MIDI files for use on the Web, you have a number of options available, as summarized in the following list.

- **Hire a musician:** Many talented composers and musicians eke out a living in a variety of pursuits, dividing their time between live gigs, jingle writing, scoring music for commercials, composing musical training exercises, teaching students, and so on. Those who are set up with the equipment to produce MIDI format files might be willing to compose original MIDI material for your use. Make sure if you work out such an arrangement that you construct a Work-for-Hire agreement to ensure that there will not be any legal or royalty hassles over your continued use of the material. Most musicians should be willing to accept this kind of agreement as long as you clearly spell out the terms.

- **Score a period piece:** Music in the public domain is yours for the taking. Given the excellent available applications that let you either transcribe or scan sheet music for conversion into MIDI data, you can quickly move music into this convenient format. For example, you might have access to the sheet music for a nineteenth century Irish folk tune that could be entered and assigned a banjo voice in MIDI. The music could be played as the backdrop on a Web site devoted to travel in the area covering Ireland. Music can serve as a valuable cue to particular cultures or parts of the world; you can integrate musical cues like this to orient people to Web site content.

- **Buy royalty-free songs**: You've heard of clip art. You can also purchase musical clips in MIDI format that are free of copyright restrictions and royalties. In other words, the music, usually contained on a CD or CD-ROM, can be freely incorporated into your multimedia works or integrated into a Web site. Many of these types of libraries can be obtained based on particular themes; for example, a collection of MIDI clips that sets a mysterious mood or that has an upbeat, driving tempo or that reflects a peaceful, New Age feel. You can also find royalty-free clips of this type on the CD-ROMs of music sequencer applications. Check the license agreement included with the software. Often these songs are available for use in your productions without restriction.

- **Capture a performance**: If you know a skilled pianist and you want to incorporate a Mozart sonata into your Web site, sit him or her down in front of your MIDI keyboard and start recording into a sequencer program. If the pianist hits a bad note or two, you can edit the mistakes later from the sequencer window. If this person can play expressively (and your MIDI keyboard is velocity sensitive), the result can be a very high-quality musical piece that you will transfer well in MIDI format to a variety of playback situations. Piano pieces in general can be transported effectively, and they sound reasonably accurate even when played back through more modest synthesizers.

- **Build a song**: Some easy-to-use programs, such as PG Music Band-in-a-Box and Jammer, let you construct songs in a number of different styles and then output your creation to MIDI file format. These packages contain the basic elements— rhythm patterns, instrument voicings, style cues, and so on—that enable you to generate a respectable simulation of a particular musical genre. For example, if you decided that it would add some flair to your Web site to have a 1910-era Rag-Time tune playing in the background, you could fashion the chords and rhythm patterns into a finished piece, even adding a custom melody line. This approach, if used indiscriminately, can sound a bit canned, but if used with some creativity can create some very interesting MIDI files in a short period of time.

Copyright Considerations

Always bear in mind that published or recorded music of recent vintage is invariably protected by copyright. If you plan to present music on your Web site, it should be music that you have either licensed for use or original music that you have created yourself. As you wander around the Web, you'll encounter many personal sites that use MIDI background music, often culled from popular music pieces that have been converted by someone into MIDI file format. The nature of MIDI makes it easy to create and distribute these files. While it's unlikely that overzealous prosecutors will attempt to levy huge fines on individuals who are using this kind of material, commercial and business sites could be targets of copyright infringement suits for unauthorized use of musical material. Even on a personal site, the use of copyrighted material is venturing into those gray legal areas where innocent intentions may be misconstrued. Given the ease with which early music (prior to 1941) can be adapted for MIDI, there is a rich source of material available for use to anyone with the tenacity to adapt these works to MIDI. You can also select from MIDI copyright-free and royalty-free libraries that provide custom music for many types of uses, usually on CD or CD-ROM, often for minimal expense. Perhaps the most fulfilling way to add music to a site, however, is to create your own. MIDI is an excellent framework to accomplish this.

 For more information about copyright issues and the correct method for copyrighting your own MIDI compositions, you can visit the site of the MIDI Manufacturer's Association at:

home.earthlink.net/~mma/smf_usco.htm

The aforementioned site also includes the necessary forms to complete and return to the U.S. Copyright office for formalizing your copyright registration. The forms are stored in Adobe Acrobat Portable Document File (PDF) format.

TIP The most recent MIDI specification includes the definition of an area within a stored MIDI file to annotate copyright information. Some MIDI players and plug-ins will display the copyright while a file is being played back. Having the copyright region filled in appropriately can help ensure that your original MIDI files are at least initially marked as your own; however, it would not be difficult for someone to modify your MIDI file and remove the copyright information.

MIDI Applications Overview

The following sections cover several different applications that let you create and edit MIDI music files, ranging from inexpensive freeware and shareware applications to high-end professional-caliber programs. You can compose some very professional-sounding pieces from even the simplest applications, so if your goal is to put music up on the Web, you don't need to immediately rush out and buy a $400 sequencer program. You can do a lot of useful work even with a $40 program.

A number of examples of how to put these MIDI applications to use appear in this chapter.

Composing on a Music Staff

If you can read music, it may be appealing for you to write music for your Web site by composing on a graphically displayed score of music staves. With just a rudimentary knowledge of music notation it is possible to compose by entering notes of different duration on the standard music staff. If you have no experience in this field, give it a try anyway. It's not as hard as you might think.

NoteWorthy Composer

NoteWorthy Composer is an inexpensive but powerful shareware program that can serve the needs of many multimedia Web site designers. This program lets you create a MIDI sound file from music you enter on the music staff using standard music notation. Even if you have only a passing familiarity with the conventions of standard musical notation, you can add the music notation symbols easily just by matching the toolbar icons in the program with the symbols on the sheet music. Ease of use is a primary consideration, but NoteWorthy Composer also contains a number of features that rival much more expensive, professional-caliber scoring applications.

The main application for NoteWorthy Composer, shown in Figure 2.7, provides a pair of toolbars. One contains the music notation symbols to be inserted onto the staff; the other, the primary tools for interacting with the program. You can start from a fresh file with an empty music staff or import an existing MIDI file and then embellish it. The program makes short work of even fairly large imported MIDI files and quickly displays the notation, supplying a staff for each instrument voice detected in the MIDI file. You can go in and add or remove staves, making it possible to easily enhance and extend existing music—perhaps adding a saxophone line to harmonize with an already recorded trumpet solo, or adding a bass line to accompany a guitar and flute.

To start a new musical piece from scratch, simply drop down the File menu and select the **New** option. Complete the file information and then click on the **Score Builder** button. Specify the number of staves to be used. You can then insert the clef symbols, time signature, musical key, expression marks, and even the MIDI patch (instrument voice) for each staff. After this very short setup sequence, you are ready to start writing music. As you compose, you can listen to your evolving work by clicking the **Play** button and previewing the musical sequence as it develops. If you make mistakes along the way, NoteWorthy Composer supports up to 100 levels of Undo, encouraging you to experiment with different musical ideas without destroying your previous sequences.

Entering notes is not particularly elegant, but it is workable. Click the appropriate note duration button (half note, quarter note, eighth note, etc.) displayed on the

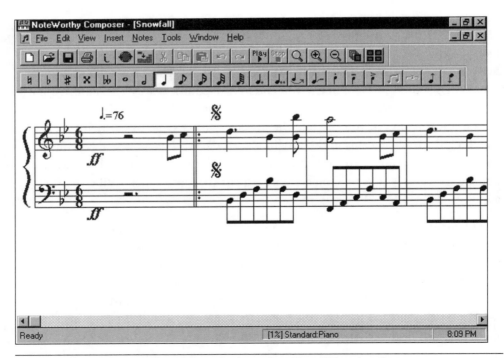

Figure 2.7 Main application window for NoteWorthy Composer.

lower toolbar. Position the cursor on the desired staff notation position and press the **Enter** key. The selected note is written to the staff. Optionally, you can position the cursor and click the right mouse button to bring up a menu of frequently used options, including an option for entering a note. This is a little faster than having to position the pointer, move from the mouse to the **Enter** key, and then back to the mouse to position the next note. However, once the note is in place, you can't physically grab it for repositioning. You can, however, select and move notes from the keyboard using a shortcut combination (**SHIFT+CTRL** while pressing the Up Arrow and Down Arrow keys). Other key combinations satisfy all of the editing functions available within the program. This feature, uncommon in products of this type, would make it possible to compose musical compositions through voice recognition programs such as Kurzweil VOICE and Dragon Dictate (see Chapter 9 for information about these products).

While editing music pieces, the active note duration button remains in effect until another note duration is selected. Using a menu or keystrokes, you can easily insert rests and special marks. Do you want a treble and bass clef like piano music, or four staves like quartet arrangements? Staves can be added and removed with ease. The program also supports flexible insertion of lyric lines—up to several different verses' worth. NoteWorthy Composer is flexible and adaptable enough to be extremely useful, yet not as complicated (read: difficult to learn) as some of the expensive music score publishing programs. You can preview (listen to) your composition at any point while you're entering notes. All of your work can be saved as a MIDI (.mid) file, making it suitable for easy Web transmission. NoteWorthy Composer also supports a number of different MIDI control features for added flexibility when composing.

NoteWorthy Player

NoteWorthy ArtWare also offers a freeware product, downloadable from their Web site, that can load and play the native file format used by NoteWorthy Composer (.nwc). This utility, called NoteWorthy Player, also can load, notate, and play standard .mid and .rmi files. This would be a handy little tool for a Web composer's toolkit, offering a compact and easily accessible means for evaluating and previewing MIDI files. Files could also be quickly converted to standard musical notation for printing or reference. You can find contact information for NoteWorthy ArtWare in Appendix C.

An Example Using NoteWorthy Composer Products such as NoteWorthy Composer offer a convenient bridge from any musical work that exists in the form of sheet music to the more visceral auditory soundscape that can be achieved using MIDI. In a fairly short period of time, you can enter and listen to any work of music, giving you a window to the musical worlds that existed in earlier times. This, of course, also gives you the ability to take any copyright-free work of music and convert it into a .mid file for distribution on the Web. If you need to add a historically accurate musical backdrop for a Web page, this is an easy route for accomplishing the task. The following example is intended to give you an idea of the steps followed in creating a usable MIDI file from sheet music.

Let's imagine that you've negotiated a contract with the Board of Directors for a small New England historical museum that wants to provide a number of historical links and topics to focus interest on their activities. One of your goals is to provide some perspective on the lives of typical New Englanders just prior to 1800. You decide that music is a great way to set the tone for exploration into these colonial times, so you begin researching in the local library. One of the songs that turns up in your research is called the Anacreontic Song, complete with sheet music. Written in England, this song celebrates the delights of wine and women, and it was often parodied in the colonies, with lyricists such as Thomas Paine and Francis Scott Key spoofing the British version. You've devised a Web page that illustrates after-hour pub activities in the colonies and decide to use the Anacreontic Song as background music when a visitor enters the room. MIDI offers the perfect way to deliver this song, since the compact files will load and start playing quickly, and both Internet Explorer and Navigator browsers support the MIDI format without plug-ins.

How do you move from the sheet music for the Anacreontic Song into MIDI file format? This is where NoteWorthy Composer comes into play.

Start by opening a new file and choosing two staves from the Score Builder window, shown in Figure 2.8. You can create a simple composition using a piano voicing and putting notes to be played by the left hand on one staff with a bass clef and the right hand on another staff. This type of arrangement can be used for many kinds of sheet music that adapt well to piano playback.

As you return to the main application window, the two staves are displayed. Using the **Clef** command from the Insert menu, you apply the treble clef to the upper staff and the bass clef to the lower. Similarly, you insert the key signature (A

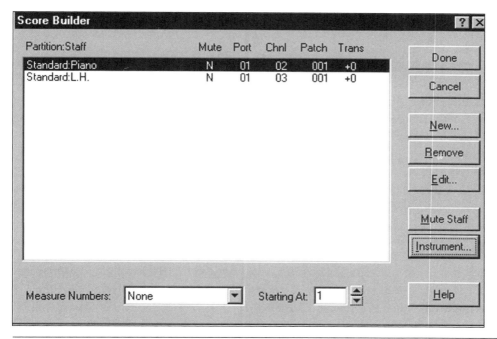

Figure 2.8 Creating two staves in the Score Builder.

Major, which is three sharps) and the time signature (3/4). The sheet music for the Anacreontic Song indicates that it should be played *With Spirit*. NoteWorthy Composer includes an option where you can specify the Performance Style (also from the Insert menu), which affects the MIDI playback. Piano voicings are a bit more subtle than other instruments, but the effect can be clearly distinguished. The performance styles are specified by the traditional Italian terms (legato, con brio, dolce, and so on), so you'd best consult a music reference if you don't speak Italian. To add some spirit to the playback, I selected the Animato performance style.

The next step is to key in the individual notes staff by staff. While many computer activities are faster by mouse, NoteWorthy Composer seems better suited in some ways to keyboard entry. There are shortcuts for most operations. It is a fairly quick matter to use the arrow keys to position the cursor, select a note value from the toolbar using the plus (+) and minus (-) keys, and press **Enter** to insert the note. To create a chord member, you simply position the cursor to the next note position and press **CTRL-ENTER** to attach the new note as a chord member with the previous note. Bar lines can be inserted with the **Tab** key, or if you're lazy, you can leave out the bar lines and Composer will automatically insert them for you later. Once you get accustomed to the system, entry goes quite quickly. Figure 2.9 shows the first few measures of the Anacreontic Song.

Song sequences appear in one long continuous staff, which is helpful if you want to view and alter part of the arrangement as you are composing. As you're playing back the song, Composer highlights the notes that are playing and automatically pans from measure-to-measure to keep you oriented. You can mute individual tracks to listen to just those parts of the music that you want to focus on. When you are ready to print, Composer takes the long strand of music notation and breaks the staves at the appropriate places, wrapping the lines to fill a standard 8.5 × 11-inch sheet. The print options, including point size, staff labeling, lyric display, and so on, can be modified to suit your preferences. A preview mode, shown in Figure 2.10, lets you see the layout of the pages before you actually print.

When you've finished your composition, you can save it in NoteWorthy Composer file format (.nwc) or export it to standard MIDI format (.mid). Once in MIDI format, you have the music in a form that can be easily delivered over the Internet (as explained further in Chapter 8).

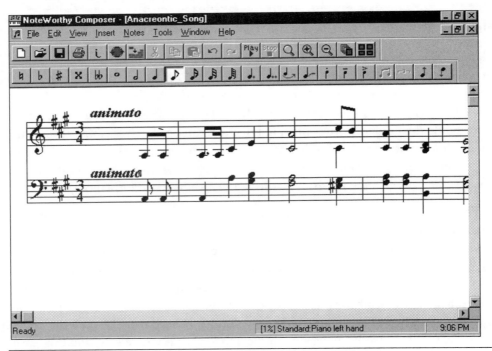

Figure 2.9 Note entry for the Anacreontic Song.

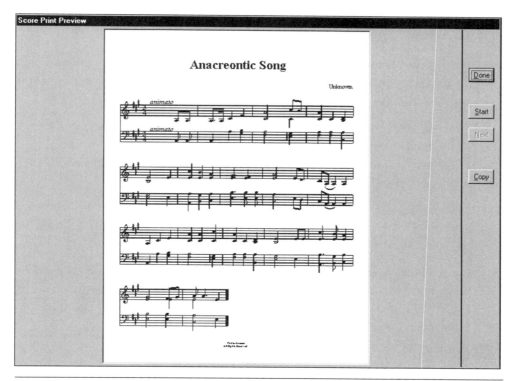

Figure 2.10 Print preview of Composer.

Delivering Sheet Music with Sound Playback

Sheet music represents another method of communicating musical information over the Web. You can actually use a program such as NoteWorthy Composer to generate the sheet music for embedding in a Microsoft Word document, Corel WordPerfect document, Adobe Acrobat portable document format, or Common Ground digital paper format. Word and WordPerfect both accept embedded objects as well, allowing you to insert the actual MIDI sequence in combination with the representation of the music notation. In other words, someone could view the sheet music and also click on a media player in the document to listen to the MIDI playing back. The resulting document could be distributed over the Web; such an approach might be a useful way to distribute music lessons to students. A student could hear the correct way to play a piece as well as practice directly from the musical notation.

From NoteWorthy Composer to Word with MIDI Object Creating these types of documents is surprisingly easy. For example, let's examine the process for creating a Word file consisting of a musical score from NoteWorthy Composer and an embedded MIDI sequence object.

1. Finish your composition in NoteWorthy Composer and save it in .nwc format for future use. Also use the **Export** option to create a MIDI file from the notation. For this example, we'll use the name kooltune.mid.

2. From the File menu, select **Print.** Choose those options from the Score Print dialog box, shown in Figure 2.11, that you want to apply to the printout. Make sure you set the Notation Size to a point value that will create a clear and legible piece of music.

3. Click the **Preview** button and then select **Copy** from the Preview display that appears. This moves the sheet music contents to a metafile in the clipboard ready for insertion into a document.

4. Open a New Word document and select **Paste** from the Edit menu. The sheet music is copied from the clipboard into your Word document, as shown in Figure 2.12. You can add introductory or explanatory text before or after the frame containing the sheet music image.

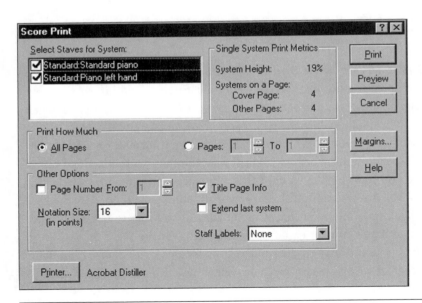

Figure 2.11 Score Print dialog box.

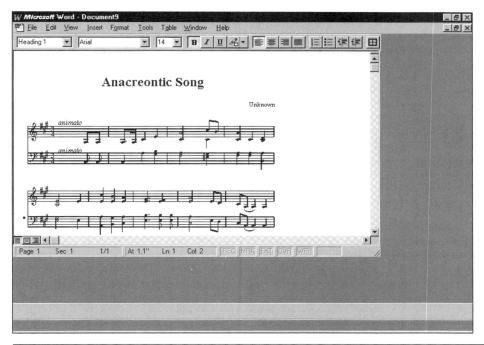

Figure 2.12 Sheet music pasted into Word.

5. To add the MIDI sequence as an object into the same document, drop down the Insert menu and select **Object**. From the list of objects that appears, select **MIDI Sequence**.

6. From the Insert Clip menu, select **MIDI Sequence**. Locate the file that you want to use (kooltune.mid) and select it. Word inserts an icon for the embedded MIDI sequence into the document, as shown in Figure 2.13, and displays the media player for the clip in a toolbar. You can sample the clip by using the transport controls in the toolbar.

7. Once the clip is embedded in this manner, the Word document can be saved and distributed as a downloadable file from an HTML document or, for Microsoft Internet Explorer users, as an ActiveX document for direct playback in Explorer. The person viewing the file only needs to double-click on the embedded object to start the sound playing.

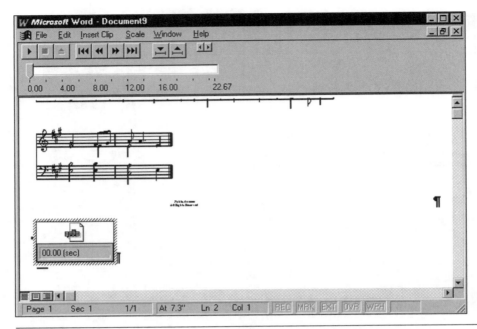

Figure 2.13 MIDI sequence icon in document.

You can accomplish a similar approach using Corel WordPerfect (7.0 or later). Select **Copy** from the NoteWorthy Composer Preview display to copy the file contents and then **Paste** the sheet music display into the WordPerfect document. Enter a paragraph return or two to make some space for the sheet music image. From the Insert menu, select **Sound**. At the prompt (.wav or .mid file?), select **.mid**. Locate and select the .mid file that you want to embed. Choose the **Store in Document** option and the MIDI sequence becomes a part of the WordPerfect document. Export the contents of the document to an HTML document using WordPerfect's conversion feature. If the resulting HTML document is brought up in a browser, a speaker icon will be displayed within it at the point that you embedded the MIDI sequence. Clicking on the speaker plays back the corresponding MIDI.

From NoteWorthy Composer to Adobe Acrobat Portable Document Format
Another useful way of exchanging musical information in the form of sheet music is through Adobe Acrobat. Acrobat format files are recognized in native mode by both Microsoft Internet Explorer and Netscape Navigator. You can also embed sound in a document created in this format so that you have both sheet music and sound.

To create an Acrobat document from NoteWorthy Composer, follow these steps:

1. Finish your composition in Composer and then save it in .nwc format.

2. Select **Print** from the File menu. The Score Print dialog box appears.

3. Select the **Printer** option and select the Acrobat Distiller print driver from your list of printers. Theoretically, the Acrobat PDF writer should also work if you embed the specialized TrueType font used for the Composer musical notation, but we ran into problems using that option. With Distiller, the notes were rendered accurately.

4. Select the **Print** button. Acrobat Distiller will create a PostScript (.ps) file to the default location that you have specified for the program.

5. When printing is done, open up Acrobat Distiller and select the .ps file to convert it into a standard Acrobat .pdf file.

The resulting .pdf file can be distributed across any browser platform where an Acrobat Reader version exists, including Unix, Macintosh, and Wintel equipment. Files can either be viewed inline within the browser or downloaded for later viewing. You can also open the .pdf file in Acrobat Exchange and insert links or objects (including sound) to enhance the sheet music. For example, you could develop a short QuickTime video clip showing the proper fingering for a violin piece (represented by the sheet music) and that clip could be played from within the Acrobat document as needed.

You can also embed sound files into the Acrobat document to accompany the sheet music display. One method to do this is to convert the MIDI file created in NoteWorthy Composer into a .wav file using MIDI-to-WAV rendering. The .wav file can then be converted into QuickTime format for embedding in the .pdf. This technique is discussed in more detail in Chapter 4 of this book.

Sites for Viewing and Hearing Music Many sites have options for viewing and downloading sheet music. Some also include the ability to view the sheet music and then play a corresponding audio file, either in MIDI format or one of the compressed (or uncompressed) digital audio formats, including .wav, .aiff, .mpeg, and .au. A number of sites have also adopted RealAudio as a means of providing a streaming version of the sound file.

Mel Bay Publications' Web site offers music training publications in a wide variety of styles, including many unusual traditional instruments, such as the mountain dulcimer and Hawaiian guitar, as well as more popular instruments, such as guitar and banjo. The site offers downloadable sheet music samples, extracted from the various books published by the company, stored in compact Adobe Acrobat .pdf format. Many of the printed music samples include both conventional notation as well as tablature, an extremely useful technique for guitarists and banjo players who want to see the fingering techniques used in a piece—as presented in the tablature—along with the musical notation. The downloadable sheet music gives a good idea of the complexity and the musical style of a piece, which could be valuable information to a musician considering purchasing one of the books. For those who don't have Acrobat Reader (or would prefer not to use it), this site also offers .gif files of the sheet music, which can be displayed in the browser, printed, or downloaded for later use. The types of music instruction offered by Mel Bay Publications should please anyone with eclectic tastes and a desire to explore some of the traditional and nontraditional approaches to music.

You can visit Mel Bay Publications' Web site at:

www.melbay.com

Another site devoted to the presentation of sheet music, but with a slightly different slant—the licensing of music—is MPL Communications. From this site, you can follow a timeline beginning in 1910 and extending to the present, including numerous musical works from various periods that have been renewed under the copyright laws and are offered for licensing for different uses. Each of the selections is showcased with a display of the sheet music (a simple melody line and lyrics). Most also have a button to preview the song through RealAudio playback. Even the early recorded tunes from the 1920s and 1930s have a crisp feel with high-quality RealAudio clips, suggesting that these earlier works may have been digitally reprocessed and enhanced from the original recordings. To license the use of songs of their music archives, MPL Communications offers memberships to individuals and organizations. This site is a good place to visit to see how RealAudio can be used effectively to deliver high-quality audio samples; the wait for the streaming audio to begin playing from the time a selection was made was rarely longer than four or five seconds.

You can visit MPL Communications at:

www.mplcommunications.com

Sheet music and tablature may not be as glamorous as streaming audio for transferring the essence of a song, but these two notational systems are read and understood by millions of amateur and professional musicians worldwide. You may have applications where this technique for sharing musical ideas makes sense in your HTML documents.

Scanning Sheet Music

Have you ever admired the elegant, pastel-shaded, ornamental graphics of an old piece of sheet music from the 1920s and really wondered what the music sounds like? Do you have some sheet music of your favorite songs and think it would be great to turn them into MIDI files? The technique for accomplishing this is reasonably simple, and it can be done with modestly priced software. Once a piece of sheet music has been imported in this manner, you can select the voicing (the instruments that apply to individual musical lines) and add other enhancements. The ease with which this technique can be accomplished should encourage everyone to try to add a bit of musical color to his or her Web site.

Musitek MidiScan

If you have a scanner connected to your computer, you can easily scan conventional sheet music into your computer and MidiScan will translate the image into a playable MIDI file. An expensive scanner is not required. A black-and-white scan of only 300 dpi (dots per inch) is sufficient; higher-resolution (larger storage size) image files are not necessary. Next time you find a colorful old piece of sheet music from the 1920s or 1890s in a curios shop, scan it, translate it, and within a short period of time you can be listening to it.

If the music turns out to be a real find, put it up for others to enjoy via your personal Web site. Musitek also has a lower-cost version of this product called PianoScan that is quite capable of taking on the vast wealth of two-stave (treble and bass clef) piano music that has been printed over the last few centuries. For more flexibility, however, particularly for use with music that includes parts for several different instruments, you will probably find MidiScan more useful for adapting music to Web site presentations.

Generating a MIDI File from MidiScan If you have a scanner that can handle 300 dots-per-inch resolution and can store files as .tiff, .bmp, or .pcx, you have the necessary hardware to work with MidiScan. While the program is fairly flexible in terms of the orientation of the page and the amount of stray noise that appears in the scanned image, you'll have better results if the image is scanned cleanly. If you use a hand scanner, you might want to use one of the frames that guides the scanner in a straight path while you're scanning. Some scanner software also has a skew function that lets you align a slightly crooked scanned image so that it is straight on the page. Also, if your scanner software has a function for cleaning up the image, either automatically or manually, you might want to eliminate stray items on the page, all the blots and noise that tend to confuse recognition packages. While MidiScan seems to achieve a high degree of accuracy in note recognition even from fairly rough images, the better the original image, the less work you will have to do within MidiScan to correct misinterpreted items on the page.

To start, create one uncompressed .tiff, .bmp, or .pcx file for each page of sheet music with your scanner. From the File menu, use the **Open** option to load the file containing the sheet music image that you want to convert. As an example, we'll bring in a .tiff file containing a song called Rondo written by Francis Hopkinson in America's colonial times. As always, the usual cautions apply about using only original material, songs in the public domain, or songs to which you have license rights. Songs from the colonial period are obviously fair game. As you open the file, the scanned image appears, as shown in Figure 2.14.

Choose **Begin Recognition** from the Recognition menu. The Recognition Setup dialog box appears, which lets you choose the basic recognition parameters, adapting the interpretation to irregular staff arrangements. Specify in the Recognition Setup box if the score is an ensemble (two or more staves per system) or a part (single contiguous staff). If the sheet music page size is unconventional, the program has some options for accommodating several different page sizes. The conversion is performed by simply clicking **OK** after completing your recognition settings and confirming the file to be converted.

MidiScan goes through the image and attempts to identify the beginning and end points for each staff and the relationship between staffs (if you have identified the piece as ensemble music). If the program runs into problems with the staff identification, you have the opportunity to specify beginnings and endings manually, using the Stave Localization floating toolbox shown in Figure 2.15.

Once you've completed the Stave Localization and selected **Done**, MidiScan converts the image into musical notation, storing it in its native file format with a .mnd extension. You can then scan through the results of the conversion, viewing the original scanned sheet music in the upper window and the musical notation that

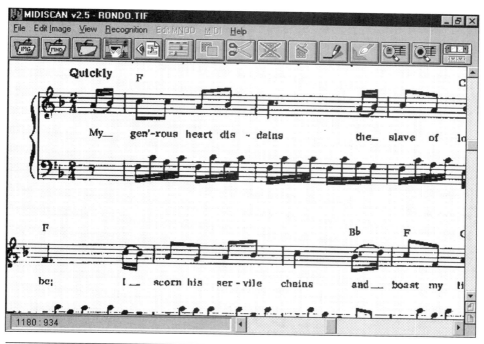

Figure 2.14 Scanned sheet music for Rondo.

MidiScan created in the lower window, as shown in Figure 2.16. While in this mode, you have the option to make any necessary corrections to the musical notation. The degree of accuracy in capturing individual notes and their durations appears to be very high, and corrections are seldom needed. MidiScan, however, sometimes misses ties between notes, which can then be corrected with the toolboxes provided.

The method for correcting and inserting notes, ties, and other musical symbols takes some practice. The toolboxes shown on the left side of the screen in Figure 2.16 control the notes or other symbols to insert. The toolbar along the top of the window controls the mode of entry of deletion, which can also be controlled from the keyboard. Until you get used to this entry method, you will spend some time hunting and pecking to select the correct symbols and get the appropriate mode activated to manipulate items on the staff you are editing. With practice, this becomes less work, and as you gain familiarity with the icons and their meanings, you can begin editing with greater speed and precision. MidiScan does most of the work, but you will probably have to do at least some touch-up of the resulting

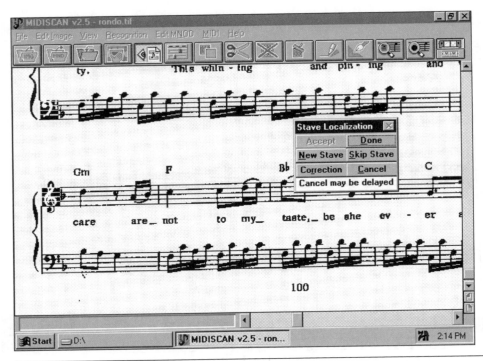

Figure 2.15 Stave Localization toolbox.

musical notation before you can duplicate the contents of the original scanned sheet music. Once you've reached the stage that you're pretty confident the musical notation matches the original, you can click a button on the toolbar to convert the notation into MIDI format. If you've selected the option for MidiScan to open its built-in synthesizer when done, it will automatically bring the completed MIDI file into the synthesizer (shown in Figure 2.17) so you can play it back. Any notation problems will be glaringly obvious in the MIDI file; you'll be able to hear notes that have been left out or timing problems, and then you can go back to correct the problem in the .mnd file.

From the built-in synthesizer, you can transpose the piece to another key, substitute different instrument voices for any of the tracks, mute individual tracks to hear parts of the performance clearly, or adjust individual track volumes. The controls provided are rudimentary and really designed just for previewing the MIDI file you have created and performing a few simple modifications.

Of course, once you have the file in MIDI format, you're free to open it in any other MIDI sequencer application and perform more complex modifications. Thus,

Figure 2.16 Viewing the .mnd file results.

a song scanned in from a simple piece of sheet music can be used as the core of a far more complex piece, as you add harmony lines, rhythm elements, and so on. You could also use one of the applications that allow MIDI music files to be synchronized with tracks composed of digital audio material (discussed later in this chapter), so that you could add a vocal singing line or a voice-over track to accompany the MIDI. Once you do this, however, you can't deliver the full performance as a MIDI file over the Web, although you could convert the entire piece (both MIDI and digital audio) to a .wav or .aiff file for distribution as digital audio. You could then also convert the file to a format to support streaming audio (such as the RealAudio or Liquid Audio file format) and distribute it for use with one of the streaming audio players. Techniques for this appear later in the book.

Uses for MidiScan MidiScan offers a number of interesting possibilities as part of a Web author's toolkit. For capturing musical performances of past centuries, any piece of music that has been recorded as sheet music can be very rapidly converted to MIDI format. Trained musicians also may be able to compose music very naturally using blank staff paper; their original compositions, if reasonably neat, could

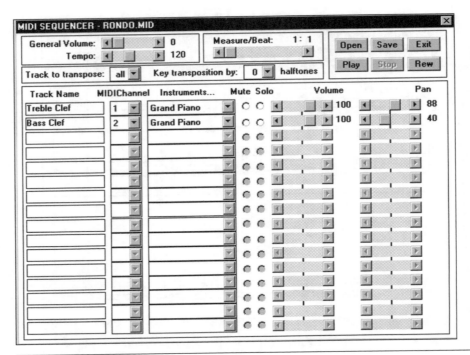

Figure 2.17 Built-in MIDI synthesizer.

be scanned in and converted to MIDI format in a matter of minutes. MidiScan opens up the vast libraries of prior music history to anyone with the imagination to import and embellish this music for accompanying a Web page presentation or serving as a standalone musical performance. You don't need to be a musician. You only need to know where to locate copyright-free music.

 A demo version of MidiScan is included on the CD-ROM bundled with this book.

Samples of Antique Instruments

Even if you can capture the recorded notes of a performance through sheet music, is there any way to replicate the sound of those antique instruments that exist only in museums or private collections? MIDI synthesizers can be extended using Sample Store techniques to include digital replicas of any kind of sound, including digital samples of rare or unusual instruments, such as crumhorns, flagolets, hurdy gurdys, old pipe organs, sackbuts, citterns, and so on. These samples can be patched into the musical instrument voices used by the synthesizer and played from a standard MIDI file. If you use these kinds of instruments for MIDI use, however, keep in mind that you can't release them for playback under General MIDI on the Web, since people using your site would be unlikely to have the antique instrument patches as part of their standard instrument voices.

NIFF Converter A new interchange format has been evolving for low-bandwidth communication of music notation data, favoring electronic transmission of the data (obviously making it ideal for Internet exchange). Based on the structure of the Microsoft Resource Interchange File Format (RIFF), this new format is called NIFF (Notation Interchange File Format). The format was developed by a coalition of music publishers, software producers of music scanning programs, music software users, and other software developers. The result is a compact, portable music storage format that allows the intricacies of scored music to be encapsulated in a common language. Remember that like spoken languages, the notational language of music is a dynamic language, subject to different approaches and interpretations and changing year by year. NIFF is designed to allow the common interchange format while still providing extensibility so that different manufacturers can handle special-purpose requirements as needed. Files structured in NIFF format can easily be exchanged among musicians, publishers, and others, presenting musical information in a form that can be precisely viewed or printed. Although the music format is not designed specifically for music playback, its structured nature suggests that it could be imported into applications and converted into MIDI data, much the way that standard sheet music can be scanned and converted.

Musitek MidiScan includes a converter that enables you to take their standard .mnd files and produce files in NIFF format for distribution. Although the NIFF format is not yet widely supported, a number of music software companies are planning to include compatibility with this format in their next software release, and most observers believe it will become an important music data exchange format. Contact information for Musitek is located in Appendix C.

Editing MIDI Files

One of the most important tools for working with MIDI files is the MIDI sequencer application. Even if you enter the initial MIDI information using one of the other techniques described in this chapter (such as keying in the notation, scanning sheet music, or going pitch-to-MIDI), odds are that you'll bring the MIDI file into a sequencer at some point to edit and refine the musical data.

MIDI sequencers often provide more than one way to edit your compositions. Initially, most MIDI recordists enter a window where tracks can be enabled and record mode set. A MIDI channel number is assigned to each MIDI track and an instrument voice (program patch) is assigned for each channel. Multiple tracks can be recorded on the same MIDI channel, but all have the same instrument voice (program patch) until a program change MIDI command is issued, which changes all the tracks on that channel to a different instrument.

MIDI sequencers often display the recorded MIDI tracks as blocks of music data referenced to the measure, bar, and beat of the music. At the track view you should be able to cut, copy, and paste down to units as small as one bar of the music (four beats in 4/4 time). If your sequencer has "piano roll" style display or the editable music staff notation option you can edit individual notes, changing their pitch as well as erasing, copying, and pasting. MIDI event editors display the actual time-stamped MIDI events of any MIDI sequence (commands and data), letting you insert or remove MIDI events from the file.

This section surveys two of the available MIDI sequencer applications to give you a sense of what it is like using these tools to work with MIDI files. For tips and ideas on enhancing the sound of MIDI files that are downloaded, refer to the later section titled "Making Your MIDI Files Sound Better." The companion section, "MIDI File Enhancement Techniques," provides additional advice on shaping the sound of MIDI files to make them more realistic and pleasing to the ear.

Voyetra Digital Orchestrator Plus

Voyetra is one of the pioneering digital sound application companies in the business. Their president, Carmine Bonanno, invented a number of the techniques that helped advance electronic music synthesis and developed the Voyetra Eight, one of the first music synthesizers to operate under computer control. Bonanno went on to develop a MIDI guitar synthesizer and a number of multiport MIDI adapters. Voyetra's software applications range from music-training CD-ROMs for students to high-power, versatile MIDI sequencer programs with the ability to support synchronized digital audio recording. Digital Orchestrator Plus includes this ability to overlay MIDI tracks with digital audio data without the need for extremely high-power computer processors. Voyetra, founded in 1975, has a reputation for solid, reliable MIDI and digital audio applications that contain many high-end features for a reasonable price.

Like the more versatile MIDI sequencer applications, Digital Orchestrator Plus (DOP) provides several different "views" of the MIDI music data. You can actually examine the contents of a MIDI file note by note in the Event List window, shown in Figure 2.18.

This type of editing provides very precise control over the parameters and timing of each individual note and also lets you specify controller commands (to execute special-purpose MIDI events), patch changes (to change instrument voicings on a track), SysEx entries (to control individual features of specific synthesizers), and so on. The Event Edit dialog box is shown in Figure 2.19.

The Track View, shown in Figure 2.20, provides a broad overview of the MIDI activity on different tracks, with each measure represented by a block. The relative density of the sound events within a block are shown by the shade of gray;

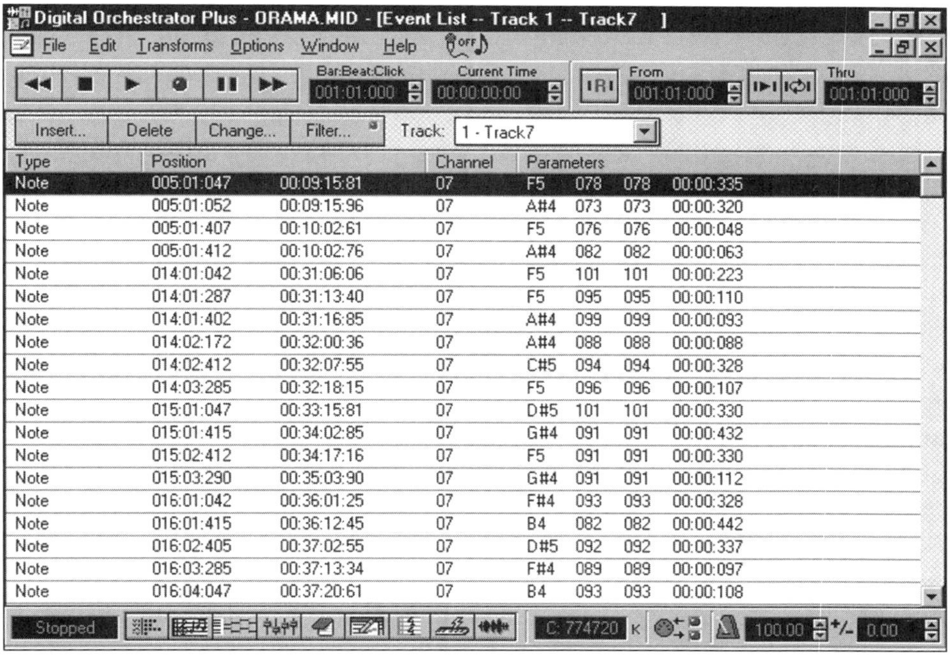

Figure 2.18 Event List window.

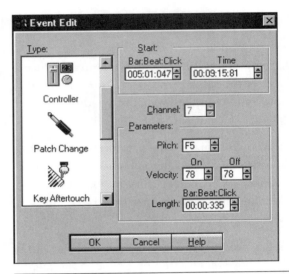

Figure 2.19 Event Edit dialog box.

white indicates silence. For large-scale editing of entire passages, you can cut and paste MIDI data much the same way you can move paragraphs and words around in a word processor. As you gain more experience working with MIDI information, this Track View window will become a familiar work area, where entire songs can be constructed out of the basic elements of a MIDI recording. From this same window, DOP also lets you interweave digital sounds either recorded over the MIDI tracks or imported as a sound file and then enhanced with MIDI tracks. If your sound board supports recording during playback, you can continue to add digital audio tracks, listening to the existing tracks while you overlay new material. This merging of the MIDI and the digital audio realm is one of the most exciting developments in digital sound applications and an extremely useful feature for the studio musician. Keep in mind, however, that as soon as you overlay digital audio in a multitrack composition, you lose the ability to distribute the finished music in MIDI format on the Web. The best you can do is to mix the entire composition down to a digital audio file and then delivery it either in one of the compressed audio formats or as streaming audio. Figure 2.20 shows the work environment offered by the Track View window.

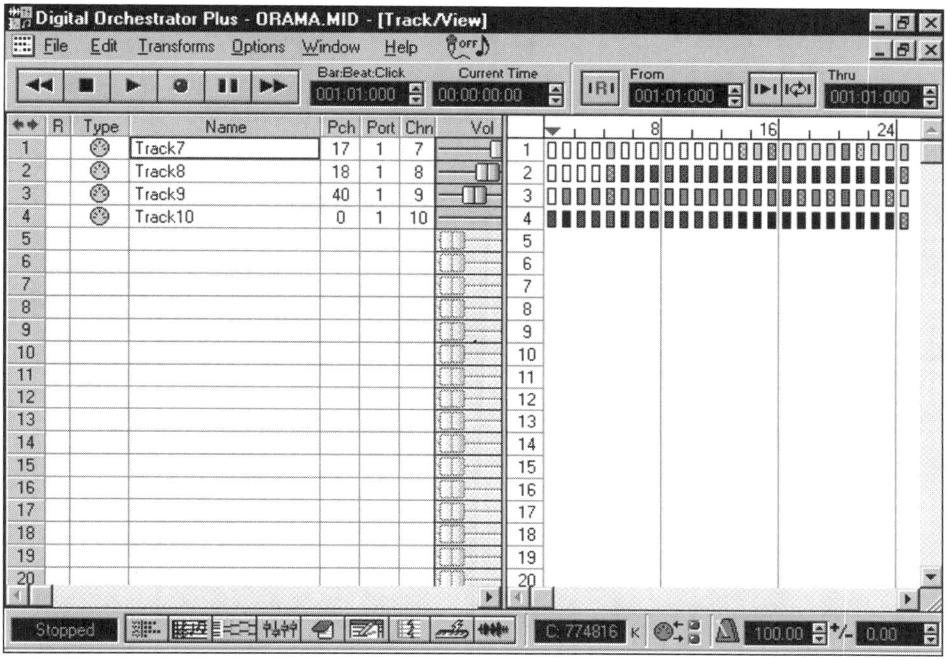

Figure 2.20 Track View window.

> **WARNING**   Your ability to work with both MIDI and digital audio
> tracks is limited to some degree by the performance of your computer.
> A 486/66 machine can typically handle one or two additional digital
> audio tracks in addition to the MIDI data. With a 586/100 computer, you
> can handle four or more tracks. Higher-power machines can manage as
> many as eight tracks of digital audio along with the MIDI data.

Looking at blocks of musical information or long lists of MIDI events in text
form doesn't always really suggest the shape and flow of a piece of music. DOP
also has a window where you can take one or more individual track and transcribe
them into standard musical notation. While you can't actually edit the notes in this
view (as you can in some other applications), this feature gives you an accurate representation of the music in a form that will be familiar to most musicians. Figure
2.21 shows the Notation window.

The remaining view available to you in DOP (and similar applications) is the
Piano Roll window. In this view, the musical data is seen as blocks that extend a

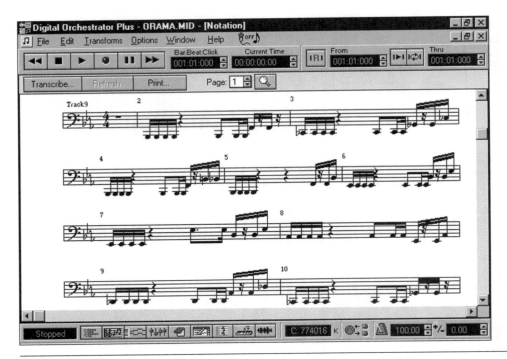

Figure 2.21 Notation window.

particular duration and are placed in time on a "piano roll," which indicates the relative pitch. The piano roll view also lets you perform editing of music sequences—you can drop individual notes onto the piano roll, slide them up and down to change their pitch, create triplets, and erase notes that may have been mistakenly added because of a slip of a finger during a MIDI recording. You can use the piano roll window to perform step editing, which allows you to enter musical notes one at a time, measure by measure, from a connected MIDI keyboard controller or by simply using your mouse pointer to select and position the notes. As you enter notes, the editor advances by a predetermined "step," making it possible to key in music that exists in sheet music form or to compose harmonies, melodies, or rhythm sequences on-the-fly. You can preview a portion of the composition using the transport controls at the upper-left corner of the window. Figure 2.22 shows the appearance of the Piano Roll window.

Digital Orchestrator Plus has many other features that support sophisticated, complex MIDI editing and sequencing. As an all-around tool for working with MIDI files, it stands up well even when compared to some much more expensive

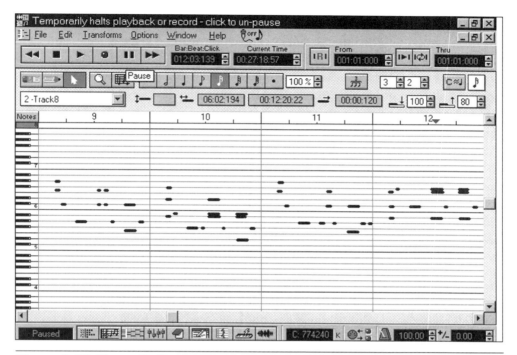

Figure 2.22 Piano Roll window.

packages. The addition of multitrack recording of digital audio along with the MIDI tracks makes DOP an excellent Swiss Army knife kind of MIDI application. Contact information for Voyetra Technologies is located in Appendix C.

 The CD-ROM included with this book features a demo version of Digital Orchestrator Plus.

PG Music Power Tracks Pro

There are a surprising number of inexpensive MIDI sequencers on the market that provide near-professional feature sets for a very low cost. Power Tracks Pro by PG Music is one of those products that has been through several generations, adding new features and refinements to the interface at each pass. Now it ranks among the best-designed products in this category.

Power Tracks Pro includes an interesting feature for drum track sequencing: the Drum Grid Editor, shown in Figure 2.23. Using this tool lets you create rhythm patterns using a collection of drum sounds and other rhythm instruments, such as shakers, tambourines, and cow bells. You specify a number to indicate the velocity (using the MIDI range from 0 to 127) of each individual percussive sound, which lets you create accents and other rhythmic effects. The drum patterns you create are saved in a native file format with a .dg extension, but you can import these drum grid files directly into a MIDI track using an **Edit menu** option, Fill Track with Drum Pattern. While the contents of each individual file contain either 16 divisions in a 4/4 pattern, or 12 divisions in a 3/4 pattern, you can link and combine several different drum patterns to create a more varying pattern from within the sequencer. Power Tracks Pro lets you fill tracks with the patterns for an indicated number of measures, so you could build a complex drum pattern to act as the groundwork for a song for a number of shorter patterns. The program includes a collection of pre-built patterns that you can drop into the sequencer and rearrange or modify to your preferences.

The editing options of Power Tracks Pro include a notation window (shown in Figure 2.24) that provides several different entry modes. You have the option of grabbing notes and moving them around the staff (and immediately hearing the new pitch play as you do) or using a piano-roll type approach where you can enter

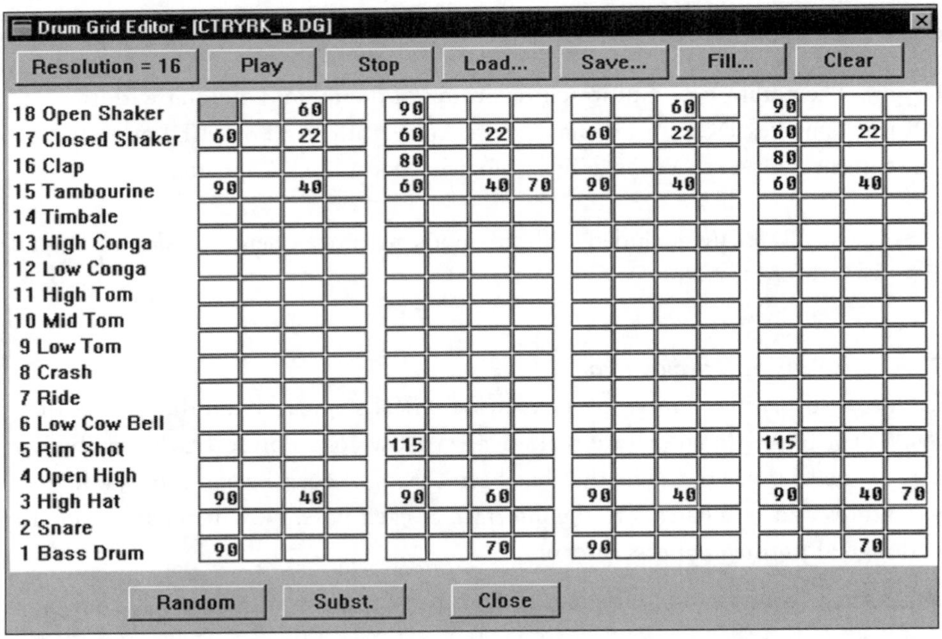

Figure 2.23 Drum Grid Editor window.

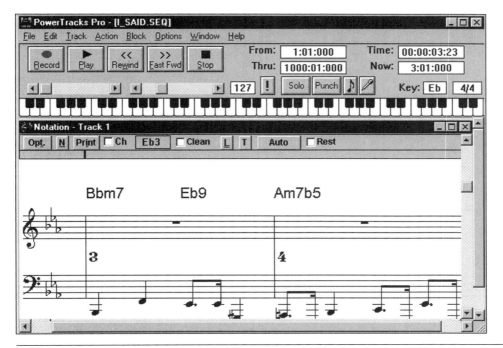

Figure 2.24 Notation Window in Power Tracks Pro.

notes by playing them on the keyboard displayed above the notation window. Power Tracks Pro lets you add both chord symbols above the staves and lyric lines for those songs that have lyrics.

One nice feature for guitarists: if you're more comfortable with a guitar fretboard than a keyboard, you can enter notes from a fretboard display, as shown in Figure 2.25. You can also watch the playback of a MIDI song as it appears on the fretboard. By slowing down the tempo of a song designed for playing on a guitar you can view the possible fingering combinations and perhaps pick up ideas on how to play a particular song.

A host of other features and options lurk beneath the surface of the deceptively simple interface, including SMPTE code generation, punch-in recording options, the ability to change the resolution of the divisions within a measure, looping and synching options, and so on. For about $40, Power Tracks Pro could be the ideal tool for a Web author looking for an inexpensive and practical means for generating MIDI files for use on the Web. Contact information for PG Music Inc. is located in Appendix C.

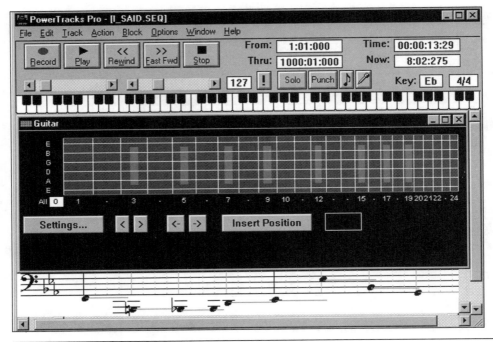

Figure 2.25 Guitar Fretboard display.

MIDI File Enhancement Techniques

If you have downloaded MIDI files from the Web that sound absolutely terrible, the problem may come from sloppy file preparation. Occasionally, MIDI files are released without the program change commands that set the initial instrument voices, or someone has inadvertently overwritten the patches. It could be an ancient MIDI file from before the General MIDI (GM) instrument-patch number specification and have patches set for an obsolete, non-GM synthesizer. Most people enjoy revoicing MIDI files so their sound card plays the MIDI file arrangement using their favorite instrument voices. It's a matter of personal taste and the performance characteristics of your computer system. While you don't have absolute control over how a MIDI file from your Web site will sound to the listener, it is wise to check the following guidelines (using a MIDI events editor) before uploading the MIDI file:

- The MIDI tempo command is specified at the beginning of the file so playback occurs at the correct tempo and not at the player's default tempo (usually 120bpm). Reserving a track for composition tempo, meter, and key signature mapping makes file management easy.

- At the start of one of the tracks assigned to each MIDI channel used, a program patch command should specify the desired instrument voice before note sequencing starts. Additional program changes can occur as the sequence progresses, changing the instrument voice assigned to the channel.

- The initial volume value for each channel used should be specified by a MIDI control command placed at the beginning of the piece.

Once you have recorded a MIDI file, you can apply some of MIDI Sequencer's editing features on the recorded tracks for enhancement. Here are some suggestions for processing MIDI files that can be performed in the tracks window of most MIDI sequencers:

- Copy the events of a recorded track onto an unused track, give the new track a different (unused) channel number, and assign an instrument voice that layers well with the voice of the original track. This, of course, can be done more than once.

- If the sequence sounds too rhythmically mechanical, create a tempo map that varies the tempo up and down by 1 or 2 beats per minute, placing the tempo changes every bar or two (as seems suitable to the musical style). The tempo change should be small, almost undetectable, and the wavering above and below the start tempo should return to the original tempo at the nodal points of the composition, in other words, by the end of a chorus or at the end of each stanza. Try to keep the excursions above and below the start tempo approximately equal so the average start tempo is not abandoned.

- If added high-end brilliance is desired for a particular track, copy its events into a new track and transpose the track up one octave (12 semitones). This will give a guitar voice a 12-string sound or cause a track that sounds buried (even after its loudness is maximized) to cut through the mix.

- If a thicker sound is desired for a track, copy the track events into a couple of new tracks, assign each an unused channel number, and slightly detune the new tracks above and below the original track. This can be done by placing a MIDI pitch bend command at the start of each of the two new tracks. You want to raise the pitch of all the contents of one of the tracks and lower the pitch of the other by an equal amount. The pitch change should be very small, much less than a semitone. It should be only a slight vibratory mistuning above and below the original track.

- Digital delay and echo effects can be created in MIDI by copying the events of a track into a new track and shifting (sometimes called sliding) the contents of the new track by a timing unit offset. In many sequencers the timing unit is the tick specified by the PPQN (Parts Per Quarter Note). The PPQN defines the resolution for recording of timed events. If the PPQN is set to 480, sliding a MIDI track 15 ticks would cause the track to follow the original after a delay equal to the duration of a 128th note at the set tempo.

- Solos can be made more legato by using pitch bend commands to enter some of the notes rather than re-attacking each note event as a new note. Careful attention to phrasing and sensible placement of the pitch bend commands can produce more realistic melodic movement. Always end a phrase containing pitch bends with a pitch bend command of 0 to the modulated channel. This sets the channel to its original pitch.

- Creative use of the MIDI panning feature along with some of the track enhancement techniques mentioned earlier can add motion within a seemingly static voice. Cross pan one voicing of MIDI events from hard left (only on left speaker) to hard right, while another voicing of the same events is panned right to left.

The inherent features of the MIDI playback synthesizer control the capabilities of any MIDI performance. MIDI compositions can utilize the Roland GS format or the Yamaha XG-MIDI format yet still be heard on regular general MIDI sound boards. In General MIDI the additional instrument banks of the GS or XG format are played by the same old orchestra.

Microphone to MIDI

For some people, the computer keyboard may be an easy system for entering notes into a MIDI sequence, but most musicians would rather use the more natural feel of the instrument that they play most frequently, whether it is a guitar or a saxophone or something else entirely. Fortunately, for those individuals, there are some programs that make it easy for you to capture your music riffs and get them down as MIDI data. Once captured as a stream of notes in MIDI format, you can further process, edit, transpose, fine tune, revoice, and embellish a musical piece. AutoScore from Wildcat Canyon Software, examined in the next section, is one such software tool.

Wildcat Canyon Software AutoScore

AutoScore features its own built-in MIDI sequencer application (shown in Figure 2.26) and, once installed, it can also appear as a toolbar icon in your favorite MIDI

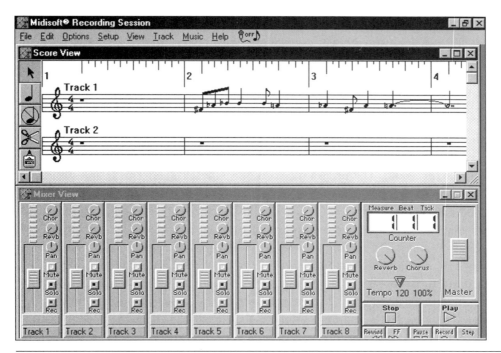

Figure 2.26 AutoScore built-in MIDI Sequencer.

program. From the toolbar, you can turn on the microphone and begin generating pitch-to-MIDI sequences by humming the notes, playing a clarinet, or playing a guitar. AutoScore drops the MIDI data directly onto the selected track where it can be further edited and mixed into an existing MIDI composition.

The note recognition works best if you spend some time tailoring the program to your microphone levels and the type of input to be used for conversion to pitch. The program provides a means for restricting the range of pitches to be converted, which improves the accuracy of the recognition. The Autoscore Instrument Settings dialog box, shown in Figure 2.27, lets you select the type of instrument, its base class (voice, wind/brass/string), the relative threshold volume for recognition, the pitch range to be analyzed, and the silent periods between notes. As you might guess, it takes some experimentation to achieve the best results under different conditions, but the recognition feature seemed to work pretty well right out of the box using the default settings. The main thing to remember is that this method of MIDI entry works only for single-line note sequences (monophonic), not harmony lines or complex instrument voicings. The technology is not yet at the point where a complex musical mix can be broken down into separate tracks of MIDI information. Of course, you can achieve the same effect by having several different musicians play MIDI-capable instruments in real time (using MIDI keyboards, drum pads, MIDI guitar pickups, and so on) and record the results into a MIDI sequencing program. AutoScore is designed to provide a means for simply and naturally entering the melodic lines of a song in a natural and effortless way.

The Music Tracking options can be set according to a number of different parameters, including constraining the tracking to a particular key (or using the full chromatic scale). The program also supports Pitch Bend Tracking (when a pitch is altered as a performance effect, such as a slide from one note to another on a guitar), volume tracking (which enables velocity information to be recorded), and a step entry mode (which allows notes to be entered one at a time, rather than in real time). The microphone level setup is crucial to the overall effectiveness of the recognition. AutoScore provides a means for adjusting the levels of a mike input to stay within the optimum levels. The AutoScore Microphone Analyzer, shown in Figure 2.28, lets you adjust your input sound to stay within the best tracking levels and to be sure that background sounds are not too loud so as to affect the recognition process.

Since AutoScore offers its functionality from within any MIDI sequencer (from its embedded toolbar icon), most musicians will probably stick to using the application they are most familiar with and simply use AutoScore as one additional input method for MIDI data. The approach should be especially effective for anyone who

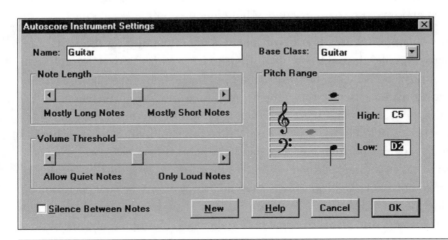

Figure 2.27 AutoScore Instrument Settings dialog box.

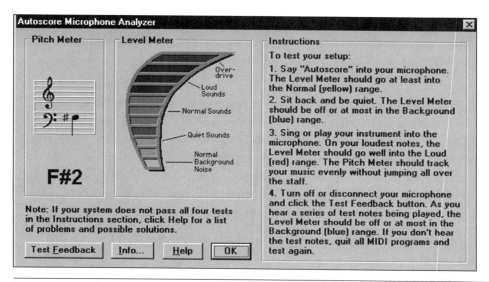

Figure 2.28 AutoScore Microphone Analyzer dialog box.

is proficient on a particular type of instrument, such as a trumpet or saxophone, but is all thumbs when it comes to playing a keyboard. For simple compositions, however, AutoScore's own Recording Session utility provides the fundamental tools for composing and mixing up to eight individual MIDI tracks, including tracks constructed using the Pitch-to-MIDI feature. Contact information for Wildcat Canyon is located in Appendix C.

Sound2MIDI

Another tool for performing conversion of pitch information into MIDI data is Audio Works' Sound2MIDI. Sing, hum, or whistle into the microphone and make your voice play back as a MIDI musical instrument voice. Capture the moment of inspiration with Sound2MIDI. Any monophonic (one note at a time) instrument, such as sax, flute, trumpet, violin, and so forth, can be used to generate MIDI event codes that include pitch, dynamics, and timing information. Record directly into your favorite MIDI sequencer or multitrack waveform recorder that has MIDI record capability. It's even possible to create drum sequences by putting Sound2MIDI in Rhythm mode. Wave samples can also be converted to MIDI.

Sound2MIDI is a Windows (95 or 3.1) program, requiring at least a 486 66MHz PC with a minimum of 8M RAM and a 16-bit soundboard with MIDI capability. It has a pitch detection range of more than six octaves and can transcribe performance done at any tempo. There are variable parameters for fine-tuning the conversion, and detection parameters can be changed on-the-fly. Automatic pitch compensation is made for instruments tuned too sharp or too flat.

If you have a MIDI sequencer or scoring program that displays MIDI events as standard notation on the music staff, you can observe your singing or playing in real time as notes on a staff, as well as hear yourself as the MIDI instrument voice you select. Ever feel like singing like a tuba, or giving your clarinet the voice of a violin? The important point here is that Sound2MIDI enables you to use your voice, or any instrument you have command over, to lay down MIDI instrument tracks. This approach is a direct and immediate way to express melodic phrases and capture them in the domain of MIDI event code.

More information on Sound2MIDI is available from AudioWork's Ltd. and located in Appendix C.

Computer-Assisted Arranging

The computer can help you create the foundation for an original musical composition. From there you can continue to build as elaborately as you want. You may simply block out some practice progressions for yourself and friends to practice or carry the work to a fanciful completion. A popular way to notate songs has been to write the melody line in standard music notation with the chord progressions labeled above the music staff. Now with inexpensive software you can easily assemble your musical concepts and nicely refine them.

PG Music Band-in-a-Box

If you've ever played guitar you've probably written down some chord progressions. If you've looked into chordal harmony you may write progressions as roman numerals, major and minor, specifying the diatonic degrees relative to a key (tonal center). This system specifies chord extensions numerically (i.e., Im7 specifies a minor seventh chord on the one or tonic root of the reigning musical key). In Nashville notation they use Arabic numerals instead of roman. If you're a singer, you may write the melodies that come to you in solfa notation (do, re, mi, etc.). Band-in-a-Box can be used to block to out arrangements, try on different rhythm and accompaniment styles, and generate a MIDI file. It's fun to try on some different hats. We put the chord progression for "Goin' to Kansas City" in a reggae style. You might try impressing a Fats Waller piano style on a familiar Beatles progression. When you get tired of playing from the large songbag that comes with the program, you will be ready to start entering your own progressions, specifying the accompaniment style and tempo. Hit play and listen. You can learn a lot about tonal harmony by viewing the chord progressions of your favorite songs in the accompanying songbag. Chord progressions can be viewed and entered in all the modes mentioned earlier (chord names, roman numerals, Nashville notation, solfa). When you get familiar with the program you can start creating unique accompaniment styles. First learn to alter existing styles and then develop your own styles for greater control and individuality.

Band-in-a-Box has been consistently upgraded and improved over the years. The first version we heard had a predominance of jazz styles. Now many different music styles are available, and it has a soloist feature. You can pick from lists of the great names in music and hear a solo played in their characteristic style over your own chord progression or one from the selections provided with the program. Contact information for PG Music Inc. is located in Appendix C.

Microsoft Music Producer

If you're not a musician or composer and you don't have a lot of money to spend for licensing music for use on your Web site, is there any other way to generate music sequences to serve as MIDI background music? Microsoft thinks so, and in response to this potential market they have released Microsoft Music Producer. This product is squarely aimed at Web authors who want to enliven their sites with MIDI music, providing an appealing interface and an assortment of musical styles that can be used as compositional guides for constructing songs. You can choose between musical styles, instrument collections, musical dynamics, and other factors to generate entire songs to a defined length. The resulting MIDI file can then be embedded in an HTML document.

The product's interface makes constructing compositions remarkably simple. All of the primary controls are located on one screen, shown in Figure 2.29. The selected instrument collections are shown as graphics in a Mixing pane that controls panning and volume. Individual instruments can be moved left and right, to adjust the left and right channel balance, and up and down to adjust the relative volume of the instrument in the MIDI mix. In other words, if you want the flute to stand out in your song, you drag the icon of the flute toward the top of the pane and the volume will increase correspondingly. If you want it to be heard more on the left stereo speaker than on the right, drag the flute icon toward the left side of the Mixing pane. This can be done in real time as you are listening to the playback,

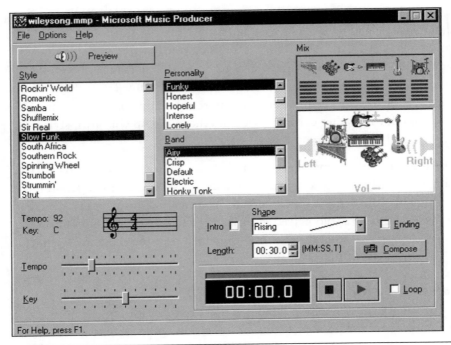

Figure 2.29 Microsoft Music Producer interface.

so you can dynamically tweak the instrument mix until you have it where you want and then save the file as a MIDI file. Since the file is a standard MIDI file, you can bring the data into any MIDI sequencer application and perform further tweaks and refinements to it.

The compositions are built from an assortment of internal algorithms based on some predefined serious styles (Beethoven, Debussy) and some whimsical ones (Hijinks, Punkarama). As a composer, you select the instruments that will be used to play your song (from the 128-voice General MIDI instrument set) and then choose the length of the music (down to a tenth of a second precision), the key, the tempo, and the musical personality.

The musical personality setting is a bit nebulous. Personalities can be: Boogie, Demented, Despairing, Noble, Searching, and a number of other categories that are equally ambiguous. Part of the fun is mixing together the combinations of factors to see what the musical output will be. For example, you can choose a Slow Funk style, select an Intense Personality, and choose an Airy Band. Once you click the **Compose** button, Music Producer constructs the sequence in a second or two and you can listen to it by using the transport controls. The Shape selection determines the overall movement of the music; for example, a Rising shape starts out simply and builds toward a more dramatic finish. The Random shape can move things in any direction. The Peaking shape builds toward a crescendo and then falls off. Even with exactly the same settings selected, if you keep pressing the **Compose** button, the program will generate a fairly different song each time through. While there is a randomness to the composition process, you can do some fairly interesting shaping of a song context using the available controls. There is an Intro checkbox and an Ending checkbox; these two options don't seem to be the strongest features of the program, which sometimes seems to stumble a bit at generating convincing beginnings and endings to songs.

Seasoned musicians may sneer at music produced in this manner, but the program manages to produce some fairly interesting sequences. The results might not be considered performance art, but you can generate a rich musical atmosphere that you would not be embarrassed to use for background music. Perhaps that's the key; while the pieces are not quite interesting enough to showcase as performance pieces, they serve well as ambient or atmospheric music. Many of them could be used to generate a solid underpinning for a MIDI number over which you could add a more interesting melody line in your favorite sequencer application. In some ways, the product is a toy, but in other ways, it perks the imagination and might lead to some very intriguing compositions. Given the variety of combinations available in the program settings, you could generate millions of different MIDI songs as fast as you can click a few buttons. The program is also expandable with additional downloadable styles that could open up even more possibilities.

 For more information, contact Microsoft Corporation at:

www.microsoft.com

Composing Precise MIDI

Composers have a special ability. In their minds they can imagine streaming musical passages, simultaneous clusters of notes, emotive inflections of melody. They are always culturing the pearl, freshly phrasing the same old human utterances that predate recollectable history. Today, we are lucky to have such sophisticated music software to offer our intellect. It is very satisfying to play a musical instrument, but it has been known for many years that even the great masters spend as much time in mental contemplation of their music as they do practicing. The computer can be programmed to calculate and verify our theories, we can teach ourselves intuitively and instinctively, day by day expressing our sentiments more deeply.

Metsan MidiText

If you have studied music, you may feel that many of the computer music composition tools are rather limited. Some border on being toys. I was delighted when I discovered MidiText. It's a powerful language for writing precisely specified MIDI music sequences in a programmer's shorthand. The final result can be translated to yield a .mid format file. If you are willing to take the challenge of learning to write in MidiText, you will find it has some interesting capabilities. It will allow you to create 5th notes, and 7th notes, and 11th notes, and so on, as well as the conventional divisions of two or three notes per beat. You can compose polyrhythmic percussion passages, split time into fractional segments, and fill segments of time with notes or chords of whatever length you specify. Those are just a few of its features. Entering characters from a keyboard into a simple text editor may not appeal to everyone as a method of making music; however, with this tool you will be able to make compositions in odd meters like 5/4 time or 7/8 time, specify dynamic modulation of pitch or controls, or enter grace notes, all by keyboard-entered programming code. If you're a studious musician, you could use MidiText as an exotic music calculator and teach yourself how to boldly play what no person has ever played.

Notes can be entered in MidiText relative to a specified clef (treble, alto, tenor, bass, or user defined), by staff note names (e, f, g, etc.), or by using a staff note numbering system (:1, :2, :3, etc.). Notes entered by one of the staff notes conventions are influenced by key signature commands just as notes on the standard music notation staff are influenced by the sharps or flats of different key signatures. Optionally, notes in MidiText can be entered by their MIDI note number (0–127) or by the MIDI note naming system used by some synthesizer manufacturers (middle C = c3). MIDI note numbers are said to be relative to the MIDI clef and must specify sharps, flats, and naturals explicitly—accidentals are not remembered.

The key signature is set by a key command:

```
key C
```

The uppercase C specifies the key signature of C major. You can specify the key signature of a minor scale using a lowercase letter. If the uppercase C is replaced with a lowercase a, then A minor, the relative minor of C, is specified.

A list of notes to be played is enclosed in braces ({}). The braces and parentheses are all separated from each other by at least one space. If MIDI note numbers are used, the individual note numbers are enclosed in parentheses. The other note naming or numbering schemes do not require parentheses for individual notes. Note names (staff or MIDI) are sharpened (+) or flattened (-) by the plus or minus character that can follow the note name. The following score uses MIDI note names to play the notes of the piano's black keys (in the octave residing directly above middle C). The plus character shows they are represented as sharpened.

```
{ c3+ d3+ f3+ g3+ a3+ }
```

Chords can be programmed by separating the note names or numbers by commas and enclosing the chord notes in parentheses. The following score in MIDI note names plays the C major and D major triad:

```
{ (c3,e3,g3) (d3,f3+,a3) }
```

Notes or chords can be repeated by appending a semicolon character and the repeat number (maximum 64). The following example uses MIDI note numbers and plays the E major triad four times:

```
{ (64,68,71)*4 }
```

In the preceding examples no duration is specified so notes and chords are played for one beat. To play a note or chord for multiple beats, precede it with a multiplier. To play a note for a fraction of a beat, attach a divisor. If the divisor is to follow a single MIDI note name, insert a period between the octave number and the divisor. In the following example middle C (MIDI note name = c3) is first played for two beats, then played for half a beat:

```
{ 2c3 c3.2 }
```

When specifying the divisor integer, no period is required following a right parentheses that encloses a note number or chord. Integer multipliers and divisors can be used simultaneously to specify any fractional duration smaller or larger than a beat. In the following example a G above middle C is played for one and a half (3/2) beats followed by an E for three-fourths (3/4) of a beat, followed by a C played for five thirds (5/3) of a beat:

```
{ 3g3.2 3e3.4 5c3.3 }
```

Using simple fractions, phrases of any number of notes can be fit into specific intervals of time and combined with standard or unfamiliar divisions of the beat. The distinctions between 4th, 5th, 6th, 7th, and so on notes are subtle and if programmed accurately can be fascinating.

Rests are inserted by using the character r (or R) to indicate the absence of a note. Timing values are added to the rest in the same way they are used to specify note or chord duration. Fractional values can be assigned. The period is never needed to isolate the divisor integer.

If you are writing drum parts to be used on MIDI channel 10, remembering what MIDI note number belongs to each percussion instrument sound can be taxing. MidiText has a set command that allows you to specify a symbolic constant (ID) that can be used in place of a number. With the set command you can associate an easily remembered name with a MIDI instrument number, a program patch (MIDI instrument) number, and other variables. Symbolic note numbers can only be explicitly specified, and parentheses are required. For example:

```
set bd=60        ; bass drum

set cm=64        ; cymbal

{ (bd) (cm) (bd) (bd) (bd,cm) }
```

In MidiText the tempo is commonly specified in beats per minute by a tempo command.

```
tempo 1=120
```

MidiText allows you to define the tempo in terms of the number of times any multiple or fraction of a beat is to occur per minute. For example:

```
tempo 3=88
```

This specifies that an interval of three beats occurs 88 times every minute yielding a tempo of 264 beats per minute. Fractional values can be used to specify a finer resolution:

```
tempo 1/2=155
```

This specifies that one half beat occurs 155 times each minute, which is equivalent to 77.5 beats per minute.

If more note separation is desired for instrument voices that are heavily sustained, the MidiText touch command can be used. Note separation can be controlled in one of three ways:

1. Specify what percentage of a note's full duration the note will actually play.

2. Specify a fraction of a beat to be subtracted from the note's full duration, where the note will end.

3. Specify a fraction of a beat that the note will play regardless of the note's full duration.

The slash character / is used to define the end of each measure. The slash must always be preceded and followed by a space. The conventional use of measures reflects the fact that music often incorporates a repeated rhythmic structure. This regular rhythmic pattern is called *meter*, and MidiText uses the meter command to control measure size. Measure sizes greater than 22 are rare; 2, 4, 6, or 8 are common. Fractional measure sizes can be specified. Measures that are not accurately programmed (have too many or too few beats) generate error statements during translation.

To fill out a measure with a rest of whatever amount of time is remaining, a minus sign preceded and followed by a space is used.

Equal temperaments other than 12 tones per octave can be tuned and played in MidiText. Since temperaments with more than 12 tones per octave have additional (non-enharmonic) sharps and flats, the extra notes residing between the common diatonic degrees are specified by appended plus (sharp) or minus (flat) symbols. In 19 tones per octave there are two discrete notes between each whole step like C to D and one enharmonic note between each semitone like B to C or E to F. The C# and Db are not the same note. In higher-number equal-temperament systems, there may be sharp, flat, enharmonic, double sharp, double flat notes between each diatonic whole step. Plus or minus symbols, as many as are needed, can be appended to the note name to specify any new note resources the temperament provides. MidiText can also be used to create just intonation (perfect pitch) tuning tables for MIDI compositions.

This is just an elementary introduction and a small sampling of the controls and commands available in MidiText. MIDI channel numbers and program patches are easily specified. All the MIDI control commands can be programmed to 14- or 7-bit accuracy, accelerating or decelerating tempos can be enacted across phrases. MidiTest can create dynamic pitch bend slurs to the smoothness (number of issued pitch bend commands) you specify. SysEx and Non-Registered Parameter Number (NRPN) commands can be made for your particular sound module or keyboard synthesizer.

As well as being a very precise way to enter music code, MidiText can be written to do looping and conditional branching like a computer program. A very powerful feature is the ability to create your own macros. A common characteristic of almost all styles of music is the existence of repetition with variation. Phrases and patterns recur with slight changes. MidiText code allows you to define macros to accept your specified parameters and embed them into sequences.

This would be a wonderful program to have on your laptop while you are commuting on the train. Wouldn't it be fun to think up (and lay down) some exotic instrumentals while you're stuck in a waiting room or traveling without your music keyboard? MidiText has a substantial learning curve, and that requires some energy on your part. It is not difficult to learn; it simply has a lot of capabilities. Programs of this complexity have a fine degree of control. Once learned, they remain useful and are not quickly outgrown. I would use MidiText to compose fine-tuned, precisely timed, MIDI sequences that originate from theoretical contemplation. The resultant .mid file can be further processed in your MIDI sequencer program or waveform rendering software.

MidiText is available from Metsan Corporation, and their contact information is located in Appendix C.

 A demo version of MidiText is included on the CD-ROM bundled with this book.

MIDI-to-Waveform Rendering

Once you are skilled at creating MIDI files, you can enhance them by computer-rendering the MIDI data as digital waveform sound files. The more exotic MIDI-to-Wave renderers allow you to create, as well as specify, the instrument wavetable samples. Of course, this creates larger sound files than the original MIDI file, but it also gives you quite a bit of sonic license. Many of these kinds of applications produce sound files of a quality that is consistent with higher-end professional synthesizer products, and for this reason, they may be the tool of choice.

This approach offers a degree of control that is more precise in some ways than the MIDI approach, since the quality of the sound is not dependent on the type of MIDI synthesizer being used for playback, but rather the nature and quality of the sound board and speakers in the user's system. The resulting sound files, depending on the application, can be generated in most of the major sound file formats—WAV, AU, AIFF, and so on.

A discussion of the tools and applications for MIDI-to-Waveform rendering appears in Chapter 3 of this book.

Aleatoric Soundscapes

If your Web site is in need of some aural ambiance, you may want background music to play as viewers indulge. Fanfares can be issued to herald the visitors' navigational achievements through your links. Sonic rewards are nice to acknowledge the receipt of visitor-submitted data. However, for extended, nonrepetitive music sequences, you may find an aleatoric music generator a handy tool. Aleatoric music is random-generated music that follows no fixed score or specified parameters. The computer can easily spin random note sequences of changing duration in a futuristic style smarting of musical anarchy. If that's a little too wild for your taste, there are algorithmic computer music generators that give you some control of the musical structure, yet produce passages full of fresh surprises. You specify the palate (pitches), the percentage of randomness for melodic movement, and some of, but not all, the rhythm and accompaniment variables.

 If you have no experience with this type of music tool check out Michiel Overtoom's SoundScape a freeware algorithmic music generator for the PC (see Figure 2.30). It can be found on the Internet at:

www.xs4all.nl/~motoom

Open and play one of the sequences that come with SoundScape. The windows that contain instrument voices display an octave of the piano keyboard, allowing you to select the notes this instrument will sound. Notice the entry area labeled probability at the bottom of the window. Click on the **Legends** button to see a list of accepted characters for the probability string. You can specify stepwise, leaping, or random melodic movement, as well as rests and repeats. Enter a string of characters (from the probability legend list) into the probability entry area for each instrument. The sequence repeats endlessly until you press **Stop**.

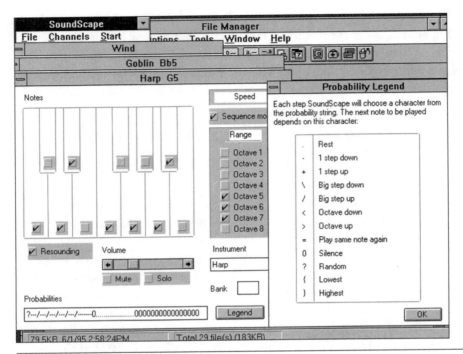

Figure 2.30 Algorithmic sound generator.

While SoundScape does not generate .mid files as output, it illustrates the power of computer music utilities. If you create a sequence that you want to keep, record it as a .wav recording by simultaneously opening a wave editor program. You may elect to process your computer music sequences off line, editing and fine-tuning as you desire, or boldly cast electrons to the wind and broadcast a permutating sequence that will play for another millennium before it repeats.

Mozart's Dice Game

Music has always had a mathematical side, and the balance between repeating and varying musical patterns has intrigued both mathematicians and musicians over the years. If you think that the notion of randomly generated computer music is a new concept, you might be surprised to learn that Mozart came up with a game in 1787 that composed Minuets and Trios from a library of 272 distinct measures based on the roll of two six-sided dice. You might think that music produced in this manner would sound horrendous, but the combination of the randomness of the dice throw and the established musical patterns in the predetermined measures creates some very interesting songs.

The subject is explored in several places on the Web and a number of individuals have come up with Web-based versions of Mozart's game. You canexplore both the nature of the game and the underlying code that is used to combine MIDI sequences based on randomly generated numbers. A good starting point is:

204.96.11.210/jchuang/Music/Mozart/

 A computer-based random number generator is used to implement a version of this game. You can set the individual MIDI voices for the right hand and the left hand. A **Make Music** button starts the playback. The resulting songs are based on the original measures composed by Mozart blending together in a pattern dictated by the computer. This site also includes a number of links to other sites that explore this same concept and offer other variations of the game. For another twist on this theme, visit:

www.cs.vu.nl/~zsofi/mozart/

This site includes some challenging quiz questions (with hidden answers) that explore the mathematics of the Musical Dice Game.

Tuning Your Recordings

Henry Cowell in his book, *New Musical Resources*, suggests that the tempo and the musical key of a piece of music are related. His theory states, if you continue to double the beats per minute (of the specified tempo), octaves higher it should coincide with a pitch of the musical scale (in standard tuning). That pitch has special significance for use as the tonal center, or key, of passages composed at the specified tempo. Take 120bpm (beats per minute), divide by 60 (60 seconds in a minute) and it equals 2 beats per second. Beats per second are considered frequencies, or vibrations, so let's call it 2 Hertz (Hz). That is a low frequency! Take that frequency of 2Hz up eight octaves (take 2 to the 8th power) and it equals 256Hz. Now a pitch of 256Hz falls between a B (~246.94Hz) and a C (~261.63Hz) in the equal tempered scale that tunes A to 440Hz. You might try detuning your music keyboard a bit flat and try playing in the key of C at 120bpm.

If you respect the A = 440Hz tuning standard (and you should tune to some pitch standard if you play music with others) the calculations can be done in

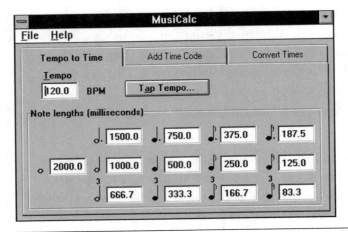

Figure 2.31 Artic MusiCalc.

reverse. Take A = 440Hz down eight octaves (divide by 2 eight times), multiply by 60 (60 seconds in a minute), and it equals ~103bpm. Of course, you can halve or double this tempo and it will still work its timely magic in the key of A.

This same theory carries into the art of setting delay times for digital delays, echos, and time-relevant effects. Utilities are available that examine your input and calculate the harmonic settings for time delays making them correlate to a specific tempo. The program or device may prompt you to tap in a measure or two of the tempo (the beats per minute). As you naturally tap your foot to keep time, the delay timing or sequence loop length is automatically adjusted and can change dynamically as you express yourself. The Artic MusiCalc program included in the Artic MIDI Music Utilities (MMU) package allows you to enter numerically or tap in the tempo in beats per minute (see Figure 2.31). Note lengths (for the specified tempo) are displayed in milliseconds for the range of whole note to sixteenth note. If you have a delay effects processor that is programmed digitally, the MusiCalc program calculates the optimized list of delay settings for your selection.

Extending MIDI: Just Intonation

If you have studied music at all or read about music theory, you've probably been exposed to the idea of the equal-tempered scale. For slightly more than 300 years, musicians playing fixed tuned instruments, such as the piano or guitar, have been trapped within the boundaries of the equal-tempered scale. The equal-tempered scale was created to allow music based on a 12-tone scale to be played in different keys on fixed tuned instruments. To do this, the frequencies of the notes within a one octave range were divided into 12 equal parts. While these frequency divisions come close to achieving pure harmonic relationships, this approach is a compromise—a given tonal interval in this system may be 4, 5, or 6Hz away from a pure harmonic relationship, resulting in a slight perceptible dissonance.

Our Western ears have grown accustomed to this dissonance, but not so much that we do not recognize pure harmonies when we hear them. The harmonies achieved by a barbershop quartet or the chamber music played by stringed instruments such as violas, violins, and cellos can be startlingly rich. Human voices and non-fretted instrument fingerboards can compensate for the limitations of the equal-tempered scale and adjust notes slightly to improve the harmonic relationships. Scales and chords that are based on mathematically precise relationships of notes are a form of *just intonation*. We hear this as a stirring, wonderfully clean blend of notes in contrast to the slightly out-of-tune, compromised equal-tempered scale.

For example, every musical tone has a fundamental pitch that is centered around a frequency, such as 100Hz. For this fundamental pitch of 100Hz, a series of harmonics exists at 200Hz, 300Hz, 400Hz, and so on. An octave, by definition is a 2-to-1 relationship of the frequencies—for example, the jump from 220Hz to 440Hz. Intervals of Fifths have a ratio of 3-to-2, Thirds have a relationship of 5-to-4—we hear these pure relationships of frequencies as pleasing, smooth blends of sound. Centuries of musical history from every conceivable culture on earth have been built around these relationships (generally without any knowledge or examination of the underlying mathematical relationships).

Even though we can hear the difference in the quality of the music when using pure harmonic relationships, we have 300-plus years of momentum supporting the current equal-tempered scale and a host of instruments designed in this framework. Prior to computer technology, the difficulties in creating keyboards that could support a variety of tunings or intonation systems was too complex to be practical. With the computer and the benefits of MIDI as a notational and performance language, dynamic adjustments can be made that alter the relationships of musical intervals to achieve pure harmonies. A variety of software products is now appearing on the market that support this approach. The better examples of these tools remove the complexity of analyzing or understanding the mathematical complexities of note and scale relationships, letting the musician focus on creating music using much cleaner, more mellow harmonic intervals.

Justonic Tuning Pitch Palette

Pitch Palette software from Justonic, a small company based in Vancouver, British Columbia, overcomes the limitations of the equal-tempered scale by offering a computer-controlled tool that can dynamically adjust the frequency of notes to support pure harmonies. Taking advantage of the microtuning possibilities available through a number of sound boards and external synthesizer units, notes are based on mathematically precise intervals based on a selected tonal center. The result is music that simply sounds better. All the discussion of mathematical relationship and frequencies becomes irrelevant to your ears. Play with the possibilities, create some songs based on this approach, and let your ears be the judge.

You have two options for playing back MIDI music files through Pitch Palette. The cleanest option is available to you if your computer system includes one of the sound boards or external MIDI devices to use for playback. This device most fully supports the MIDI tuning standard, which allows microtuning of individual notes. Microtuning is the ability to create musical notes with a very precise frequency resolution over the entire range of the keyboard. Supported MIDI devices include the Turtle Beach Multisound sound board; Yamaha's MU-50 and MU-80 tone generators; Ensoniq MR series; Kurzweil K2000, K2500, and K150; E-mu Proteus, Classic Keys, Vintage Keys Plus; and several other models. Justonic has also been working in combination with a British firm to create their own synthesizer, called the Justonic Tone Palette. The design offers increased tuning flexibility with a resolution of about 0.01Hz throughout the full range of the keyboard. The entire synthesizer can also be retuned in the span of several milliseconds. This equipment would be the way to go if you want to take maximum advantage of the flexibility of the Pitch Palette software.

The other option is to use a software synthesizer product that allows microtuning. In one of their packages, Justonic offers the popular Roland Sound Canvas software, which provides software synthesis for MIDI file playback. Software synthesis, described in several places in this book, places demands on the computer processor, which must deal with rapid generation of waveforms for output from a library of disk-stored instrument samples. This approach rules out low-performance machines, but isn't everyone running a Pentium these days? I didn't think so.

The Pitch Palette software consists of a set of tools (some of them shown in Figure 2.32), providing a number of different means for tinkering with scales and harmonic relationships and viewing these relationships graphically. A Chord Detector can be used to automatically detect the tuning root and dynamically adjust interval relationships to maintain pure harmonic tones. An onscreen digital Oscilloscope shows graphically the interaction of two or more tonal frequencies, displaying Lissajous patterns in response to the frequency inputs. Other tools let you select scales from predefined interval relationships and then view the output in a bar-chart format that displays the individual elements of the scale and their newly defined frequencies. Of course, any of these settings can be used for playing back a MIDI file, and you can compose individual pieces that take advantage of the many options available through Pitch Palette. Justonic refers to their approach as using a three-dimensional scale. In live playing, as a keyboardist cycles through chords or modulates keys, the Pitch Palette software interprets the harmonic structure and almost instantly makes microtuning adjustments to maintain the harmonic relationships. Music sounds sweeter. Justonic believes this will be the way music will be made in the twenty-first century. Without the computer, none of these rapid tuning adjustments could be accomplished.

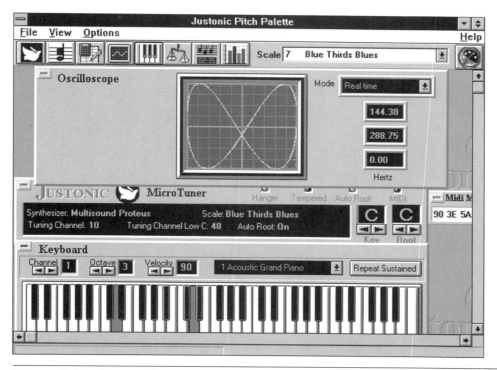

Figure 2.32. Some of the tools available through the Pitch Palette software.

More information on Justonic Tuning, Inc can be obtained by contacting at the address listed in Appendix C.

Working with MIDI

You can deliver sound to the Web without ever looking at or touching a MIDI file, but to do so is to ignore one of the more useful, malleable, and compact music formats. MIDI delivers a high concentration of musical contents with a minimal consumption of bandwidth. While you might argue that the Web author loses vital control over the sound being played back, even modestly equipped systems usually contain some form of sound synthesis capable of at least delivering some facsimile of music. With the increased prevalence of wavetable synthesis in sound boards and software synthesis technique, the quality of MIDI sound is now higher than it has ever been.

Chapter 8 discusses MIDI techniques further, describing the means by which you can deliver MIDI files from an HTML document.

The Digital
Sound Studio

*This chapter introduces the tools and techniques for working
with sound in a desktop computer studio. The techniques
described can be used to process sound files for use on the
Internet and to perfect existing recordings to get exactly the
effect you desire. A number of guidelines for recording successfully using digital techniques and converting sounds from
one format to another are included.*

Recording has never been more fun! With the graphical soundwave editing capability of your desktop computer, you can remove the mistakes and
sweeten to perfection the favorite parts of your sound files. You can do multitrack recording, sound on sound, vocal and instrument arrangements, and
sonic enhancements. Sounds can be generated electronically and/or combined
with audio recorded from a microphone, stage mixer output, home entertainment equipment, and so forth. Once the sound is digitized and stored on
your hard disk, the magical sound file processing can begin. In processing
your sound files for Web site playback you will inevitably resort to some
kind of data reduction scheme to reduce the file size. Tomorrow may bring
faster data transmission rates, but we must design with and for what is available today. You may find that a little intelligent computer processing can
make your sound files much smaller and yet still sound very good. Learn to
listen to the audio spectrum as a whole and experiment with equalization,

delays, and modulation. You will find great delight and reward in computer-enhancing your sound files, so much that you'll be proud to upload them for everyone in the wide world.

Going from Analog to Digital

More and more, everything is going to digital technology. Digital cameras, digital recorders, digital telephones, digital assistants—it's too good to contest. However, sound is still recorded with microphones and still taken from the outputs of traditional musical instruments as analog audio waveforms. The process of converting sound from the analog (real) world to the digital (binary) domain is performed by circuitry that rapidly measures the instantaneous voltage of the live audio waveform and assigns a corresponding binary number that represents the measured (sampled) voltage. Like a highly accurate digital voltmeter, it strobes the instantaneous amplitude measurements tens of thousands of times a second, writing them to the computer's hard drive. Very little chaos goes unnoticed. The lightning speed of modern electronics has made the digital age a reality.

A number of devices can make digital recordings of sound. Some machines commonly used today for capturing live audio are:

- **Digital Tape recorders:** Digital Audio Tape (DAT), Alesis Digital Audio Tape (ADAT)

- **Hard Disk recorders:** Computer with sound card, dedicated hard disk recorder workstation

- **MiniDisc recorders:** Writable magneto-optical disc devices

- **Flash RAM recorders:** Nonvolatile RAM recorders (no moving parts)

Once your recording is in the digital domain, other digital copies can be made with no loss of sound quality. With your music loaded into the computer's hard drive, digital processing effects (delays, echos, reverbs) can be done without loss of sound quality or the injection of noise. Music on the hard drive can be accessed like memory, in a random-access fashion. You do not need to sequentially progress from beginning to end like the tape medium. And, last but not least, you are granted the ability to perform an undo! If you delete a selection of your recording to edit a mistake but find the selected area you cut was not properly specified, you can immediately undo the operation and the file is restored to its last saved version.

Sampling Analog Waveforms

Analog input audio is converted to the digital domain by analog-to-digital (A/D) circuitry on your sound board. Binary numbers are generated that represent each instantaneous voltage amplitude sample of the analog input waveform. These numeric amplitude values are stored to the computer's hard disk. Hence, it is called hard disk recording. The binary coded, instantaneous voltage levels are sampled at tens of thousands of times per second.

When you use your computer as a digital waveform recorder, you first must determine how much recording time your system resources can provide. Your computer must have enough empty disk space to supply 5Mbytes of memory per recorded second for a monaural recording sampled at 44.KHz and, double that, 10Mbytes per second, for a stereo recording. Sampling at half that sampling rate (22KHz) reduces both of these figures by one-half.

When you click to initiate a new recording, most recording utilities first present the Record Settings window. Here the sample rate, resolution (16-bit or 8-bit), and the stereo/mono options are provided. Radio buttons are often provided for you to specify the recording format. If this screen is not automatically presented when you proceed to do a new recording, check the menus and first set the recording format. Figure 3.1 shows a typical window for specifying the record format.

With the sample rate, resolution, and stereo/mono settings specified, you need to check only the record gain setting before clicking the **Record** button. It is not difficult to adjust the record gain accurately; the computer will display either a signal strength bar graph indicator or oscillograph display of the live input waveform allowing you to instantly see if your input signal is robust, weak, or so strong it's going off the scale (a sure sign of clipping). When digitally recording from an analog source you want to capture the strongest signal possible without clipping off the peaks of the loudest (largest) samples. A record gain fine adjustment in the form of a volume slider may require adjustment. Figure 3.2 shows the record gain adjustment screen of the SoundBlaster Creative WaveStudio software. If you require more record gain than the mixer adjustment allows, enter the Recording Settings screen (available via a drop-down menu from the mixer screen). The Gain box in the Recording Settings window shown in the figure permits the record gain to be boosted by 2 or 4 with separate adjustments for the right and left channels. Most sound cards will allow a similar coarse adjustment of the record gain sensitivity.

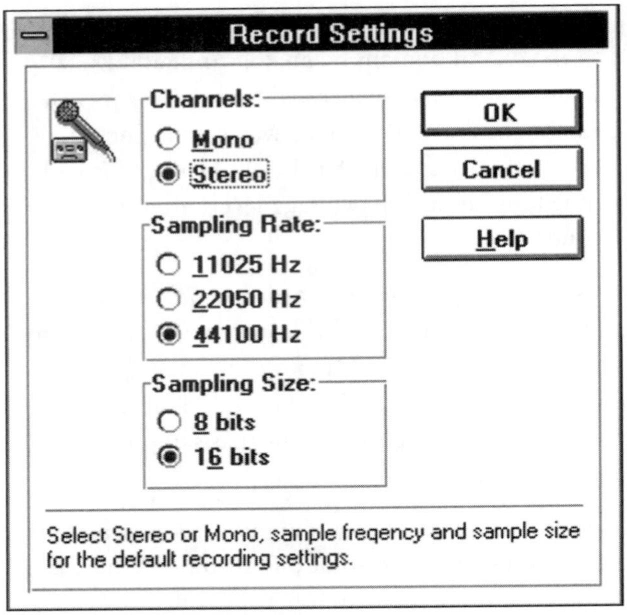

Figure 3.1 Record settings.

Boosting the record gain to acquire more sensitivity because a microphone signal is very weak can lead to an intolerable noise increase in some situations. A respected alternative is to keep the record gain setting at a moderate level, purchase a microphone preamplifier, and input the line level signal from the preamplifier into the line inputs of the sound card. This technique is discussed in further detail later in the chapter.

A good place to start is to use the computer to make short digital sound event samples. Record utterances, honks, bells, creaks, cracks, pops, and snaps and store each as an individual sound file. If you're a musician you can use your computer to make instrument sound samples (wavetable sound) that can be rendered across the musical scale and performed or rendered by MIDI control. Processing waveforms of digitally recorded audio can take minutes (or more, depending on the operation) because digital sound is dense, contiguous, binary information. Working on short sound clips initially will allow you to familiarize yourself with new sound processing software and reduce the frustration that often accompanies large file processing. After first covering the basics, we will discuss recording and synthesizing sound samples so you can do it yourself.

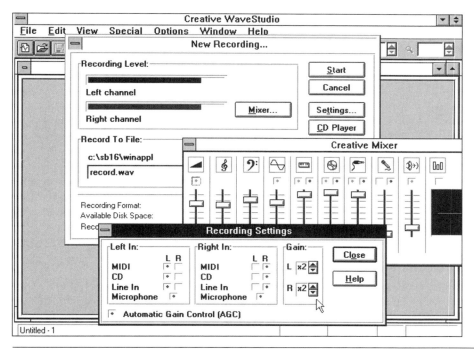

Figure 3.2 Record gain adjustment.

A-to-D through Sound Board

It is common for a sound board to have two analog input jacks: one for a microphone and another for a line level audio signal (see Figure 3.3). The microphone input is the most sensitive. It should have enough gain to amplify the minute signal from the microphone to a signal volume that can be accurately recorded. The line input jack accepts electrical audio signals in the range of 1/2 volt to 2 volts rms and can accept a stereo signal from a variety of sources. The stereo analog outputs from a cassette recorder, television, radio, record player, CD player, the aux output of your home entertainment system; they all present suitable and recordable output signals. Also, the analog outputs from a music keyboard, guitar effects rack, or sound mixer can be ported into the line input jack of the computer's sound board. Some devices will output stronger signals than others, and you will occasionally need to fine-adjust the record gain to accommodate an odd signal source.

At this point in history, there are a lot of sound cards in use that can record 16-bit stereo sound. They are adequate for preprocessing sound for Web site use.

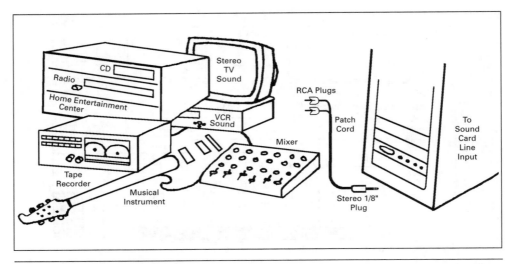

Figure 3.3 Analog inputs.

However, the microphone inputs on most of these sound cards (professional recording gear excluded) are better used for voice communications (as an Internet telephone mic or audio chat mic) or for vocally commanding the computer to perform specific operations. Voice-to-text dictation has become a feasible alternative for inputting data. All these applications have been designed for live mic use within the fan noise and circus dungeon acoustics of the modern office cubicle. The cooling fan noise of the computer presents the biggest problem when recording audio live with a microphone plugged into the mic input of the sound card. A longer microphone cable can be used to distance yourself from the noise source, but unbalanced microphone cable cannot be run hundreds of feet without signal loss or additional noise pickup.

Don't be afraid to experiment. Try capturing some sound from a diverse collection of sources and compare the results. Once in the digital domain, digital signal processing can be used to mix, modulate, enhance, and alter your recordings. Try plugging an electric guitar directly into your sound board and recording. You will need an monaural patch cord that has a ¼-inch phone plug on one end (to insert into the guitar) and a ⅛-inch phone plug on the other end, to insert into the sound card. (I'm assuming your guitar isn't stereo; if it is then use a stereo version of the same patch cord.) First try plugging into the line input of the sound card and recording. The signal output strength of guitars can vary greatly depending on their pickup types or internal circuitry. Humbucking pickups tend to have higher output signals than models with single coil pickups. The term *humbucking* refers to the ability of this type of pickup to neutralize hum by using two individual coils within the pickup wired out of phase with each other. Also, if you're playing the instrument through an effects rack, the effects circuits probably have some signal gain, so definitely use the line input of the sound card for inputting your signal.

> **WARNING**   Is it a good idea to plug a mono jack into a stereo input? It's safe to plug a mono patch cord into a stereo input jack. One of the stereo input channels simply receives 0 volts (no signal) because it contacts ground via the plug. Caution should be observed that the mono patch cord is not accidentally inserted into one of the sound card's output jacks like the stereo line output or stereo speaker output jack. This would short one of the output channels to ground, a practice that is not recommended. It could cause damage to the equipment.

If you're not recording stereo, set up the recording as monaural so only the active signal channel records. Otherwise, the silent channel will also record, doubling the size of the sound file. It uses just as much memory to record silence as it does to record signal. If the record gain cannot be optimized, the guitar signal may be too weak for the line level inputs, so the microphone input must be used.

A-to-D through Recorder

Recording digitally to tape is a reasonably inexpensive way to capture your audio sessions. The tape hiss and mediocre signal-to-noise characteristics of analog tape recordings are now the vestiges of a bygone era. If you have a digital recorder you may feel more comfortable recording remote from the computer and later transferring the "good takes" to your computer's hard disk for editing. If you don't have a digital recorder, by all means use your analog tape recorder. We have brought many sounds to our computer for digital processing after recording them on an analog cassette recorder. Use the best quality equipment available, but don't talk yourself out of trying because you don't have the latest and greatest equipment. You may be very surprised at what can be done on a limited budget.

The most popular digital recorders are the DAT and ADAT. The DAT (Digital Audio Tape) inputs stereo sound, converts it to the digital domain (if you're recording analog), and stores it to tape cassette or cartridge, depending on the specific machine. Most DAT machines have both analog and digital active record inputs that can be selected by a switch on the recorder. ADATs also usually have both analog and digital outputs.

The consumer-grade DAT machines contain the Serial Code Management System (SCMS), which prevents copying of digital material under certain circumstances. SCMS limits the number of digital copies you can make to one. It prevents protected CD material from being copied and interferes with communications between some digital audio workstations and DAT machines. Machines with an SCMS defeat function are available.

The Alesis Digital Audio Tape (ADAT) is a multitrack recording device that can record up to eight channels of audio data onto videotape. These devices use the same ½-inch S-VHS video tape cartridges that you feed your camcorder, but the tape is run at 3¾-inches per second—much faster than the tape is run when used in a camcorder. Using a 120 S-VHS tape you can get 40 minutes of recording when using the 48KHz sampling rate. That rises to 53 minutes of recording time when using a 160-minute tape. Tapes must be precoded with a timecode to establish synchronization. A single optical cable (sometimes called a light pipe) carries all eight tracks of digital audio to the computer.

ADAT machines use the same kind of rotary recording/playback head with helical scan that is used for video recording. Converters are available that can combine pairs of tracks into AES3 or S/PDIF formats. The original ADAT format was developed by Alesis, but equipment has also been produced by Matsushita.

MiniDisc Recorder MiniDisc (MD) recorders are digital sound recorders that use magneto-optical technology for recording to a small (64mm) optical disc. Some units now available are consumer-grade recorders limited to a few tracks, but the format has also gained popularity in the field of professional radio broadcasting where it has largely replaced analog cassettes.

Less expensive MD recorders use analog mixing stages and often contain no digital effects processing capability. Rerecording a track destructively writes over the old track; there are no multiple levels of undo. So far, the MiniDisc format has been largely targeted to the music collector, but portable studio units for musicians have also been introduced. MiniDisc units can be used for collecting sound samples, and some units are equipped with an optical digital output. The small portable units have not been designed for track level editing.

Staying in the Digital Domain

Once the recorder has converted audio into the digital domain it is preferable to transfer the audio as digital sound to the computer. Do not convert a recording back and forth between the analog and digital domain. Once sound has been transformed from analog to digital, keep it in the digital domain. Each conversion increases the quantization error in the signal and cumulative signal degradation occurs. To transfer a digital recording from a digital tape recorder to the computer requires a sound board or module that has a digital signal input (see Figure 3.4). These are becoming more popular, and if you don't have one already, it should definitely be a requested feature at your next sound card purchase. If you like to use digital rack mount effects modules, shop for models with digital signal input and output capability. Many hardware digital effects boxes do yet another internal A/D and D/A conversion, so digital input and output capability is very desirable if the effects are to be used in an all-digital recording chain.

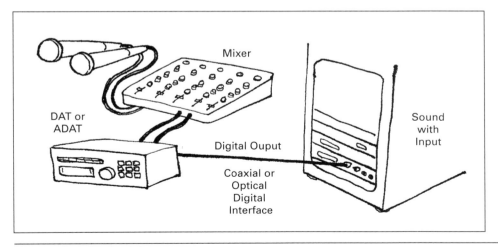

Figure 3.4 Digital inputs.

Direct Digital from CD

Many sound cards, while having only analog inputs exposed to the outside world, have an onboard connector that inputs digital sound from the computer's CD/CD-ROM player, thus bypassing the A/D circuitry on the sound card. The music on any CD is already in the digital domain, and it would only be degraded by the errors of successive quantization if the analog output of the CD player was routed to the sound card for yet another analog-to-digital conversion.

Not all CD players and CD-ROM drives are capable of being accessed directly; the term applied to this technique is *digital extraction*. Software applications, such as OMI's Disc-to-Disk, can be used to initiate the digital transfer from the audio CD to the computer's hard disk drive.

Digital Signal Interfaces

As digital signal input and output capability becomes a more common feature on computer sound cards, we need to take a look at the interface standards.

AES/EBU The Audio Engineering Society/European Broadcast Union (AES/EBU) has developed a digital audio interface standard that is used by professional and consumer digital audio devices. It is a serial communications protocol for transferring digital audio over a single transmission line. The single line carries both channels of stereo digital audio at resolutions up to 24 bits per sample. Control and status information are also transmitted on the line. The sample rate of the transmitted sound data is derived from the bitstream (a clock signal is synthesized from the transmitted bits). The AES/EUB standard recognizes sample rates of 32KHz, 44.1KHz, and 48KHz.

A variety of physical connection methods is found on equipment using the AES/EUB standard:

- **Balanced (differential) line:** Using two conductors and a shield and outfitted with XLR connectors (like a balanced line microphone cable)

- **Unbalanced (single-ended) line:** Using a single conductor and a shield audio coax cable, outfitted with RCA plugs (like a VCR video cable with RCA connectors)

- **Optical cable:** A fiber-optic light pipe

S/PDIF The Sony/Phillips Digital Interface Format (S/PDIF) for the most part equates to being the AES/EUB standard operated in consumer mode using an unbalanced line with RCA connectors. Consumer mode means that many of the professional mode channel status bits (sample number, word length, alphanumeric channel origin and destination, time of day, etc.) are not supported. The S/PDIF interface does include copy protection information.

The physical implementation of an S/PDIF interface will have a single RCA jack for stereo digital in and another single RCA jack for stereo digital out. The single conductor, serial transmission carries both the left and right channel information for stereo program material.

Sound Effects and Samples Your digital audio work need not start from raw source recordings. There are a number of different sources of professional-quality sound effects and digital sound samples that can be incorporated into your work, either as a starting point for further enhancement or as individual elements that can be used in a variety of ways in HTML documents.

One source of audio clips, as well as voice talent, is EDnet, a company that works closely with the broadcasting and entertainment industry to exchange high-quality audio, compressed video, and multimedia data. Their sound site, which uses a variation of the Liquid Audio software discussed in Chapter 7, offers download-able sound effects that can be purchased and licensed for project use.

Sound samples are also well represented on the Web. Rarefaction produces CDs containing hundreds of "sound sculptures" engineered for inclusion in many different types of audio projects—as sound effects, as instrument samples in a MIDI setup, or as source audio for modifying further in imaginative ways. CDs such as their *Poke in the Ear with a Sharp Stick* offer original and unique sound libraries that will provide audio fuel for many creative efforts.

 You can visit EDnet's Web site at:

www.ednet.com

and Rarefaction's Web site at:

www.rarefaction.com

Appendix C, "Internet Sound Resources", suggests a number of other sources where you can obtain audio files for various uses.

Music Recordings (Royalty-Free) Composing professional quality music for Web audio applications is not a task for the faint at heart. Even skilled musicians need a good deal of recording experience to be able to construct musical works at a professional level. If you're looking for musical accompaniment that you can weave through your Web pages, you might want to investigate royalty-free music. These types of music require a single initial fee, after which you can use the material as you see fit—in interactive authoring, in videos, in multimedia projects, and so on.

One company that offers excellent quality music of this type is QCCS Productions. Their Professional Background Theme Music (PBTM) series includes full-length songs and shorter segments for use as lead-ins or trailers in various categories, such as suspense, nature, sports, and so on. Samples can be obtained on compact disc or cassette tape. Contact information for QCCS Productions is located in Appendix C.

Digital-Only Sound Boards

Digital-only audio cards that contain no onboard analog-to-digital or digital-to-analog converters are now popular for professional computer hard-disk recording systems. These boards may or may not be equipped with MIDI-capable circuitry. The digital-only audio cards require that A-to-D and D-to-A conversion be done externally. They are equipped with S/PDIF connectors and/or optical connectors for use with DAT or ADAT recorders or any effects device with digital signal interface capability.

The digital-only audio cards have one electrical (rather than optical) digital input jack and one electrical digital output jack. These physically resemble standard mono RCA jacks, a connector that has been common on audio equipment for half a century. Each jack carries the left and right information of the digitized stereo information in its single serial signal path. The ultrasonic frequency burden of these serial digital signal paths requires the use of signal cables better than audio quality. Good quality 75-ohm coaxial video cables equipped with the RCA-style plugs are recommended.

The optical (light pipe) connectors, one for input and one for output, permit an ADAT recorder to send eight tracks of digital audio serially into or out of the computer via a digital-only audio card.

If you have a DAT recorder and a digital-only sound card, a tapeless studio of good sound quality can be created. Put the DAT on record pause and use the analog inputs of the DAT while routing its digital output to the input of the digital-only card. Some DAT machines require a tape to be in the machine before they will enter pause mode. If you have a second DAT machine, also put it on record pause and route the digital output from the card to the digital input of the DAT, using the analog outputs from its D/A for playback.

Zefiro Acoustics ZA2 One good choice for a professional-quality digital sound board for your computer that won't cost you more than the computer itself is the Zefiro Acoustics ZA2. Equipped with both S/PDIF (Sony/Phillips Digital Interface Format) and AES/EBU (Audio Engineering Society/European Broadcasters Union), the ZA2 is designed for a standard ISA bus slot in an IBM-compatible PC. A break-out cable included with the board provides a variety of inputs and outputs, including coaxial S/PDIF inputs and outputs, fiber optic S/PDIF inputs and outputs, XLR AES/EBU inputs and outputs, and stereo analog line outputs.

A pop-up control panel can be used under Windows95 to set your sample rates, choose input and output options, and perform other selections. An included DOS utility even lets you back up your hard disk drive to DAT tape. If you're going to do serious digital audio work on your computer, it's very helpful to have an interface that will support direct digital signals in and out. Keep in mind that every time you perform an additional audio conversion—from digital-to-analog or from analog-to-digital—you introduce some additional signal degradation. If you can keep your music and voice data in the digital realm, the quality of your recording and sound processing will be much higher.

More information on the ZA2 can be obtained from Zefiro Acoustics; their contact information is located in Appendix C.

Studio Setup

Working in a computer-based sound studio may require some adjustments to the way you've worked with your computer in the past. If you're going to be doing any live recording, you'll need to pay some attention to the acoustics of the room in which you're recording and the surrounding sounds. Things you don't notice, or filter out, in the course of everyday activities can become a part of your digital recording if you're not careful. That barking dog next door can make an interesting accompaniment to your serious recorded narration for your Web page design. Passing airplanes and cars can become inextricably mixed with your acoustic guitar recording to your chagrin. Even the fan noise generated by your PC can work its way into your recording efforts. Successfully doing digital recording requires constant awareness of the sound environment within which you are working and the acoustics of everything around you.

Learning the equipment associated with recording is also an important part of the process. Soundwave signals move through a variety of paths on their way to their ultimate destination—hopefully, your HTML document. Moving signals cleanly requires lots of cables and connections, and there are lots of chances for the signals to get distorted or degraded along the way. This section is designed to lead you through the worst pitfalls and help you get set up for successful recording.

Using Analog Recording Inputs

Don't assume your sound card's microphone input is stereo because the microphone that came with it has a stereo plug at the end of its cord. Check the specifications; the microphone input jack on some sound boards is designed for a mono (single channel) microphone. The microphone that's included with the sound card is often a cheap condenser mic; its plug appears stereo because the ring connector of the plug is used to supply voltage from the sound card to the microphone. Electret condensor microphones require a power source. If you want stereo microphone inputs, check the specs carefully before purchasing a sound board and make sure they're present.

If a dynamic microphone with a mono ⅛-inch plug at the end of its cord is inserted into the sound card microphone input described previously, it will not cause damage to the sound card. The voltage source for the condensor mic will contact the ground of the microphone cable, but it is always current limited by an internal resistor. Of course, if your sound card mic input is a true stereo input, you can use a stereo microphone that has a stereo ⅛-inch phone plug at the end of its cord. But, what about using two microphones separated from each other?

An adapter is available that accepts two mono ¼-inch phone plugs (from the two microphones) and routes them as the left and right channels of a ⅛-inch stereo male plug. If this adapter is too bulky to physically fit in the close quarters behind the computer, find one terminated in a ⅛-inch female jack instead of male plug, and use a stereo patch cord terminated in ⅛-inch phone plugs to connect the adapter to the computer.

Another very viable option is to purchase a stereo microphone preamplifier or stereo mixer that has built-in microphone preamplifiers. Plug the microphones into this device and cable its stereo outputs to the line level inputs of the sound card. This method allows you to boost the microphone outputs to a strong signal level before inputting. Unless your sound card is a professional-quality model with balanced line inputs, this method is probably the best method for recording sound from live mics. A low-noise preamplifier with adequate gain can produce superior results over using the microphone inputs of most commercial-grade sound cards. Often the gain of the sound card mic input signal has to be set so high for optimized recording level that noise is injected in the signal path from EMI in the computer cabinet.

Microphone Recording Techniques

The microphone is an electro-acoustic transducer that reacts to sound pressure waves and produces an electrical analog. No transducer is ideal—there is always some nonlinearity and power loss. Also, be aware that the microphone you use can subtly impart its tonality onto your recording. Professional microphones can have very small output signals, as low as 1 millivolt. Often, the sensitivity (record gain) of the sound board must be increased to accommodate a pro-quality microphone at the mic input.

Types of Microphones Microphones are rated for their sensitivity and frequency response. The sensitivity rating really expresses how much of the incoming acoustical signal energy at the microphone's input is converted to usable electrical signal. Often sensitivity will be given as a negative value of decibels (db) measured at 1000Hz. In comparing two microphones, the one having the greater minus db rating is the least sensitive. The frequency response tells what range of frequencies the microphone is capable of transducing. A frequency response graph is often provided to show the deviation in sensitivity throughout the frequency range of the specific microphone. The ideal microphone has a flat frequency response, no deviation, through the entire audio spectrum. Since all microphones have some deviation across their frequency response, choose a microphone that suits the sound source being recorded. If you are recording a band instrument like flute or clarinet, choose a mic with a relatively flat frequency response in the frequency range of the instrument. These instruments do not play deep bass notes, so the lower end of the microphone's frequency response curve need not be perfectly flat. Just remember, when a microphone is used it is the first device to accept the sound. It initially defines the quality of the sound for the rest of the recording or amplifying chain.

Microphone Polar Patterns Microphones are also categorized by their field or polar pattern, often referred to as their directional characteristic. The pattern defines the shape of the most sensitive sound pickup area around the microphone input. Figure 3.5 shows three of the most common mic polar patterns.

Cardiod mics exhibit a heart-shaped polar pattern that is most sensitive to sound directly in front of the mic. They are also called unidirectional microphones. Super-cardiod mics have tighter, more exaggerated cardiod patterns. Cardiod microphones are traditionally used by performing vocalists because they have reduced sensitivity to sound entering from behind the mic, and this lowers the possibility of feedback through the amplifiers they are driving. Cardiod mics can still feedback in this environment; they merely allow the amplifier to be used 3 to 6 db louder before feedback. The consequences of using a cardiod mic for recording are twofold. First, they rarely have as flat a frequency response curve as omnidirectional mics. Second, in some situations the pickup pattern can be too tight, forcing the singer to stand unnaturally fixed in front of the mic or too close to the mic, causing a bass boost effect while recording. A mere glance to the side or turn of the head can cause the signal level to drop off.

An omnidirectional microphone picks up sound from all directions. Omnidirectional mics usually yield the most natural sounding recording because they often have the flattest frequency response that often extends to 15,000 or

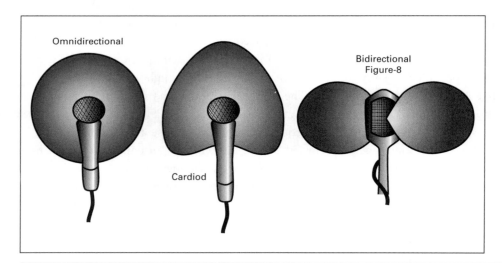

Figure 3.5 Microphone polar patterns.

20,000Hz. They are less susceptible to handling noise, popping, wind noise, and proximity effects. You will be able to record cymbals and the overtones and harmonics of instruments. A fact of nature is that the higher audio frequencies are more directional than lower frequencies, so an omnidirectional mic may seem to be responding like a unidirectional at higher frequencies. They are a good choice for recording if you enjoy the warmth of natural room acoustics and delight in hyper-realism. They are not the natural choice for recording industrial-strength, youthfully spirited garage band music.

There are bidirectional pattern mics and stereo microphones. The bidirectional microphone polar pattern is shaped like a figure-8. Ribbon microphones have traditionally shown this characteristic. Today, stereo microphones are available where each lobe of the figure-8 pattern serves as the sensing domain of the related channel, left or right.

Dynamic Microphones The dynamic mic is rugged and dependable. It can handle high sound pressure levels and does not require a power source like the electret condensor microphone. Cheaper varieties tend to have a limited frequency response, especially on the high end. They are available in many polar patterns including unidirectional and omnidirectional. Many dynamic mics are built more for rugged touring abuse and stage acrobatics than for sensitive recording. This can translate to poor transient response and can yield a less crisp, muted recording quality, especially from budget-priced models. Omnidirectional dynamics tend to have better frequency response characteristics and can sound more natural, but they must be carefully placed when used in stereo to avoid phase cancellation.

Electret Condensor Condensor microphones have superior frequency response and excellent transient response. They require a power source from a battery or external phantom power supply. They do not handle high sound pressure levels well and can be more easily overdriven than the dynamic microphone. Many have a high frequency peak in their response that must be rolled off above 10KHz to obtain a more natural recording. Condensor mics are often preferred for recording acoustic guitars and for capturing the crispness of the snare drum. They are suitable for some types of vocal recording, but they are not recommended for mic-swallowing screamers.

Ribbon Microphones Ribbon microphones are sensitive devices usually manufactured only as professional-quality devices. Once they were considered the ultimate studio mic because of their warm sonic tonality. They are somewhat susceptible to wind pops and vocal fricative problems and must be used properly. These problems can be avoided with foam windscreens and by placing the mic a respectable distance from the vocalist. The ribbon microphone does not tolerate the intimate mic techniques that many singers employ. Excellent sounding recordings can be made with these devices if the singer can be trained not to swallow the microphone. They are usually heavy since a large permanent magnet is used in their construction, and they are somewhat fragile because they have an ultra-light metal ribbon as the sound sensor. The common monaural ribbon microphone has a figure-8 directional characteristic. Sound can enter from either side of the internal ribbon; however, sound entering from opposite sides will be 180 degrees out of phase.

Mic Positioning Recording mono with a single microphone is easy. If the sound source is stationary, experiment by recording with the mic at different distances from the sound source. Try mics that have different polar patterns and determine how much coloration from the natural room acoustics (ambiance) you want in the background. The more distant from the sound source the mic is placed, the more room ambiance, reflections, echos, and so forth appear in the recording. However, the output signal strength of a mic falls off quickly (by the inverse square law) as the distance from sound source to mic increases. Sound-only media with no video imaging of the speaker's lips usually demands a quieter background ambient noise level for easy understandability. But, on some occasions, a little background sound can lend warmth, presence, and realism.

Use a microphone stand or suspend the mic from the ceiling by a hanging mount. Avoid recording from a hand-held mic if possible. Anything that rubs against the mic, its cable, or the mic stand can create noise that will be recorded. When recording voice or singing, high-frequency whistling sounds called sibilants occur when certain consonants are pronounced. When the microphone is placed directly in front of the speaker or singer these sounds can be exaggerated by some microphones, and a very unnatural and annoying effect is created. You can reduce sibilance by placing the mic above, below, or to one side of the mouth; no loss of frequency response occurs as long as the mic is still pointed directly at the artist's mouth. This placement technique is also useful for reducing plosives, the popping sounds from consonants like b and p. They can produce ugly thumps in the sound.

If you want to record stereo and want to focus the mics to collect sound in a specific space, the stereo V alignment may be used. Try recording someone singing and playing the acoustic guitar, by setting up two omnidirectional condensor microphones on gooseneck extensions from the same mic stand. With the mics placed approximately 10.5 inches apart (at their windscreen centers), the two mics point in, their extended centerlines coinciding approximately 9 or 10 inches in front of them, making an angle of about 75 degrees. Adjust the mic stand height so the microphones are at the same level as the singer's mouth. This arrangement will capture good clear vocals with a guitar-to-vocal balance that is often satisfactory. Avoid getting too close to the omnidirectional mics. Encourage the singer to stay 10 to 12 inches away from the microphone at the center focal point.

Mid-side stereo recording is an old technique that has again become popular among videographers. A mono bidirectional microphone (figure-8 polar pattern) is positioned at right angles to the sound source (like the ears on your head), and a directional mic is positioned toward the sound source (between the lobes of the bidirectional pattern). The raw stereo recording done in this field has the middle channel sound from the directional mic on one track and the side channel sound from the figure-8, bidirectional mic on the other track. Sound recorded in this manner can be mixed via a simple M-S (Mid-Side) matrix decoder, allowing you in post production to choose between mono (on both channels), wide stereo, or a mixture of both. Straight mono mixed in this way has none of the phase cancellation problems that can occur when stereo signals are mixed to mono.

 Mike Sokol in his Sound Advice for Computer/Video #6 found on the World Wide Web at:

www.soundav.com/link2.html

illustrates how to wire a phase-inverted balanced-line Y connector cable that will do the M-S decoding.

The mid-side stereo technique is very useful for recording in situations where sound sources are moving around in an active sound field. For example, if your recording is an outdoor capture of a newscaster speaking, interesting environmental sounds can later be brought out in the mix by panning to a wide stereo setting during the vocal pauses. See Figure 3.6 for an illustration of a mid-side mic assembly and an example of stereo V mic placement.

Noise Factors

It's not impossible to record at home using microphones. Simply do the best you can to avoid picking up the common household noise makers like refrigerators, air conditioners, fans, washing machines, vehicle motors, fluorescent light hum, heaters, fans, and sounds entering through open windows. Recording close to your computer

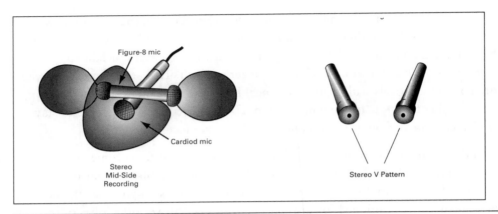

Figure 3.6 Mic Placement.

can cause the computer cooling fan noise and disk access chatter sounds to get into the live microphone. Computers that have been engineered for minimum noise emission can be purchased. However, with good common sense most of the noise problems associated with air recording near the computer can be subdued. Always use shielded cable for your microphone connection and route the microphone cable away from the monitor and computer fan to avoid noise pickup.

EMI Electromagnetic Interference (EMI) is a common problem encountered whenever you're working with electronic components. Electromagnetic waves, such as radio frequency waves from power supplies and monitors, get induced into surrounding cables to disrupt and distort the signal fidelity. This is apparent in audio signals as hums, static, and other kinds of audio distortions. Even the low-frequency waves generated by the AC outlets in your home at 60Hz can find their way into your audio signals if the conditions are right.

Avoiding the perils of EMI—one of the biggest enemies to pristine quality recordings—can require careful attention to your entire recording setup. Consider the following guidelines:

- Use the shortest cables possible for all your connections. Longer cables can act as antennas and any stray EMI can be picked up. Unterminated cables (cables that have only one end plugged into an input) are a particular problem. Unplug them completely.

- Route your signal cables away from power cords or DC transformers (often called *wall warts*) to avoid picking up any EMI from these sources.

- Try different slot locations for your computer sound board. Try to keep the board as far away from the power supply as possible.

- Keep a distance from anything with a large motor in it. Obvious culprits are refrigerators, air conditioners, copiers, and so on, but even fans can create problems. Having these devices on the same AC line as your recording equipment can be an invitation to problems.

- Don't use fluorescent lighting in or around your studio. Fluorescent lights generate high amounts of EMI that can easily be picked up by your recording gear.

It can take some effort to remove all the sources of EMI from around your recording gear, but the result of these efforts will be cleaner, hum-free recordings.

Digital Recording Fundamentals

The basic rules of digital recording are covered in this section. Many of these terms and techniques are discussed throughout the rest of the book, so if you're unfamiliar with these concepts, it might be helpful to spend some time reading through this section.

Sample Rate/Resolution

The two main characteristics of digital recording are sample rate and sample size:

- **Sample Rate**: The number of analog-to-digital conversions per second performed as the sound is recorded into the digital domain. This same value or sample rate must be used during playback as each sample is converted from digital to analog, or the playback will be pitch shifted.

- **Sample Size**: The precision of the analog-to-digital conversion specified in bits. An 8-bit sample size permits each incoming waveform amplitude sample to be recorded as one of 256 discrete voltage levels equally spaced across the dynamic input range of the converter. A 16-bit sample size records to a resolution of 65,536 discrete voltage levels within the converter's input range.

The number of input channels is also important. Stereo sound is perceived as having more depth than monaural (single channel) sound (called mono as opposed to stereo). Stereo is a widely accepted convention; monoaural recordings tend to sound flat to us because we are used to stereo sound. However, stereo means twice as many channels, and that means twice as many bytes of storage are required.

Sound cards with four discrete audio inputs (for simultaneously recording from four microphones, or line-level inputs) are now available for high-speed computer systems. But, surprisingly, many sound collectors have libraries of 16-bit mono as well as stereo sound files. Why? Because it is easy to pan a monaural sample into the stereo field of another recording. You can place the sound equally on both the right and left speakers or put it more on the left and complement it with an alternate take of the same recorded material panned more to the right channel.

So what's the downside of digital sound? The enormous size of sound files in the tens or hundreds of megabytes is one. In the early days of digital recording some artists complained of a cold lifelessness to the sound quality. This problem has been reduced by using digital delays to enhance the feeling of ambiance in the recording, and using vacuum tube compression preamplifiers during recording. However, digital recording all on its own, has given birth to some unique forms of signal distortion, named alias distortion and quantization error.

Alias Distortion

Alias distortion in the analog-to-digital sampling process occurs when frequencies (fundamental or harmonics of lower fundamentals) are not recorded with adequate precision because they exceed half the digital sampling rate (recording frequency). Aliasing may generate moire patterns in the recording, appearing as new, unwanted, lower-frequency difference tones or the cancellation of certain frequencies. Most A/D converters use an input low-pass filter (called an anti-aliasing filter) with a sharp cut-off frequency set at half the sampling rate. This removes all frequencies that cannot be accurately sampled. If the sound board has been properly engineered, alias distortion should not be detectable. It is not something you will lose sleep over unless aging insomniacs remove their sound board input filters and create loud and highly distorted music with maximized quantization error within earshot of your bedroom.

Quantization Errors

Quantization errors occur during analog-to-digital conversion as each amplitude sample value (of the input waveform) is rounded to the nearest digital amplitude approximation. Quantization error is reduced as sample size is increased. Doing 16-bit recording (65,536 possible amplitude levels) reduces quantization error greatly over 8-bit recording (256 possible amplitude levels). Low levels of accuracy can cause noise due to quantization errors. Keep in mind when recording analog input signals with your computer that if the record input levels are set too low you are not capturing a highly accurate digitization of the input. However, if the record input levels are set too high the digital recording of the analog input will be clipped.

Recording Guidelines

The effects available to you through digital recording applications can shape wave-forms in a tremendous number of ways by manipulating the stored bit patterns mathematically. This allows you to achieve effects in a desktop computer studio that previously were available only at very high cost through professional recording studios. The following sections cover some of the more common effects that you can apply to ensure the most accurate sound reproduction.

Dynamic Range

The real beauty of digital sound is its greatly increased usable dynamic range. Analog recordings done on professional equipment, even using noise reduction cir-cuitry, rarely achieved signal-to-noise ratios of -80db. Digital audio sampled at 44.1KHz can achieve a signal-to-noise ratio of -94db or more. This means that soft musical passages can be heard clearly and not be buried in a floor of noise. It also means that once your ear has comfortably adjusted to listening to that soft musical passage, you can be startled by crystal clear loud fanfares that are not distorted or clipped. Music properly mastered for the digital domain can definitely sound more realistic than an analog recording. Less compression is required because there is more dynamic range in which to perform.

Down converting a file from 16-bit resolution to 8-bit resolution will reduce its dynamic range. Make your initial recording as professional and low noise as possi-ble. The ambient background noise floor of the recording will seem more promi-nent as resolution is reduced. In some instances it may be better to reduce frequency response by downsampling instead of reducing resolution by converting from 16- to 8-bit format.

Normalizing

A feature commonly found on digital wave editors is normalization. This operation scans the selected area of the recorded waveform samples, finds the peak amplitude samples, and adjusts the overall volume of the selection to the maximum amplitude permissible without clipping any of the samples. When using this function, or doing any volume level adjustments, be aware that increasing the signal amplitude of a signal that has initially been recorded at too low a record gain setting will not improve the resolution of the waveform. Good resolution must be inherent in the initial recording of the waveform. However, if you record robust samples initially, intelligent use of normalization can be useful. It is wise to refrain from normalizing a sound file until it is near completion. Do not normalize first because doing sample mixing, sound-on-sound pastes, even effects processing will increase the amplitude of the waveform and clipping will occur. When all editing, mixing, and effects processing are finished, then normalize the whole waveform. Occasionally it is very useful to use normalization to increase the volume of singular sound events in a recording. A specific cymbal crash can be brought up by selecting and normalizing only its wave samples. If a singer or orator changes volume drastically during a recording, you can normalize the waveform phrase by phrase, or verse by verse, and compress the dynamics as much as required.

Compression/Limiting

Some sounds are difficult to record. As the bass drum of a drum kit is thumped by the foot pedal, the event has a very high amplitude attack portion as the beater strikes the drumhead. After this follows the low ring of the drum shell resonance, much lower in volume. This has always been difficult to record. It is easy to overdrive and clip the attack portion while trying to get adequate signal level for recording the resonant portion. Likewise, snapped bass strings have always been difficult to record.

Compression and limiting are two techniques for avoiding overdriving your input sources. Compression ensures that any peaks that would normally clip are reduced to below 0dB. Most effects of this type use a nonvarying gain to prevent any hard clipping from occurring.

Limiting sets an absolute threshold and prevents the signal from exceeding it. Signals that go above the threshold are clamped to the maximum allowable level.

Compression and limiting are often used together to successfully record loud volume sound sources that have frequent transient peaks. Many of the digital recording applications, such as SoundEdit 16 and Sound Forge, have this feature available when you are processing digital waveforms.

Working with Earlier Computers

If your computer is not the latest or fastest, the trick to obtaining successful digital recordings is to avoid overtaxing your equipment. The fewer processes taking place during the recording, the better your odds of success. When recording at high sample rates, turn off any active waveform displays (oscilloscope or bar graph) once your record level has been set. This type of display is very useful during playback for recognizing clicks or pops and should be used for presetting the recording level, but during the actual recording process it's another burdensome and timely task the computer must perform while also sampling your audio input signals at tens of thousands of times per second.

To avoid degraded audio quality, or, even worse, gaps or drop-outs in the recording, avoid all software utilities that require some processor overhead while recording. Try increasing the size of your record buffer in the control setup menu of your digital recording software to improve the recording quality of your system.

Disk compression utilities can be a source of problems, even on some newer machines. The compression and decompression cycles steal a certain number of processor cycles to pack data down to its most compact level or to expand it once again when it is being accessed. If you try to use these utilities on earlier computer equipment used for digital recording, you're basically looking for trouble. Most early equipment will have a hard enough time just keeping up with the stream of audio data without having to expand or compress this data stream at the same time. Also, digitized audio waveforms, by their contiguous nature, do not compress nondestructively like text, photos, or some other forms of data.

Preamplification/Impedance Matching

Microphone signal outputs can be extremely low compared to the signals generated at line level by other types of electronic equipment. To ensure adequate signal levels during recording, it is sometimes necessary to boost the gain on the microphone levels by using a preamplifier of some sort, as shown in Figure 3.7. Some audio mixers, such as the Mackie product line, routinely include gain control on the microphone inputs to give the recordist the ability to raise the signal level as necessary to ensure a sufficient recording level.

Impedance matching is also an issue when connecting different kinds of music recording gear. Impedance is a combination of all of the electronic factors—resistance, capacitance, and inductance. It is resistance whose value changes depending

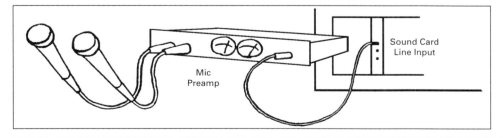

Figure 3.7 Microphone preamplification.

on the frequency applied. Every piece of equipment that you work with has a particular set of characteristics and input and output impedance ratings (generally listed in the specifications). The output impedance of one device should be much lower (one tenth or more) than the input impedance of the device that it is driving so that maximum signal (voltage) transfer occurs. Mismatched impedances can cause loss of signal level. High impedance microphones work properly only in high impedance inputs. Low impedance microphones will usually work in either high or low impedance inputs. Transformers for converting the impedance of a piece of equipment or a microphone can often be obtained to eliminate impedance mismatch problems. The mic input of most consumer-grade sound cards is an input impedance of approximately 10,000 to 15,000 ohms. This is not a high or a low impedance. Low impedance mics will perform better in this medium impedance; high impedance mics may suffer signal loss or frequency response degradation.

Direct Box and Speaker Emulators

It would be nice if you could simply plug your guitar straight into your computer sound board and start recording the rhythm line for a multitrack recording. In reality, if you do this, the resulting recording will usually sound inert and lifeless. If the sound you are looking for is that nice, fat amplified sound that you get when you plug into your guitar amplifier and crank up the volume, maybe with a touch of saturation dialed in, you may want to investigate the use of a direct box or speaker-emulator effects box. These devices use a number of electronic components to simulate the signal processing that takes place in an amplifier and do a fair job of letting you do direct recording and still get that nice, juicy, amplified sound.

This type of component is widely available through companies that offer music gear. One possible source is Musician's Friend, and their contact information is located in Appendix C.

Sound File Processing

Always work on uncompressed sound files. Your sound-related software may have numerous options for compressed storage. Do not save your sound file in a compressed format until it is complete and you are ready to archive. Once compressed it must be decompressed each time before use, and with any compression scheme there is the danger of some loss of quality. The decompression algorithm adds more latency to the start-up of playback, so digital sound samples for sequenced playback are never used in a compressed format.

Waveform Editing

All waveform editors should perform Cut, Copy, and Paste functions like a word processor. Any portion of the displayed waveform can be selected for cropping, duplication, additional processing, or erasure. When examining a new wave editor, first open a sound file and determine the required method for selecting (highlighting) a portion of the recorded waveform. Many programs accept the click-and-drag mouse technique to highlight a portion of the displayed sound wave. The GoldWave waveform editor uses the left mouse button to set selection start and the right mouse button to specify selection end (since these can also be placed "on the fly" as the file is playing). Once a portion of sound wave is selected, play it back to ensure the selection starts and stops at the desired spots, without start hesitation or premature truncation. A copied portion of sound can be saved under a unique filename, precisely pasted over (mixed with) an existing recorded waveform, or inserted (spliced) into the original or another waveform at the specified selection point.

DSP

The DSP (Digital Signal Processing) functions performed by your sound card make up a list equivalent to the capabilities of traditional analog electronic music synthesis hardware: mixing, filtering, frequency and amplitude modulation, envelope shaping, gating, and compression. All the effects created by the use of signal delays—echo, reverb, chorus, flange, and so forth—are done by DSP processing. The difference is that DSP (hardware, software, often both) can perform these functions on your digital waveforms. Many sound cards contain a DSP integrated circuit designed to function with, and speed up, the signal processing routines.

Waveform Editing Tools

There are an incredible number of applications available now that let you perform waveform editing on your computer. These start from inexpensive shareware programs, which can often provide significant value for a beginning sound recordist, to sophisticated tools combining digital audio and MIDI. The following sections describe some of the options available in this area.

GoldWave Digital Audio Editor

GoldWave is an excellent, yet inexpensive, digital audio stereo waveform editor for Windows. It supports many file formats (.wav, .au, .iff, .voc, .snd, .mat, .aiff, and raw data) and can convert files between any of these. It can handle large files (up to 1GB) and has a multiple document interface for editing clips between dozens of files in one session. Editing can be done in RAM (to minimize processing time) or from the hard disk. Visually, it's an attractive package. The device control window includes a real-time oscilloscope that can display signal amplitude waveforms, frequency spectrum, equalizer bands, and spectrograms (frequency versus time). It has an impressive list of digital effects that include dynamic control of pitch, volume, and distortion characteristics, as well as echo, filtering, offset adjustment, panning, pitch transposition, phase inversion, resampling, and more. Intelligent editing automatically converts samples to ensure perfect mix and paste operations.

The first thing to learn when using GoldWave is how to select a portion of a displayed waveform. GoldWave does not use the standard Windows *click and drag* method to paint (highlight) a section of the active window waveform. The start marker of a selection is placed by clicking the left mouse button on the waveform at the appropriate place. The finish marker is placed by clicking the right mouse button on the waveform at the appropriate place. This can be done very accurately with the display zoomed if necessary. By entering the device setup window, you can program the user **Play** button to play the selected or the unselected portion of the waveform. Playing the unselected portion of the waveform allows you to determine if the markers are properly placed before you delete the selected area, a very handy feature during editing sessions. GoldWave also has a trim function that crops (removes) all the waveform except the selected portion, handy for reducing the file to one isolated sound event. The editor permits mix as well as paste operations. Mix allows you to perform a digital sound-on-sound paste operation. Perhaps your recording has a dull spot between the end of the vocal and before the instrument solo starts. You can copy a sound event from another wave file—a cymbal crash or the sound of a cuckoo clock—and mix it with the existing sound by placing the start marker at the correct point rhythmically in the sequence. When you apply the mix function you are prompted to specify the amplitude value for the event being pasted in the mix. You must be careful to avoid clipping when mixing together signals—if their combined amplitude is too great the signal exceeds the maximum voltage extremes of the recorder. However, working in this manner, you can do some exciting sound-on-sound work while remaining in the stereo format.

GoldWave supports direct-to-disk editing, RAM editing, and a time-saving flash feature. During direct-to-disk editing, the sound file is stored in a temporary file on the hard disk where it can be modified. In RAM editing, a copy of the sound is stored in RAM where processing and editing can occur much faster; however, the file must be small enough to fit in the amount of RAM installed on the computer.

The flash feature allows large files to be opened instantly. The entire file is not copied to temporary disk storage, and only one second's worth is loaded into RAM. While this system requires a fast computer, it is quick and a good way to open several large files for playback (no modification).

Another interesting feature of GoldWave is the ability to directly edit samples. Zoom in on the displayed waveform until you can see the actual individual cycles of sound vibration. Place the mouse directly over the trace of the waveform. The cursor arrow will change to a thin horizontal with two small arrows pointing in. Click and hold the left mouse button while moving the mouse up, down, left, or right. The waveshape will deform according to your command. This is useful for smoothing out discontinuities caused by inaccurate cut or paste operations or for freehand waveshaping at the sample level.

In the next section we examine one of the many possible uses of the GoldWave Expression Evaluator.

Waveform Synthesis Using GoldWave The sound vibrations that we think of as musical instrument sounds are complex pendular vibrations that contain an array of whole number multiple vibrations called harmonics. The presence or absence of these harmonics, and the relative amplitude of each harmonic within the sound, make up its overtone structure. It is this array of harmonic partials that gives each tone its uniqueness. By using a process called additive synthesis, you can create instrument sound samples (digital waveform files) that can be triggered by MIDI sequencing.

The growth pattern on many plants that emit shoots from their stem follows a sequence called the Fibonacci sequence. The sequence starts 0, 1, 1, 2, 3, 5, 8, and so on (each new number is equal to the sum of the two previous integers). Let's make an organ voice waveform whose harmonic series follows the Fibonacci sequence. GoldWave has a versatile tool for manipulating and generating digital sound called the Expression Evaluator. By additive synthesis we can use the Expression Evaluator to calculate any complex waveform. Expressions can be entered by clicking on the calculator style buttons, typing from the keyboard, or selecting expressions from the drop-down Group and Expression name list.

To be in tune, let's make the fundamental frequency 220Hz (the A below middle C). If we assume 1 to be our fundamental frequency, let's add harmonics at two, three, five, and eight times as many vibrations per second. As higher harmonics are added they must be decreased in amplitude or they will overpower the fundamental and it will not be heard. However, changing the relative intensities of the harmonics can greatly alter the tone color. The mathematical equation for the sine wave is $y = \sin(\,2\ \text{pi}\ f\ t)$ where f is the frequency, t is the time, and pi = 3.14159.

You can read more about Fibonacci spirals at:

www.zometool.com.80/deepzome/golden.html

As shown in Figure 3.8, we have entered the following expression into the Expression Evaluator:

```
(0.6*sin(2*pi*f*t) + 0.3*sin(2*pi*3*f*t) + 0.2*sin(2*pi*5*f*t) +
0.15*sin(2*pi*8*f*t))
```

Notice that in each sine wave expression after the first, the frequency (f) term is preceded by a multiplier representing the desired harmonic (2, 3, 5, 8). The decimal multiplier before each sine statement sets the relative amplitude of the harmonic. The desired value for the fundamental frequency (f) is entered in the $f=$ variables

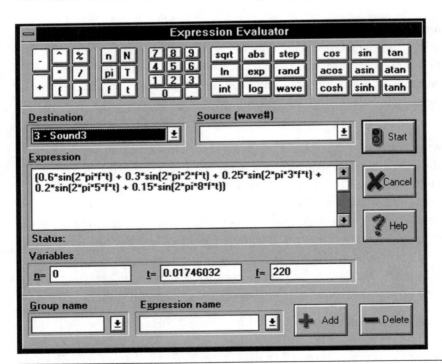

Figure 3.8 GoldWave Expression Evaluator.

window below the main expression window. We have entered 220 to specify our selected fundamental frequency of 220Hz. Calculation of the complex waveform begins when we click the start icon. When the calculation is complete, cancel out of the Expression Evaluator and go to the destination window where the new waveform resides.

The Expression Evaluator can also be used to modulate any recorded sound file.

Making Sound Events and Clips

To gain experience editing sound files, record two or three minutes of sound events onto your hard disk, specify a filename, and save the recording in uncompressed format. Then open a wave editor program and examine the recorded waveform. Wave editors often give you several options for working with your waveform. You may edit in precise slices of time (useful if you are editing strictly rhythmic material), actual samples, or bytes.

Precisely crop the sample you have displayed so it starts without delay and ends without sounding clipped off or lingering in ambient noise. Examine the amplitude of the sample. If it is going to be used alone as a system event alarm you might increase its amplitude to the maximum allowable, just under clipping. If you are going to paste, mix, or attach it to a sequence of other sounds, determine a good signal amplitude to work with that won't push the mix into clipping.

Time/Rate Compression

X Audio tape machines with rotating heads were developed during WWII. These machines enabled recorded speech and music to be played at a faster rate yet retain their natural pitch. Simply speeding up a tape increases the rate and the pitch. A few decades later it was realized that this technology had great benefit for the blind, who often can listen and comprehend audio information at greatly accelerated rates. Students also began using cassette recorders that could enable them to listen to the day's lectures in shorter periods of time. Today the DSP capability of computers has made time/rate compression a popular subject again. Now it has been refined to the point that it can be used for sound processing.

CoolEdit

CoolEdit provides a versatile environment for detailed editing. Many sound file formats can be accessed and converted to other formats by this program. One of its most outstanding features is its time/rate compression capability, called Stretch. A digital recording can be sped up or slowed down without the pitch of the recording being changed. Conversely, the pitch of the recording can be raised or lowered without slowing down or speeding up its rate (tempo). And, the pitch and rate can be increased or decreased simultaneously, like a tape recorder with a speed control. Figure 3.9 shows the CoolEdit Stretch window. Notice that an initial and final value can be specified as a changing variable. The changing function(s) can be stretched or compressed linearly from one ratio to another. This equates to slowing down or speeding up the tempo, or raising or lowering the pitch as time progresses. Setting the initial and final percentage ratios to the same value will cause a constant increase for values greater than 100 percent and a decrease for values less than 100 percent. Notice the radio buttons that permit you to select Preserve Pitch, Preserve Tempo, and Preserve neither.

When rate or time is compressed, the waveform must be smoothly stretched or shortened to retain its intelligence without adding annoying distortion. The interval overlap method outputs tiny chunks of the original wave, overlapping each with the previously transformed chunk. The interval rate determines the size of the chunk. When rates above 50Hz are used they become audible. If the rate is too low, echos will be distinguishable when raising pitch or slowing down tempo. Syllables become choppy when lowering pitch or speeding up the tempo. Values between 20 and 40Hz are usually satisfactory. The overlapping of chunks can sometimes cause a chorusing effect. Lowering the overlapping percentage can reduce this. When adjusting the overlapping you must strike a balance between choppiness and chorusing. When fractional interval overlapping is selected, a reverb/echo effect can sometimes be noticed. If stretching is done at rates lower than 60 percent or higher than 175 percent, desirable results can be obtained. Interval rates of 15 down to 7 seem to work best with fractional interval overlapping.

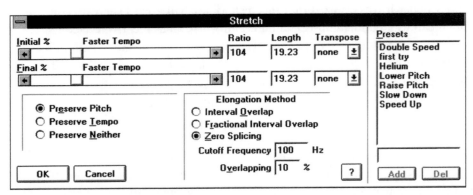

Figure 3.9 CoolEdit Stretch.

The quality of mono pure tone samples that are being stretched can be improved by the use of an interval rate that is evenly divisible into the frequency of the sample. This does not work for non-tonal or noise samples.

Zero splicing works well on samples that are derived from a single source. A single instrument or voice will work fine. The wave is broken into chunks that begin and end when the waveform crosses zero. Chunks are repeated or discarded depending on the compression ratio and the cutoff frequency. Chunks smaller than the cutoff frequency will not be thrown out or repeated. Experiment with cutoff frequencies between 50 and 300Hz when using zero splicing.

Tools

As you gain experience with digital audio editing, some tools will become an indispensable part of your work environment. Some of the best applications make it possible to directly create the types of sound files that you will need for distribution on the Internet. Sound Forge, for example, lets you generate sound files in RealAudio formats. These files can then be distributed directly for RealAudio streaming playback, either through a server or through an individual ISP. Macromedia's SoundEdit 16, a Macintosh-based application, lets you generate Shockwave audio formats, which can then be used either as standalone audio files, for playback on the Web, or embedded in Shockwave productions that include video or animation. More tools are being introduced every day, but both Sound Forge and SoundEdit 16 are excellent choices for the computer-based studio.

Sound Forge

Sound Forge by Sonic Foundry (under the umbrella of Macromedia) is one of the premier sound editing tools on the market. It includes almost every conceivable type of digital processing in the base application and also offers a number of plug-ins that provide specialized processing such as noise reduction, spectrum analysis, and batch conversion of sound files. The online help system includes much more than the usual text description of features, offering animated sequences of how to use different product features with voice-over narration. You can actually learn how to implement many of Sound Forge's most interesting features through the online help.

The main application window of Sound Forge, shown in Figure 3.10, lets you display stereo waveforms at many different zoom settings. Zooming in on very small portions of a signal lets you perform exacting cut and paste operations.

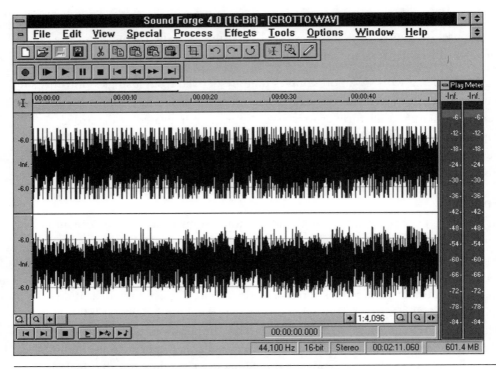

Figure 3.10 Sound Forge main application window.

The program works very well with both very long sound files and very short files. You can preview effects for long sound files without having to perform the complete file processing (which could take many minutes). You can also save settings for many of the common effects, such as equalization, to use for later processing—using any name that will help you remember the setting, as shown in Figure 3.11.

The feature list and capabilities of Sound Forge are extensive. Probably the best way to get familiar with the program's capabilities is to try the demo version included on the CD-ROM bundled with this book.

Noise Reduction Plug-In One of the more powerful plug-ins available for Sound Forge users is the Noise reduction plug-in. This plug-in, which installs under Sound Forge and then becomes accessible through the program menus, includes noise-reduction algorithms that are optimized for various types of signal processing, such as removing the clicks and pops from a vinyl recording that you are converting into digital format.

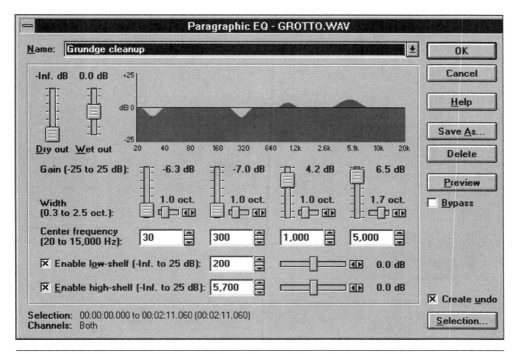

Figure 3.11 Paragraphic equalization options in Sound Forge.

The algorithms available also work for other types of noise, such as tape hiss, electrical hum, machinery rumble, and so on. The noise reduction process identifies a particular set of frequency components, creates a noiseprint, and then selectively separates the unwanted noise from the original signal.

The Noise Reduction window, shown in Figure 3.12, lets you either apply your own custom presets or choose from any of the factory presets provided by Sonic Foundry.

Spectrum Analyzer Spectrum analysis has become a common feature in waveform editors and multitrack digital recording software packages. These exotic, sometimes three-dimensional, graphs show the energy domains of your recording, relative to frequency (and if three-dimensional, time). What is it good for? If used in conjunction with graphic or parametric equalization (also common in many of the waveform editing and recorder packages), you can alter the amplitude of different parts of the recording's sound spectrum. An exaggerated but fun analogy would be the funhouse mirror that enlarges and shrinks different sections of your body. Let's take a look at the common equalization zones of the sound spectrum.

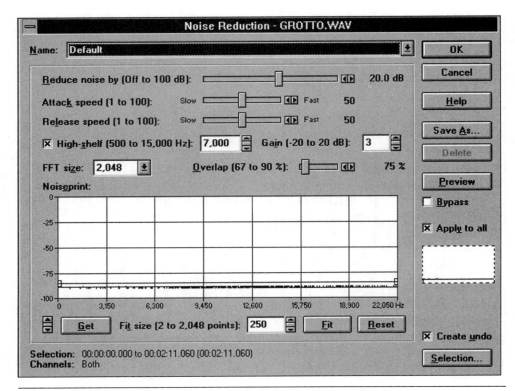

Figure 3.12 Noise Reduction window in Sound Forge.

- **20Hz to 150Hz:** These are the low end of the bass sounds and lower. They are often perceived as being felt more than heard. Too much amplitude boost in this region can result in muddiness. Some instruments exhibit subharmonics below 50Hz that should be cut.

- **150Hz to 300Hz:** Voice can be boosted or cut at approximately 150Hz; however, boosting it at 250Hz may cause booming. Many rhythm section sounds can be made to sound fat or thin by equalization in this region.

- **300Hz to 2000Hz:** Instrument resonances can be equalized by boosting or cutting in the 300 to 500Hz region. Boosting in the 300Hz area can make instruments sound more horn-like. Too much boosting in the 1000 to 2000Hz range can create a tinny quality. Violin and organ sounds often have wonderful midband sounds that can be brought out from the 1200 to 2000Hz region.

- **2000Hz to 5000Hz**: Cutting at around 3000Hz can help to bring buried vocals to the top. Too much overall boosting in this region can cause listener fatigue and lost lyrics. Boosting the 3000 to 5000Hz range slightly can bring clarity to acoustic guitar.

- **5000Hz to 10,000Hz**: Boosts in this region can enhance the feeling of presence and give the illusion that the overall volume has been increased greatly. Cuts in this region can result in a distant or faraway feel. The shimmer of cymbals is enhanced by boosts in the 8000 to 10,000Hz range.

- **10,000Hz to 15,000Hz**: Sibilance and brightness are controlled by equalization in this region.

The spectrum analysis shown in Figure 3.13 is from Sound Forge.

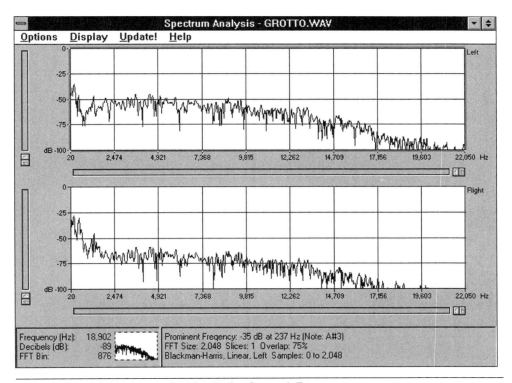

Figure 3.13 Spectrum Analysis in Sound Forge.

Demonstration versions of Sound Forge and several of its plug-in are included on the CD-ROM bundled with this book.

SoundEdit 16 Version 2

SoundEdit 16, produced by Macromedia, has been a favorite of Macintosh users since its introduction several years ago. The latest iteration, Version 2, includes features that should appeal to anyone interested in creating sound files for Internet use.

The new Automator feature lets you perform group conversions of sound files, choosing formats, sample rates, bit depths, and so on. For example, you could start with a group of Macintosh AU files and convert them all to Windows WAV files in 16-bit, 11KHz format using one command.

Capture of digital audio extracted directly from a CD can also be useful to audio engineers, and this form of audio extraction is now available in SoundEdit 16. A variety of new compression standards have been added, such as ADPCM and mu-Law, and SoundEdit can be extended with an Xtra (similar to a plug-in) to create Shockwave audio files. The main application window is shown in Figure 3.14.

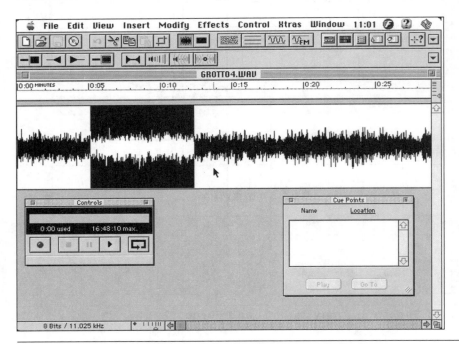

Figure 3.14 SoundEdit 16 main application window.

Generally, SoundEdit 16 is a true workhorse application for all types of audio editing work and worth consideration if most of your audio processing will be on the Macintosh.

MIDI and Multitrack Tools

One of the more recent trends in digital audio editing is to combine MIDI tracks with synchronized digital audio output. This can be an extremely useful way to create complex music. The MIDI tracks can be used to lay down rhythm tracks, drum patterns, piano arpeggios, and so on, while the digital audio tracks can be reserved for vocals, wind instruments, guitar solos, and those components that are more difficult (or impossible) to recreate in MIDI form. An example of one of the leading applications in this area, Voyetra Digital Orchestrator Plus, follows.

Voyetra Digital Orchestrator Plus

Voyetra Digital Orchestrator Plus (DOP) has the ability to merge MIDI and WAV files, creating complex mixes that combine these two sound file formats. The net result is a desktop computer multitrack studio that lets you accomplish effects that would normally require the services of a professional recording studio.

Voyetra's MIDI sequencing capabilities are impressive by themselves, providing features such as a collection of MIDI transforms including Humanize, Quantize, Swing, Scaling, Tap Tempo, Fit Time, Acclerando, and so on. These transforms can do much to reduce the mechanical quality that plagues much MIDI music by introducing those elements that we're accustomed to in live music. For example, soloing just a fraction ahead of the beat or introducing slight timing differences in a drum pattern can make MIDI music sound much more realistic.

The number of digital audio tracks available varies with the processing power of your computer, though even users with 486/66 machines should be able to get two tracks of audio. More powerful Pentium equipment should be capable of handling as many as eight digital audio tracks.

DOP provides the ability to synchronize to external devices using MIDI Time Codes, SMPTE coding, or Song Position Pointers. This enables you to synchronize your music with other tape decks or video equipment, also a useful feature in the studio environment.

Digital Orchestrator Plus - FLUFF11.ORC - [Track/View]

__File__ __Edit__ __Transforms__ __Options__ __Window__ __Help__

	R	Type	Name	Port	Pch	Chn	Vol	Trans	S	M	Pan	Reve			
1			"Fluff 'n' Stuff"	1	--	--		0:0			<0>	--	1		
2			Composed by John Pavlik	1	--	--		0:0			<0>	--	2		
3			Copyright ©1995	1	--	--		0:0			<0>	--	3		
4			Voyetra Technologies	1	--	--		0:0			<0>	--	4		
5			All Rights Reserved	1	--	--		0:0			<0>	--	5		
6				1	--	--		0:0			<0>	--	6		
7			Final Mix Down	1	--	--		0:0			<0>	--	7		
8				1	--	--		0:0			<0>	--	8		
9			final mix left	1					S	M	<64		9		
10			final mix right	1					S	M	63>		10		
11				1	--	--		0:0			<0>	--	11		
12			original midi tracks	1	--	--		0:0			<0>	--	12		
13				1	--	--		0:0			<0>	--	13		
14		◎	Tambourine	1	16	10		0:0		M	<0>	128	14		
15		◎	drums	1	16	10		0:0		M	<0>	128	15		
16		◎	bass guitar	1	37	3		0:0		M	<9	23	16		
17		◎	brass falls	1	62	2		0:0		M	63>	72	17		
18		◎	brass hits	1	62	1		0:0		M	<41	36	18		
19		◎	brass hits	1	57	4		0:0		M	7>	72	19		
20		◎	brass hits	1	67	5		1:0 v		M	<17	72	20		
21			lead guitar	1						M	<5		21		
22			ardut2	1						M	<64		22		

Stopped   C: 623168 K   90.00   +/- 0.00

Figure 3.15 Merged MIDI and WAV files in DOP.

The program also has the ability to cut and paste between a number of different open windows. For example, you can grab a segment of MIDI data from one window and drop it into another Orchestrator song that you are composing. The main DOP application window, showing merged MIDI and WAV files, is shown in Figure 3.15.

 A demonstration version of Digital Orchestrator Plus appears on the CD-ROM bundled with this book.

More information on Voyetra products is located in Appendix C.

MIDI-to-Wave Rendering

WAVmaker is an inexpensive, shareware MIDI-to-WAV rendering and audio FX package. It runs under Windows95, Windows NT, and Windows 3.1 on PCs equipped with a 386 CPU or better. You can create CD-quality .wav files with virtually unlimited polyphony from your MIDI sound files. It has a large selection of

Digital Signal Processor functions, allowing you to create new timbres for your personalized instrument patch sample library.

WAVmaker lets you MIDI sequence the .wav file samples in its wav directory. Figure 3.16 shows WAVmaker's main window. A full-featured wav recording and editing window is provided for making samples, or you can import the samples from the large libraries of samples that are available. The wave editing includes DSP capabilities that provide lots of options for enhancement and gives you the ability to set loop points to specify the sustained portion of the sample. The PRG (program) directory holds .prg files that correspond to the MIDI instrument sounds. In these files the .wav samples are mapped to MIDI keyboard notes. Samples of two adjacent base notes for each octave are often sufficient; the other notes are obtained by resampling. You can choose to work MOD style, sample just one note, and derive all others from it. This is done by assigning a large key range to the sample. Percussion sounds for MIDI channel 10 must each be set as a unique .wav sample. The PRG editor is a full-featured window that lets you specify envelope and expression characteristics as well as the .wav samples. Playlists are created for each MIDI file to be rendered. The playlists, stored as .lst files in the LST directory, contain musical event information extracted from the MIDI file

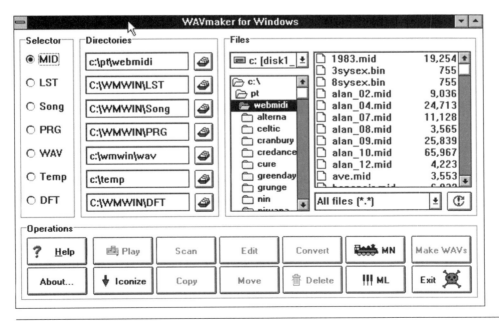

Figure 3.16 WAVmaker MIDI-to-WAV rendering.

and performance parameters. The LST files can be viewed and edited by any text editor program. Both MIDI and .wav files can be scanned for a report of vital content information. MIDI files can first be converted to playlist (.lst) to determine what program (.prg) files are called. The .wav samples referenced in the PRG file must be present in the current .wav directory.

 Mellosoftron (a live virtual sampler) and MIDInight Express (a real-time MIDI renderer) are standalone programs that can be launched from within WAVmaker. The WAVmaker home page is at:

http://www.abc.se/~m9303/index.html

and from there you will find links to the Mellosoftron and MIDInight Express homepages.

Downsampling and File Conversion

Always record and edit at the highest resolution your equipment is capable of performing. When you find you must down convert to a lower resolution or sample rate, or from stereo to mono to meet the requirements imposed by the bandwidth of your typical Internet audience, determine the best conversion path for the specific recording. If the recording does not exploit stereo panning, perhaps you can tolerate converting the file to mono, reducing its size in half. Try converting from 16-bit resolution to 8-bit resolution; this will reduce the file size by one half. Keep looking at the file size and make judgments as to what you will audibly tolerate to reduce the file size as much as possible. Try another conversion that reduces the sample rate by one half. Keep the original file (the one having the highest resolution and sampling rate) unaltered and make all your conversions from it, or from a copy of it. Try converting from 16-bit to 8-bit and from 44.1KHz to 22KHz. Never do sequential down conversions or downsampling operations on the same file, as errors will be compounded. Always start fresh from the highest-quality version of the recording.

Down convert the file's sampling frequency to 11KHz and compare its playback to the original. Determine how severely the high frequencies have been cut. Try down conversions to 8Khz, and notice how the high-frequency edge of the recording is even more severely attenuated, resulting in a muted and somewhat canned sound. Also notice the size reduction of the down converted file. You must decide how much sampling frequency down conversion you can tolerate depending of the content of the recorded material. Some recordings can be made quite small without terrible loss; others will lose their percussion sounds or will start to break up in unpleasant distortion when too much sampling frequency down conversion is employed.

It is sometimes unnerving to engineer sound for a limited bandwidth. Those with a background in high-quality audio often find it a most disturbing chore to down convert or downsample digital audio. You must keep reminding yourself that you cannot expect visitors to your Web site to wait 10 or 20 minutes or more for one of your recordings to start playing. If you are working with 16-bit sound, doing hard disk recording with your computer, it is probably wise to use the 44.1KHz sampling rate since the common lower sample rates (22Khz and 11KHz) are simply half and one-fourth the rate. Note that 22KHz is an abbreviation; it is really 22.05KHz, and 11KHz is really 11.025KHz. Recording done at 48KHz or 32KHz requires additional interpolation to be downsampled to 22KHz or 11KHz.

File Conversion Tools

Utility programs are available that can convert digital sound files from one file type to a different file type. Perhaps you have two sound file processing programs but each is designed for a proprietary file type. You can convert your file, work in the other sound editing program, and have the best of both worlds. Most of these programs determine the file format type from the filename extension. However, you must be familiar with the basic characteristics of the file formats you are working with to determine if any sound quality reduction will occur during the conversion. One simple way to determine if sound quality is reduced (before listening) is to examine the size of the file and its converted version. If the original format was a 16-bit stereo format at 22KHz sampling rate and the converted format is by nature 8-bit, 11KHz, the converted file size may be only one-fourth as many bytes. Some sound quality has been lost in the conversion.

AWAVE

If you have a PC running Windows95, AWAVE is an up-to-date sound file converter. It won't run on Windows 3.1 machines even with the win32 extension code installed. If you're running an older machine and your waveform editor will not let you save your sound file in a particular format, I recommend SoX.

SoX

SoX (short for SOund eXchange) is a freeware, universal sound file translator that accepts many different sound file formats. The list includes .au, .hcom, .raw, .st, .voc, .auto, .cdr, .dat, .wav, .aif, .snd, and many more. Versions of SoX are available for Unix and DOS (PC). It determines the file format from the file extension, but it also has an auto detect feature that attempts to classify unmarked samples. SoX can also do sample rate conversion and some sound effects processing.

 You can download a free version of SoX from the Internet as well as tutorials and cookbooks for basic SoX invocations. Try downloading SoX from:

www.spies.com/Sox/

or let your favorite search engine ferret out a download site. The URL given here links to pages of examples and tips for using SoX.

You will have to study the command-line protocol to learn how to use this tool. Here's a file format conversion example for the DOS version of SoX.

You want to convert a .au file to .wav format. Make your machine go to the DOS prompt, change to the directory containing the SoX program, and type:

```
sox    filename.au    filename.wav
```

This creates a .wav version of the source .au file. If desired, a new filename can be specified for the destination filename with the .wav extension.

File Formats for the Web

Internet communications have made it possible for many types of computer platforms to intercommunicate. Each computer operating system has its own sound file formats; some formats are proprietary to music software running on that particular computer. The Net has started a trend toward fewer, more standardized, audio file formats. However, there are quite a number of viable audio file formats in use today, and, in reality, more will appear in the future. It's not really a problem! Don't be frustrated into a state of indecision attempting to find the ultimate sound file format. Determine the file format most common to the type of computer and operating system software you are running. As long as you're running software that is compatible with your system you should have no problems. Use your machine to its best advantage.

Summary

As a musician or composer working in a modern desktop computer recording studio you have access to an astonishing variety of tools and processes that can transform sound in many different ways. You can spend hours reading all the manuals and learning the theoretical aspects of sound recording, but, while this is useful information in its own way, you won't really learn recording techniques until you jump in and start trying things. The right sound is what you are after, and, as much as anything else, you need to train your ears to learn what effect signal processing can have on a particular sound. Sometimes, the best processing is no processing at all. Other times, you can recover what appears to be a hopeless piece of audio recording by using the right tools. Spend as much time recording, editing, and becoming familiar with sound as you can. The ultimate test is compressing sound for use on the Web without losing its essence or character. The digital tools are there; enjoy learning how to use them.

Part Two

Presenting Audio on the Internet

Basic HTML
Audio Techniques

This chapter covers the most fundamental means for integrating sound files into HTML documents, including the built-in support provided by both Netscape Navigator and Microsoft Internet Explorer. The techniques presented can be used even by someone with little experience in HTML coding.

Microsoft and Netscape, as well as other browser manufacturers, had the foresight to include support for a number of native sound formats within their browser architecture. Even relatively early browsers had the ability to play back basic sound files, including WAV, AU, and AIFF formats, and many browsers also included the ability to handle MIDI sound file playback. This feature can be used in a variety of ways. You can place a sound file within an HTML document and either play it back automatically as the page loads or place controls on the page to put playback under user control. You can place the sound files under the control of JavaScript or VBScript and have playback conditional on some event taking place.

For example, you can use the onMouseOver event handler in JavaScript to play a sound file each time the mouse pointer is positioned over a particular graphic on screen. You may just want to use a sound file to play background music as someone is viewing a Web page; however, keep in mind that many websters prefer to have some control over whether music and images download automatically, to avoid long download cycles while they are touring pages. There are a number of simple techniques you can use to include the audio content as an optional downloadable item, subject to the viewer's preferences. Some of these techniques appear in this chapter and the next.

The level of sophistication for handling sound files has advanced dramatically in more recent browser releases. Microsoft has added support for streaming digital media with their ActiveMovie technology and ActiveX multimedia plug-ins. Netscape has also designed their Media Player to handle streaming formats, much in the same manner as Liquid Audio and RealAudio. Streaming digital media is covered in more detail in Chapter 7. This chapter deals with the fundamentals—the easiest means for incorporating sound into your HTML documents. If you're unfamiliar with HTML, Appendix A provides a quick introduction to the most recent officially sanctioned standard, HTML 3.2, and suggests some additional references for obtaining more experience working with this markup language.

Native File Support

Some audio support requires the use of browser plug-ins or helper applications. No matter how motivated your audience is to experience your spine-tingling audio content, there is always resistance against downloading and installing another plug-in or helper. You will lose some percentage of your audience each time you rely on one of these plug-ins rather than native file support.

You can, however, accomplish quite a bit in the audio domain without venturing outside the built-in support offered by Microsoft and Netscape in their browsers. The trinity of audio file formats supported by both browsers includes AU, WAV, and AIFF. These formats can be created in a number of common digital sound processing applications, at varying resolutions and sample rates. Both browser platforms also support MIDI file formats with built-in MIDI players. The way to ensure the widest possible audience for your audio content is to take advantage of native file support.

The easiest way to include sound in an HTML document is simply to embed a supported sound file format onto the page using the <EMBED> tag. This tag is supported by both Netscape Navigator and Microsoft Internet Explorer with minor variations for each platform. <EMBED> entries can include a number of additional attributes that provide precise control over the sound playback, including the start and end times of the sound, the type of console and controls that will appear, the alignment of the console, whether the sound starts immediately, and the name of the sound being included with the tag. Volume controls are even provided for those sound boards that support dynamic control of the volume. Tampering with the volume, however, runs the risk of either generating an error message during playback (when the sound board doesn't support this feature), or blasting the ears of those visiting your site if they already have their speaker volume turned up fairly loud.

Netscape calls their sound environment LiveAudio and has engineered JavaScript support for LiveAudio components. LiveAudio playback of embedded sound file formats can either include a small console that provides control over the audio material (featuring controls similar to a cassette player—these consoles are sometimes called transports). Optionally, the console can be hidden; instructions for the playback of audio are contained within the brackets of the <EMBED> command. For example, an audio selection can be looped (restarted each time it reaches the end) with the addition of a LOOP=TRUE entry within the <EMBED> command.

Bare-Bones Sound

The easiest way to get a sound onto a Web page is by using the most minimal form of the <EMBED> statement. The only required attribute is the source file for the sound, but additional attributes can help control playback, as shown in the following example:

```
<EMBED SRC="birdsong.wav" HIDDEN=TRUE AUTOSTART=TRUE>
```

The browser loads the sound and built-in plug-in when it loads the HTML document. No audio console appears on the page and the sound plays once as it is loaded. Obviously, the larger the WAV file that you embed, the longer it will take the page to download. If you're not going to give visitors the opportunity to choose whether or not to download the sound, keep the file sizes small (less than 60K).

If you don't use the HIDDEN or AUTOSTART attributes, a partial console appears on the page (since no console dimensions have been specified) and the sound does not play at once. Since the user can't get to the necessary transport controls to play the sound, there is no way to hear it. Consider the <EMBED> entry in the context of the following simple HTML document.

```
<HTML>

<HEAD><TITLE>Infinite Sound Resources</TITLE>
```

```
</HEAD>

<BODY BGCOLOR="#FFFF00" TEXT="#0000FF">

<CENTER><H1>Sounds of the Industrial Fringe</H1></CENTER><P.

<HR>

<P>Consider the following sounds:<P>

<EMBED SRC="birdsong.wav">

<HR>

<ADDRESS>

Elishu Purcell<BR>

<AHREF="mailto:elishu_purcell@infinite_sound.net">

elishu_purcell@infinite_sound.net</A><BR>

</ADDRESS><P>

</BODY>

</HTML>
```

The resulting Web page, when displayed, would appear as shown in Figure 4.1.

Clearly, a page with a partial console isn't going to be very helpful to anyone. To avoid this, the <EMBED> tag includes attributes that specify the minimal dimensions of the audio console. The default console, displayed if you don't use the SMALLCONSOLE attribute, requires the attributes WIDTH=144 and HEIGHT=60. The entire <EMBED> entry would read as follows:

```
<EMBED SRC="birdsong.wav" WIDTH=144 HEIGHT=60>
```

With this statement entered into the previously displayed HTML code, the page would include the full console, complete with volume lever, as shown in Figure 4.2.

Viewing the available controls from left to right, the console allows someone to stop the sound file playback, start playback, or pause playback. Unless the sound is more than several seconds long, the stop and pause controls don't serve much purpose. The sliding volume level controls the relative volume of the sound playback

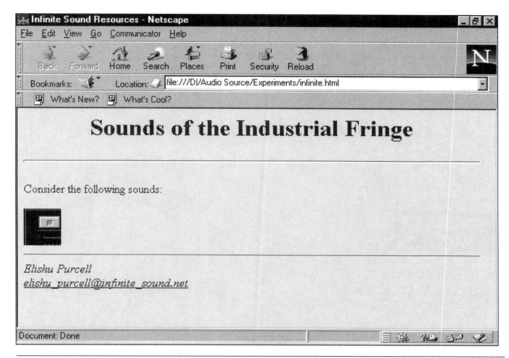

Figure 4.1 Partial audio console embedded in page.

on those systems that support this option. Not all do. The green indicator bar below the volume lever displays the approximate dynamic range of the sound to be played back, given the current volume setting.

You can also use a streamlined audio console, which is specified by using the CONTROLS=SMALLCONSOLE attribute within the <EMBED> entry. This console occupies a different space on the page, so you also need to modify the height setting to read: HEIGHT=15. The small audio console lacks a volume control lever or pause control. In most cases, where you are providing an audio console linked to a particular sound, you will want to label the console as well. The following two lines would embed a small console linked to the file "spacey1.wav" and label the console in italic type.

```
<I>First space contact</I><P>
```

```
<EMBED SRC="spacey1.wav" WIDTH=144 HEIGHT=15>
```

The resulting display, if inserted as part of the previous HTML example, would appear as shown in Figure 4.3.

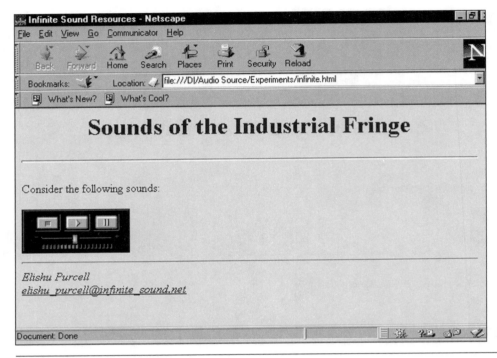

Figure 4.2 Full-sized audio console.

The console method of presenting audio can be used flexibly for a number of different applications. As discussed in a later section on the EMBED attributes, you can insert individual controls onto a page, such as a play button or volume lever, without the rest of the console. A single control can be used to link to one sound file or several different sound files, as determined by how the sound files are referenced through HTML and JavaScript or VBScript. Or, several different controls can be used to influence the playback of a single audio file.

As an example of the practical applications, you might use the <EMBED> technique for dropping the following kinds of sound onto a page:

- **A Short, Lower-quality Version of an Audio File:** This will serve as a preview to someone prior to downloading a larger, higher-quality version. For example, this might be a sample of an original song being showcased to spark interest in an audio CD being released by an unsigned band.

- **A Section of a Speech:** With voice-grade resolution, an audio clip of a prominent individual could be 30 seconds long without creating an impossibly long

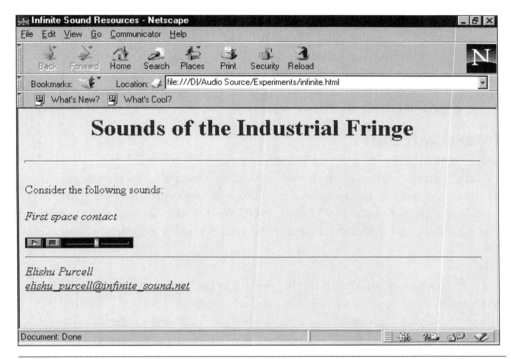

Figure 4.3 Streamlined audio console (SMALLCONSOLE).

download time. Thirty seconds may not seem like enough time to cover much ground, but in our news-byte oriented society, 30 seconds can stretch on forever. Try reading a page from a book or magazine to see how far through it you can get in 30 seconds; the results might surprise you.

- **A Sound Effect**: A good sound effect can enhance onscreen presentation immeasurably. For example, if your page is displaying images of the birds of New Mexico, you could include selective audio clips of the songs of scrub jays, orioles, and finches. If your site is showing an image of the Tequila Junction Café and discussing open mic night, you could have a 20-second clip of an amateur performance concluding in wild applause and cheers to capture the ambiance of the occasion. A site offering custom-made replicas of medieval musical instruments could have 12-second clips below the image of each instrument to demonstrate its sound.

- **A Short Introductory Greeting**: The greeting that will play when someone visits your Web page might be voice-quality ("Welcome to the site of the Frazier

Monastery!") or a short music sample (the opening strains of Beethoven's Fifth Symphony). Using the HIDDEN=TRUE and AUTOSTART=TRUE attributes with <EMBED> ensures that the clip will play immediately on page loading and display no console. You might want to offer this page as a path to visitors only after they have selected a "sound-enhanced" option offered on a prior Web page (providing a non-audio branch for those who choose it).

EMBED Attributes

Since the <EMBED> tag plays an important role in the presentation of files that are supported native formats through most browsers, let's take a closer look at the attributes and options that you have available when using this tag. Some of these attributes, such as NAME and MASTERSOUND, become essential if you are going to use JavaScript or VBScript to control the behavior of an embedded sound clip.

SRC

The source attribute, shortened to SRC, identifies the location of the sound file to be accessed, which can either be a relative (local) path or a full URL. If the file named "bark.wav" is located in a directory on the local server called "dog_sounds," the SRC could be specified as:

```
SRC="/dog_sounds/bark.wav"
```

If the sound file is stored on another Web site, you can provide the full path to access it, such as:

```
SRC="http://www.dogs_r_us.org/dog_sounds/bark.wav"
```

The most direct way to access it, of course, is if the sound file is located in the same directory as the HTML document, so the SRC attribute needs no additional path information, such as:

```
SRC="bark.wav"
```

In the audio realm, the digital sound files should be stored in one of the appropriate formats with the appropriate header (supplied when the file is saved by a sound application or converted from another format). The valid digital audio file formats are as follows:

- **AU:** Extension is .au. Supports monaural and stereo files with a resolution of 8 to 16 bits, sampled at 8KHz to 48KHz. Originated on the Unix platform, but also supported by numerous PC and Mac applications.

- **AIFF**: Extension is .aif (Audio Interchange File Format). Supports uncompressed audio in mono, stereo, or multichannel formats. A wide variety of sampling rates and resolutions is included in this format, up to CD quality (16-bit resolution and 44KHz sample rates). Originated on the Macintosh platform but widely supported under Unix and PC.

- **WAV**: Extension is .wav (Waveform Audio). Supports audio in mono, stereo, or multichannel formats with sampling rates up to 44KHz with 16-bit samples. The WAV format originated on the Windows platform with the release of Windows 3.1; WAV is now one of the most popular sound file formats on the Internet. WAV is similar in structure to .aif, but with different header information.

- **MID**: Extension is .mid (Musical Instrument Data Interchange). Supports Standard MIDI File (SMF) data on systems equipped for MIDI playback (with some form of sound synthesis).

No special setup is required to inform the browser that a file is being stored in a particular format at a particular sampling rate and resolution. The file extension and the header information that is automatically appended to the file when it is stored contain all the information that the browser needs to initiate playback.

AUTOSTART

By default, an embedded sound file does not begin to play until someone clicks the **Play** button on the audio console that represents the file. You can, however, use the AUTOSTART attribute to initiate playback as soon as the file is loaded. The AUTOSTART attribute accepts two values: TRUE or FALSE.

For example, if you wanted to play the AU file "shriek.au" immediately on loading, you could use the following statement:

```
<EMBED SRC="shriek.au" HIDDEN=TRUE AUTOSTART=TRUE>
```

In this example, the file would play without displaying the audio console.

The AUTOSTART attribute could be assigned to a variable under JavaScript or VBScript, and then set according to user preferences or some other condition. The appropriate <EMBED> entry could then be written into the body of the HTML document using the writeln method in JavaScript. Using a technique such as this, you could determine whether it was appropriate to begin playing a sound file following page loading and proceed to dynamically construct the page in JavaScript.

If you want to drive your listeners mad, hide the audio console, set the AUTOSTART attribute TRUE, and set the LOOP attribute TRUE. Set the SRC to a short, annoying sound file and each time someone enters the page, the sound will play incessantly without the ability to turn the audio off through the console. For those brazen enough to offend their site visitors with this approach, for an annoying file named "frenzy.wav" the <EMBED> entry should read:

```
<EMBED SRC="frenzy.wav" HIDDEN=TRUE AUTOSTART=TRUE LOOP=TRUE>
```

This is an excellent way to ensure that no one will ever visit your site twice.

LOOP

The LOOP attribute determines whether the sound file should continue playing again once it reaches the end. You can also specify how many cycles a particular file should play. To indicate that the sound should continue playing indefinitely, use the LOOP=TRUE attribute, as shown in the example for the file "jango.aif":

```
<EMBED SRC="jango.aif" HEIGHT=60 WIDTH=144 LOOP=TRUE>
```

Since this statement doesn't include the AUTOSTART attribute set to TRUE, it would loop the selection "jango.aif" only after the site visitor clicked the **Play** button on the full-sized console. Once started, the file would continue to play until stopped on the console or until the page was exited.

You can also use the LOOP attribute to specify the number of times the file should play. The value entered for the attribute should be an integer (whole number). To play the file "croak.wav" seven times on the small console, you could use the following entry:

```
<EMBED SRC="croak.wav" CONSOLE=SMALLCONSOLE HEIGHT=15 WIDTH=144 AUTOSTART=TRUE
LOOP=7>
```

If the site visitor grows tired of listening to the audio, he or she can use the console to turn it off.

Setting LOOP=FALSE ensures that the selection will play only once. Realistically, you don't need to specify this, since the default setting is FALSE, but in some circumstances where you might be setting this option through JavaScript or VBScript, you might want to use a variable to represent the attribute setting.

STARTTIME

The STARTTIME attribute identifies the position within the sound file, specified in minutes and seconds, to initiate playback. For example, if you wanted to start 15 seconds into the sound file, you would use the entry STARTTIME = 00:15. If you wanted to start the sound file "longwail.aif" playing at 15 seconds into the file, you could use the entry:

```
<EMBED SRC="longwail.aif" HEIGHT=60 WIDTH=144 STARTTIME=00:15>
```

At the point where the site visitor clicked the **Play** button on the console to start playback, the sound would begin playing 15 seconds into the file.

ENDTIME

Using the same basic construction as the STARTTIME attribute, the ENDTIME attribute identifies the position within the sound file, specified in minutes and seconds, to discontinue playback. For example, if you wanted to stop 55 seconds into the sound file, you would use the entry ENDTIME = 00:55. If you wanted to stop the sound file "longwail.aif" from playing at 1 minute 10 seconds into the file, you could use the entry:

```
<EMBED SRC="longwail.aif" HEIGHT=60 WIDTH=144 ENDTIME=01:10>
```

At the point where the site visitor clicked the **Play** button on the console to start playback, the sound would stop playing 1 minute and 10 seconds into the file.

VOLUME

For those systems that support it, the VOLUME attribute specifies the volume level as a percentage of maximum volume, ranging from 0 to 100. This entry can be overridden by the MASTERVOLUME attribute (which assigns a set volume to a collection of control elements or places them under a single central control). The MASTERVOLUME setting always takes precedence over individual volume settings.

To set the volume to 50 percent of the maximum level for sound file playback, use an entry as follows:

```
<EMBED SRC="cymbals.wav" HEIGHT=60 WIDTH=144 VOLUME=50>
```

Use this control with discretion. Setting the volume to 100 on a system where the speaker volume is cranked up loudly could cause painful oscillations of the listener's eardrums.

WIDTH

The WIDTH attribute reserves a space on the page for an audio console, or some part of the console, such as a volume slider. The value represents the number of pixels in the width. The width should correspond to the appropriate width for the console chosen. For example, if you use the default console, the minimum width is 144. If you specify a width *less* than this, part of the console image will be cut off as it is displayed on the Web page. If you specify a width *greater* than this, extra white space will appear as padding around the console. The console generally looks best on the page when you match the width exactly. For reserving a space for a console, both a WIDTH and a HEIGHT setting should appear in the <EMBED> statement.

To reserve a space for the SMALLCONSOLE, you could use an entry as follows:

```
<EMBED SRC="regalia.au" CONTROLS=SMALLCONSOLE HEIGHT=15 WIDTH=144>
```

The small console would fit neatly within the perimeters defined by the WIDTH and HEIGHT settings.

TIP The WIDTH setting issue gets tricky if you are working with third-party plug-ins, such as the many MIDI plug-ins. In some cases, you may not be able to determine which MIDI plug-in is being used on a particular browser, and this creates difficulties in determining a width to use. You could, however, use JavaScript to identify the plug-in enabled for MIDI and then set the console width accordingly.

HEIGHT

The HEIGHT setting is also expressed in pixels. It determines the vertical space on the page to be reserved for the audio console. For example, the setting HEIGHT=60 reserves the precise space required for the default audio console on the page. There should always be a WIDTH setting to accompany the HEIGHT setting. The following example reserves space for the default console to present the sound file titled "loudsong.wav"

```
<EMBED SRC="loudsong.wav" HEIGHT=60 WIDTH=144 AUTOSTART=TRUE>
```

In this example, the default console is displayed within the perimeter indicated, and the sound file begins playing immediately.

ALIGN

The ALIGN attribute positions text in relation to the displayed audio console. This primarily controls text flow in much the same way that the ALIGN attributes are used with the HTML <IMG> tag. The available attributes for ALIGN are:

- TOP

- BOTTOM

- CENTER

- BASELINE

- LEFT

- RIGHT

- TEXTTOP

- MIDDLE

- ABSMIDDLE

- ABSBOTTOM

The ALIGN statement controls the flow of those elements that are on the same line (not separated by paragraph tags). For example, consider the following lines of HTML code that include an audio console:

```
<I>First space contact</I>

<EMBED SRC="spacey1.wav" ALIGN=BASELINE HEIGHT=60 WIDTH=144>

<I>The unedited voice of a captured alien...</I>
```

If these entries were included in the same HTML example as was used to generate Figure 4.2, the resulting text flow would appear as shown in Figure 4.4.

Notice how the text conforms with the BASELINE of the audio console. The other ALIGN statements work in similar fashion, each expressing the characteristic of the text flow in relation to the embedded audio console. Since the ALIGN attribute can produce clumsy word wrapping if not used carefully, spend some time experimenting with these different settings and checking the browser window at different sizes to ensure that you achieve the flow that you are looking for.

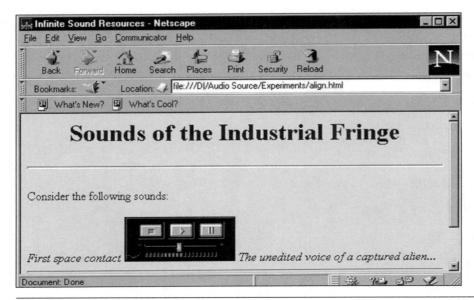

Figure 4.4 ALIGN attribute set to BASELINE.

CONTROLS

The CONTROLS attribute indicates which of the available control objects will be embedded onto the page. The <EMBED> tag allows you to specify individual elements from the console transport controls; for example, you could drop a Play button onto the page to initiate playback of a file. The Stop button could be positioned as a separate element another paragraph away.

The available controls are:

- CONSOLE

- SMALLCONSOLE

- PLAYBUTTON

- PAUSEBUTTON

- STOPBUTTON

- VOLUMELEVER

Buttons occupy less space than consoles, so you should adjust the WIDTH and HEIGHT requirements accordingly. The minimal HEIGHT for a button (including the PLAYBUTTON, PAUSEBUTTON, and STOPBUTTON) should be 22. The WIDTH should be 37.

To embed a single button using the <EMBED> tag, the entry should be similar to the following:

```
<EMBED SRC="spacey1.wav" CONTROLS=PLAYBUTTON ALIGN=BASELINE HEIGHT=22 WIDTH=37>
```

Applied to our running example, this line of HTML code results in the display shown in Figure 4.5.

Of course, you can use the ALIGN attribute to choose another means of controlling the text flow around the button. If you are going to use more than one control to handle a single sound file, you need to identify the master sound file using the MASTERSOUND attribute, explained in a later section. You also need to use the NAME attribute to group the individual control elements that will be interacting with the designated MASTERSOUND. This is also explained in a later section.

HIDDEN

The HIDDEN attribute supports only one value: TRUE. You do not need to specify the HIDDEN attribute unless you are using it to indicate that the specified sound

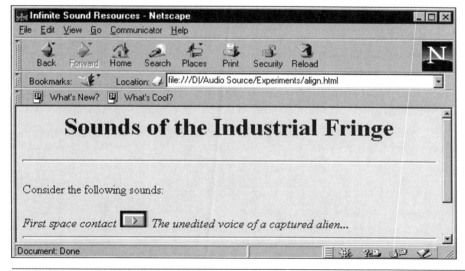

Figure 4.5 Embedding a single play button.

should be played without a console. For example, the following entry causes the file "sunrise.aif" to be played when the page is loaded.

```
<EMBED SRC="sunrise.aif" HIDDEN=TRUE AUTOSTART=TRUE>
```

Because there is no other way to initiate the playback, you should always include the AUTOSTART=TRUE attribute to play back the sound file following page loading. Ideally, this tag should be used only in instances where the viewer has stated a preference for hearing audio on the page or when the sound file specified by the SRC attribute is short enough not to cause undue slowdowns when loading the page. If you include a 500Kb CD-quality audio introduction that loads and plays without user knowledge or permission, your site visitors will be fleeing like lemmings in a monsoon before playback ever begins.

T I P Microsoft Internet Explorer recognizes another attribute, BGSOUND, that identifies a sound file as an element to be played in the background without a displayed console. The BGSOUND attribute, however, is not recognized by Netscape Navigator

---

MASTERSOUND

MASTERSOUND serves as an identifier for a sound file to be actually played when several control elements all reference the same file. Grouping is accomplished using the NAME attribute. In other words, when you separate an audio console into individual components (a play button, stop button, and so on), these components can be combined under a common name. The MASTERSOUND file is the sound to be controlled; the other components are associated with stub files, which are short dummy files intended to initiate the LiveAudio interaction.

If this sounds complicated, it is actually easier to implement than it sounds. The entry to designate a particular file, "eons.wav," as the MASTERSOUND for playback (through a single play button) would be as follows:

```
<EMBED SRC="eons.wav" HEIGHT=22 WIDTH=37 CONTROLS=PLAYBUTTON NAME="ergo"
MASTERSOUND>
```

Note that the MASTERSOUND attribute doesn't require any additional value; it stands by itself. The group of controls, in this case, is identified by the NAME="ergo" entry. This example is expanded in the following section.

NAME

The NAME attribute designates a title to be applied to a collection of controls that will all refer to the same sound file. This activity takes a bit of extra work, as each of the other controls (those not included as part of the MASTERSOUND entry) must be pointed at a stub file, which is a short dummy file for satisfying the LiveAudio requirements.

Using a control as part of a group requires only that you use the same NAME attribute. For example, to embed a PAUSEBUTTON as part of the group NAME="ergo", you could use the following entry:

```
<EMBED SRC="dummy1.wav" HEIGHT=22 WIDTH=37 CONTROLS=PAUSEBUTTON NAME="ergo">
```

This entry assumes that you have created another <EMBED> tag that has been designated as the MASTERSOUND and that the "dummy1.wav" is a stub file, which is not intended for playback (the only sound file in a group that is actually played back is the one designated as the MASTERSOUND).

As an example of how this works, consider the following HTML code:

```
<HTML>

<HEAD><TITLE>Vampire Study Institute</TITLE>

</HEAD>

<CENTER><H1>Interviews with Prominent Vampires</H1></CENTER><P>

<HR>

<P>We've collected the best of the interviews with some of the leading vampires

in Lithuania, captured before a late night dinner party.<P>

<I>Interview with Peter Brashinski</I>

<EMBED SRC="noise1.wav" CONTROLS=PLAYBUTTON ALIGN=BASELINE HEIGHT=22 WIDTH=37

MASTERSOUND NAME="ergo">

<I>Peter balks at the microphone</I>
```

```
<P>If the discussion becomes too intense, you can pause

<EMBED SRC="dummy1.wav" CONTROLS=PAUSEBUTTON HEIGHT=22 WIDTH=37 NAME="ergo">

<I>Catch your breath here</I>

<P>If you feel things are totally out of control, you can stop the interview at

any point

<EMBED SPC="dummy2.wav" CONTROLS=STOPBUTTON HEIGHT=22 WIDTH=37 NAME="ergo">

<I>Time to bail out!</I>

<HR>

</BODY>

</HTML>
```

The two stub files, "dummy1.wav" and "dummy2.wav," never play. You can supply an extremely short audio clip to serve as the stub, but it must be actually available in the designated directory, or the browser will display a broken link symbol in place of the corresponding transport control. To create the stub, just take any audio file of the appropriate format and trim it down to a second or two in length. Save it using the filename indicated in your HTML code.

The NAME="ergo" entry ensures that each of the three controls—the play button, pause button, and stop button—will all control the sound file indicated as the MASTERSOUND. If you assembled this HTML code (and the necessary sound files), the resulting browser display would be as shown in Figure 4.6.

You can see that the controls are spread out over several lines in the Web page, but they all interact with the sound file titled "noise1.wav." If you started the playback using the single play button, you could then pause it using the pause button a couple of lines down, or stop it using the stop button. Any number of console controls can be distributed about a page in this manner, each of them controlling the same original SRC file.

This approach, of course, is effective only if you make it clear by your Web page design that the individual transport controls are linked in some manner. You can do this by placing them around a common graphic element, clustering them within adjacent areas in a block of text, or using titles on the controls that clearly identify their functions.

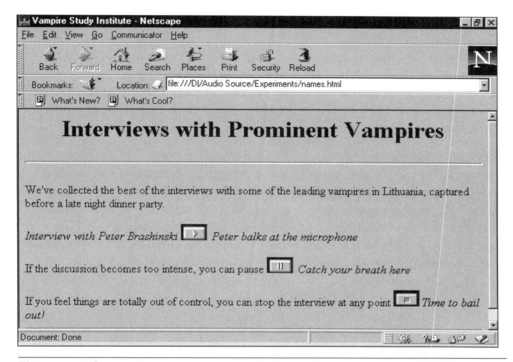

Figure 4.6 Separate console controls linked by a common NAME.

Sound Format Considerations

So far we've dealt only with those sound file formats that have native support within the mainstream browsers. You don't need to download or install any additional plug-ins to be able to play them. While this is the simplest way to include sound files on a Web page, you might wonder what the differences are between choosing the different formats—AU, AIFF, and WAV—for practical applications. This section provides some fundamental information on these formats to help guide your decision as to which to use.

WAV Files

The common WAV file, which soared in popularity with the release of Microsoft Windows 3.1, has become one of the most ubiquitous file formats appearing on the Web. Formally, the format is known as the RIFF WAVE audio file format, based on the Resource Interchange File Format Waveform standard described by Microsoft as part of their multimedia programming specifications. As you might suspect, the format is most widely supported on computers running Intel processors, although players and conversion utilities exist for this format on both the Macintosh and Unix platforms. You can confidently post WAV files on a World Wide Web site or FTP site with the assurance that your audience will have little trouble finding an application to play them. Of course, these files can be played from directly within the browser environment for Navigator and Explorer, which is a practical alternative only if the file sizes are fairly small or the data transfer speeds of your Internet connection are at least ISDN rates or higher.

The WAV file format bears much in common with the Macintosh-oriented AIFF format; both of these audio formats originated with the idea of offering an interchange medium for exchanging audio data. WAV files are found in both compressed and uncompressed formats, ranging from 8KHz, 8-bit, mono samples to 44KHz, 16-bit stereo samples. A 12-bit storage format is also supported, but rarely seen. When compression is applied, most commonly using the IMA/ADPCM compression standards, compression ratios of 4:1 can be achieved with slight signal loss. This compression standard has native support in Windows95 and other current operating systems. For earlier operating systems, users may have to obtain a special driver to be able to play back the compressed files.

You would have to hunt diligently to find a sound processing application on the Windows platform that does not support WAV files. Both high-end programs such as Sound Forge and more modest bundled utilities such as the Sound Recorder program included with Windows can edit and save audio in WAV file format. On the Macintosh platform, leading products such as SoundEdit 16 version 2 (Macromedia) allow you to import and export WAV files. Support for this format, however, is not universal in Macintosh applications, and it is supported only by newer applications in the Unix domain.

WAV is a good choice for presenting audio files if your primary audience consists of Windows users. If you suspect that a fair number of your audience will be running Macintosh equipment (or machines with Motorola processors), you may want to post both WAV and AIFF versions of audio files that you want to distribute. It's a little extra work to create the files in both formats, but a touch that your Macintosh audience is sure to appreciate.

AIFF Files

Apple Computer originated the AIFF format to support uncompressed audio file interchange at sample rates ranging from 8KHz, 8-bit mono to 48KHz, 16-bit stereo. Short for Audio Interchange File Format, AIFF enjoys wide support on machines equipped with Motorola processors, but it also can be found in many Windows sound processing applications and on applications designed for Silicon Graphics workstations. As a native file format for the Navigator and Explorer browsers, AIFF is a safe bet for distributing audio content on the Internet.

A variation of AIFF, referred to as AIFF-C, supports compressed data as well as uncompressed. Using the MACE or IMA/ADPCM compression schemes, AIFF-C can achieve audio compression ratios as high as 6:1. At the higher levels of compression, sound quality begins to drop off.

AIFF tends to be used as a "pure" sound file storage format, rather than a multimedia format, because it does not separate data and other file parameters, making it difficult to incorporate into multitrack operations, such as overdubbing and merging of tracks. If you are offering audio content intended for both Macintosh and Windows users, you might want to consider placing both WAV and AIFF formats for download. Many Windows users are not overly familiar with AIFF, even though their sound processing applications may support it. Internally, AIFF and WAV files are very similar; only the header information in the file differentiates the two.

AU Files

The "mother" of Internet sound, AU files originated on Sun Microsystems workstations and quickly became dispersed throughout the Internet as voice mail attachments to e-mail, downloadable sound files, and interactive sound effects. The format is now used as the chief means of adding sound content to Java applets. Despite its Unix origins, this file format is commonly supported under Macintosh and Windows applications, including native browser support in Explorer and Navigator. Both stereo and mono audio files can be created with sample rates ranging from 8KHz to 48KHz and bit resolutions of 8-bits or 16-bits. AU files can be compressed using the ADPCM compression scheme or another scheme common on Unix platforms known as µlaw (pronounced me-ew law).

If your primary audience consists of Unix users, you might want to post audio content using the AU format; otherwise, your audience would probably be better served with WAV or AIFF formats. Although most Windows and Mac users have tools that can read, edit, and play AU, this format tends to be unfamiliar to many of them and may generate some confusion and a reluctance to download the content. Shorter AU files, however, designed for immediate playback in a browser audio console or as content within a Java applet, provide more practical applications.

Fast and Clean Conversions

If you perform a lot of sound file conversions and you need a streamlined program for maintaining the highest possible audio quality during conversions, a company called Waves offers a program called WaveConvert that quickly converts many of the most common audio file formats. WaveConvert includes Windows and Mac versions in the same package and supports AIFF, SND, SDII, QuickTime, and WAV, as well as raw audio (PCM) data. The product is optimized to reduce the impact of downsampling and bit-reduction errors, using proprietary algorithms to ensure the best audio fidelity throughout the conversion process.

  For details, check out Waves' Web site:

www.waves.com.

Supporting Simple File Downloads

As you can see, it's a fairly easy matter to embed short sound files into an HTML document and play them back either automatically or through an audio console under manual control. This approach works best for low-resolution sound files that can be quickly downloaded and accessed in a reasonable length of time. What's reasonable? Many websters get impatient if they have to spend more than a few seconds waiting for a page to load. If you're working with WAV, AIFF, or AU file formats, this limits you to mono files sampled at 11KHz or 22KHz, 8-bit resolution, that run for a few seconds. The audio quality will not be impeccable, but with care you can deliver voice-quality sound or simple music with respectable fidelity. If you use MIDI files, of course, you can deliver much longer and more complex musical sequences, but the quality of playback depends on the sound equipment available to the user. You lose a certain measure of control when you trust your playback to an unknown MIDI synthesizer, maybe installed in a conservative schoolteacher's 386SX machine in upstate Idaho on an 8-bit sound board using FM synthesis. The resulting MIDI playback will suffer the pangs of Faustian torment.

As you gain more fidelity with a digital sound file (by increasing the sampling rate and the bit resolution), the required file storage space expands accordingly and the necessary download times for files posted on the Internet rise. Compression standards, such as MPEG and ADPCM, let you reduce the overall size of the digital file, but they require decoding before playback. If you want to deliver high-quality audio in real time, you can turn to streaming audio formats (discussed in Chapter 7). For simply providing samples of sounds for playback, however, the easiest method is to offer the native file formats as linked files that can be downloaded. This can be accomplished very easily in an HTML document, and this approach is frequently used by musicians, broadcast buffs, and others who want to make samples of the sound—containing music or voice—available for offline listening. You do, however, need to strike a balance between the size of a downloadable file and the fidelity of the sound.

Tweaking the Sound File Size

It almost always makes sense to record your original sound source at the highest possible resolution and sampling rate and then to downsample for achieving a balance between fidelity and file size. For example, assume you've got a completed song mixed to CD quality (44,100Hz, 16-bit stereo) that you want to showcase on the Web. The length of the song, stored as a WAV file, is 2 minutes, 10 seconds. The uncompressed file size for this tune is 22Mb, a very unlikely download size for anyone with a dial-up connection.

The first step to making this file more accessible for Web access is to downsample the waveform, which reduces the number of samples per second used to represent the sound data. Reducing the sample rate affects the high-frequency data (remember the Nyquist rate, discussed in Chapter 3) and also can generate distortion in the downsampled signal by causing aliasing errors. For this reason, many sound-processing applications include an anti-aliasing filter that is applied when downsampling a sound file to serve as a low-pass filter and reduce aliasing error.

If you downsample the file, using a sampling rate of 22,050Hz, the resulting sound file is effectively reduced to 11.29Mb. We're still looking at a pretty hefty download size, but if you play the song back at this sampling rate, you will find that the sound quality is still very high. We've slipped a bit from the previous audiophile CD quality, but overall most people would have trouble distinguishing just what is different between this sound file and the one prior to downsampling.

Can you go one more downsample pass to 11,025Hz? This sampling rate will generate audible deterioration of the signal to a degree that most of your listeners will probably notice the difference, but the effect can be managed to keep the resulting sound within acceptable limits. The high-frequency components of the signal will be less prominent, and the low end will tend to predominate. With a sound file resampled to this sampling rate, you might want to try running equalization on the waveform to boost the high frequencies and lessen the boominess of the low end. With this last downsampling, you've reduced the sound file size to 5.64Mb, which is probably on the outer edge of what someone might be inclined to download if they wanted to listen to your work.

Music downsampled to 8KHz loses much of its vibrancy and tends to sound "flat" and lifeless. The background music that you hear while on hold on the telephone has this flattened quality; music doesn't travel well through the phone lines, nor does it sound much like music at 8KHz sampling. If you exclude the option of downsampling to 8KHz, you have three choices at this point if you want to squeeze the sound data down even further. You can mix the two stereo tracks down to a single monaural track, change the sample size (the bit resolution) to 8-bits, or you can cut the length of the song. You can also try combining these options—for example, you can mix the two tracks to one monaural track and change the sample rate to 8-bits. This brings the WAV file size down to 1.41Mb, certainly well within the download range for someone who is seriously interested in listening to a sample of your music. If you want to go one more step, you can shorten the length of the song to 1 minute, 5 seconds, resulting in a file size around 700Kb.

These types of operations—downsampling, mixing from stereo to mono, changing the sample rate, adjusting equalization—can be performed in most typical sound-processing applications. Sound Forge (by Sonic Foundry) is a good choice for Windows users; Macintosh users frequently turn to Macromedia's SoundEdit 16. Because even a 700Kb sound file is going to take several minutes to download for most users with 28.8Kbps modems, you might want to provide a short 10 or 12-second audio clip of the selection for previewing prior to downloading.

Keep in mind that these techniques are not the only techniques you have to choose from, just those techniques designed to keep the sound file in a native file format without using a codec (coder/decoder) for compression and decompression of the sound information. Additional techniques, including streaming audio formats and MPEG compression, are discussed in other places in this book, and these approaches may make sense for your particular application.

As a summary, consider the sound file sizes through the entire reduction process, starting from the unaltered 2-minute, 10-second audio selection:

- **22 Megabytes**: 44KHz, 16-bit, stereo; CD-quality sound

- **11.29 Megabytes**: 22KHz, 16-bit, stereo; high-fidelity sound, some high-frequency loss

- **5.64 Megabytes**: 11KHz, 16-bit stereo; medium-quality sound, significant high-frequency loss

- **2.82 Megabytes**: 11KHz, 16-bit mono; medium-quality sound, loss of stereo ambiance

- **1.41 Megabytes**: 11KHz, 8-bit mono; quality close to AM radio, overall flattening and loss of vibrancy

- **.7 Megabytes**: 11KHz, 8-bit mono, edited to 50 percent of original length; same as above, only shorter

If you value the sonic integrity of your original work, all of these downsample and reformatting decisions are going to be difficult because each involves a degree of fidelity loss in exchange for a file size that is more easily distributable over the Internet. Do everything you can during the downsampling process—including anti-aliasing and equalization—to maintain the best possible sound quality. At some point, however, you need to make an aesthetic judgment as to what constitutes acceptable sound quality and then turn your creation loose on the Internet for public consumption. In many cases, you may be extending audio material to tempt someone to buy your audio CD or come to your next performance at the Black Cat Café. Be realistic about what someone is willing to download, and you will increase the size of your audience significantly. File sizes around 1Mb or below are probably your best bet for general-purpose use.

Downsampling Voice Files

If your sound material consists of recorded voice, whether from a radio broadcast or speech or poetry reading, you can generally downsample to much more compact file sizes because voice recordings use much less of the audible frequency range. A voice file resampled to 11KHz, 8-bit, mono will not suffer the same degradation that a complex music piece will undergo at the same sample rate. You should, however, still record the original source material at the highest possible sampling rate available to you, although you may want to consider recording to mono, rather than stereo. There are also a number of codecs (discussed in more detail in Chapter 10) that are optimized to compress voice material significantly while minimizing signal distortion. Some of these, such as EchoSpeech, can also deliver audio files in streaming mode without requiring elaborate server setup. You should consider these options when determining the best way to deliver sound files consisting of voice recordings onto the Web.

Posting Sound Files in HTML

An HTML document can contain any kind of content that is available for down-loading by placing the appropriate filenames within a pair of <A> tags. When a Web-page visitor clicks on the link, the browser offers a choice of options as to how to deal with the type of file pointed to by the link. The browser can then facilitate downloading or playback of the file contents.

This simple technique is used by many music groups and organizations that want to make files available on the Web for basic downloading. Consider the following HTML code example:

```
<HTML>

<HEAD><TITLE>Squalling Lizard's Music Emporium</TITLE></HEAD>

<CENTER><H1>Latest cuts from the Squalling Lizards</H1></CENTER><P>

<HR>

To all you sun-loving lizard heads out there—here are some releases from our

upcoming CD, "Squashed on the Wall."<P>

<I>A Radiant Burst of Energy</I><P>

<A HREF="burst.wav">Download 723Kb, WAV format</A><P>

<I>Singing in the Bathtub</I><P>

<A HREF="bathtub.wav">Download 640Kb, WAV format</A><P>

<I>Basic bog blues</I><P>

<A HREF="bogblues.wav">Download 812Kb, WAV format</A><P>

<HR>

</BODY>

</HTML>
```

Make sure that you give your site visitors fair warning about the size of the download. Including the file format is also an important part of making the audio content available. The display resulting from this HTML code is shown in Figure 4.7.

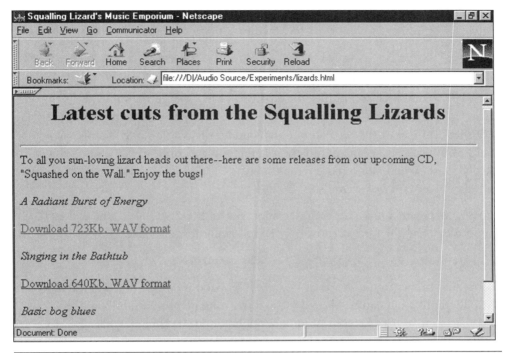

Figure 4.7 Sample WAV file downloads.

The HREF= entry inside the <A> tags can point to a file through a relative path or through another site. For example, if your sound files are stored on the server one directory below the HTML document in a directory named "skinks," your reference should read:

```
<A HREF="skinks/burst.wav">Download 723Kb, WAV format</A><P>
```

You could also add a link to files stored at another Web site, as shown in the following code:

```
<A HREF="http://www.lizard_kings.net/skinks/burst.wav">Download 723Kb, WAV
format</A><P>
```

If your ISP limits your space for storing HTML documents and resources but you have access to another site using the FTP protocol, you could also include a pointer to the appropriate FTP site, as shown in the following code:

```
<A HREF="ftp://lizard_kings.net/skinks/burst.wav">Download 723Kb, WAV
format</A><P>
```

To expand your potential audience, you might want to also provide a set of matching AIFF files as a courtesy to Macintosh users who might prefer the format over WAV.

Previewing Posted Sound Files

The 600Kb to 800Kb sound files for download discussed in the previous example are hefty enough that a preview playback might encourage someone to sample a very short snippet of the file before downloading the whole thing. The preview files could be accessed using the audio console method described earlier in this chapter. Ideally, these would be no more than 40 or 50Kb so that each file would download and play in a matter of seconds.

You can create a link that contains an image and textual link to the preview sound file, using the format shown in the following line of code:

```
<A HREF="preview1.wav"><IMG SRC="notes.gif">Preview song...</A><P>
```

The link points to the short preview file, "preview1.wav." The IMG referenced is a small graphic that can be clicked to start the song playback. Optionally, the text "Preview song..." can be used to initiate the link and the song playback.

With this line inserted just after the entry for the first song from our previous HTML example, the code appears as follows:

```
<HTML>

<HEAD><TITLE>Squalling Lizard's Music Emporium</TITLE></HEAD>

<CENTER><H1>Latest cuts from the Squalling Lizards</H1></CENTER><P>

<HR>

To all you sun-loving lizard heads out there—here are some releases from our

upcoming CD, "Squashed on the Wall." Enjoy the bugs!<P>

<I>A Radiant Burst of Energy</I><P>

<A HREF="preview1.wav"><IMG SRC="notes.gif">Preview song...</A><P>

<A HREF="burst.wav">Download 723Kb, WAV format</A><P>

<I>Singing in the Bathtub</I><P>

<A HREF="bathtub.wav">Download 640Kb, WAV format</A><P>
```

```
<I>Basic bog blues</I><P>

<A HREF="bogblues.wav">Download 812Kb, WAV format</A><P>

<HR>

</BODY>

</HTML>
```

If you view this page in Navigator, as shown in Figure 4.8, you'll see that the embedded image (the small notes graphic) serves as an active link to start the preview playback. Click the image and the audio console appears in the browser window. Visitors to this page can listen to the short sample on the audio console to determine if they want to download the larger file.

Sound Files on the Web

If you're looking for music on the Web, you'll find many examples of bands that have posted their original material for you to listen to. Often, this is in a blatant

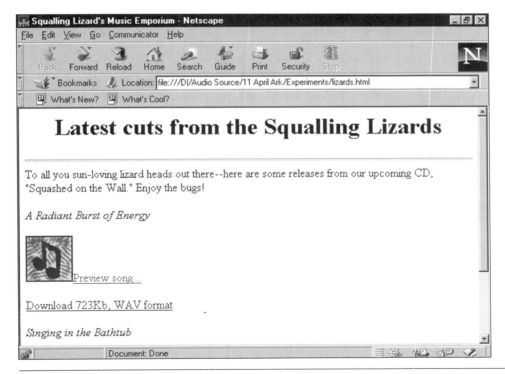

Figure 4.8 Embedded notes graphic.

attempt to persuade you to buy their CD or go to their next concert, but if you enjoy sampling different kinds of music, there is no better way to listen to the latest and greatest releases. You'll find a wide mix of styles and an equally wide range of talent—from the most raw garage band to professional musicians who may be recording on their own label or preparing to sign with a record company to complete their first album. If you're interested in posting your own music or other audio content, spend some time first looking at how others have accomplished this (and listen to their results). Three or four hours of touring music and audio sites will give you a clear picture of what works and what doesn't. Remember that the simplest approaches generally favor the largest audiences. As you move outside the native browser file formats, thereby requiring plug-ins, players, decoders, and helper applications, you'll be steadily reducing your potential audience.

One example of an active band with downloadable songs on their Web site is Belizbeha, a Burlington, Vermont-based band with a sound sometimes described as Acid Jazz. You can view a diary describing some of the band's recent gigs, scan through a collection of reviews from local and national media, read quotes from other musicians that have been turned on to Belizbeha's sound (such as Jon Fishman of Phish, another popular Vermont band), and check out the current concert schedule.

Belizbeha offers both real audio samples of their music, set up for real-time streaming, and downloadable AU files for more leisurely offline listening. Figure 4.9 shows the Web page that contains the downloadable files. The technique used to present these files is the same as demonstrated in the previous example—a simple link on the page referencing the sound file content. Note that the band gives you the file size right beside the link to avoid any interminable download surprises.

 You can sample Belizbeha's latest material at:

> **http://www.belizbeha.com**

If you have a RealAudio 3.0 Player installed, you can also sample their streaming audio content. A link is provided to the Progressive Network's site for those who need to download the player.

Sources of Sound Files

Using the techniques presented in Chapter 3, you can record many of your own sound effects or music and process the waveforms to create sound files for use on

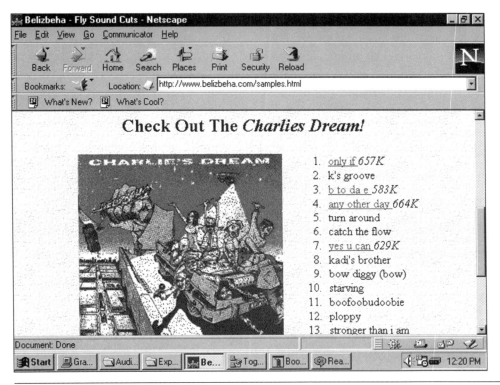

Figure 4.9 Download page for Belizbeha.

the Web. In many cases, though, you may want to rely on professionally recorded sound samples or royalty-free music clips. Sound clip libraries are becoming more common, with diverse selections of music and effects suitable for any conceivable Web application. The types of sounds available in a variety of formats range from the insipid strains of grocery-store music to the works of cutting-edge sound sculptors who contribute snippets to the libraries of Rarefaction (including *A Poke in the Ear with a Sharp Stick* and *A Diffusion of Noise*, discussed in the following section). Choose your Web persona carefully. You can recreate the ambiance of a Minneapolis mall or an industrial workshop in a future colony orbiting one of the moons of Jupiter or the turbulence of a Louisiana bayou during a violent summer thunderstorm. Sound has a powerful ability to shape emotions and create vivid impressions.

Working with Useful Noise

Sound design using modern digital audio tools is both an art and a science. Rarefaction, a new company that arose when Macromedia swallowed up OSC (a small San Francisco-based company primarily known for their Macintosh digital recorded program: Deck) showcases the work of sound sculptors and acoustic designers on a series of audio CDs. Spurning sample libraries that contain one more English horn variation and one more grand piano, Rarefaction packs their CDs with the strangest assortment of other-worldly sounds ever experienced by human ears. These short, high-quality audio clips, enhanced using a technique that Rarefaction calls Hyper-Stereo, can be freely used in multimedia work, films, Web presentations, video projects, and musical compositions. All selections are 16-bit digital audio; Rarefaction offers both conventional audio CDs and Macintosh-format CD-ROMs; earlier Macintosh-based releases are being converted to more accessible audio CDs. Utilities such as OMI's Disc-to-Disk allow digital audio tracks to be retrieved directly from a CD for computer storage and use, maintaining the digital format throughout the retrieval, so the contents of audio CDs can be used without introducing sound error in additional analog-to-digital and digital-to-analog cycles when acquiring the data.

Many of the sounds have a dark, foreboding quality—this library series does not specialize in bird songs, burbling brooks, and laughing children. Instead, you'll hear sounds identified with short descriptions such as Eerie Stuff, CyberDoom, Kaos, Sharkcage, Assorted Weird-ass, Asylum 100, and Oakland Jail Ambiance. One of the first collections converted from Mac format to audio CD format, *A Poke in the Ear with a Sharp Stick*, includes the work of internationally acknowledged sound designers, whose work often appears in cutting-edge films and video projects. *A Diffusion of Useful Noise* carries on the tradition established by the original *Poke in the Ear* release, with audio clips described as Alternate Atmospheres, Hard FX, Complex Ambiance, Digital and Analog Oscillators, Ambient Textures, and so on. If you're looking for unique sounds to enhance a Web project or create an awe-inspiring musical composition, this library contains the sounds to spur your creativity.

For Web presentations, sounds such as the ones in the *Poke in the Ear* library can be used in a number of different ways. You could use an audio clip behind a Shockwave animation that appears when a certain area on the site is entered. You could use Metallic Percussion sounds stored as a sample in a synthesizer to use while constructing a unique drum pattern to play in the background of a page. You could use clips as sound effects that play when a certain object is selected on a page or when the visitor exits from a particular area of the site. It will take some skill to compress the 16-bit audio clips down to a size that can be effectively used on the Web, but the latest generation of digital sound processing tools is capable of the

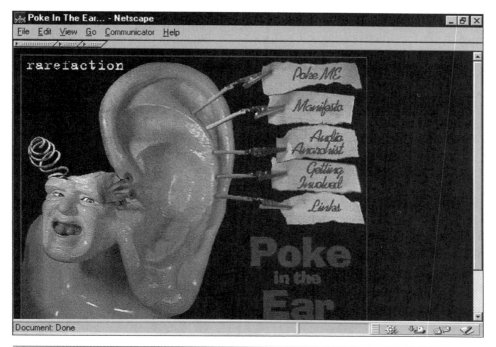

Figure 4.10 Rarefaction Web site.

job. Sound sculpting can be a satisfying preoccupation and an expressive medium for communicating.

 More information on recent Rarefaction releases can be obtained from their Web site (shown in Figure 4.10):

www.rarefaction.com

Royalty-Free Music

Not all of us are gifted with the instincts and talents for composing music. Tasteful use of music on a Web site can do a great deal to provide a certain atmosphere, if used with discretion, but how do you present high-quality music and deal with the licensing and copyright issues? In other words, if you can't write songs yourself, where do you get them?

One possible option is through royalty-free music libraries. An entire genre of royalty-free music has burst forth in the industry to support multimedia projects, video endeavors, computer game design, independent film, and Web presentations. One of the more effective companies working in this area is QCCS Productions, based in Eugene, Oregon, with a collection of audio CDs and cassettes organized by musical themes. You can purchase a CD full of mystery music, with audio selections presented in several different lengths from 30-second and 60-second lead-ins and trailers to complete songs that run three or four minutes. Other categories include suspense, humor, nature, sports, and so on. The music is consistently high quality, professionally performed, and easily accessible from CD or cassette. The *Professional Background Theme Music* (PBTM) series offers just about any type of music you can think of and any of these pieces can be dropped into a Web presentation or multimedia production without the usual "needle-drop fees" that are often associated with music licensed for broadcast use. Sometimes called buyout music, you can obtain a CD from QCCS Productions with about 10 songs (some with several different lengths) for around $60; cassettes cost $50. Once you buy them, you can freely drop any of the pieces into your Web work without concern for additional licensing or royalty fees. The only stipulation is that you don't try to redistribute the music outside of a production.

The music libraries at QCCS Productions continue to grow. You can find contact information for QCCS Productions in Appendix C.

Other Sources of Stock Music and Sound

 Royalty Free Music (catchy title) offers royalty-free music that can be purchased from their Web site at (you guessed it):

www.royaltyfree.com

You can obtain three CDs' worth of songs at the Royalty Free site to drop into projects of any type, including Web presentations. Gary Lamb, the composer of these royalty-free pieces, offers previews of selections on the Web site. The previews are sampled down, using techniques similar to those discussed in this chapter, to an 11KHz sampling rate with 8-bit samples. These short samples average around 350Kb in length and run long enough to get a good sense of the style and the quality of the music (generally, 15 to 25 seconds). A page from this site is shown in Figure 4.11. The site includes online ordering; you can obtain three CDs for $149.95. No additional licensing or royalties are required for use.

Gary Lamb has successfully broken into the top 10 in the *Billboard Magazine* charts, a rare feat for an independent recording label. The Web site includes

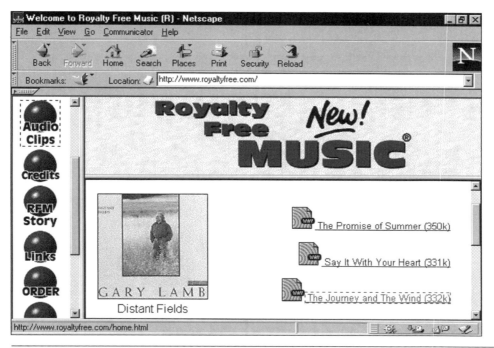

Figure 4.11 Royalty Free Music site.

suggestions as to how to use the material provided. Users are encouraged to use the music on many different types of projects, and a royalty-free waiver gives the purchaser of each disc unlimited rights for use of the music. The only stipulation is that the music not be resold and that the composer, Gary Lamb, be given credit wherever possible.

The Music Bakery is another source of audio material sold without license restrictions. They offer samples of their CD-quality works in AIFF, WAV, and RealAudio formats. These samples run about 10 to 15 seconds in length and are captured at a sample rate of 22KHz with 8-bit samples. You can notice the boost in sound quality as compared to samples done at 11KHz, but the tradeoff involves the length of each sample. Most of the samples at the Music Bakery are shorter segments to keep the download times from becoming prohibitive. As a Web author, you will continually be faced with this issue—should you make samples higher quality to showcase your recorded material in the best possible light, resulting in larger downloads, or should you economize on the sound quality to shorten download times?

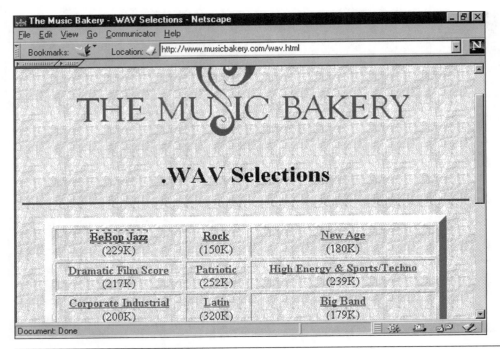

Figure 4.12 A table full of songs at the Music Bakery.

Samples are organized in table format, as shown in Figure 4.12. At the lengths provided, these clips take 15 or 20 seconds to download at a 28.8Kbps connection rate and play for several seconds. The RealAudio clips start playing slightly more quickly—as soon as the RealAudio Player buffer fills.

Cambium Sound Choice

Cambium Sound Choice offers musical cuts on CD-ROM, with categories ranging from classical through new age to jazz. There are original composed pieces, recordings of the works of the great composers (Bach and Beethoven, among others), lively jazz material—all royalty-free, with much of this music available for sampling online. This site (illustrated in Figure 4.13) includes some discussions of the different sound formats offered and the arrangement of material on their CD-ROM (which is designed to support multimedia editing and simplified selection).

Individual volumes contain somewhere around 28 main songs, with most selections running about 60 seconds and additional shorter variations that Cambium calls bumpers. Bumpers are very short clips that have been pre-edited and designed

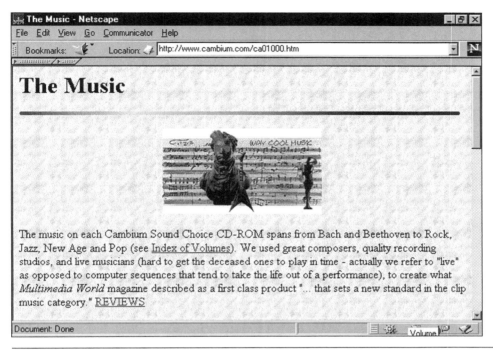

Figure 4.13 Musical selections at Cambium Sound Choice.

to be dropped into place as transitions, introductions, grand finales, and similar applications. These shorter pieces are designed to work with and be used in combination with the longer selections, so that you can easily create a running theme for a multimedia piece or Web creation.

One interesting feature of the sample clips that Cambium provides online in WAV format is that many of them are presented using the Microsoft ADPCM compression scheme. This level of compression allows high-quality 22KHz stereo files to be distributed in files that contain about 1.3Mb of data per minute of sound. The ADPCM compression achieves a 4:1 compression ratio (in other words, you can cut the size of the sound files down to one-quarter of their original size). The tradeoff is that unless your audience is running Windows95, it may have to install special drivers to play back these compressed files—an obstacle for Windows 3.1, Macintosh, and Unix users. Most machines can be equipped to play ADPCM WAV, but it is definitely a hindrance for non-Windows95 site visitors.

Cambium includes samples as low as 11KHz sampled, monaural, ADPCM-compressed files, but warns that the sound quality will not exactly dazzle you.

The general tone and character that prevails on this site is witty and engaging; you might want to stop for a visit at:

www.cambium.com

Searching for Sounds

The Lycos search engine (**www.lycos.com**) lets you conduct a search based on sounds, retrieving all matches that include the search term and an audio component of some type (WAV, AIFF, or AU). For a quick tour of how different folks are using sound on the Web, try running a few searches from Lycos with the **Sound** option selected. You're guaranteed to retrieve some fascinating and bizarre material. Keep in mind that with this option selected, the search engine points to and selects audio material directly. You can preview a description, which may or may not be informative, but once you click on it, the browser will begin downloading the selected audio content, and as soon as the audio console in your browser can manage it, playback begins. As you might expect, a lot of this audio content is silly, illegal, or pointless, but if you're curious about the current Web soundscape, this **Lycos** option might keep you amused for long hours on a Saturday night. Some of the items retrieved during a recent Lycos search included a live (bootlegged) recording of a Jimmy Page trill, a clip of a well-known TV sitcom character (first name hint: Jamie) imploring "I want to have sex!," some unidentifiable mumblings and scuffling sounds that somehow evoked an image of a Czechoslovakian radio station being overthrown, and an extremely bad recording of some garage band from somewhere in the Midwest. The sounds are out there, if your ears can stand them.

 You can access the Lycos search engine at:

www.Lycos.com

Internet Music Kit

When it comes to creating Web pages, some Web authors like getting down to the lowest possible level and working (or grappling) with the tags required to construct the page. Others would prefer not to ever look at a page full of tags and generally choose tools that let them work at a higher level, designing the basic elements of a page and then letting the HTML editor output the necessary code. Adobe's Page

Mill is an example of a program that lets you build HTML documents at a higher level, without become immersed in the coding conventions. Microsoft's Front Page is another example.

Internet Music Kit, by Wildcat Canyon Software, uses a similar high-level approach to streamline the process of embedding sound into a Web page. The program is designed to let you add soundtracks to a Web page in a minimal amount of time without extensive knowledge of HTML coding. If you have an aversion to working with the nitty-gritty tags and conventions associated with HTML, Internet Music Kit can help you compose and deliver music from your Web pages by means of a straightforward interface and some simple commands.

The program boils the music creation and embedding process down to a three-step procedure. The files used as source material are any files stored as Standard MIDI File format (SMF), but Internet Music Kit performs a conversion to prepare the files for playback in its own native format. A plug-in, referred to as WebTracks, is required for playback. The toolbar for the WebTracks plug-in gets embedded in a designated location, or it can be displayed as a floating toolbar and positioned any-where on the desktop. If the person viewing the page doesn't already have the plug-in, the toolbar provides a quick link to allow it to be downloaded and installed.

For source material, you can use MIDI files that you have created in another application, or you can use a program that was developed by Roland Corporation, bundled with Internet Music Kit, called DoReMix. DoReMix lets you quickly assemble MIDI music pieces by manipulating blocks that represent musical phrases in a variety of styles. A number of sample pieces are included that you can use as a starting point for your own composition, or you can trust the fates and use the *Shaker* option, a method of creating computer-generated music through random selection from the library of phrases. Although the process may seem a bit lame, the resulting music is surprisingly good. Roland's long experience with computer-controlled drum machines, synthesizers, and sound board technology comes through the mix, generating MIDI songs with strong drum patterns and rhythm lines. Melodically, these computer-generated works are a bit weak, but you have the option of exported the MIDI file to another sequencer application and embellishing the song further before bringing it into Internet Music Kit for conversion to their Web-based format.

If you're anxious to get music up on your site, but you don't have any original music and you're eager to experiment without spending several days learning

HTML, Internet Music Kit can be the most direct way to satisfy your requirements. The following procedure illustrates the process.

The initial Internet Music Kit screen, shown in Figure 4.14, belies the notion that producing music for the Internet is difficult. Three buttons—**Create Music**, **Convert Music**, and **Embed Music**—guide you through the process. You can be playing music from your Web site within about 20 minutes from the time you first start using this program—if you don't run into snags.

Create Music

Click the **Create Music** button to begin the process of adding music to your Web site. The Internet Music Kit gives you a choice of three options for composition. You can immediately launch the bundled companion program, DoReMiX, and construct a musical composition from phrases; you can grab music from the Web (make sure it is public domain or royalty-free before using it); or you can use your own personal composition application to compose a song.

Figure 4.14 Initial screen for the Internet Music Kit.

If you choose to grab music from the Web, the program initially hooks up to the Wildcat Canyon Web site, where you can pick from an assortment of pre-built songs in their NetMusic directory. You are free to download and use these songs on your pages; you might want to use this option initially to get some source material for using this program.

If you launch DoReMix, the fastest way to build a song is to select a musical style from the Settings menu. You can choose from selections such as classical, rock, house, and world music. The style selected determines the musical phrases that will be available to you as you're building a composition.

Once the musical style has been selected, you can drag the Shaker icon, shown in the lower-left portion of the window in Figure 4.15, to the first frame. A random series of musical phrases is then filled into several of the tracks. You can move frame by frame through the piece and allow the shaker to fill up the song with phrases, choosing from that range of musical instruments that is appropriate for the style you have chosen.

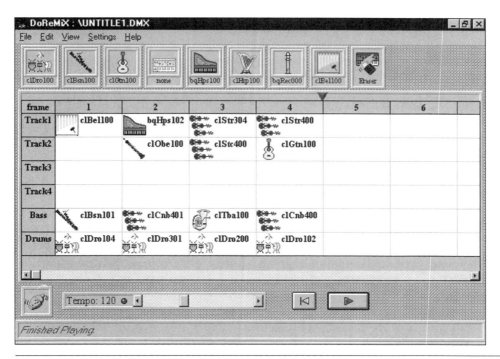

Figure 4.15 Building a musical composition randomly.

You might think the resulting music would consist of hideous cacophony, but the program does a nice job of creating a fluid, well-coordinated musical piece. You can then embellish the song further by dragging musical phrases from the upper toolbar onto frames and tracks. The **Play** button lets you sample this creation at any stage in the process. The Tempo slidebar lets you determine an appropriate tempo for your work.

You can save the song as a Standard Midi Format file (SMF), which is the correct format for importing into Internet Music Kit. You might also want to save it in the native DMX format for later editing and refinement. At this stage, you're ready to **Convert the Music** for Web distribution.

Convert the Music

The raw musical fuel for conversion to WebTracks format is standard MIDI. You can start with a song you created in DoReMiX or another MIDI file. The conversion utility processes the file and saves it in WTX format. When you click the **Convert the Music** button, Internet Music Kit prompts you for the source file for the conversion, as shown in Figure 4.16.

Step 2 in this procedure takes only about 10 seconds to complete. Once you have a valid WTX format file, you're ready to plug it into a Web page.

Embed Music

The Embed Music procedure is guided by a wizard. Internet Music Kit takes you through the process of inserting the selected song into a page that you can then preview in the Web browser of your choice. The wizard lets you choose a page, a WTX file, the correct means for displaying the WebTracks plug-in on the page (floating or fixed), whether the song should loop continuously or play once, and other display options. The program will then launch your Web browser for you and let you sample the resulting playback. Figure 4.17 shows a Web page prepped for WebTracks playback exactly as it will appear to someone who accesses the page. The WebTracks plug-in appears in the upper-left corner of the window. Controls accessible by clicking the plug-in let someone change the volume, adjust settings, or download the necessary WebTracks audio component from the Wildcat Canyon site to be able to hear the WTX file.

This is probably the fastest way to get music onto your Web site. The auto-generated music may not receive any Academy Award nominations for best musical score, but the works originating in DoReMiX were surprisingly coherent and

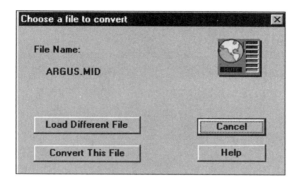

Figure 4.16 Conversion from MIDI to WebTracks format.

engaging in that computer-music sort of way. If you don't like auto-generated music, of course, you're free to embed your own MIDI composition, and many Web authors will probably choose this option. Internet Music Kit is fun, immediately usable, and adaptable for many kinds of Web-authoring applications where music is involved.

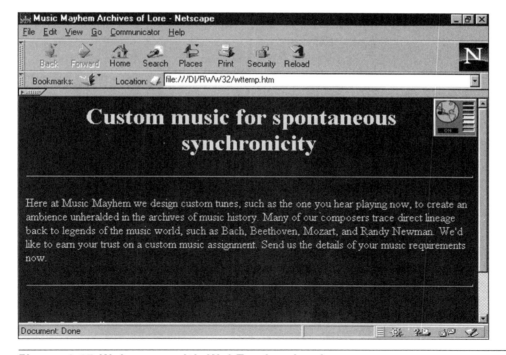

Figure 4.17 Web page with WebTracks plug-in.

More Complex HTML Applications

This chapter covered the fundamental techniques for putting audio material up on a Web site. Even if you started out not knowing much about HTML, you shouldn't have had any problem executing the examples given here and adapting them for your own audio-based Web pages.

The next chapter looks at some more advanced techniques, some of them involving JavaScript, for providing Web audio more selectively. Your users will be able to turn audio options on or off and determine what they want to listen to (if anything). JavaScript takes a bit of work to master, but the benefits are well worth the time invested because you can provide considerable control over your HTML documents using very simple JavaScripts. A good tool for learning this language, Acadia Software's Infuse, is included on the CD-ROM bundled with this book.

More HTML
Audio Techniques

The previous chapter dealt with audio in the context of built-in playback features of common browsers, such as Microsoft Internet Explorer and Netscape Navigator. This chapter extends the audio playback options even further by discussing ways that you can provide effective audio content that is embedded in an HTML document through the use of plug-ins and other options. This approach is not quite as direct as using native file formats for the sound content, but it can have certain advantages, as will be demonstrated by the examples within this chapter.

Audio is popping up in a variety of places these days: inside word processing documents, as audio attachments to e-mail messages, as spoken greetings as you enter a Web page. Once you get beyond the boundaries of the built-in capabilities of common browsers, there are a number of techniques that let you incorporate audio in ways that you might not suspect.

Audio Content within an Acrobat File

One of the simplest ways to distribute audio content over the Internet is to insert an object containing the sound in an appropriate format into a container, such as a document designed to hold audio or video objects, and then distribute the document. You can do this conveniently using word processor document files that include the ability to present MIDI or digital sound files. Microsoft Word and Corel WordPerfect are two examples of word processors that support embedded audio objects, including digital sound files and MIDI files. The embedded objects typically show up on the document page as a small player console or an easily identifiable icon. Clicking the appropriate control triggers playback.

Another technique is to use a portable document file (PDF) created by Adobe Acrobat with the sound embedded as a QuickTime file or other sound file format. The QuickTime file format can support standalone audio content as well as video, so it provides a convenient cross-platform means of distributed audio content. Adobe Acrobat files can also contain embedded WAV and AIFF files that are accessible through hypertext links in the document, through pushbuttons associated with document forms, and as embedded sound files that are attached to a page in an Acrobat document. Each of these techniques will be discussed in this chapter.

Within the framework of an Adobe Acrobat document, the sound file can be presented in a polished, professional manner with the typographical benefits offered by Acrobat (providing much more flexibility than you can achieve using HTML). Adobe Acrobat PDF (portable document file) format files are supported as a native file format in both Netscape Navigator and Microsoft Internet Explorer, so you don't have to be concerned about plug-ins being available, unless your viewer has a very early version of Explorer or Navigator (prior to version 3.0 for both). The Acrobat documents can either be embedded (using the <EMBED> tag) in an HTML document or they can be referenced through a link. Acrobat documents created using version 3.0 or above can be optimized so as to be delivered by the Web server a page at a time, rather than requiring that an entire PDF file be downloaded at once. Graphics stored in a PDF file are automatically compressed by Acrobat, so the display of graphic-heavy content can often be faster than it is when delivered from an HTML document.

The PDF file can be easily detached from its Web-based display and distributed separately, complete with the embedded audio content. This, of course, can also be accomplished easily in the current versions of Explorer and in the Netscape Communicator package, which allow HTML documents to be distributed (complete with links and all other content) through e-mail or Internet conference data exchanges. PDF files also make effective self-contained electronic publishing vehicles, allowing distribution through FTP sites, gopher sites, and other Internet repositories of downloadable files. A PDF file is a good choice if your potential audience includes a significant population that uses Internet tools outside of the Web. While

PDF documents can be easily viewed from within browsers, they can also be viewed separately using the freely available Adobe Acrobat Reader, which comes in versions for the Macintosh, Unix, and Wintel platforms.

Acrobat documents are free of the formatting irregularities that exist in a conventional browser window. For example, if you change the font preference for a browser to a size that is somewhat different from the default, the odds are that any documents that you view that contain a lot of graphics will be quite scrambled. HTML also offers less control of typography and fewer choices of fonts (although this is changing with the introduction of cascading style sheets). With Acrobat, you ensure that your site visitors will see the same page layout you design, including the same fonts, and the layout won't change if someone resizes the browser window dimensions. Acrobat provides typographical stability, a fixed page layout, portability throughout the Windows, Mac, Unix worlds, and strong support for audio content. With these glowing recommendations behind it, let's look at some methods for creating Acrobat documents for Web distribution that contain sound.

Creating a Simple Acrobat Document with Sound

Adobe Acrobat files can be created using almost any application that you can use to print: word processing applications, paint programs, desktop publishing programs, spreadsheets, and so on. Instead of printing the file directly to a printer, you can either print to create a PostScript printer file or create a PDF file directly from the source application. For example, Word 7 for Windows95, as well as many other applications, contains a **Create Adobe PDF** option on its File menu, allowing you to generate the PDF from within any open Word document. If you go the interim step and create a PostScript printer file, which is sometimes necessary if your source document contains encapsulated PostScript graphics (EPS files), you then run Adobe Distiller to convert the PostScript file to Portable Document Format.

A file in Portable Document Format contains all of the same elements as the source document, including page dimensions, graphics layout, and typography. You have the option of embedding any fonts that might not be available to the person viewing the file. The Acrobat reader and Acrobat browser plug-in both substitute fonts if a specified font in a PDF file is not available on the system being used for playback. If you embed the fonts with the Acrobat document, the file size of the document increases slightly, but the viewer will see the pages exactly as you intended. The precision of Adobe Acrobat in rendering page layouts and typography is so good that many lithographic printing facilities that accept computer files for page masters request that clients use Acrobat for submitting material for printing. The same degree of precision carries forward to Web display. Acrobat documents displayed in a browser can be zoomed and examined without loss of detail up to the capabilities of the system displaying the documents. For example, a viewer can zoom in on a particular graphic to pick up the detail from within the browser window. You can create hyperlinks to Web URLs within an Acrobat document—a feature that is very useful for expanding the reach of an Acrobat document beyond the confines of the browser window.

To create a PDF file, start by composing a document in your preferred word processing or publishing tool. Figure 5.1 shows a reasonably simple Word document with an embedded graphic and some fairly unusual font usage: Copperplate Gothic Light and Lucida Handwriting.

You can't enter text, except as labels and identifiers, within Acrobat, so before you create the PDF file, complete the displayed document to your preferences. If you're using special-purpose fonts or display fonts, you might want to check the current settings for the Acrobat PDFWriter printer driver or Acrobat Distiller (depending on which driver you intend to print to) to ensure that all of the fonts

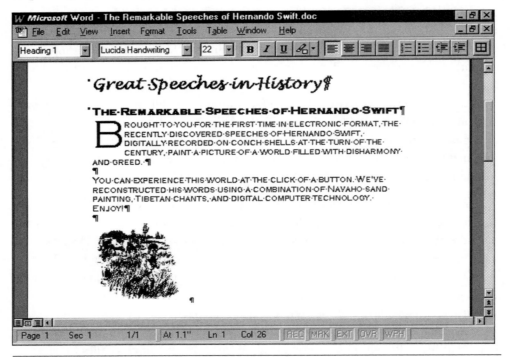

Figure 5.1 Initial Word document.

used in the document will be embedded. You also have options for controlling the compression of the Acrobat document contents and general page layout. The setup is slightly different from the Mac to Unix to Wintel platforms, so follow the documentation for your particular platform for the necessary details to tweak the printer driver settings. Figure 5.2 shows the Font Embedding dialog box as it appears on the Windows95 platform.

Choose the **Create Adobe PDF** option from the File menu and supply a filename for the PDF file that you are going to create. Word displays the Printer message box as it generates the PDF file. Files rendered in this manner generally print as fast or a bit faster than files being sent to an actual printer. When printing is complete, open Acrobat Exchange. Acrobat Exchange is the application that provides:

- **Link creation**: Either to hyperlink points within the PDF file or to other external PDF files or URLs. Links can also be set to refer to multimedia objects, such as QuickTime movies or WAV sound files.

- **Embedding of objects**: For example, movies or sound files.

- **Setting of action lists**: These lists cause certain events to occur when a PDF page is opened or closed. For example, you can include an action in the PDF file so that a particular song stored in a WAV file is played when the page is first opened.

- **Creation of a hierarchical contents listing**: The listing can be displayed in a separate pane beside the main viewing window (in either Acrobat Reader or from within the browser window). The contents page can be used to quickly guide visitors to a particular topic in a long and involved document.

T I P If you have one of the programs that support direct creation of PDF files, you may have a feature that allows you to automatically generate a table of contents and an index with live hypertext links. FrameMaker, a product acquired by Adobe from Frame Technology, can produce a fully hyperlinked PDF document, right down to links within an extensive multipage index, just by selecting one option prior to printing. Other Acrobat-savvy applications can perform similar feats; check the documentation for your word processor or desktop publishing program. (Hint: *If it's an Adobe product, it probably has this capability*).

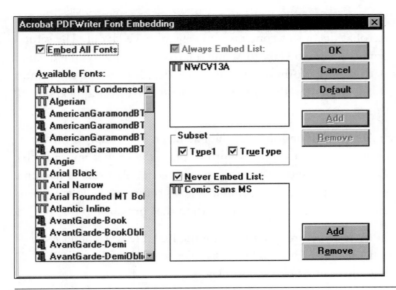

Figure 5.2 Font Embedding options.

When you use Acrobat Exchange to open up the document created in Word and saved in PDF format, the PDF version appears as shown in Figure 5.3. As you can see, it bears a very close resemblance to the original Word document.

One of the easiest ways to add sound to a PDF document is to use one of the form options. Acrobat supports some fairly sophisticated form data collection and transfer features, oriented toward Web interchange of forms data, but you can accomplish quite a bit just using rudimentary controls.

To add a pushbutton to the PDF document, choose the Form tool from the Tools menu and draw the form field where you want it. The Field Properties dialog box pops up, as shown in Figure 5.4. If you select the type of field as a Button and give it a name (shown as Swift_speech in the figure), you can refer to the button from other points in Acrobat, such as the action lists.

For this example, let's add the text "Play speech" to the button **Appearance** when UP and "Speech playing" to the button **Appearance** when PUSHED. These two entries appear on the button surface: One appears when the button is dormant on the page (**Play speech**), indicating the action that button initiates; the other appears when the button is pressed (**Speech playing**), indicating that the audio is playing back. Acrobat also offers an option of using an icon on the button, but for simplicity, we'll skip that step in this example.

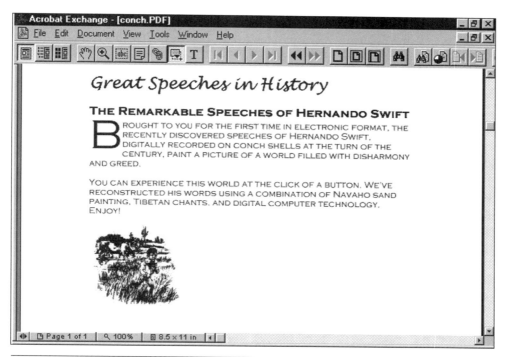

Figure 5.3 PDF document in Acrobat Exchange.

Figure 5.4 Field Properties for a button.

You can use the Appearance tab in this dialog box to control the looks of the button, but for the moment cosmetics aren't that important. The next important element is to set the Actions to be performed by the button, a feature that is included on the Actions tab (shown in Figure 5.5). If you set the Mouse Up action, you can choose the **Add** button and select **Sound** as the action to be performed. Acrobat lets you browse through your subdirectories and choose the sound file (WAV or AIFF) that you want to associate with this button.

When you confirm this addition, Acrobat displays the button on the screen, as shown in Figure 5.6. Clicking the button (from Acrobat Reader or from within a browser) triggers the playback of the designated sound file. While the file is playing, the button is consider PUSHED, so it displays the legend "Speech playing." The button also darkens during the playback to indicate the activity.

Once you save the modified PDF document in Acrobat Exchange, with the newly embedded button, the file can be distributed over the Internet, complete with audio. The file could be stored on an FTP site for download and playback with Acrobat Reader, embedded in an HTML document where it would then be accessed as an inline document, or referenced through a hyperlink in an HTML document (either for download for storage or for immediate loading into the browser window).

Figure 5.5 Mouse Up action.

Figure 5.6 Play Speech Button.

QuickTime Movies versus Sound Files

Adobe Acrobat supports both audio contained in QuickTime Movies (in other words, a QuickTime movie file that contains audio content but no video content) or sound files (AIFF or WAV). If you reference a QuickTime Movie from within an Acrobat document, it creates an external link to the movie file. The movie file has to accompany the Acrobat document that refers to it to ensure playback. Sound files, on the other hand, are actually embedded in the Acrobat document and become part of the PDF file (so you don't have to include the source sound file when you distribute the Acrobat document). The sound will play back from within the Acrobat document without needing any external references.

WARNING Acrobat does not support compressed audio file formats (such as ADPCM), so if you have a sound file using one of the compression schemes, you should convert it to uncompressed form in one of the digital sound processing applications (such as Sound Forge or SoundEdit 2). As is the case for presenting any form of audio on the Web, you should always reduce the sampling rate and sample size to the most compact size acceptable for the sound quality that you want. Embedded Acrobat sound files, if prepared carefully, work well at 11KHz sample rate, 8-bit samples, in mono format. Keep in mind that the sound file becomes part of the Acrobat document and will boost the PDF file size accordingly. Multiple sound files on a single Acrobat page may slow down the page-at-a-time loading that is available for PDF files optimized under Acrobat version 3. You might want to consider distributing multiple sound files across several pages to provide faster individual page loading.

Accessing an Acrobat Document from HTML

Acrobat files can be included in HTML documents in a number of different ways. The display of these files is dependent on the selected browser and its current settings. One of the most reliable means of providing access to PDF content is through a simple link. If we take the PDF file created in the previous section and make it accessible through an HTML document, the resulting code might look something like the following example:

```
<HTML>

<HEAD><TITLE>Great Speeches from History</TITLE>

</HEAD>

<CENTER><H1>Memorable Speeches in Time</H1></CENTER>

<HR>

<BODY>

We've gathered together some of the finest speeches of the last 500 years on

this unique Web site. You can sample them with descriptions and full audio

through the following links...<P>

<I>Hernando Swift's soliloquies</I><P>

<A HREF="conch.pdf">Swift speech</A><P>

.....other links inserted here...

</BODY>

</HTML>
```

Clicking on the link in this example will retrieve the PDF file referenced in the HREF entry. In most cases, this will result in the PDF document being shown in line within the browser window, as illustrated in Figure 5.7. Note that the full range of Acrobat controls appears on the toolbar inside the browser window, so you can navigate, zoom, search, and perform the full assortment of Acrobat functions. For some browsers, particularly those predating versions 3.0 of Internet Explorer and Navigator, clicking the link may launch Adobe Acrobat Reader as a helper application (if it is installed on the client system).

Another option that works well for recent browsers is to use the <EMBED> tag. The <EMBED> tag can be recognized reliably by versions 3.0 of Internet Explorer and Navigator, as well as compatible browsers. In v3.0 Internet Explorer, this places the entire document into the Web page with the full Acrobat toolbar. In v3.0 Navigator, only the document—not the controls—appears. Links are also enabled only for the first page. Whereas Explorer supports the full range of links on each page, the Netscape Communicator package, with Navigator 4, supports the <EMBED> entry a bit differently. For example, the following <EMBED> entry

Figure 5.7 Acrobat document displayed in the browser window.

places an image of the Acrobat document into the Web page as a thumbnail (a *large* thumbnail, as shown in Figure 5.8).

```
<EMBED SRC="conch.pdf WIDTH=25% HEIGHT=200>  Swift speech<P>
```

If you right-click on the thumbnail image, Navigator 4 lets you download the referenced Acrobat document, which is displayed full screen with all controls.

Using the <OBJECT> Tag

For a viewing audience that includes Internet Explorer 3.0 and later browsers, the <OBJECT> tag can be used to embed PDF documents in an HTML document. Using this option, of course, creates an incompatibility for Navigator users, so you would either want to automatically detect the browser type using JavaScript and direct page flow accordingly or provide a user-controlled branch in HTML for an alternate path.

The <OBJECT> tag provides some options beyond the <EMBED> tag, including the ability to provide interactions with a PDF document using JavaScript or VBScript. You can use the Print and AboutBox methods in the ActiveX control.

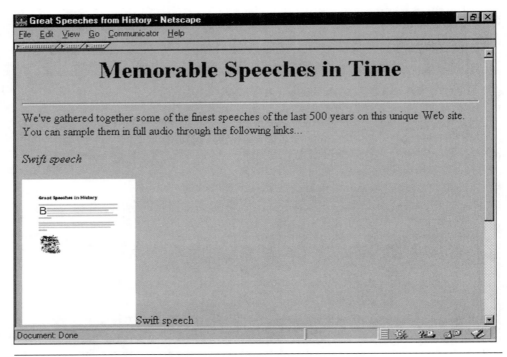

Figure 5.8 Navigator 4 thumbnail display.

This feature makes it possible to construct a **Print** button that appears in the HTML page and will print the entire range of pages in the PDF document. If you try to print an embedded PDF document using the browser **Print** option, only the first page of the document will be printed, so this is a valuable addition. Someone who wants to print a PDF document in its entirety can always save the PDF document file, open it in Acrobat Reader, and print from Reader, but this is obviously a much more roundabout technique.

If your goal is to insert a PDF file (called legend.pdf) into an HTML file using the <OBJECT> tag, the following code will work:

```
<OBJECT CLASSID="clsid:CA8A9780-280D-11CF-A24D-44455354000 WIDTH=423 HEIGHT=333
ID=Pdf1>

<PARAM NAME="SRC" VALUE="legend.pdf">

</OBJECT>
```

For scenarios where you want to provide support for browsers that don't recognize the <OBJECT> tag, you can use <EMBED> and/or <NOEMBED> entries as shown in the following example (using a sample PDF file name of "lore.pdf"):

```
<OBJECT CLASSID="clsid:CA8A9780-280D-11CF-A24D-44455354000 WIDTH=423 HEIGHT=333
ID=Pdf1>

<PARAM NAME="SRC" VALUE="lore.pdf">

<EMBED SRC="lore.pdf" HEIGHT=423 WIDTH=333>

<NOEMBED>

<IMG SRC="lore_pic.gif" alt="Lore pamphlett" WIDTH=179 HEIGHT=134>

</NOEMBED>

</OBJECT>
```

The <NOEMBED> option, in this case, displays a GIF image in place of the embedded content.

Page-at-a-Time Viewing

The cleanest way to deliver PDF files to your site visitors is through page-at-a-time viewing. If a browser supports PDF files for direct viewing and the server supports byte serving, Acrobat documents are displayed page-by-page (rather than downloading an entire PDF file prior to viewing anything). For viewing and navigating through large PDF documents, this can obviously save a considerable amount of time. Download delays are quite short—about what you can expect when accessing streaming audio files. The person viewing your PDF documents doesn't have to do anything to enable page-at-a-time viewing, but the server does have to be set up for this option, either through a CGI application or built-in support.

 Adobe posts a list of server applications that support this byte-serving approach at:

www.adobe.com/acrobat/moreinfo.

There is one option that viewers can select to continue downloading the remainder of a PDF document while one page is being displayed. Selecting the **Allow Background Download of Entire File** option in the General Preferences menu of Navigator activates this option.

Adobe Acrobat offers a reliable vehicle for transporting audio information over the Web and has the advantage that the content can be freely accessed outside the confines of the browser window—for example, the free Acrobat player can be bundled on a recordable CD along with a collection of PDF files (or on other removable media, such as Zip or Jaz cartridges). Many organizations (such as the Internal Revenue Service) use PDF files to shuttle forms and other formatted data across the Internet. There's no reason you can't use the same distribution method for a file full of howling rock stars or an audio sampling of the birdsongs of North America.

Audio Embedded in Movie Formats

Audio content on the World Wide Web can come in many sizes and shapes. One particularly useful means for delivering audio material is through well-understood, well-supported "movie" formats. Shockwave and QuickTime are two examples of strongly supported industry standards, which support movie content (animation and video) through the use of plug-ins. Movie content, of course, has both an audio and a video component; there is no reason you can't use the audio component as a stable means for delivering sound through an HTML document. Macromedia's Shockwave and Apple's QuickTime are both busily improving support for event synchronization, something that is always difficult given the asynchronous operation of the Web.

For situations where you may want to coordinate the audio content with other events going on within a Web page, perhaps through the use of JavaScript or VBScript, the controlled environments offered by Shockwave and QuickTime can be preferable over other methods of synchronizing audio with onscreen activities.

Working with QuickTime

The Apple Macintosh is still the chosen platform for the vast majority of multimedia development, and the application tools available for work in this area are often superior to those you can find for use under Windows. The careful integration of multimedia support into the MacOS creates far fewer problems that you're likely to encounter under Windows when working with audio, video, complex graphics, animation, or 3D rendering. For these reasons, it's worth considering using QuickTime as the means for delivering audio material across the Web. To do this, you only need to create a QuickTime Movie that contains audio data and then save it in a format that can be used on both platforms.

Creating a QuickTime Audio Clip

To illustrate the process of creating an audio clip that runs under QuickTime on both Mac and Windows platforms, let's start on the Macintosh and create a QuickTime movie with embedded audio (and no video). This example uses Avid VideoShop to create the QuickTime movie, but you could just as easily use Adobe Premiere or another application with QuickTime production capabilities.

Avid VideoShop shows the movie contents as a series of tracks, as shown in Figure 5.9, with the available clips, consisting of audio, video, animations, and MIDI files, shown in a separate window (labeled Tutorial Clips in this example). Creating a movie involves dragging clips onto the appropriate tracks and assembling them into the correctly timed sequence.

The two tracks shown in the default window support video and digital audio; if you were creating a movie containing these two elements, you could simply drag each appropriate clip onto an individual track and then VideoShop combines the two within the movie. For this example, we'll drag the clip containing MIDI data into the Sequencer window. Each track corresponds with a particular data type, so first you need to use the **Add Track** command. Click and hold the button titled **Add Tracks** in the Sequencer window to pull down the options and select the **Track** type—in this case, a MIDI Track. VideoShow adds an additional track for MIDI data to the Sequencer window.

Figure 5.9 Work environment within Avid VideoShop.

For this example, we've dragged a MIDI clip entitled "Nina's Eyes" onto the track. When you drag a MIDI clip onto the track designated for MIDI data, VideoShop displays a dialog box for further specifying the MIDI options. The dialog box (Figure 5.10) shows the two individual MIDI tracks and their selected voices, as determined when the General MIDI file was first saved—in this case, two tracks designated using the Acoustic Grand Piano voice. You can freely choose different voices for the MIDI tracks, including any of those General MIDI instruments supported as part of the GM standard, by clicking the **Instrument** button and making a selection. You can also choose the synthesizer type for playback. The **Best Synthesizer** option allows an external synthesizer to be used in place of the built-in QuickTime playback. You can sample the playback right from this dialog box, allowing you to check the effects of different voices on the song contents.

After you've chosen the options for MIDI playback, select **OK** and then drag the icon for the clip to the starting point of the MIDI track in the Sequencer window. Because you need only the single audio track, pull down the Sequence menu and choose the **Remove Track** command with the Sound Track selected. This deletes the

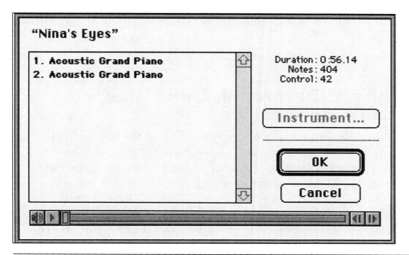

Figure 5.10 MIDI options for "Nina's Eyes."

track from the sequence. You can use this same command to remove the Video Track, leaving only the single MIDI Track sequence. Save the file as a movie, making sure that the **Cross Platform format** option is checked, and you have a QuickTime file ready for playback when embedded in an HTML document (or through the MoviePlayer utility available on both the Windows and Mac platforms). The most remarkable part of this process is the compactness of the resulting files. The MIDI file, Nina's Song, used in this example, when saved in movie file format (MOV) occupies only 4K, yet the song provides about a minute of music. When played back using the sound synthesis built into QuickTime, the quality is impressive, equal to many of the wavetable synthesizer sound boards that rely on stored samples of GM instruments.

Digital audio files can be contained in a VideoShop movie in exactly the same manner. You simply drag a clip designated as an AIFF sound file into the appropriate point in the Sequencer window. A series of clips could be stacked and combined and then saved as a movie. Depending on the sample rate and resolution of the audio file, the movie size will be significantly larger than a comparable MIDI file, but judicious processing and compacting can still achieve reasonable quality in a small file size.

The player that appears for QuickTime playback relies on the QuickTime plug-in being available for the browser. Figure 5.11 shows the QuickTime plug-in as implemented for playback of a file at the OpCode Systems Web site, a company that offers a wide range of MIDI and digital audio products. As with similar types of multimedia players, the QuickTime player occupies its own window independent of the window from which it was called from the browser.

High-Quality MIDI through QuickTime Music Architecture

One of the classic difficulties with putting MIDI files on the Web is that the Web author can't control the quality of playback because it is impossible to predict what kind of sound board or MIDI synthesizer the person accessing the file has. This worry becomes less important through the use of Apple's QuickTime Music Architecture (QTMA). QTMA utilizes software synthesis—the sounds of individual MIDI voices are shaped through wavetable synthesis based on Roland's *Sound Canvas* library of instrument sounds. This well-respected collection of sounds has been ported to both the Mac and Windows platforms through the QuickTime architecture, and the result is a rich, expressive means for delivering MIDI-based music through almost any kind of sound board (or through the built-in sound-handling abilities of the Macintosh). Users, of course, have the option of choosing another MIDI output device—other than the QuickTime synthesis—such as a full-sized synthesizer attached to a MIDI port on the computer or an internal sound board that also performs wavetable synthesis. The advantage, of course, is that the lowest common denominator offered through QTMA is far superior to any kind of FM synthesis, so that websters with inexpensive sound boards can still hear excellent MIDI music with the lowest bandwidth requirements of any kind of Web-delivered sound.

Embedding QuickTime

By now you've probably realized that when we talk about embedding something in an HTML document, we're talking about using the <EMBED> tag. QuickTime files are no exception. Movies that contain video content require a HEIGHT and WIDTH entry to determine the correct size to display the player. For audio content, these entries are optional. If you don't include a HEIGHT and WIDTH entry, the QuickTime player inserts a compact pair of controls consisting of a small speaker icon (for volume control) and a single play button. Apple, however, states that the WIDTH and HEIGHT parameters are mandatory, so—even though this approach seems to work—it might be safer to specify the WIDTH and HEIGHT in all cases. With the minimal panel, the **Play** button converts to a pause button once playback begins. If you specify a minimal WIDTH=136 entry, QuickTime also provides a slider control that allows someone to selectively play different segments of the audio selection.

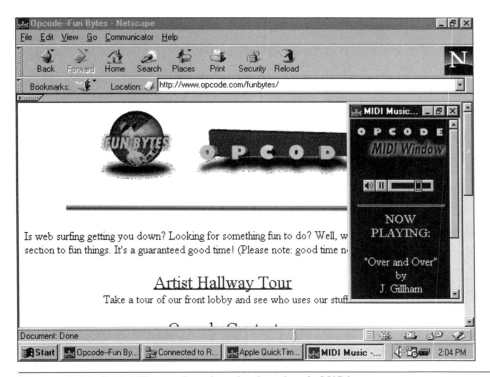

Figure 5.11 QuickTime plug-in playing back MIDI.

To embed a QuickTime movie (containing audio only) titled "parade.mov" with the smallest audio player, the <EMBED> entry should read as follows:

```
<EMBED SRC="parade.mov">
```

If you want to provide a larger player with a slider bar for moving to different parts of the audio clip, the entry should read:

```
<EMBED SRC="parade.mov" HEIGHT=18 WIDTH=136>
```

As an example of how a QuickTime movie might appear in a typical HTML document, consider the following code:

```
<HTML>

<HEAD><TITLE>Music Machinations</TITLE>

</HEAD>

<CENTER><H1>A Preview of Nina's Eyes</H1></CENTER><P>
```

```
<HR>

<P>Noted pianist Clara Brittonia will be performing "Nina's Eyes", as well as

other classical pieces, Friday, October 24th, at Plaza Stadium. A brief excerpt

follows:<P>

<I>"Nina's Eyes"</I>

<EMBED SRC="nina2.mov" HEIGHT=18 WIDTH=136 AUTOPLAY=TRUE>

<I>Performed by Clara Brittonia</I>

<P>We hope to see you there.

<HR>

</BODY>

</HTML>
```

This HTML document displayed in a browser appears as shown in Figure 5.12.

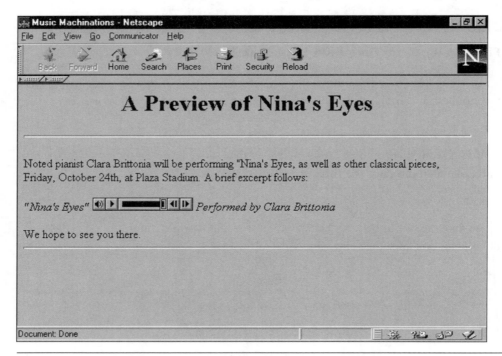

Figure 5.12 QuickTime player in an HTML document.

Because the AUTOPLAY=TRUE entry was included between the <EMBED> tags, the QuickTime player will begin playing back the MIDI clip immediately on downloading. The controls provided in the QuickTime player console allow someone to stop or repeat sections of the song. QuickTime includes a number of additional features that work within the <EMBED> tags, as described in the following section.

EMBED Syntax for QuickTime

There are some additional parameters available to the QuickTime player that are unique to this plug-in. Some of these are appropriate only to special-purpose QuickTime operations, such as displaying VRML sequences, but others can be used effectively with audio. Only those with audio significance are listed.

CACHE The CACHE parameter indicates whether a QuickTime movie should be stored in the browser cache region in the same manner as previously viewed documents are stored. Caching a movie makes it quicker to access because it doesn't have to be downloaded a second time if the viewer returns to the same page containing the movie file. The CACHE parameter accepts either TRUE or FALSE values. For example, if you want to enable caching for a movie titled "breakout.mov," the entry should read:

```
<EMBED SRC="breakout.mov" HEIGHT=18 WIDTH=136 CACHE=TRUE>
```

This parameter works only in Netscape Navigator.

VOLUME The VOLUME parameter lets you determine a relative volume level setting for the audio playback ranging from 0 to 256. The default volume setting is maximum (256). If you wanted to set the volume level to half for playing back the movie "nuisance.mov," the entry would be:

```
<EMBED SRC="nusiance.mov" VOLUME=128 HEIGHT=176 WIDTH=136>
```

The HEIGHT and WIDTH settings assume that the movie contains video as well as sound.

PLUGINSPAGE By specifying a URL, you can indicate the address to download the latest QuickTime plug-in with this parameter. The browser displays a message indicating that the plug-in can be downloaded and requests instructions as to how to proceed. To point the browser to the correct site for loading the QuickTime plug-in, the entry should read as follows:

```
<EMBED SRC="sample.mov" HEIGHT=18 WIDTH=136
PLUGINSPAGE="http://quicktime.apple.com">
```

WIDTH This required parameter indicates the width on an HTML page to reserve for the embedded QuickTime movie. It always works in combination with the HEIGHT parameter. If your movie contains video content, as well as audio, and you don't know the exact size of the movie, you can use the MoviePlayer program supplied with QuickTime to obtain the correct size. Drop down the Movie menu and choose the **Get Movie Info** option.

The WIDTH settings affects which of the audio control panels to display if a QuickTime movie consists of only audio content. With a WIDTH of 136, the control panel includes a volume button, a play button, a slider, and forward and reverse buttons. As you drop down the WIDTH below 136, the forward and reverse buttons are dropped and the slider is reduced in size. At a WIDTH of 48, the player displays only a volume button and a play/pause button. Drop down to a WIDTH of 24, and you'll see only the **Play** button. Choose a WIDTH setting that provides the appropriate controls for the audio that you want to present. For a short speech, you might want to use only the volume and a play button, as supported by the following code:

```
<EMBED SRC="speech.mov" HEIGHT=18 WIDTH=48>
```

The resulting display would include only the volume button and play button. If you use a WIDTH setting that is larger than the maximum size audio console, QuickTime centers the player within the specified space.

HEIGHT The HEIGHT parameter is also required for a QuickTime entry. If your QuickTime audio includes a video component as well, use the height of the movie frame (as determined from the **Get Movie Info** option of the MoviePlayer utility). Add 24 pixels to this height if you want to include the console controls for movie playback, which appear directly below the frame. Apple recommends that you do not specify a HEIGHT setting less than 2. If you're trying to completely eliminate display of the player, use the HIDDEN parameter, rather than reducing the HEIGHT or WIDTH options. For a typical movie with both audio and video content, the <EMBED> entry might read:

```
<EMBED SRC="gorilla.mov" HEIGHT=176 WIDTH=136>
```

HIDDEN The HIDDEN setting prevents the display of any player components or movie frames. Because no controls are available to initiate playback, you should use this in combination with the AUTOPLAY=TRUE entry. This parameter is most frequently used to initiate playback of a sound-only movie without controls; you might also want to use it to play audio from an existing movie without displaying the video content. A typical entry might read:

```
<EMBED SRC="hat_song.mov" HIDDEN>
```

Note that the HIDDEN parameter doesn't require any attributes.

AUTOPLAY The AUTOPLAY=TRUE entry instructs the QuickTime player to start playback immediately. If the QuickTime version 2.5 Movie Player has been used to convert the file, playback begins shortly after the first frame of the movie is downloaded (rather than after the entire file is downloaded). QuickTime triggers playback at the point in time that it estimates that it can keep the movie streaming without having to pause for additional data. By default, AUTOPLAY=FALSE is set.

CONTROLLER The CONTROLLER setting determines whether the movie controller will be visible on the page. A setting of CONTROLLER=TRUE makes it visible; CONTROLLER=FALSE hides it.

LOOP The LOOP setting determines whether the movie should be played continuously. TRUE indicates the selection should loop; FALSE indicates that the movie should not loop. Another interesting parameter, PALINDROME, causes a movie to play forward and then backward. This might be used to alternately display an animation moving forward and backward, but it doesn't make sense for audio and has no effect on MIDI file playback. To set a movie to cycle forward and backward, you could use this entry:

```
<EMBED SRC="bo_ball.mov" LOOP=PALINDROME HEIGHT=176 WIDTH=136>
```

 The other QuickTime parameters have relevance only for QuickTime VR Objects and Panoramas. If you're interested in this aspect of QuickTime presentations, you can get more information from:

quicktime.apple.com

Accelerating QuickTime Playback

Version 2.5 of QuickTime includes features that accelerate the playback of an embedded QuickTime movie. To achieve these benefits, regardless of the source of the movie, you should open and save it with the MoviePlayer program that ships with QuickTime 2.5. With the movie prepared in this manner, the initial frame of a movie begins playing back almost immediately. Using a technique similar to streaming audio, the frame is displayed and the movie starts playback while the remainder of the movie file is still being downloaded from the Web. If the AUTO-PLAY=TRUE entry is added within the <EMBED> tags, audio files begin playing almost immediately after the download begins.

Apple also offers a batch conversion tool called the Internet Movie Tool that performs file modification on earlier QuickTime movies to give them this accelerated edge. The Internet Movie Tool can be downloaded from Apple's QuickTime Software Page. It works on the Macintosh platform and implements the conversion simply by dragging any QuickTime movie file to the Internet Movie Tool icon and dropping it. The conversion begins immediately. This conversion process ensures that the QuickTime movie file contains appropriate information in the resource fork for cross-platform playback and that all file data is in the cross-platform format. This tool also moves any *meta* data from the end of a QuickTime movie to the beginning where, under QuickTime 2.5, this information can be used to accelerate the start of playback.

QuickTime Support for MPEG

Apple has bolstered the QuickTime multimedia environment by extending it to support MPEG-1 (Moving Picture Experts Group). The QuickTime MPEG extension, available initially only for PowerPC Mac OS machines, provides full-screen playback of MPEG-1 and VideoCD audio and video files. This is a software-only solution that uses streaming techniques to begin playback of MPEG content shortly after the file begins loading. The MPEG extension is designed to be fully compatible with the QuickTime plug-ins that operate with Microsoft Internet Explorer and Netscape Navigator, and the architecture is intended to reduce the normal multimedia delays that occur because of slow dial-up interconnections.

MPEG-encoded audio streams at CD-quality sample levels (44KHz, 16-bit, stereo) can be delivered using this technology. The integration of MPEG into the QuickTime Media Layer architecture offers some powerful options to developers, including:

- The ability to use MPEG embedded bookmarks, allowing applications to interact with specific points in a file

- Advance and reverse through a multimedia sequence frame-by frame

- Incorporation of different media types into an MPEG file through clipboard insertions

- Access to advanced controls for movie productions, including movie layering, compositing, and graphic-mode controls

- Adding new tracks consisting of audio files or MIDI sound files into a stream of MPEG material

Web authors looking to gain an advantage in the swiftly changing multimedia game are encouraged to look further into the possibilities offered by this latest QuickTime development.

Using Shockwave for Audio

The folks at Macromedia, long-time leaders in multimedia authoring and development for desktop and CD-ROM applications, have channeled a good percentage of their recent efforts toward making multimedia content easily accessible through the World Wide Web. One of the main vehicles in this drive is Shockwave, available as a plug-in that essentially provides run-time support for many of Macromedia's leading multimedia products within the browser window. Support for Macromedia Director, Authorware, Freehand, and Flash allows developers to work in familiar multimedia authoring environments while creating files that can add some multimedia flair to the Internet. Shockwave plug-ins are available for most of the major computing platforms. Not one to overlook the benefits of audio, Macromedia has also focused some of their attention on refining the audio components of Shockwave so that properly prepared files (stored in Shockwave Audio format with an .swa extension) can be delivered in streaming mode. Shockwave audio files can be prepared directly in Macromedia's SoundEdit 16 version 2 digital audio processing application using a variety of sample rates and formats. Macromedia provides various-size players that can be stored as Director movies and used in combination with Shockwave audio files to provide streaming audio output. The setup is fairly simple, and the entire configuration can be dropped into an HTML document using the ubiquitous <EMBED> entry.

One of the strengths of using Shockwave audio is that clever use of Macromedia's scripting language—Lingo—can interactively control the audio playback. Lingo sees the audio as what it refers to as a Streaming Cast member with definable properties. By manipulating these properties, a Web author can exert more control over the audio dimension than with some of the other methods for delivering sound. Lingo requires some effort to master, as does its parent application, Macromedia Director, but there are some benefits to learning a scripting language that can be so tightly mapped to online multimedia components.

Creating a Shockwave Audio File

Macromedia has devised a special format for Shockwave audio files that is necessary to support the streaming audio behavior. Sound files embedded in a Director movie destined for Shockwave conversion are converted into this format automatically as part of the Shockwave transformation. Director 5 and later versions require that a Shockwave plug-in resides in the Xtras folder to carry out this conversion. You can also create the Shockwave audio files directly from Macromedia's SoundEdit 16 version 2 from the **Export** option on the File menu. The conversion technique includes selecting the estimated rate—in bits per second—that the audio material will be delivered. Determining the appropriate rate will influence how effectively the streaming feature works on slower dial-up connections to the Internet (14.4Kbps to 56Kbps).

If your Shockwave audio content is contained within a Director movie, you can follow the conventional technique for producing a Shocked Director movie (the Shockwave equivalent to a standard movie file). If you're running Director 5 under Windows or the Macintosh, you may need to obtain or update the Xtras plug-in for Shockwave.

The Xtras plug-in is available for free from Macromedia's Web site at:

www.macromedia.com

This site tends to have a lot of traffic, and the URLs change quite frequently, so we won't try to give you the precise download area for Shockwave files. The path will be easily identified from the introductory Web page.

To create a Shocked Director movie:

1. Complete the movie, making sure that you don't use those Director features that don't translate to Web delivery (the list is small—check the current documentation). The behavior of Director movies in a browser can vary slightly from desktop delivery. Take care with high-calorie embedded content—such as audio and video clips—as these can significantly increase download times. Be aware of data transmission issues.

2. With the movie saved, select the **Afterburner** option from the Director 5 Xtras menu. This appears as an option only if you have obtained and installed the Shockwave plug-in.

3. Complete the conversion using Afterburner and save the file to the appropriate folder. The default extension is .dcr; for recognition by browsers, you should keep this extension.

4. Transfer the shocked movie file to the HTTP Web server that will be distributing it. The server must be configured to handle Director movies in Shockwave format.

5. Access the Director files from any Shockwave-compatible browser, such as versions 3.0 or later of Microsoft Internet Explorer or Netscape Navigator.

To create a Shockwave audio file for use in streaming mode through an appropriately configured player:

1. Prepare the audio content in a sound processing application, such as Macromedia SoundEdit 16 version 2.

2. Downsample to obtain an appropriate file size. For fast Web playback, you might want to use 8-bit sample, 11KHz, mono format. For higher quality, use 16-bit, 22KHz, mono format. Stereo is a luxury on the Web. Use it only if essential. Figure 5.13 shows a WAV file downsampled to 8-bit, 11KHz mono ready for export to Shockwave audio format from SoundEdit 16.

3. From the Xtras menu, select **Shockwave for Audio Settings**.

4. Choose a bit rate that is appropriate for your intended delivery method. If your target audience is running 28.8Kbps modems, a bit rate of 16KBits/second is conservative. You can try 24KBits/second with the understanding that this may not be a realistic level during peak Internet traffic. This setting will not affect the quality of the sound in the file, but it may affect whether there are skips or pauses during the streaming playback. If the bit rate supports it, you can keep a selection in Stereo format, but at rates under 48KBits/second, the compression utility automatically converts to mono format.

5. From the File menu, select **Export**. From the Export Type menu, select **SWA** file and assign a filename and destination folder.

6. Click **Save** to start the conversion process. The SWA Exporter box provides a progress bar as the conversion takes place. A two-minute WAV file should only take a couple of minutes or so to convert.

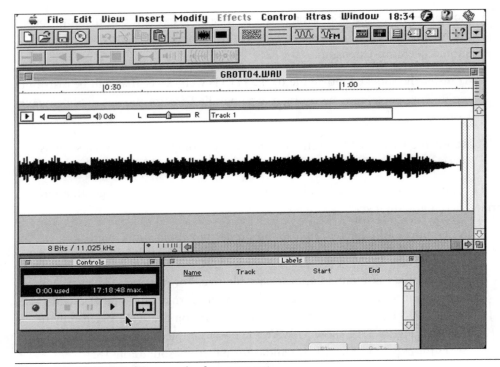

Figure 5.13 WAV file ready for export.

Once you have the file in SWA format, it's ready to drop into an HTML document, as explained in the following section.

Embedding a Shockwave Audio File in an HTML Document

Shockwave audio provides a convenient means for offering streaming audio playback in a simple manner. The package that is provided with the Shockwave Audio Xtras plug-in includes a sample player, constructed as a Director movie file (player.dcr) that can be used in combination with the <EMBED> command in an HTML document. Depending on the size specified in the HEIGHT and WIDTH settings within EMBED, the player can occupy four different sizes with a different display and controls for each. The following example shows a size that presents a simple Shockwave pushbutton to start and stop playback, a title window that can be set to display the name of the selection playing, and a progress bar that indicates the playback progress.

The player.dcr file and the converted Shockwave Audio file should be stored in the same directory as the HTML document referencing them, or the appropriate URL should be provided as part of the <EMBED> entries. Use the technique described in the previous section to create the appropriately formatted Shockwave audio file to use with the player.

The HTML code for this example follows:

```
<HTML>

<HEAD><TITLE>Shockwave Streaming Audio</TITLE>

</HEAD>

<CENTER><H1>Journey to the Grotto</H1></CENTER><P>

<HR>

<P>We have the honor to showcase the latest work of David Purcell, "At the

Grotto," soon to be released on his new CD.<P>

<I>"At the Grotto"</I><P>

<EMBED WIDTH=295 HEIGHT=32 SRC="player.dcr" SW1=off swURL="grotto.swa"

swText="At the Grotto" swPreLoadTime=3 sw2=0 sw3=1>

<P><I>Coming to a music dealer near you...</I>

<P>Thanks for listening!

<HR>

</BODY>

</HTML>
```

This code displays the player, which is enclosed in the simple Director movie—player.dcr—and begins playing the Shockwave audio file as soon as someone clicks the **Shockwave** button. Figure 5.14 shows how the player appears in the browser window.

Reducing the dimensions of the HEIGHT and WIDTH can shrink the player down to a simple Shockwave rectangle that can be clicked to start playback and clicked again to pause. Note that the <EMBED> entry also contains three switches: SW1, SW2, and SW3.

SW1 is a debugger mode. When set to SW1=ON, the Player movie provides messages and authoring details that help debug playback from your site. Make sure this switch is set to SW=OFF before you place a movie on the site for final delivery.

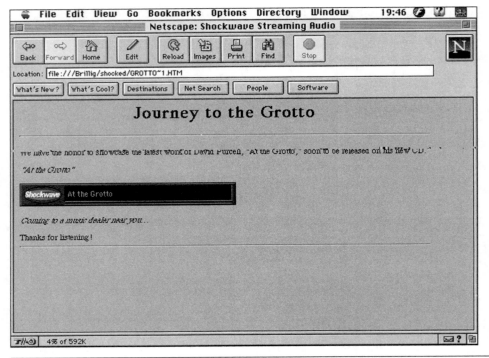

Figure 5.14 Shockwave Audio player in action.

SW2 is the AUTOPLAY switch. If you set SW2=1, the player will begin playing the indicated song as soon as the streaming audio content is partially downloaded. SW3 is what Macromedia calls LOGOMODE; we are still trying to figure out exactly what it does.

Note that the title of the Shocked Audio file appears following the swURL= entry. You could use a URL other than the local folder to access a more remote file, such as:

```
swURL="http://www.bungie_jump.com/screams/scream1.swa"
```

The player itself could be stored at another location and accessed with a URL, such as:

```
SRC="http://www.squid.com/multimedia/player.dcr"
```

Use the SW1=ON setting to debug playback from whatever site locations you choose until you have the streaming audio operating efficiently.

Download Guidelines

Just as a basic guideline as to how long downloads will take, Macromedia has calculated the following estimates. For a tiny movie consisting of small graphics and simple animation, approximately 30Kb of data, downloading will take 30 seconds with a 14.4Kbps connection and 10 seconds with a 28.8Kbps connection. A compact Director movie, ranging in size from 100 to 200Kb, will take 180 to 300 seconds at 14.4Kbps and 90 to 180 seconds at 28.8Kbps. If your movie contains a video clip and is around 500Kb, Macromedia considers the download time excessive for 14.4Kbps. For 28.8Kbps connections, the download will take about 120 to 240 seconds. Plan your movie content wisely to avoid annoying your users. The current generation of 56Kbps modems should help open up some additional multimedia options as they become more prevalent.

Server Configuration for Shockwave

Plug-ins invariably require some server setup to provide support for the file types—referred to as MIME types—that will be handled during data transfers. Each server has a different means for configuring MIME types, but the same basic setup actions usually apply.

If you obtain your Internet access through an Internet Service Provider, ask your ISP to add the following MIME types to the server where your public directory space is located. If you're administering the server yourself, the following MIME type entries should be made for Director files:

- application/x-director dir

- application/x-director dcr

- application/x-director dxr

These settings are commonly made using an AddType entry, such as:

```
AddType application/x-director dir
```

The Shockwave Audio format is supported through the director MIME types shown. No additional setup is required to configure the server for audio playback of Shockwave files.

Odds are that if you're getting Web space through an ISP, the server is already set up to handle Director movies in Shockwave format. This particular format has achieved a good deal of popularity across the Web.

Using Basic JavaScript for Audio Control

JavaScript is a compact, adaptable scripting language for controlling objects in an HTML document (not to be confused with Java). For Web authors looking for new ways to deliver information, including audio content, over the Web, JavaScript offers considerable flexibility and control. JavaScript operates like a streamlined, special-purpose version of the C++ language (sharing many of the same constructions) that is targeted for maximum interaction with the elements of a typical HTML document: forms, frames, body content, links, embedded objects, applets, and so on. JavaScript can even be combined with VBScript (in some environments) for even more control of everything that appears in HTML form, including ActiveX controls.

The downside of this, of course, is that you have to learn a new language in order to use JavaScript effectively. The learning curve is not as difficult as something like Java or C++; the language elements are fewer and the architecture is far more forgiving. However, it is still a programming language at heart, and it is a bit more difficult to master than learning how to mark up a document with HTML. Without a lot of training, you can drop short scripts into your HTML documents to accomplish certain tasks, usually without having to change very much of a script. Some of the examples given in this section are simple enough to do this. More extensive examples appear in the next chapter.

Resources for Learning JavaScript

If you're not familiar with programming in JavaScript, and this section spurs your interest, you might want to obtain a book to guide you through the learning process. Three possibilities include: *The JavaScript Sourcebook* by Gordon McComb (published by John Wiley & Sons, 1996); *JavaScript for the World Wide Web* by Ted Gesing and Jeremy Schneider (published by Peachpit Press, 1997); and *The ABC's of JavaScript* by Lee Purcell (hmmm...does that name sound familiar?) and Mary Jane Mara (published by Sybex, 1997). All of these are a good bet to get you off to a strong start toward becoming an effective JavaScript programmer.

Simple JavaScript Example

JavaScript can be used to control the playback in a number of different ways. Sounds can be played when a page loads, when a certain condition is satisfied, when the mouse passes over an object in the browser window, or when a link is accessed. The following example shows how a link associated with an image can be used to playback an audio clip.

```
<HTML>

<HEAD><TITLE>The Calls of Flying Grackles</TITLE>

<SCRIPT LANGUAGE="JavaScript">

function play(){

        window.location="grackles.wav"

}

</SCRIPT>

</HEAD>

<CENTER><H1>Grackle Calls Central</H1></CENTER><P>

<STRONG>Ornithologist F. T. Catte has collected samples of grackle migrations.

Click on the image to hear a sample audio clip. </STRONG><P>

<A HREF="javascript:play()"><IMG SRC="felix.gif" BORDER=1></A>

<HR>

</BODY>

</HTML>
```

The JavaScript function defined in the <HEAD> of the HTML document called play() uses the location property of the document window to point to the audio content, in this case, a file named "grackles.wav." This is enough to trigger audio playback using Netscape's LiveAudio plug-in or the equivalent audio handling in Microsoft Internet Explorer. A player is displayed in a separate window and the audio begins playing as soon as it is loaded.

The link itself contains an entry that indicates that the JavaScript play() function should be called—javascript:play()—when the link is clicked. When the link is clicked and the play() function called, JavaScript accesses the specified audio clip and playback begins. The browser displays the page contents as shown in Figure 5.15.

This is one of the simplest ways to use JavaScript to initiate audio playback. The link itself could be modified in any of the available ways provided in HTML; for

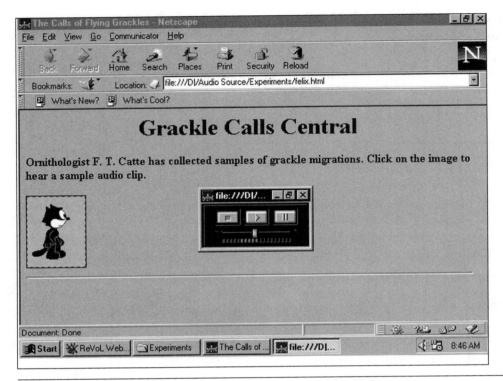

Figure 5.15 Triggering audio playback through a link.

example, you could substitute a descriptive text string in place of the image to identify the sound file to be played and to list its size.

Getting Permission to Play

Not everyone appreciates having audio content thrust on them as they are browsing the Web. For example, in an office setting, you don't want an unexpected audio clip from the latest release of Nine Inch Nails spewing from the speakers unannounced. You can use JavaScript to query visitors to your pages whether they want to hear audio content.

The following script determines whether or not to play the audio based on the response of the site visitor.

```
<HTML>

<HEAD><TITLE>The Calls of Flying Grackles</TITLE>

<SCRIPT LANGUAGE="JavaScript">
```

```
if (confirm("Would you like to hear grackles singing while you browse this
⌐site?")) {

        document.write("<EMBED SRC="grackles.wav" HEIGHT=62 WIDTH=160
AUTOSTART=TRUE LOOP=TRUE>")

} else {

alert("You don't know what you're missing...")

}

</SCRIPT>

</HEAD>

<CENTER><H1>Grackle Calls Central</H1></CENTER><P>

<STRONG>Welcome, fellow bird lovers!</STRONG><P>

<HR>

</BODY>

</HTML>
```

The first thing this code does is place a prompt on screen, as shown in Figure 5.16, that asks the users, "Would you like to hear grackles singing as you browse this site?" If the user answers "Yes" to the prompt, the If portion of the clause is executed, and the document.write method writes the <EMBED> entry into the body of the HTML document. This brings up an audio player and begins playing the specified file immediately (AUTOSTART=TRUE).

The LOOP=TRUE entry ensures that the sound will keep recycling over and over until the user grows tired of hearing it and clicks the **Stop** button or until another page is accessed. Use the **LOOP** option with discretion; certain audio sequences could get very annoying in a fairly short period of time.

If the user selects "Cancel" to the initial prompt, JavaScript displays an alert box assuring them, "You don't know what you're missing." The page then continues loading without the embedded audio content. This is a simple technique, but one that is bound to be appreciated by those websters who prefer silent browsing.

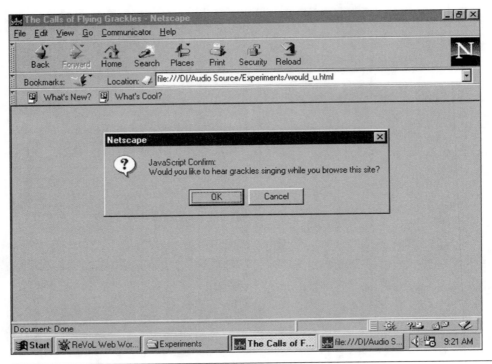

Figure 5.16 Would you like to hear grackles singing?

More Complex Scripting

The HTML and JavaScript examples presented so far use only the most basic techniques available for presenting audio. You can achieve much more interesting audio interaction within an HTML document by using more complex scripting, either through JavaScript or VBScript or by using Java applets with multimedia components included within them. The next chapter discusses these types of approaches and provides a number of techniques to increase your audio-authoring prowess.

6

Scripting Techniques
for Internet Audio

*This chapter provides a series of examples in JavaScript
and Java showing some of the more effective means for
incorporating audio into your site. A number of useful
development tools are discussed to help simplify the
authoring tasks involved.*

A CD player without any kind of controls wouldn't be very successful in
the marketplace, nor would it win any accolades from consumers. If you
couldn't turn it on or off, or you couldn't select the song to play, or you
couldn't adjust the volume—odds are that you would pretty quickly throw it
in the trash.

Internet audio without controls presents problems as well. Site visitors might
not want music or sound and might quickly look for a way to turn it off. The
music might be a style that is annoying to a visitor; he or she might prefer classical to techno-industrial background music. Music and sound options are subject to personal preferences. Using controls available through JavaScript and
Java, you can provide the options for musical accompaniments and give site
visitors some choices without inflicting your personal tastes on someone.

This chapter looks at several different techniques, using JavaScript and
Java, to control the way music and sound are presented on your Web site.
Because not everyone has the ability to immediately start programming in

Java, two applications that allow you to construct Java applets quickly are introduced. Symantec's Visual Café uses a drag-and-drop approach to create and modify the objects that form the basis of Java applets. Aimtech's Jamba simplifies applet construction even further, allowing you to add multimedia elements to Web pages using point-and-click authoring. Both these products are used to provide audio enhancements to a Web page through a series of examples.

JavaScript is certainly a simpler language with which to work, but it also requires a fairly imposing learning curve to master. To help out in that regard, we've included a demo version of Acadia Software's Infuse on the CD-ROM bundled with this book. Infuse organizes the elements and components available to a JavaScript author into a streamlined interface. Single-click access to descriptions of each component and debugging tools makes it a simple process to construct effective, error-free JavaScript code.

Netscape's LiveConnect

The nature of object-oriented programming revolves around the concept of *objects* and their associated *properties* and *methods*. Within the domain of HTML documents, objects can be any of the things you typically find referenced on a page: forms, images, Java applets, or plug-ins. Objects are essentially just a means of organizing information about something, whether you're talking about a document object (an HTML file), a forms object (the checkboxes and text-edit boxes on a page), or an embedded object in the context of a plug-in (for example, the LiveAudio player).

You can control objects by changing their properties; but this may sound a bit abstract, in practice the concept is fairly simple. One of the properties of an HTML document is the background color that applies to the page. If you change the background color of a page from white to blue, the effect is immediately noticeable and easy to visualize. If you change the property of an image from visible to hidden, it disappears from view on the page. JavaScript provides an easy way to reference and change the properties of all of those elements that you are used to working with in an HTML document. Because JavaScript is a programming language, these changes can be keyed to events that occur while someone is browsing a page, such as selecting an item listed by a radio button or passing the mouse over a particular object on the page. They can also be keyed to changing conditions—for example, when a particular day arrives (as indicated by the Date object) you could cause the page background color to change in response to this condition.

You can also apply *methods* to objects. Methods control the behavior of objects. One of the simplest JavaScript methods is document.write( ). Applying the write( ) method to the document object causes a particular action to take place. In this case, it causes the text or other elements contained in parentheses to be written to the HTML page. Entering the line document.write("Hello, Earthling!") into your JavaScript program causes the text "Hello, Earthling!" to be written to the body of the HTML document. Other methods control things like the submission of a form to a server—submit( )—or accessing the current day of the week from a Date object—getDate. Note that each particular method corresponds to a type of object. You can't try to apply the getDate method to a document object and expect to get any kind of response. Methods define the range of behavior that can be controlled through program interaction.

To a large degree, programming in JavaScript is a simple matter of connecting events that occur within an HTML document to changes that are applied to the properties of objects contained in the document. Objects are also controlled by the application of methods in response to various conditions. While this is an oversimplification, we hope it serves to demystify the programming aspects of JavaScript. Outside of the purview of HTML, JavaScript is utterly worthless. Without a browser to interpret the JavaScript code, you cannot run a JavaScript program. Once inside the browser, however, you can interact with objects on the page even more directly than you can with Java. To return to the events and properties correlation, you could create a simple JavaScript sequence that used the onMouseOver event to trigger the changing of the property associated with the background color of a page. For example, the JavaScript event handler for onMouseOver could be programmed to change the page background from white to blue each time the mouse passes over a link. To look at this in audio terms, you could also use the same event handler to indicate that a particular sound be played each time the mouse pointer passes over a link. We'll provide examples of how to do that later in this chapter.

Similarly, plug-ins and Java applets have properties. Properties that are exposed —that is, properties that have been made available for programming access—can be controlled through HTML and JavaScript from within the Web page. Note that only those properties that have been designed to be changed by external program access can be manipulated. Methods are also used in respect to plug-ins and applets. Methods that are available through Java are defined as public methods. Plug-ins also have defined methods based on the design of the plug-in. For example, some of the newer MIDI player consoles, such as LiveUpdate's Crescendo and

Headspace's Beatnik, have plug-ins designed with exposed properties and available methods. You can use JavaScript to turn them on and off, rewind a selection, and—in the case of Beatnik—even play individual MIDI notes. The exact means of controlling a plug-in varies according to those design features and controls that have been built into the software.

LiveConnect is Netscape's architecture for providing access to the full range of elements that can interact in an HTML document, including Netscape plug-ins, Java applets, and JavaScript functions. LiveConnect appeared on the scene with the version 3.0 release of Navigator—you can't use the techniques described in this chapter to work with earlier versions of the browser.

Methods That Apply to LiveAudio

The LiveAudio plug-in that is available in Navigator 3.0 has the following defined methods:

- **play( )**: Starts audio playback from the current position

- **stop( )**: Halts audio playback and returns to the start of the audio file

- **rewind( )**: Returns to the beginning of the audio segment

- **seek(*n*)**: Sets the playback position to the point indicated by *n* (an integer representing the number of seconds into the audio file)

These controls are fairly rudimentary compared to what some of the other audio plug-ins, such as Beatnik and Crescendo, can accomplish, but they at least provide a measure of control over the audio playback.

You can use the play( ) method in combination with a link on an HTML page. The method triggers the playback of the sound file referenced in the link. An <EMBED> entry in the HTML document specifies the name of the sound, allowing it to be referenced from within the link entry. The code appears as follows:

```
<HTML>

<HEAD></HEAD>

<BODY>

<EMBED SRC="120ride.wav" HIDDEN=TRUE NAME="awk" MASTERSOUND>

<A HREF="javascript:document.awk.play(false)">Make a joyful noise!</A>
```

```
</BODY>

</HTML>
```

The MASTERSOUND tag is required whenever a NAME attribute appears in reference to an <EMBED> entry destined for LiveAudio handling. In this case, the name of the sound file, as designated by the SRC attribute, is "120ride.wav." The NAME attribute allows you to link to the sound file through the <EMBED> entry by using the assigned name, awk. When a user clicks on the link, JavaScript uses the play( ) method through the LiveAudio plug-in to play the 120ride.wav sound file.

T I P Note that if a different plug-in were assigned to handle the WAV file MIME type, the player associated with that file type would be loaded in place of the LiveAudio player. In many cases, the players will support the same methods. For example, if the Beatnik player were assigned to handle WAV files, when this script was executed, the Beatnik player would be loaded and would play back the file. Since the HIDDEN=TRUE attribute is present in the <EMBED> entry, this wouldn't make any difference to someone viewing the page. The audio playback would sound about the same. However, if a player is assigned to the MIME type that doesn't support the play( ) method, the script would not execute properly.

In this example, the WAV file, 120ride.wav, loads at the same time as the HTML document. This increases the download time for the page by a certain amount depending on the size of the WAV file. You can devise a simple script that waits until a user actually clicks the link before downloading the sound file. This script relies on what is called a "stub" file, which is essentially a dummy WAV file that must be present to satisfy the <EMBED> syntax. The stub file should consist of the shortest WAV file you can create—perhaps a 5K file. Use a sound editing application to trim any file down to this size. It will be loaded with the page, but never played.

A JavaScript function is used to specify playback of the actual sound file. This is called only if the link is called, and at that time the WAV file that you really mean to play is loaded (the stub file is ignored). The script to accomplish this follows:

```
<HTML>

<HEAD>

<SCRIPT LANGUAGE=JavaScript>

<!-- Let ancient browsers beware

function playtime()

        {

        document.chorus.play(false, 'http://www.sound_place/bin/120ride.wav')

        }

// -->

</SCRIPT>

</HEAD>

<BODY>

<EMBED SRC="dummy2.wav" HIDDEN=TRUE NAME="chorus" MASTERSOUND>

<A HREF="javascript:playtime()">Download and play the ethereal chorus....</A>

</BODY>

</HTML>
```

These examples only touch on the capabilities of JavaScript control over audio player activities. Later scripts show how you can expand on these capabilities to control more aspects of sound playback.

Acadia Software Infuse

Even though JavaScript is not an incredibly difficult language to learn, it still requires some discipline and attention to detail while you are learning the interrelationships of the different components, the terminology, and the syntax of JavaScript statements. To help you along in this goal, and to provide a supportive programming environment, Acadia's Infuse provides the ideal workspace for both new and experienced JavaScript coders.

The main application window, shown in Figure 6.1, provides a large area for code construction and smaller windows to the left that provide access to the functions and objects of your script while you are building it. The tabbed panels in the bottom-left portion of the screen provide drag-and-drop elements that you can incorporate in a script. For example, if you want to create an if...else statement, you can drag the icon for this statement type from the Language panel to the program area, and Infuse inserts the syntax-perfect framework for this statement. All you need to do is fill in the rest of the statement. HTML tags are provided on the HTML panel and JavaScript built-in objects, such as history objects, window objects, and Array objects can be dropped into the code as well. Infuse provides support for Netscape's LiveWire server software, allowing you to create server-side JavaScripts to be used in the LiveWire environment.

At any point in your code development, you can preview the current status in either Microsoft Internet Explorer or Netscape Navigator, usually a wise idea since the two browsers don't always agree on their JavaScript implementations. If you

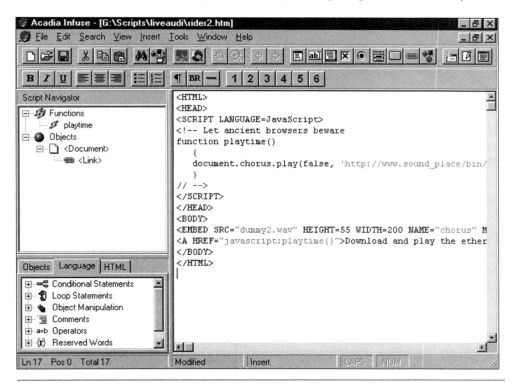

Figure 6.1 Infuse main application window.

forget a particular JavaScript construction, Infuse includes the entire JavaScript Authoring Guide (as developed by Netscape), accessible through the Windows help system. You can click on any language element and the help system will return a full description of the element.

Specialized characters that require extra text handling in the code, such as carriage returns and new-line characters, can also be inserted using drag-and-drop techniques from a tree-structured framework. Your scripting efforts are also accelerated by a feature that helps eliminate one of the most common scripting errors: braces that are not matched in pairs. Infuse will diligently scan your script to identify the closing brace from any opening brace that you identify. You can quickly spot mismatched braces and correct any script problems that would result from this situation. This also helps in confirming the proper construction of statements in JavaScript.

Another helpful aid while working on scripts is immediate access to the full JavaScript object model, which can be expanded and collapsed from its hierarchical tree structure, as shown in Figure 6.2. The interrelationships between objects in

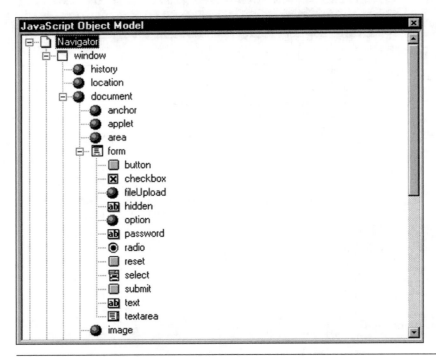

Figure 6.2 JavaScript object model.

JavaScript is a key consideration when constructing scripts. The hierarchy plays an important role in naming and identifying objects, so having this model available within a floating window can be extremely useful for Web authors.

Infuse includes a library of frequently needed scripts that can be dragged into your program whenever needed. Short scripts are available for such things as getting the actual date and year, creating dynamic text based on the detected browser, checking for blank required fields on a form to be submitted, simulating a pushbutton that depresses when clicked, and retrieving a value from a selected object. You can also expand this library of scripts with your own additions, so that many of the more common coding tasks can be accomplished by dragging a prewritten script into the programming window. Infuse provides a framework that supports full use of JavaScript's features and options in an environment that can be quickly mastered by novice coders.

 A demonstration version of Infuse is included on the CD-ROM bundled with this book.

You can find contact information for Acadia Software in Appendix C.

Sound Embedded in Java Applets

Placing your audio content inside Java applets removes the necessity for requiring a specific plug-in to support playback. If a browser is enabled for Java support (as versions 3.0 of Microsoft Internet Explorer and Netscape Navigator are), you have access to the full capabilities of the Java Virtual Machine for your individual platform. The built-in sound capabilities of Java have been limited to AU sound file formats, but that situation has changed since Sun Microsystems licensed Headspace's audio technology to provide support for Rich Music Format files. The audio engine designed by Headspace uses software synthesis to produce extremely rich MIDI playback, and the same engine can handle other common PCM-based sound file formats (such as WAV and AIFF).

In the meantime, while you're waiting for this technology to filter down to the masses, you can still accomplish quite a bit using audio in combination with Java applets. This format provides portability—since applets can be freely distributed among platforms—and a controlled environment for playback, allowing you to synchronize events occurring in the browser window. Probably the most difficult aspect of using Java for providing audio playback on the Internet is Java itself. Learning to program in Java requires a major investment in time and energy.

Capsule Summary of Java

Using some of the visual development tools, you can effectively work with Java components without having to know much about the Java architecture. Understanding how the Java architecture is structured, however, can still be helpful when creating and distributing Java applets. Java applets are programs that run under a Java-compliant browser. Standalone Java applets can also run on a computer equipped to support the Java architecture through its operating system. Each Java-compliant browser contains a Java interpreter, which translates the byte code contained in the applets and performs the operations required by the program.

Applets consist of a series of class files, rather than a single executable program. When referred to as a group, these class files are generally known as a class library. The class files are distributed to the browser on recognition of the <APPLET> tag in an HTML document. The <APPLET> entry can also contain additional parameters that control the manner in which the class files are executed within the browser. Class files include references to fundamental objects that have properties. Properties are characteristics of an object that can usually be modified by a program. Objects can also be controlled by methods. If the methods are designated as external or public, they can be used to control behavior of the applet from an outside source—for example, controlling the applet behavior through JavaScript. When a Java applet is distributed to a browser, all of the class files that it uses must be transferred, as well as any objects that are used within the applet—such as images or audio files. Transfer of these files can be simplified by using one of the Java applet archive formats. Microsoft Internet Explorer uses the CAB format; Netscape Navigator uses the ZIP format. The packages are compressed to reduce transfer times.

Fortunately, there are some tools available that simplify the creation of Java applets. One example is Jamba, a product made by a New Hampshire-based company called Aimtech. Jamba concentrates on the creation of multimedia elements for Web pages. Using the capabilities of Jamba, you can develop applets that contain audio, animation, forms elements, and so on. The simplicity of the interface should appeal to beginning Web designers, but the program's capabilities extend to include interactivity with JavaScript functions and support for CGI Objects.

Another tool aimed more at professional programmers, Symantec's Visual Café includes both a simplified means of creating applets by dragging and dropping objects into a programming window and full support for all aspects of Java programming. In other words, you can accelerate the creation of many different types of multimedia and forms support functions while still having the ability to drop down to full programming level and work with code line by line.

We can't hope to teach you Java in this book, but the examples provided of creating audio material using Jamba and Visual Café should give you a sense of what it is like to work with Java. As the Java Virtual Machine is enhanced with the Headspace Beatnik audio engine, the possibilities for audio interaction will be increased considerably. An example of some of the things you can accomplish through Beatnik appears later in this chapter.

Creating Audio Applets in Jamba

About the easiest way available to create Java applets with multimedia components is to use a program like Jamba. Aimtech's Jamba eliminates the reliance on plug-ins to play back multimedia contents, such as audio material or animations, since the resulting applets consist of platform-independent byte-code that should run under any browser that supports the Java Virtual Machine (assuming that Java support has been enabled in the browser preference settings). Keep in mind that some people, particularly business users with a fear of demonic applets running loose on their equipment, turn off Java routinely; if you rely entirely on applets for your Web page content, these people won't be able to use your pages. On the other hand, most people don't worry about downloading applets from trusted sources, so Java is certainly worth considering as a means for introducing audio to your site visitors.

Audio can be played in response to specified events, such as when a page is started or the mouse pointer is positioned over a graphic object. Because of restrictions imposed by Java, the only type of sound files supported for inclusion in applets are AU format files in mono. If, however, your source files are in stereo WAV file format, Jamba will perform the necessary conversion for you to prepare the files for use (converting them to mono AU format).

The following Jamba example demonstrates the process of creating a simple applet that plays audio in response to pointing at a graphic on screen.

1. Start Jamba and select the **New** option from the File menu. This creates a new project window and allows you to assign a name to the Jamba project. Jamba creates individual subdirectories under the directory you specify for project storage and uses those directories to store graphics, text items, and other elements of an applet.

2. Double-click the **StartPage** thumbnail to open up a work area, called the Page Layout Editor, as shown in Figure 6.3. The thin strip of icons along the far left are the objects that you can drag into the work area for inclusion in the applet. This is called the Object Palette. The column shown with the Name heading lists the items that you have incorporated into a script—so far, it is just the single start page.

3. To introduce a graphic to the Editor, select the Graphic object from the Object Palette and drag it across to the work area. When the graphic box appears, click on it with the right mouse button to open the Properties list. A list of

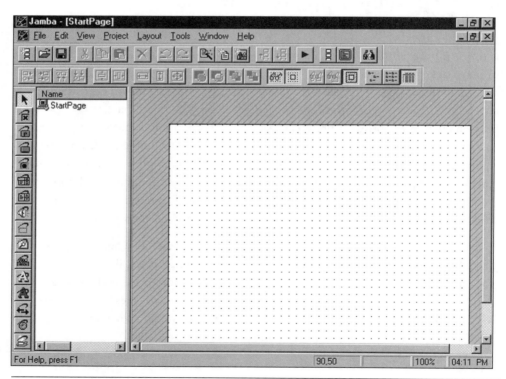

Figure 6.3 Page Layout Editor.

properties appears. By setting the DrawStyle property to SizeByGraphic, you ensure that Jamba will automatically scale the size of the area designated for the graphic to match the dimensions of the graphic.

4. Locate the Filename property and double-click the value field. This brings up a dialog box that allows you to select the name of the graphic to be inserted onto the page. For this example, we've selected the image of a microphone titled mic.gif.

5. Use the same technique to drag a Text object from the Object Palette and then use the cursor to create a text block. Once again, clicking on the block with the right mouse button opens the Properties list. You can enter text, choose the font and point size, and perform similar edits in this list. For our example, we'll enter text that reads, "Welcome to the Talking Druid's Workshop". The graphic and text block added appear as shown in Figure 6.4.

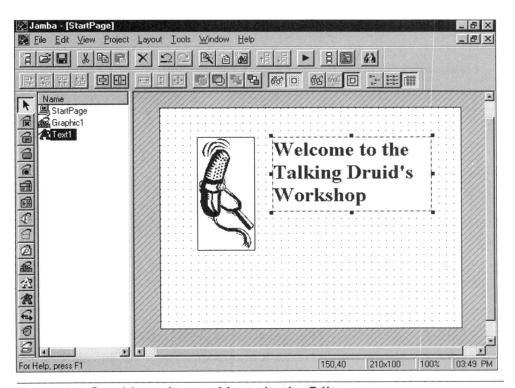

Figure 6.4 Graphic and text objects in the Editor.

6. You can add an audio object in the same manner. Drag the audio icon from the Object Palette to the Editor. An audio icon appears in the work area, but it's only for your reference—the icon won't appear in the final applet.

7. Right-click on the audio object and display its properties. You select the name of the file that you want for the audio by double-clicking the value field under Filename. In this case, we've picked a file called druid.au, as shown in Figure 6.5. You can also assign a name to the audio file, which will be displayed under the list of applet objects for the page. The name "talking_druid" should help identify the file.

8. If you reselect the Image object (the microphone graphic) and right-click on it, you can open the ToDo List for the image. This list associates certain events with any of the objects available to us and triggers an action for the object in response to the event. The drop-down listbox shows the available events, one of which is called Enter. Enter signifies that the mouse pointer has entered the area occupied by the graphic.

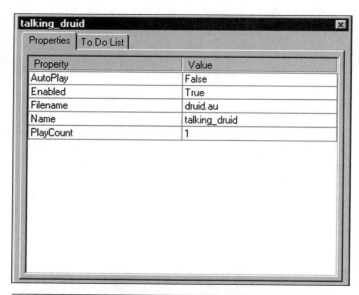

Figure 6.5 Properties list for an audio object.

9. If you select the New To Do icon from the toolbar, you can select the audio object, talking_druid, and then choose "What to do" from the list of audio actions, as shown in Figure 6.6. In this case, we've chosen Play( ). This indicates that when the mouse pointer enters the image area, the applet should play the audio file titled talking_druid.

10. In a similar manner, you can use the Leave event (when the mouse pointer leaves the graphic area) to trigger a Stop( ) action for the talking_druid audio. When the mouse pointer leaves the graphic, the audio is turned off.

You might want to add a quick text field to let people know what happens on the page. In this case, we added the block "To start the talking, move the mouse pointer over the microphone." You can test the applet using the **Run** command from the Project menu. Jamba brings up a Java runtime window, shown in Figure 6.7, and lets you ensure that the interactivity you designed into the applet is working correctly.

This is about the simplest way you will find for creating a Java applet, which can then be embedded into any HTML document. Jamba includes additional functions that let you liven up the presentation even more—you could add animation to the microphone graphic so that the mouse pointer entering the area would make it appear to vibrate as the sound played. Most of the functions in Jamba are handled in a similar manner; by manipulating the properties of objects and associating

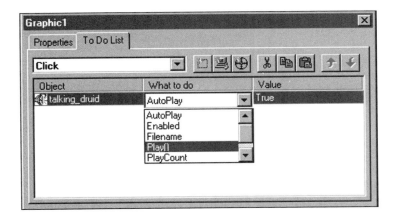

Figure 6.6 To Do List for Graphic1.

6.7 Jamba Viewer for testing applet.

certain actions with events, you can produce interactive applets in a minimal amount of time. You don't actually work directly with the Java code, but you do have precise control over the many properties for each object and the interactions that will be performed. Beginners to Java applet creation should have no trouble mastering this tool, and even experienced pros may want to take advantage of some of the special features offered by Jamba, such as the ability to create strip animations quickly and easily.

Distributing Jamba-Created Projects

Jamba includes a distribution wizard that provides several different methods of transferring the project files to ensure appropriate delivery over the Internet. You have the option of using compression standards, such as the CABinet compression and repository technology recognized by Microsoft Internet Explorer and the ZIP compression utilized by Netscape Navigator. You can also distribute all the necessary class files in uncompressed format to ensure accessibility by all Java-compliant browsers. Jamba provides the option of distributing the Java files directly to an indicated Web or FTP site. The distribution wizard thoughtfully creates a structure with subdirectories for project items. Optionally, class files can be stored in a relative directory path, a fully specified directory path, or the default directory. File storage is an important aspect of applet distribution; without the required files and classes available, an applet will not be able to run.

 A demonstration version of Jamba is included on the CD-ROM bundled with this book.

Contact information for Aimtech appears in Appendix C.

Audio Handling in Visual Café

Like Aimtech's Jamba, Symantec's Visual Café is designed to simplify the creation of Java applets within a visual workspace, using drag-and-drop techniques to create objects and manipulate them in a variety of ways. Unlike Jamba, Visual Café expects that you may be working directly on the Java code and provides a supporting programming environment for doing so. If you want a quick path for learning Java, Visual Café can provide a solid foundation to work from, since you can examine the code created using the drag-and-drop techniques and use it as a model for any programming tasks that you want to master. Throughout the development process, Visual Café lets you freely switch between a visual view of the code and a text-based view. Much in the same way that Acadia Software's Infuse accelerates the process of creating JavaScripts, Visual Café accelerates the process of creating Java applications in minimal time.

Visual Café uses the project as the main organizing element. Projects contain a number of forms and each form serves as a container for any of the elements used for applet construction, including menubars, graphic images, scrollbars, buttons, and audio content. Audio is handled in Visual Café as an object available from the Multimedia panel, and you can work with audio objects by manipulating their properties and associating them with events. Figure 6.8 shows the basic working environment within Visual Café. Applet 1 in the Form Designer window is a form in progress containing components that have dropped into place from the panels directly above the window. As you add new components to the project, they appear in the Project window to the left on a collapsible tree. The tree indicates the contents of the complete package—those components that have become part of the Java applet being created.

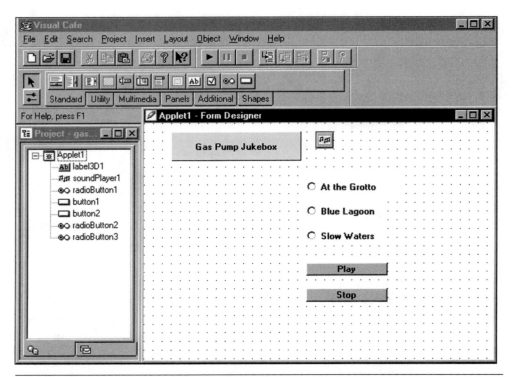

Figure 6.8 Workspace in Visual Café showing Form Designer.

To give a sense of how a simple audio-oriented applet can be created in Visual Café, we'll go through the process of embedding an audio object and then constructing a play list for it using songs selected through radio buttons.

To get started with the creation of a new applet, select **New** from the File menu. Visual Café gives you a choice of templates, as shown in Figure 6.9. The Basic Applet is the template that lets you build an applet for use with a browser.

Choose a name and destination for your new project. Visual Café keeps track of all of the different project components and can track and examine them as needed from the Project tree. Once you've named your project, Visual Café opens up a blank Form Designer window. This is where you'll add those elements that will be used in the applet.

Select the Multimedia tab from the panel cluster in the toolbar group of Visual Café. The last icon in the Multimedia group is the SoundPlayer, which provides audio controls for applets. If you click the icon and move the mouse pointer back

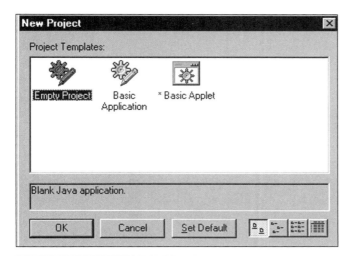

Figure 6.9 Selecting a template.

to the form window, the cursor changes to crosshairs. You can drop the SoundPlayer icon anywhere within the window—location isn't important because it doesn't show up in the applet. It's basically a placeholder for audio content.

If you right-click on the SoundPlayer icon, you can select the Property List, as shown in Figure 6.10. The Class, which can't be changed, is symantec.itools.multimedia.SoundPlayer. This Class represents one component that must be included in the applet package for the sound to function. You can select a different Name for the SoundPlayer, choose the number of times the sound should repeat, and choose how synchronization is handled. The sound itself is identified by the URL list, which can include one or more AU format sound files that will be associated with the SoundPlayer. For this example, we'll leave the URL list empty and then load audio files later by selecting them with radio buttons.

In the same manner as you dragged the SoundPlayer into the window, you can select a radio button from the Standard tab and position it on the form. The radio button also has a set of properties that can be accessed by right-clicking the object and then choosing **Properties** from the menu. For radio buttons, these include items such as the font, color, initial state of the button, and the label of the button. For this example, we've changed the label to "At the Grotto," the name that will then appear on the button face. The two other radio buttons, as shown back in Figure 6.8, have labels reading Blue Lagoon and Slow Waters. These names are intended to identify the song selections to be played.

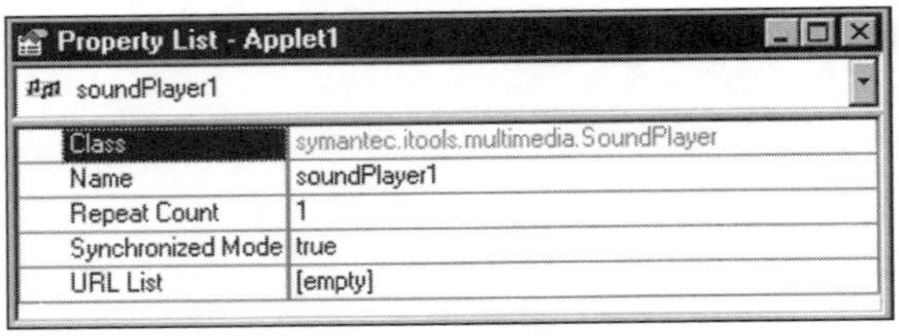

Figure 6.10 Property List for sounds.

Visual Café lets you add interactions to objects using an Interaction Wizard. If you select a radio button, right-click, and choose **Add Interaction**, the Interaction Wizard appears, as shown in Figure 6.11. This is where the strength of Visual Café is most evident—it provides the capability of establishing interactions between objects without writing code. Visual Café constructs the appropriate code based on your instructions and drops it into the program. You're free to edit it if you like, but you can actually create entire programs without venturing down to the code level.

For this example, we want to choose **Action** and then select the soundPlayer1 as the item to interact with. The final step is to choose what you want to happen. In

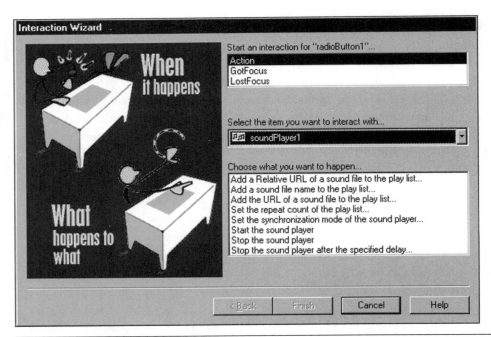

Figure 6.11 Interaction Wizard.

this case, you want to "Add a Relative URL of a sound file to the play list." Sounds added to the play list will be played in order when the play method is applied to the SoundPlayer. Assign a different sound file and its corresponding URL to each of the radio buttons in turn. You've established a means to add songs to the player through the applet as it is running. Next you need to get the player to Start and Stop.

Buttons are the most common control element for many applets. Using the same drag-and-drop techniques, select two buttons from the Standard tab, move them into the form, name one of them "**Play**" and the other "**Stop**" through their Property List, and you can then assign the interaction using the Interaction Wizard. This time the interaction for the first button is Clicked, as shown in Figure 6.12. Once again, you want to interact with soundPlayer1, and you want the click to "Start the sound player."

The **Stop** button is then set up exactly the same way, but this time you set the Clicked interaction to trigger "Stop the sound player." You've just created buttons that can start and stop the playback of sound from the embedded sound player in your applet. You've also designed a means to select the songs to be played and add them to a list that will be sequenced by the player.

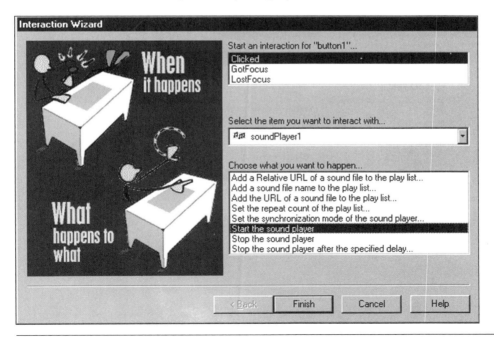

Figure 6.12 Button interaction.

You can then add images and labels to give some orientation to the viewer of the applet. In this case, we've named the player the "Gas Pump Jukebox," using a Label drawn from the Standard panel.

To add an image to the display, go to the Multimedia panel and select the ImageViewer icon. You can then use the mouse crosshairs to select the region where you want the image to appear. As with the sound files, the Property List lets you select a URL representing the source of the image file. Visual Café immediately drops it into place in the WYSIWYG window. You can position any of the elements in the window, even after you've added interactive elements to them. Visual Café simply changes the positioning data that appears in the Java code automatically. You can dynamically jump back and forth between the visual display and the text display. Changing one causes the other to immediately reflect the changes for the other. In other words, if you do change the position of the graphic, you can immediately see the new positioning data in the code window. Visual Café is unique in this ability to support what they call "two-way" programming.

Once you save all the components in the applet, Visual Café offers you a chance to compile and preview your work in a RunTime window The applet displays, as

Figure 6.13 Running applet.

shown in Figure 6.13, and you can test all the features and interactions. Problems can be eliminated by returning to the Edit window and then running a step-by-step debug sequence.

This example adds the specified song to the play list and then Plays or Stops the selection using the two buttons. Practically, this isn't an applet you would want to use on your site because the play list keeps growing larger and larger and there is no way to delete files from the list once you start playing. Getting into a more realistic playback situation—where the user can manipulate the contents of the play list—requires some more coding. We primarily wanted to show you the steps involved in creating a workable applet in Visual Café and the ways in which audio content can be handled. Understand that even using visual programming tools, it can be a fair amount of work to devise a program that runs the way you want it to and doesn't contain any unexpected surprises to spring on Web visitors.

New Audio Engine for Java

In its current iteration, Java does not provide a particularly robust means for dealing with sound, nor does it offer much support for anything more interesting than bare-bones AU file playback. The SoundPlayer class built into Symantec's library seems to be fixed to 8-bit sound files sampled at 11KHz, not exactly an awe-inspiring means of impressing your listeners. Sun Microsystems, however, has licensed the audio engine that Headspace uses in its Beatnik player, which is definitely cause for celebration. Any Java-enabled platform will have the capabilities of playing Rich Music Format files. The audio capabilities of the next release of Java should rise markedly. You can, of course, use Java to interact with higher-quality sound processing tools—plug-ins, players, or ActiveX controls—and this can make up somewhat for the internal sound handling deficits. It does, however, require some programming gyrations to accomplish, which somewhat defeats the benefit that Java offers in providing a means of distributing platform-independent applets throughout the browser community. We'll watch with interest to see how the audio capabilities improve next time around.

Programming for Beatnik

The Beatnik system, brainchild of Headspace, Inc., provides an entirely new level of interactive control for music on the Web. The Beatnik plug-in, which works with the Netscape Navigator Windows and Macintosh browser, uses files created using the Beatnik Editor, an application that digests WAV, AIFF, AU, SDII, MOD, and MIDI files and outputs Rich Music Format (RMF) files. RMF files are compact and portable, and they contain copyright protection in the form of internal watermarks that employ 40-bit data encryption. The Beatnik system is limited to Navigator interaction—Microsoft's Internet Explorer is not supported.

Although compatible with General MIDI, Beatnik goes a step further, allowing individual music samples to be imported to expand the range of available instrument voices. Beatnik's software synthesizer ensures consistent, predictable playback on all platforms, regardless of the type of MIDI equipment installed on a system. The synthesizer includes filtering, reverb, ADSRs, LFOs, and other sound processing features typically encountered in high-end professional synthesizers.

Using the Type Attribute for Beatnik

The Beatnik plug-in can be accessed through an <EMBED> entry in an HTML document. The use of the TYPE attribute removes the requirement for MIME type setup at the server level (as is the case for the LiveUpdate Crescendo plug-in). For embedding a single RMF file in an HTML document, a simple <EMBED> entry would read:

```
<EMBED SRC="cooltune.rmf" TYPE="audio/rmf" WIDTH=144 HEIGHT=60 DISPLAY=SYSTEM
MODE=METERS AUTOSTART=TRUE LOOP=TRUE>
```

This entry will begin playing the specified RMF file (cooltune.rmf, in this case) as soon as it is downloaded, while displaying the standard Beatnik player console. The MODE=METERS attributes displays the Beatnik meters that pulse to the music during playback. Optionally, you can display the oscilloscope on the console by using the MODE=SCOPE attribute.

For browsers that are configured to use Beatnik to play back other types of sound files, the TYPE attribute can be configured to accommodate MOD files (TYPE="audio/MOD"), WAV files (TYPE="audio/WAV"), or MIDI (TYPE="audio/MIDI").

Interacting with Groovoids

Beatnik's internal library of sound effects, called Groovoids, are the most rapid means of utilizing sound available to Web authors. Because Groovoids are stored internally within the Beatnik player, they can provide near-instantaneous audio in response to events such as clicking a link or button, passing the mouse pointer over an image or link, or performing a submit. Groovoids can be used in a simple <EMBED> entry, as shown in the following example:

```
<EMBED SRC="stub.mid" GROOVOID="Fanfare-Majesty" TYPE="audio/rmf" WIDTH=2
HEIGHT=2 HIDDEN AUTOSTART=TRUE>
```

This Groovoid plays a stirring trumpet chorus when the page containing this <EMBED> entry is first downloaded. The stub.mid file is a dummy file that is required for proper syntax in an <EMBED> entry. It doesn't matter what is in the file but it should be short, and a file of the specified name should be present in the local directory.

Groovoids are also handy for providing audio feedback for user-triggered events. For example, you could set up a button graphic so that a distinct Groovoid click sounds when someone clicks the button. To do this requires two separate statements: one to add the sound to the HTML document with a specific name, and the other to provide the link containing the button graphic that is clicked. As an example, the two statements could read:

```
<EMBED SRC="stub.mid" TYPE="audio/rmf" NAME=pluggo WIDTH=2 HEIGHT=2 HIDDEN
AUTOSTART=TRUE LOOP=FALSE>

<A HREF="javascript:document.pluggo.play(false,'groovoid://UI-

SimpleClick1')"><IMG SRC="push.gif" WIDTH=60 HEIGHT=20></A>
```

The pushbutton referenced within this link will provide a reassuring audio "click," generated by the Groovoid, when someone clicks it. Note that once again the <EMBED> entry uses a stub file entry—"stub.mid"—to satisfy the syntax requirements. The sound is identified by the name supplied in the <EMBED> entry, so it can be referenced and played using the play( ) method in JavaScript.

Beatnik Plug-In musicObject Functions

To fully interact with the Beatnik plug-in, you can take advantage of a library of JavaScript code that has been developed by Headspace. This library, music-object.js, can be referenced from the Headspace Web site; JavaScript code specified in an external reference in this manner becomes available to any running script.

 musicObject is located at:

www.headspace.com/beatnik/doc/music-object.js

Optionally, you can download this file and make it available on your own site. By simply referencing the locally stored file, you expand the range of operations you can perform interactively using the Beatnik plug-in. The musicObject library takes care of the communication with Netscape's LiveConnect architecture to ensure that all of the features will be available to the Web author. To add a reference to this external JavaScript library within your own code, assuming the file is stored locally with the rest of your HTML files, you would add the line:

```
<SCRIPT SRC="music-object.js"></SCRIPT>
```

You can also specify a path. For example, if the library file was located at **www.ice_house.net/music_bin/** you would enter:

```
<SCRIPT SRC="http://www.ice_house.net/music_bin/music-object.js"></SCRIPT>
```

To incorporate the functionality of musicObjects in an HTML document, you need to create an object based on a new instance of the musicObject; this is one of the features made available through the JavaScript library. Once the musicObject is associated with the Beatnik plug-in, through the <EMBED> entry, you can implement the functions available through the musicObject. Headspace suggests the following code for creating the new musicObject and making it ready for use in an HTML document.

```
<SCRIPT SRC="correct-path-here/music-object.js"></SCRIPT>

<SCRIPT LANGUAGE="JavaScript"><!--//

nameOfMusicObject=new musicObject("nameOfMusicObject")

function execute_a_musicObject_function( ) {

        nameOfMusicObject.setTranspose(12); //transposes  the music up by an
octave

}

</SCRIPT>

<FORM>

        <INPUT TYPE="button" VALUE="execute a musicObject function"

ONCLICK="execute_a_musicObject_function( )">

</FORM>

<EMBED SRC="your-music-file.mid" TYPE="audio/midi"
```

```
PLUGINSPAGE="http://www.headspace.com/beatnik/plug-in/index.html" WIDTH=2

HEIGHT=2 HIDDEN NAME="nameOfMusicObjectPlugin"

ONREADY="nameOfMusicObject.setReady( )">

//--></SCRIPT>
```

This basic template can be used to access multiple occurrences of a Beatnik plug-in simply by following the basic layout of the script and substituting the appropriate names of files and objects. The attribute titled ONREADY calls a function to determine if the plug-in referenced is present and ready for communication. If not, the musicObject ignores subsequent calls to execute specific functions from the extended library. Many of the functions are fully compatible with Netscape's LiveAudio and can be used with the LiveAudio plug-in as well as the Beatnik plug-in.

The library provides a collection of both control and status functions. A quick summary of the functions follows.

Control Functions

- **play( )**: Starts playback of an indicated file.

- **stop( )**: Halts playback and unloads the song.

- **pause( )**: Temporarily halts playback allowing it to be resumed at the same point.

- **setLoop( )**: Indicates the number of times that a file should repeat. Overrides <EMBED> entries.

- **setAutoStart( )**: Determines whether the indicated plug-in should start playback automatically. Affects all subsequent files.

- **fadeTo( )**: Diminishes the volume level to an indicated value.

- **fadeFromTo( )**: Creates a fade between two specified levels.

- **playNote( )**: Plays an indicated MIDI note to a specified channel. Channel numbers, bank numbers, velocity, duration, and program numbers can be specified.

- **noteOn( )**: Starts a note playing on the indicated MIDI channel.

- **noteOff( )**: Switches off a note that is playing.

- **getNoteName( )**: Retrieves the name of a note from an indicated MIDI note number.

- **getNoteNumber( )**: Retrieves the MIDI note number that corresponds with a given note name.

- **setVolume( )**: Adjusts the master volume setting for playback.

- **setTranspose( )**: Transposes the pitch of a song by the specified interval.

- **setReverbType( )**: Selects from one of several available reverb types to be used during playback.

- **setTempo( )**: Controls the playback speed of a specific file.

- **setController( )**: Selects a particular type of MIDI controller from a list of supported types.

- **setProgram( )**: Specifies a MIDI program change.

- **setTrackMute( )**: Mutes or unmutes a designated MIDI track.

- **setChannelMute( )**: Mutes or unmutes a specified MIDI channel.

- **setTrackSolo( )**: Determines the solo status of an indicated track.

- **setChannelSolo( )**: Selects the solo status of an indicated channel.

- **setMonophonic( )**: Determines whether an indicated channel is to be played in monophonic mode.

Status Functions

The following functions of the musicObject library retrieve status of the plug-in and playback status.

- **getLoop( )**: Retrieves the loop status of a particular file.

- **getAutoStart( )**: Determines the Autostart setting for a plug-in.

- **getReverbType( )**: Retrieves the currently set reverb type.

- **getTempo( )**: Determines the current tempo setting.

- **getTranspose( )**: Retrieves the current transposition setting.

- **getController:** Retrieves the identity of the indicated MIDI controller.

- **getProgram( )**: Retrieves the program number that applies to the designated MIDI channel.

- **getVolume( )**: Determines the current master volume setting.

- **getTrackMute( )**: Retrieves the setting of the mute on the specified track.

- **getChannelMute( )**: Retrieves the mute status of the indicated MIDI channel.

- **getTrackSolo( )**: Returns the solo status of the designated track.

- **getChannelSolo( )**: Returns the solo status of the channel specified.

- **getMonophonic( )**: Retrieves the value indicating what the monophonic setting is currently.

- **isPaused( )**: Determines if a file is paused or in play or stopped.

- **isPlaying( )**: Determines if a file is currently playing.

- **isReady( )**: Determines if a particular plug-in is available and ready to play.

 More documentation on the functions available through the musicObject library can be obtained from:

www.headspace.com/beatnik/doc/authoring/reference.html

Playing MIDI Notes through Beatnik

As described in the previous section, Beatnik has the ability to play individual MIDI notes and instrument voices through JavaScript statements. Such playback can also be handy to provide audio feedback to link and image clicking, but some innovative Web authors have used this feature to create interactive instruments that play notes in response to onMouseOver events detected over an image. The Interactive Magical Harp, designed by Paul Sebastien (Director of Production at Headspace, Inc.), is one such approach.

 The Interactive Magical Harp can be viewed at:

http://www.headspace.com

This JavaScript-based sound environment provides music and sound effects in response to the mouse pointer passing over an elaborate graphic of a harp. The JavaScript program makes extensive use of the fact that Beatnik supports generation of MIDI notes that can be played directly through JavaScript and Navigator's LiveConnect facility.

Another of Paul Sebastien's scripts, The Interactive Cave, appears in Appendix D, where the JavaScript code can be viewed and the musicObject library can be examined.

You can use the ability to generate MIDI notes using different instrument voices to enhance the audio feedback on your site. For example, to add the sound of an orchestra hit to the clicking of a link enter your link with the ONCLICK attribute. An <EMBED> entry is not needed. This is shown in the following statement:

```
<A HREF="anchor_point"
ONCLICK="with(document.musicPlugin){setProgram(1,55);playNote(1,60,80,1600)}">Link
to somewhere interesting.</A>
```

This entry will play back the orchestra hit (MIDI program change 55) on channel 1 at C4. The velocity is set to medium and the duration is 1.6 seconds (1600 milliseconds). This type of MIDI support offers a wide range of options to developers, who can play back melodies based on a string of MIDI notes, embed audio cues for site visitors in response to specific interactions, and provide musical training in an economical and easily programmed manner.

 Beatnik plug-ins for Windows and Macintosh users (for Netscape Navigator) are provided on the CD-ROM included with this book.

Random Music Generated for Site Visitors

The following short guest script, courtesy of Headspace, Inc., makes it possible to play a different MIDI song through Beatnik each time a visitor enters your site. It uses the random method associated with JavaScript's Math object to generate a different number each time, which is referenced to a set of MIDI files. To use this script, you first need to set up a collection of MIDI files that use numbers in combination with a common name string. For example, if you want to use the string INTRO with the filenames, the first file should be called INTRO1.MID, the second INTRO2.MID, and so on.

To use this technique, place the following script somewhere close to the end of your HTML file. The location should be a good spot for the Beatnik player to appear on the page, so choose the spot carefully.

```
<SCRIPT LANGUAGE= "JavaScript">

<!--Beware, old browsers...
```

```
total_files=15;

files_name="INTRO";

with (Math) {document.writeln('<EMBED SRC="' +files_name+(round(random() *
↳(total_files-1))+1)+ '.MID"AUTOSTART=TRUE WIDTH=2 HEIGHT=2 VOLUME=100
↳LOOP=TRUE>')}

//-->

</SCRIPT>
```

Pay particular attention to the single- and double-quotation marks as they appear for the <EMBED> entries. Single quotes are used to surround the entire text string as it will be written to the HTML document by JavaScript. Double quotes surround the entire SRC= attribute, which also includes single quotes to identify the variables and text that are concatenated to create the entire string to be written to the page. If you get any of the quotes out of position, the script will not work.

The with (Math) used in combination with the curly braces is a compact way of ensuring that the random number operation will be associated with JavaScript's Math object. Note that the random number that is produced is scaled to the total_files variable, which in this example has been assigned the number 15. The random() method in JavaScript produces a decimal value between 0 and 1. In the script, you then multiply this value by 14 (total_files minus 1) and round the number off. To ensure that you don't generate the value "0", a "1" is added to the rounded number. This is a quick and elegant way to let JavaScript choose an integer value ranging from 1 to 15. Note that if you change the number assigned to the total_files variable, it will scale the random number produced to the number of files that you have specified.

The concatenation (stringing together individual pieces) indicated by the "+" sign allows you to construct the entry that will appear within the <EMBED> tags. For example, assume that the random method generated the number 7. The text that would be written by the document.writeln() statement would be as follows:

```
<EMBED SRC="INTRO7.MID"AUTOSTART=TRUE WIDTH=2 HEIGHT=2 VOLUME=100 LOOP=TRUE>
```

With this line entered into the body of your HTML document, the currently active player for the MIDI MIME type would be loaded and the MIDI selection titled intro7.mid would then be played. If you were feeling ambitious, you could generate 48 MIDI files and use them in combination with this script to give an even wider range of selections that could potentially be heard by your site visitors. People enjoy seeing and hearing something different when they visit a site; this is one technique that ensures you'll always have fresh and different music to greet your visitors.

More JavaScript Examples

JavaScript provides infinite flexibility for shaping and structuring an audio environment to enrich your Web site. The following two examples may suggest some additional techniques that you want to extend and modify for use on your own site.

Triggering Sound from the Mouse Pointer

Because JavaScript can respond to specific events that occur within the browser, you can use those events to trigger audio playback. For example, the onMouseOver event handler can be used with an image to initiate the playback of an audio clip. Consider the following script:

```
<HTML>

<HEAD>

function riptime(name) {

document.embeds[name].play()

}

</HEAD>

<BODY>

<H1>Riff City: Home of the Hottest Licks</H1><BR>

Guitarists--sample the latest hot riff from Alex Bejing.

<EMBED NAME="dru" SRC="dru.wav" HIDDEN=TRUE AUTOSTART=FALSE MASTERSOUND>

<A HREF="#" onMouseOver="riptime('dru')"><IMG SRC="guitar.gif" HEIGHT=133

WIDTH=66></A>

</BODY>

</HTML>
```

As this script loads, the guitar image appears below the text, as shown in Figure 6.14.

The function riptime( ) plays the embedded sound file through JavaScript. The name of the sound file is passed as an argument to the function when it is called from the link—the onMouseOver event handler calls the function when the pointer passes over the guitar image, the name assigned to the embedded file ('dru') gets passed to the function, and then the function plays the sound file. As explained earlier in the chapter, JavaScript uses the play( ) method to play back audio files through the LiveAudio player. If another audio player is assigned to handle the indicated MIME type—in this case, a .wav file—that player will be substituted. For a substitute player to work, it must also be capable of handling the play( ) method through JavaScript.

The onMouseOver event handler can also be used effectively with Beatnik's Groovoids, which are built-in sounds that can be called from the player itself,

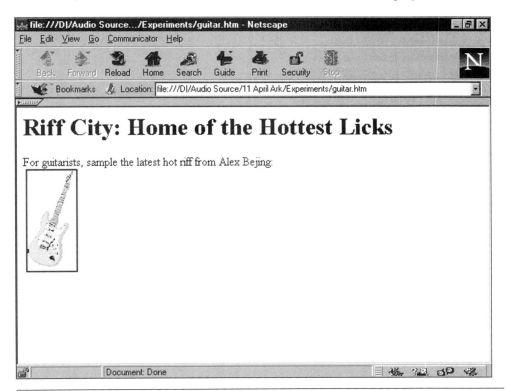

Figure 6.14 Guitar image connected to onMouseOver handler.

rather than having to download and access a separate sound file. Groovoids are a more data-efficient means of providing simple sound effects in response to Web browsing events.

Summary

Interactive control of audio through scripting languages or Java applets can provide sonic feedback for many common Web browser events—such as clicking a button or selecting a link—as well as providing a source for background music that can be turned on or off. You can even give site visitors the ability to choose their own background music from a list of selections. Learning a scripting language or Java development tools requires some work, but the rewards can be enhanced delivery of audio that is carefully integrated into the interactive components on your site.

Part Three

Pushing the Envelope

Streaming Audio
on the Web

This chapter looks at the various methods of streaming audio and the means by which they are implemented. The focus is on music-quality streaming techniques; Chapter 10 discusses streaming techniques that are custom tailored to delivering voice-quality data over the Web. The approach offered by Liquid Audio is examined in some detail, since their approach is a start-to-finish model for encoding, previewing, distributing, and tracking music sales, with protections for copyrights and against illicit copying. CEO Gerry Kearby sometimes refers to the product as offering a "record-company-in-a-box." Interviews with Liquid Audio staff members are included in the chapter.

Interest in and awareness of streaming audio on the Web have risen sharply in recent months. Tens of millions of RealAudio players have been downloaded by websters eager to tune into Internet-delivered broadcasts of music and sound. Streaming techniques built into QuickTime v2.5 and Shockwave have made it possible to deliver sound and visual data only seconds after file downloads begin. Liquid Audio with their commerce model for distributing music over the Internet promises to revolutionize the way that music reaches an audience, opening up new channels for both independent labels and the established record companies. Xing's StreamWorks makes it possible to perform real-time broadcasting of events over the Internet, and more than 7 million of their players have been downloaded. Streaming audio is among the most important new uses of the Web, and a growing number of companies and individuals are taking advantage of this new communication channel.

Most of the technologies required to deliver streaming audio remain within the grasp of even small independents, although server software and licensing fee costs—depending on the chosen technology—can add up in a hurry. Simple streaming methods as implemented in QuickTime and Shockwave can be enjoyed by any Web author, even those whose server space resides on an ISP. Dedicated servers required for RealAudio or Liquid Audio streaming delivery up the ante a bit, but enterprising musicians and independent labels are already taking advantage of this avenue for previewing and selling their music. The investment is minor when compared to typical business start-up costs, and the potential for quickly reaching new audiences for music or radio broadcast-style material is enormous.

The salient characteristic of streaming audio is that it is composed of compressed digital audio data that is designed to begin playing back shortly after the file download begins. Earlier techniques for transmitting audio files on the Internet involved downloading the entire file and then playing back the contents with a helper application or player. Even compacted digital audio files tend to be very large, and it can take several minutes to download even a relatively short segment of music or voice. In comparison, when you access a streaming audio file through an inline player in your browser window, the file contents begin downloading into a designated buffer area maintained by the browser on your system. When the buffer is sufficiently full to ensure uninterrupted playback, the player begins pulling audio data out of the buffer and playing it back while more data is being pumped into the buffer. If all goes well and Web traffic is not too heavy, the player can deliver the audio with a minimum of dropouts and pauses.

Compression techniques are typically geared to the anticipated transfer rate of the data and balanced between keeping the quality of the sound as high as possible and keeping the streamed file sizes as compact as possible to ensure fast transfers. Thus, a file compressed for streaming delivery at 28.8Kbps can contain significantly higher-quality sound than a file compacted for use with a 14.4Kbps interconnection (because it doesn't have to be as severely compressed and less signal loss occurs). The usual rule-of-thumb is that 14.4Kbps interconnections can support sound quality roughly equal to an AM radio (with loss of some of the high-frequency bandwidth). Sound files designed for streaming at 28.8Kbps interconnections deliver roughly FM radio quality, with a slight drop-off of the high-end frequencies. Sound files shipped to those lucky people who have ISDN connections to the Internet can achieve near CD quality in streaming mode. The technology can support enormous file sizes (essentially unlimited), which can be streamed in real time, making it possible to produce streaming audio coverage of live sporting events, government hearings, political conventions, live concerts, and so on.

The streaming audio encoders currently on the market seem to be geared for either 14.4Kbps to 28.8Kbps modems with the next jump in quality to ISDN connections. The new crop of 33.6Kbps and 57.2Kbps modems promises to support higher-quality sound in streaming mode as soon as the encoding software is set up to handle the corresponding compression rates.

Streaming Audio Tools and Techniques

To deliver streaming audio on the Internet, you have a choice of several different delivery platforms, each with its own advantages and disadvantages. Some require specialized tools for creation and encoding of the files. Some require dedicated server software to control the output of the streams, whereas others can be distributed as simple MIME file types that are handled dynamically by their plug-in or ActiveX players from within a visitor's browser.

This section surveys some of the leading tools and explains what is required to creating streaming audio files with these tools and to distribute the files over the Internet.

Progressive Networks' RealAudio

RealAudio is the product that many think of as synonymous with streaming audio on the Web. The base version of the RealAudio player is free, it installs easily and works well, and for many it is their first exposure to the wonders of real-time streaming audio. Hundreds of RealAudio servers have already been set up across the Internet dispersing an eclectic mix of counter-culture news, alternative music, interviews with celebrities and government officials, sports event commentary, as well as providing an additional outlet for mainstream radio stations and music stores selling albums over the Internet. The technology is not difficult to set up and use. To produce RealAudio files, an encoder (which is available for free from the Progressive Networks' Web site) processes digital audio files for delivery at a selected Internet connection rate. These files are then distributed through server software (which is not available for free) designed by Progressive Networks, with a licensing fee paid based on the number of streams to be supported.

The standard (free) RealAudio player does the job of playing back streaming audio in a no-nonsense kind of way, but for a small outlay of cash you can obtain the RealAudio Player Plus, shown in Figure 7.1, which boasts a number of extra features. A number of presets, similar to the programmable buttons on your car radio, let you set up quick, pushbutton access to your favorite RealAudio stations. A Scan function cycles through addresses on the Web and tunes into those that are broadcasting RealAudio material. If you've ever played around with a wide-band radio, cycling through the frequencies to pick up broadcasts from all over the world, you'll have similar fun with the Scan function on the RealAudio Player Plus. The quantity and variety of stations that are online already is staggering, and you can pick up anything from abysmal garage bands in Malibu Beach despoiling the air waves with bad rock to live concerts featuring world-class groups. News and information stations, as you might expect, also proliferate. The worldwide reach of Internet broadcasting makes it possible to produce material for specialized or niche audiences and markets, so you can find news, interviews, and information that appeals to every political persuasion and every interest.

The Player has a **Record** button, but this feature is activated only if the content providers have prepared the source material so that recording is enabled. In other words, you can't record material from a RealAudio stream unless the content provider says you can. You won't often find this the case for many kinds of material, such as retransmitted broadcast material from radio stations or interview segments with various figures of renown. The File menu offers an option called **PerfectPlay Mode**. If enabled, this mode increases the portion of the streaming file that is buffered, which delays the playback a bit but enhances the sound quality for Internet connections at normal dial-up rates: 14.4Kbps or 28.8Kbps.

Figure 7.1 RealAudio Player Plus controls.

If your intention simply is to distribute files compressed to RealAudio format in nonstreaming mode for offline playback by anyone with a RealAudio player, you can download and use the encoder software that handles conversions from Progressive Networks' Web site. The conversion process is simple, and there is an option to listen to the file in preview mode as it is being converted. At the very least, you'll want to play converted files back over your Internet link (after uploading them to your Web site) to hear the effect of the compression on the sound quality. Preprocessing the digital audio files before conversion can often improve the quality of sound in the converted file. Guidelines for sound processing are offered by Progressive Networks in a 115-page manual downloadable in Adobe Acrobat format that walks through most of the common functions and explains how to achieve the best conversion results.

Encoding Files for RealAudio

The RealAudio Encoder, shown in Figure 7.2, provides a straightforward means of converting common digital audio file formats into RealAudio formats. Source files can be in any of the following formats: WAV, AU, or PCM. You can also further process files in the native RealAudio file format (saved with a .ra extension). The Encoder works only with uncompressed file formats, so, for example, if you have an AU file that was saved using mu-law compression, you'll need to convert it to uncompressed form before using the Encoder on it. WAV and PCM files can be accommodated in several sample rates and bit resolutions, including 8KHz, 11KHz, 22KHz, or 44KHz sample rates with either 8-bit or 16-bit samples. Files should be stored as a single monophonic track if intended for monophonic playback; stereo file formats are supported only if you choose RealAudio 3.0 28.8Kbps or ISDN conversions. If you're using AU source files, they can be sampled at 8KHz, 22KHz, or 44KHz in mono format.

The Encoder window provides a place for you to enter the title, author, and copyright information about the recorded material, as shown in the lower-left portion of the screen in Figure 7.2. This is the information that will appear in the RealAudio Player window when the clip is being played back. If you enable the **PerfectPlay conversion** option, by clicking the checkbox, someone listening to the file through the Player will be able to turn on the **PerfectPlay** option to improve the sound quality during playback.

Set the compression option to correspond with the application that most closely matches your intended use of the audio material. For example, if you're trying to

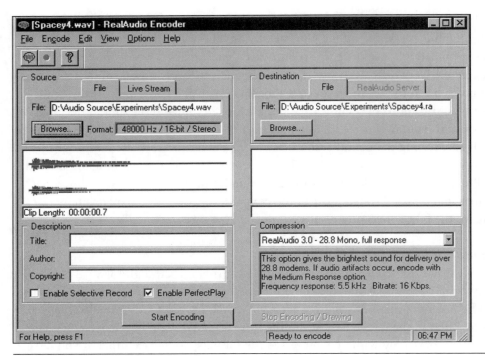

Figure 7.2 RealAudio Encoder.

create a clean RA file containing complex classical music, the RealAudio 3.0 28.8 full response (mono) option may be your best bet. This setting produces files that support a bit-rate of 16Kbps, capable of streaming successfully with most 28.8Kbps Internet connections during normal traffic. The Encoder also provides backward compatibility for RealAudio formats used with earlier versions of the Player (versions 1.0 and 2.0) because there is a large installed base of server software and many people continue to use the earlier players and formats. Other settings offer tradeoffs between the support bit transfer rates and the overall sound quality, dynamics, and frequency response. Generally, the more reliably you want the streaming to be (in other words, the setting corresponds with the slowest bit transfer rate), the more your higher frequencies and dynamic range will suffer from the compression. At ISDN rates, you can clearly produce the files with the most fidelity, but the ISDN settings to be effective require a bit transfer rate of 40Kbps, beyond the range of a typical dial-up connection. ISDN compression settings, however, would work well for files intended for distribution within well-connected workstations in a corporate intranet.

Although the **Play While Encoding** option, located on the Options menu, provides some indication of the compressed sound quality, you get a more realistic preview by opening the file in the RealAudio Player after it has been converted. If you produce certain kinds of audio material, such as talk-show format shows or live interviews, you will probably be able to choose one of the compression settings that will consistently work with all your recorded source files. However, if you generate a substantial number of files, the RealAudio Encoder may not be the best way to perform the conversion because it doesn't support batch file processing. Sonic Foundry's Sound Forge 4.0 and later offers an optional Batch Converter plug-in that can work through a list of files to automatically perform conversion to RealAudio format, using the settings that you establish. Until the RealAudio Encoder is equipped with a batch function, Sound Forge is a much more realistic tool for producing RA files for anyone serious about doing this kind of work.

To achieve the necessary data compression, portions of the audio content—those areas of the frequency spectrum that contain the least information in a given selection—are discarded. This characteristic is what makes it possible to achieve the high levels of compression and also the reason that the different compressions are tailored to different types of source input. The voice settings, for example, trim off too much of the high-frequency component to be useful for music. The discarded audio content does to some degree "color" musical selections so that some listeners claim that even at CD-quality compression settings, the music sounds quite different from genuine CD quality. Others say that the differences are almost indiscernible. Depending on your own personal subjective judgment, the quality ranges from good to excellent for much streaming audio. Given that bit transfer rates are increasing over the Internet as improved modems and digital links become more prevalent and compression techniques are also being refined, the overall quality of streaming audio should continue to improve.

Live streaming is also supported by an enhanced version of the RealAudio Encoder. The tab for this feature is present but not active in the free downloadable version. Using live streaming, you can convert the digitized sound from an event, such as a radio broadcast or concert, into a RealAudio file that is immediately directed onto the Internet to anyone who is logged into the address.

If you are going to be working with large numbers of sound files, Sound Forge 4.0 can smooth out and automate the process. The Batch Converter plug-in makes it possible to assemble a list of source files, choose the appropriate conversion, and apply presets or other Sound Forge processing options during the conversion. This is a vast improvement over Progressive Networks' own freely distributed RealAudio Encoder and an absolute necessity if you're producing a steady output of sound files for Internet distribution. The initial window for the Batch Converter tool, shown in Figure 7.3, shows the list of files as you assemble it for processing.

Through the Options menu, you can tweak the conversion settings. A number of preset conversions are available by name; for example, the RealAudio (bandwidth negotiation) conversion setting (shown selected in Figure 7.4) creates a folder containing both 14.4Kbps and 28.8Kbps versions of the RealAudio output so that when the bandwidth is negotiated with the RealAudio server, the appropriate file can be selected from the file.

The checkbox titled "Add or remove Summary and Extra Information" allows specific details about a selection to be added to the file for possible use by the server. The "Use Plug-Ins" checkbox supports the use of additional effects or processing options during the RealAudio conversion. Preset values, established from

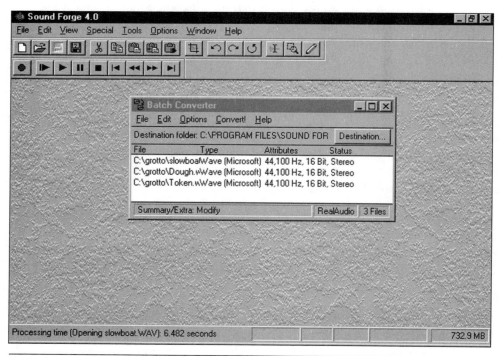

Figure 7.3 Batch Converter tool in Sound Forge.

existing libraries or custom-designed options created in Sound Forge, can be applied during the conversion. For example, you could choose to boost the high-frequency regions of a file by 6dB during conversion to the 14.4Kbps compression size to make up for the high-frequency loss that occurs at this degree of compression.

The **Preview** button included in this dialog box lets you test the current settings by running a conversion on a small portion of the currently selected file. This short sample, about six or seven seconds in length, lets you determine if you have chosen the optimum settings, and then you can actually listen to the resulting output before you take several minutes or longer to convert the entire batched file set.

The RealAudio Settings dialog box, shown in Figure 7.5, provides a place to fine-tune the compression type and other aspects of the conversion. Note that this dialog box gives you the option of turning on the Bandwidth Negotiation feature, allowing the server to select the best file to send depending on the detected bandwidth of an individual connection.

The checkbox titled "Automatically generate RealAudio Metafiles (RAM)," if enabled, adds additional information to the file that helps the server determine the

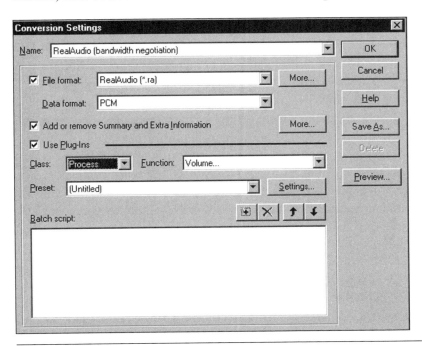

Figure 7.4 Conversion Settings dialog box.

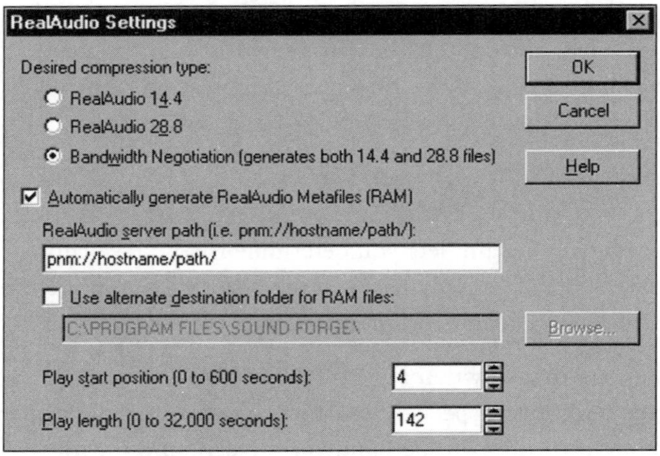

Figure 7.5 RealAudio settings.

appropriate ways to manage the file content. If this option is selected, a start position—measured in seconds—can be specified for a file to start playback at a particular point, or you can use the "Play length" value to determine how much of a file to play.

Achieving the best sounding output from a RealAudio-compressed file takes some practice because the compression techniques are somewhat different from those you might be familiar with for other kinds of digital audio work. Keep in mind that the compression is scaled to the anticipated Internet connection and the intention is to maintain the highest-quality sound output at a selected bit transfer rate for a particular kind of audio content. Music compression will sound different from voice compression, and 14.4Kbps selections will differ from ISDN selection. Although Sound Forge doesn't equate the compression settings with different types of audio content, as the RealAudio Encoder does, you can establish complex presets that can greatly improve the playback of RealAudio files. The addition of Sound Forge's excellent digital sound processing features, and the ability to assign particular effects during the conversion, make it possible to creatively refine the output for the best aesthetic results possible with this technology.

Guidelines for Creating RealAudio Files
Even if you are familiar with compressing audio files using nonstreaming formats, such as mu-law or ADPCM, you may still need to familiarize yourself with encoding techniques used for streaming audio, which scale the degree of compression to the anticipated bit rate of the Internet connection between the client and the

server. As with similar compression formats, such as the Dolby Digital AC3 format, the RealAudio encoder removes data from an audio file by determining which information is most important to the sound fidelity and then extracting the less important data. The perceptual difference between other types of audio compression can be quite noticeable, so we encourage you to experiment with different settings and different types of audio material to see what effects are obtained under different conditions.

Many of the tips for achieving good results when recording sounds apply to any type of recording, but a number of factors are of special importance when producing files for encoding. To get the best results when creating RealAudio files, consider the following guidelines:

- Start with the highest-quality sound file that you possibly can. If you are using a microphone for recording, use a professional-caliber microphone (not the little plastic job that came with your computer sound board). Music stored in digital format on CD or DAT offers cleaner source files than analog tapes or vinyl records. Any noise in a recording will create problems and distortion during the encoding process.

- When digitizing sounds, use the highest-available sampling rate and sample size: Ideally, this should be 44.1KHz with 16-bit samples. Don't sample at lower than 22KHz. Make sure that your recording input levels are set to the highest possible level without clipping the signal. Minor digital clipping can be removed by some sound editors, such as Sound Forge, but it's better to avoid it in the first place.

- Choose the codec for the file conversion carefully. The RealAudio Encoder offers several codecs, each geared to a particular type of music and connection rate. The appropriate codec will give you the best balance between file size and signal fidelity. If your listeners, for example, are all on a high-speed corporate intranet, use the ISDN codec with full stereo enabled. If you're transmitting voice-grade material, try one of the codecs tailored for voice delivery. RealAudio 4.0 includes a low bit rate codec for 8.5Kbps transmission rates that can do a fair job of handling music at low bit rates. Preview your selections after encoding to see if the resulting sound file is acceptable.

- Perform any sound processing necessary to achieve optimum signal fidelity prior to performing the RealAudio encoding. Sound processing effects such as equalization, normalization, compression, gating, and removing DC offset can cause a dramatic improvement in the sound file fidelity. Most sound editing applications provide these processing effects. Learn how to use them successfully. Files being processed for low bit-rate transfers generally require more processing than files destined for high bit-rate delivery. Boosting midrange frequencies for low bit-rate files (around 2500Hz) can brighten up the sound that is otherwise flattened by the effects of downsampling.

- Use the best-quality recording gear that you can afford—professional quality, if possible. Every component in your recording system has an effect on the recorded sound and one weak link—even an inferior cable—can reduce the fidelity of the recorded signal.

Embedding RealAudio Controls onto a Web Page

RealAudio files can be streamed from a Web site provided by an ISP, if the correct MIME type is registered for the ISP's server, but streaming is more effective when delivered from a server equipped with RealAudio server software. If you have purchased RealAudio server software from Progressive Networks, the administrator guidelines offer a full description of how to prepare files for streaming and how to set up links through a Web page.

If you want to set up RealAudio streaming through an ISP, the following description applies. Given the popularity of RealAudio on the Internet, many servers are automatically configured to recognize the RealAudio MIME types. However, you should ensure that your ISP adds the following entries to the server MIME registry:

- **.ra and .ram file extensions:** audio/x-pn-realaudio

- **.rpm file extensions:** audio/x-pn-realaudio-plugin

A metafile, containing a pointer to the source of the RealAudio file, is used as a reference within <EMBED> entries or a link entry. To create the metafile, you use any line editor to create a file with a .ram extension or .rpm extension, containing the URL of the RealAudio file that you want to have played when someone clicks the appropriate link or activates the player controls. The .ram extension is typically used in links to access a RealAudio file when the link is clicked; the .rpm extension specifies the plug-in as it is installed within an <EMBED> entry. If the RealAudio file is stored at www.sounder.net/beacon/howdy.ra, then you would enter this line in the metafile and store it in the some directory on your ISP site as the RealAudio source file will be stored. Let's assume that you give the metafile the name "greeting.rpm." A typical <EMBED> statement would be as follows:

```
<EMBED SRC="greeting.rpm" WIDTH=300 HEIGHT=134>
```

This loads the RealAudio plug-in, using the indicated size, and then references and loads the RealAudio file specified in the metafile "greeting.rpm."

Optionally, you can create a metafile using the .ram extension, which can then be used within a link. For example, to create a link to the RealAudio file from the previous example, your link entry should read:

```
<A HREF "http://www.sounder.net/beacon/greeting.ram">
```

Both of these techniques deliver streaming audio, so that playback begins a few seconds after the RealAudio file is accessed. This approach, however, works well only if you don't anticipate a high volume of activity at your ISP site. If multiple requests begin arriving for the RealAudio file, the server will probably not be able to maintain streaming mode. In situations where more than casual file access is expected, the RealAudio server software is a better solution because it is designed to be able to maintain multiple audiostreams.

ActiveX Access RealAudio functions can be used under ActiveX control for those websters who are running Microsoft Internet Explorer 3.0 and above. The ActiveX controls can be accessed through VBScript or JavaScript to allow interactive use of the RealAudio functions, a useful means of providing programmable audio functions on a Web page.

To embed the RealAudio Control for ActiveX onto an HTML page, you use the Object tag, as shown in the following example:

```
<OBJECT

ID=RAOCX

CLASSID="clsid:CFCDAA03-8BE4-11cf-B84B-0020AFBBCCFA"

HEIGHT=140

WIDTH=312>

<PARAM NAME="SRC"

VALUE="http://www.yow.com/hi.rpm">

<PARAM NAME="CONTROLS" VALUE="all">

</OBJECT>
```

The SRC entry should point to the RealAudio file to be used, either by using a metafile entry of HTTP reference or through the associated VALUE. The Class ID is fixed; this identifier should always be used when referring to the RealAudio ActiveX control.

Xing StreamWorks

Xing Technology Corporation has been involved in various forms of data compression since their founding in 1990. They developed the first compression software for JPEG images and licensed the technology to Microsoft, Creative Labs, Analog Devices, and others. Turning their sights to MPEG, Xing went on to develop techniques for compressing digital video and audio using parallel-processing hardware architectures as well as software-only solutions. Work on developing a wide-area digital video distribution system proved the viability of using packet transfers under TCP/IP to air a commercial video production—the first two channels, under the umbrella of NBC Desktop Video, carried financial news and data.

StreamWorks is an extension of all Xing's previous work, providing a compact and reliable means for streaming audio or video content over the Internet. Using MPEG as the basis for the compression, StreamWorks can provide up to full-screen, full-color video accompanied by audio at pristine 44.1KHz sample rates. On a more modest scale, the StreamWorks audio player does well with dial-up modem bit transfer rates, delivering clear audio content to users with 14.4Kbps and 28.8Kbps modems. The StreamWorks player accommodates all the major platforms—Macintosh, Windows, and X-Windows—and can be scaled for a variety of data rates ranging from 8.5Kbps to 2.0Mbps. The quality of the compressed audio and video material compares favorably with other compression techniques available on the Internet.

MPEG works well for audio and video compression, supporting file sizes approximately 10 to 15 percent of the original file size with minimal loss of quality. In other words, you can take about two minutes of CD quality audio—roughly 20Mb of data—and compress it down to 2Mb with little discernible loss. Xing Technology has created some proprietary enhancements to the MPEG standard to facilitate low bit-rate transfers—the standard compression rate available within MPEG is designed at a minimum for 32Kbps, a little fast for 28.8Kbps modem connections. Two major MPEG variations exist. MPEG 1 was originally designed for CD-ROM data delivery, allowing compressed audio and video material to be retrieved from single-speed CD-

ROM drives. MPEG 2 was tailored to broadcast systems, particularly HDTV components, for audio and video delivery. Within these two standards, three separate layers are defined, from Layer 1 to Layer 3, each handling a specific range of sampling frequencies and bit rates. Layer 3 decoders can handle all three layers; Layer 2 decoders can only handle Layers 2 and 1. The proprietary extensions to MPEG that are incorporated in StreamWorks handle bit rates as low as 8Kbps.

StreamWorks uses IP unicasting techniques to be able to simultaneously support thousands of streams from the multimedia server without restrictions due to bandwidth requirements. The server software available from Xing includes a component called StreamWorks Transmitter that can handle live encoding of audio or video material, supporting real-time broadcasting over the Internet. Once set up, broadcasting through this system is essentially as simple as hooking up your audio or video source material and streaming data to the world. MPEG variables, such as frame intervals, can be controlled within this environment, referred to by Xing as the StreamWorks Architecture. StreamWorks has been the method of choice for several major Webcasting events that proved the viability of the Internet as a communication medium capable of handling streaming video, as well as audio.

A variety of licensing agreements and software combinations are available to provide server support for StreamWorks. Rather than charging per stream, Xing charges based on the bandwidth to be delivered. The base entry point allows you to support a total bandwidth of 128Kbps, so you could stream 4 28.8Kbps transmissions or 16 8Kbps streams. The high-end license offers unlimited streams. Xing also offers a feature that lets one server propagate streams to another server to relieve traffic demands. The system is well constructed to handle industrial-strength audio and video streaming, if necessary, and this technology has found acceptance with companies such as Reuters, Capitol Records, Microsoft, Hewlett Packard, Intel, and so on.

The audio portion of StreamWorks is used frequently for providing samples of material from a record company's catalog to entice potential buyers and showcase the artist's talents. The site at Blue Note, shown in Figure 7.6, provides short clips of modern and classic jazz performances, stored in streaming audio format. The compact StreamWorks player is shown in the lower-right portion of the window.

The live broadcasting capabilities of StreamWorks can also be seen in action on the Web. A radio broadcast in Stockholm, Sweden—Power 106—provides an assortment of music in both live and prerecorded formats, as shown in Figure 7.7.

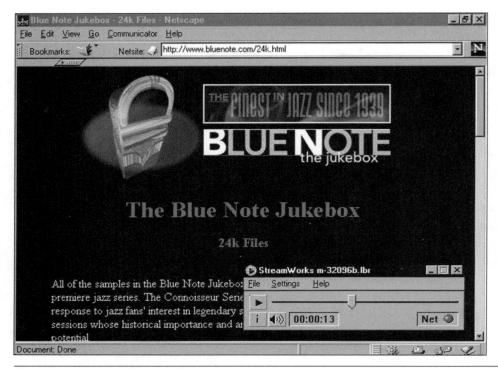

Figure 7.6 Blue Note Web site and StreamWorks player.

If your Swedish is a bit rusty, the station offers a JavaScript-enabled button that redraws the page with English text.

With its MPEG compression and flexible server architecture, StreamWorks is a good choice for medium- to large-scale audio streaming with the additional advantage that it can stream video as well. The pricing favors corporate and organizational site providers, but the entry point pricing is not too high to rule out small companies or independents. The quality of the streamed content ranks near the top of the list for this category.

Liquid Audio In-Depth Profile

One of the more important Web-based technologies to emerge recently, Liquid Audio is the first turnkey system for previewing, selling, and distributing music on the Internet. Despite the pressure of software-release deadlines and upcoming trade shows, staff members were generous with their time, allowing us to do an in-depth

Figure 7.7 Power 106 in Stockholm, Sweden, streams audio.

examination of Liquid Audio's origins, tools, and future. We talked with Tom Murphy, Electronic Marketing Manager at Liquid Audio; Steve Ansell, the staff server expert; and Jason Brownell, an audio engineer who has perfected many of the encoding techniques used by Liquid Audio. Many of the views and information presented in the following sections are based on information obtained through a series of telephone interviews with these staff members.

Liquid Audio in a Nutshell

From the beginning, co-founder and CEO Gerry Kearby visualized Liquid Audio as a complete process—a completely integrated method for producing, distributing, and selling music on the Web. The Liquid Audio product consists of a package of software components that offer an integrated approach to presenting and selling audio material on the Web. The encoding software allows developers to create files suitable for playback through the Liquid Audio player; files that are optimized for different rates of streaming data transfer. The server software provides an environment for managing the delivery of Liquid Audio files, extracting and presenting information from properly encoded files within the player window. More than just a codec approach, Liquid Audio creates a media and environment on the Internet where people can preview, purchase, and handle the actual distribution of copyrighted music content.

While audio data compression and streaming are included in the Liquid Audio package, the model is based on a scenario where Web site visitors preview and then can purchase music. For example, as you're browsing a Web site with music content in Liquid Audio format, you click on a selection to hear it at whatever fidelity your system can handle. The assumption is that you're listening because you anticipate making a purchase. If you sample the music and it suits your taste, you can click another button to initiate the whole commerce mechanism. The server software supports the entry of a credit card number or CyberCash account or other Internet cash system, and the selected music gets delivered over the Net to you. In cases where you may have a CD recorder available, in an hour or so (after the full download), you can burn a CD and then play it in your car or drop it into your CD player. The Internet is used as a vehicle to move music around, but it clearly doesn't have to just stay within the domain of the computer.

As part of the sale and delivery process, a number of accounting features are built in to ensure that the artist gets paid and the label gets paid and whoever has rights to the music gets paid. The entire mechanism is designed to take advantage of the convenience of the Internet for accessing and previewing music and also to allow visitors to obtain the music on demand to copy to CD, cassette, DAT, or other media formats. The system can also support the sale of pressed CDs for anyone who prefers to obtain a finished product.

To encourage industry acceptance of this technology, Liquid Audio includes technologies that provide watermarking and encryption. Without this kind of protection, you run the risk that the Internet will become the world's most efficient and fastest bootleg vehicle. Musicians and the labels and everyone who has a vested interest in protecting their works are more likely to accept this technology if built-in protections lessen the chances that bootlegging will occur.

The CD recorder option has not been included with version 1.0 of the Liquid Audio software, but it is slated for release in the near future. With CD recorder prices down to approximately $300 for internal units, it won't be long before many computer systems are bundled with built-in recorders, just as CD-ROM drives are now included with almost all systems. For more comprehensive information on CD recording technology, consult *The Complete CD-Recordable Guide* by Lee Purcell and David Martin (released by Sybex in June 1997).

Until the product includes the CD recorder feature, users will have to rely on an order-button approach. Click on an order button, fill out an online form, and a CD can be drop-shipped to you directly from the artist or a label.

Musicians and conventional audio broadcasters sometimes use RealAudio as a tool for distributing encoded files in streaming mode for playback on the Web. Generally, this approach is used as a promotional tool—as a way for previewing song selections or gaining an audience outside the range of a conventional radio broadcast. Liquid Audio, in comparison, is more like a record store than this radio station model. The focus is on the commerce—previewing and selling music on the Internet—and protecting artist's original works. RealAudio makes more sense when the goal is to showcase a portion of a song or a number of songs on a CD to encourage someone to buy the album; Liquid Audio makes more sense when the system is set up to allow the purchase of selections, either through online ordering or direct downloading of the music to be copied to other media.

Other Liquid Audio Features

Besides the use of Dolby Digital compression technology and the streaming protocol that is integrated into Liquid Audio, the package includes other components recognized as critical to a music commerce system, including:

- Supporting integration with databases

- Serving not just audio, but information and data about music selections

- Displaying album covers and lyrics

- Providing details about the participating musicians and the studios

These are the types of things you typically see when you are thumbing through a CD jacket. Liquid Audio can deliver the media data about the song to allow the developer to provide a complete preview of an album or selection.

Database support allows full accounting for licensing agencies, royalty tracking, copyright management and protection, and support for various levels of reporting structures. Those people who have rights and licensing to any kind of music will be able to track and get paid for any transactions that take place. When someone buys a CD, the reporting process is easy because it is tied to physical inventory. The database integration including in Liquid Audio allows the same type of accounting and database management for transactions that are carried out in electronic form as well.

Preventing Illegal Copying

One of the potential dangers in distributing music electronically is that once someone has purchased a song, they can easily make copies of it to pass around and give to other people. Liquid Audio utilizes a form of watermarking technology, which is essentially like a digital fingerprint that embeds information about the music within the actual audio signal. If any copies of a Liquid Audio file are distributed, watermarking allows the source to be traced. Adding accountability and recognition is one of the key elements in helping to prevent piracy. If you can identify music and identify where it came from and who purchased it, this should lessen the likelihood that anyone will make copies of it because each of the copies points directly back to the source.

This approach, however, doesn't prevent people from making copies. Another built-in feature of Liquid Audio is a copy protection scheme that uses encryption to verify that only a certain individual has access to a specific piece of music. For example, you don't get CD-quality sound unless the purchase transaction was for CD-quality sound. You're prevented from downloading a piece of music unless you can be identified as a person who has purchased it.

If someone makes a copy of the music and puts it on another system, Liquid Audio recognizes the different environment and prevents playback. The combined copy protection and copy management schemes keep people from making copies of songs to give away. All of this functionality is integral to the audio data formats and the mechanisms by which the clients and the servers interact.

Interview with Tom Murphy

Tom Murphy, Electronic Marketing Manager at Liquid Audio, spent five years at Digidesign before joining Liquid Audio. In a telephone interview, Tom spent some time discussing Liquid Audio's history and development.

I understand the compression technique used in Liquid Audio is different from some of the other audio compression formats.

To begin with, we are the only company that has license for the Dolby Digital compression. Phil Wiser, co-founder and the V.P. of Engineering, worked in the audio signal processing area for many years. As the founders were working on a CD-ROM-based audio device, he developed optimizations for AC-3 in a general-purpose computing environment. AC-3 was designed to function in consumer electronic environments that were less flexible than a PC. The Liquid Audio optimizations resulted in a significant quality improvement.

We realize that as compression technology evolves, there probably will be other codecs available. The Liquid Audio architecture is designed so that if better compression technologies arise, we can build them into our system quickly and easily—and keep the environment backward-compatible. As other technologies evolve, we'll be able to ensure that we have the cleanest and best audio fidelity available.

Does the compression scale itself in any way to the target download bandwidth?

In addition to the codec alone, there is the whole streaming technology side of things. We are the first company to utilize RTP, the Real-Time Protocol. This is the basis for Progressive's Real Media proposal for RTSP. RTP allows us to negotiate the bandwidth between the client and the server. It allows you to determine how you are connected and how to deliver the audio content.

Does the watermarking and copyright protection and artist information actually get plugged into the file by Liquifier Pro?

Absolutely. Both are there and on the server. There are a lot of database fields; there is a whole section in the encoder—in Liquifier Pro—where you are typing in all this information about licensing agencies and who has copyrights and publishing rights. You're encoding and binding and locking it with the data itself—it's married together, they are inseparable.

The watermarking puts this information actually within the audio signal, so even if you made an analog copy of it, it's still in there. When you publish it to the server, the server has all this data at its disposal as well. Both Shockwave and RealAudio have some mechanisms where you can use any server you want to stream your music, but they don't have any of those database connections or any of the protections involved. If it's just a file on a Web server, it's basically public access.

Can you explain the use of the encoding tool, Liquifier Pro?

Many of the people in this company have come from the audio workstation business, so we've spent a lot of time making recording and editing tools, and doing dynamics and compression and processing—working on the highly professional level, from pro tools systems and doing film post-production and so on. Liquifier Pro encompasses many of those tools and techniques, but focuses specifically on creating Internet master content.

So there are actually sound processing tools as part of the Liquifier Pro encoder software?

Correct. The software has a dynamics module and an EQ module. Depending on what your modem speed is, your fidelity changes dramatically. What you hear through a 14.4Kbps modem isn't what you hear through an ISDN line. What we allow you to do is to optimize the fidelity of the processing for each of the data rates. In the preview window, you can highlight a portion of your CD master file and then process it at each of the different data rates, adding EQ and compression for each data rate. Since you lose so much high end at the 14.4Kbpsrate, you can bump up the high frequencies a bit before you process it. The version that you have processed at 14.4Kbps is a little different from your 16-bit stereo ISDN connection.

RTP Packet Transmissions

Liquid Audio represents one of the first commercial products to incorporate Real Time Protocol (RTP) into its handling of streaming data formats. RTP works at the packet level with TCP/IP to perform two-way communication during real-time data transmissions. If you are dropping packets, RTP can send an appropriate message to the server and the server can then scale itself to the optimal transfer rate.

Under conventional TCP/IP packet transmissions you can lose packets, which is not an acceptable means of data handling if you're trying to delivery CD-quality audio data. The conventional approach to data delivery under TCP/IP presents serious problems when working with multimedia content. Do you wait for late packets? Do you leave gaps in the audio? Do you try to fill in the missing data? To some degree, you cannot escape the problem of losing packets on the Internet. You may or may not be able to wait for that data to come in before you have to play it. If, however, you are downloading data to ensure CD-quality content, gaps are unacceptable. To ensure the necessary quality, you must wait until you can fill in the gaps caused by missing packets. By instituting communication between the server and the data source, RTP goes a long way toward reducing the problem of data disruption and supporting streaming of different types of data.

Server Software Options

The Liquid Audio product line is being expanded to include several different variations, each providing a different entry point (and different associated costs) to developers and sites interested in providing this functionality on their Web site. The initial server model is geared more toward the higher-end commercial environment where commerce is the primary interest. Potentially, however, there are many different uses for this technology. The range extends from the major labels that have thousands of titles that they want to make available to the public, to small, independent producers that prefer to market their wares on the Internet rather than compete with the major labels in the record stores.

Many mid-sized independent labels have a number of popular artists that can quickly and easily recover the cost of the server. Web site administrators and developers who suspect they will be able to move a fair volume of albums may want to investigate Liquid Audio's pricing plans to see if they fit their business model. Another option that will probably increase in popularity is the potential for straight service providers to offer space on the server for audio content in Liquid Audio format. For example, IUMA has purchased a Liquid Audio server and is going to license out pieces of it. IUMA acts as a kind of a musician's Internet Service Provider. Beyond the simple leasing of Web space, you also get audio space on the server.

Other server models may include simplified versions of the product that don't have all of the functions enabled. For example, if someone doesn't need to do the CD-quality audio distribution, but they have warehouses of audio discs that they want to distribute physically, a Liquid Audio server could enable their customers to preview and purchase selections. All order processing could be handled by the components of this simplified server.

Tom Murphy described the Liquid Audio commitment to the widest range of individuals as follows: "There are thousands of independent record labels out there that have everything from a single artist to hundreds of artists. It's impossible to make one product that is going to fit everyone's needs, so we have the challenge of trying to make the appropriate tools for the appropriate markets. Initially, we intend to be working with the professional community, but we also want to provide benefits to the independent labels."

Stream Fees

Some companies involved in streaming audio, such as Progressive Networks, charge a per-stream fee as part of their server license structure. Liquid Audio, however, does not place these limitations on the server software. Users of the product can stream any audio data up to the capacity of the server hardware and software without accruing any additional costs for high-traffic demands. Whether you have an ISDN line or T1 or more, the bandwidth really defines how many simultaneous connections you can have. The current Liquid Audio server platform is designed for Sun SPARCstations and Silicon Graphics Indy systems, which are recognized as platforms with a lot of horsepower built in. By the time you read this, Liquid Audio should also have a Windows NT server available.

Overview of Liquifier Pro

The starting point for many audio projects involving Liquid Audio will be a CD-quality master. To convert this audio content to the appropriate file format requires running Liquifier Pro, a Microsoft Windows applications that uses a wizard-like approach through a series of panels to complete the file processing and data entry for the audio content. Liquifier Pro goes through a series of steps, beginning with the media window where you type in all the information about the song—the name of the song, how long it is, the band, the album name, the musicians, the recording studio, and so on.

The next step is either to import or record the song. You can record the audio through a sound board with analog or digital inputs. If you have a sound board with an SPD/IF input, you can record directly from a DAT master. Optionally, you can record the audio directly from a CD, if you already have a finished audio CD available directly from within the Liquifier record window. This feature allows you to bring in the contents of a CD's tracks without performing any additional analog-to-digital or digital-to-analog conversions, therefore eliminating any degradation of the sound fidelity during the transfer. The basic assumption by Liquifier Pro is that it will be working with a 16-bit stereo master PCM file.

Recording input can be processed through an edit window. Editing options are fairly fundamental: you can trim the top and tail of each piece—to have clean beginnings and ends to all the songs. You can copy and paste music segments within the editor. Whenever you do the copying and pasting, Liquifier Pro builds in cross fades, so you always have clean splices. This eliminates the tics, clicks, and pops in transition areas (which are a very common problem for many workstation-based sound editing tools).

Editing is destructive, in that the changes you specify are applied to the indicated sound files. Nondestructive sound editing tools, such as Hohner-Midia's Samplitude Studio, let you work in a virtual environment where the source files remain unaltered and only the effects and processing are stored in a separate file. You can use more sophisticated sound processing tools to create the PCM file format for import into Liquifier Pro, and in cases where significant sound processing may be required, this approach will yield the best results.

Liquifier Pro is focused on those types of tasks that allow music to be presented and delivered on the Web. For example, you can highlight a region that is going to be a clip—so that you can have an entire song available—and highlight a 30-second clip that is the chorus or hook. You can also set fade-in and fade-out times for both the song and the clip. Each clip that you specify can have a fade-out, which provides a professional touch when the music is previewed. You can also set both the clip and song markers, and you can set fade times. The fades are actually implemented by the Liquid Audio player—they do not result in the creation of separate files that you have to keep track of.

The end result of the editing in Liquifier Pro creates a single master file for each song. You don't need to worry about creating separate versions of the song for different data rates and then creating a metafile that points to the appropriate file when the server interaction begins. One master file contains all the media data and the information for each separate data rate that has been selected for inclusion. All of this information is encapsulated into one master file that is published on the Liquid Audio Server.

Pointers in the master file can extract whatever information is requested on the client end. Once you've set your clip and your song in Liquifier Pro, you generally proceed to the Preview menu. You can highlight a certain segment of a song, and Liquifier Pro will encode for each of those selected data rates. For example, you might highlight the chorus of a song and then click the 14.4Kbps rate. Liquifier Pro encodes the audio data and you can then listen to it and make judgment calls as to the quality. You are free to set all the parameters and tweaks of the processing versus the compression for each data rate. In this manner, you very quickly hear what the

14.4Kbps rate is going to sound like, the 28.8 rate, the ISDN rate, and the full CD quality. With the Preview window still open, you can make whatever modifications or tweaks to the files that are necessary to achieve the sound balance that you want.

Once you've picked exactly the parameters of how you want it to sound at all the various data rates, you go to the Print window. The Print window lets you select whether you encode the entire song or the only the clip for each of the data rates. For example, you choose to select all of the 14.4Kbps clips to create preview clips for the streaming data access and then select the option to download a full version of the CD-quality song. Or, maybe you encode both a clip and a song and create a larger file that has the entire song at all the data rates, but then on some portions of the Web site, visitors can listen to just the 30-second clip or, on other portions of the Web site, they can hear the whole thing. Because this all takes place with changes made to one file, you don't need to make separate versions for different uses.

Liquifier Pro lets you selectively determine what file sizes and data rates you will be using; then the last step is to publish the material. You type in the address of your server and an account password, if you have one, and press the **Upload** button. Liquifier Pro takes the selected file, connects to the server, and negotiates uploading. The server then deals with extracting the media information from the file and also oversees the archiving and file management. All you need supply to facilitate the upload is one URL. The file consists of a unique Liquid Audio MIME type that gets spawned—the server and the client deal with all the rest of the maintenance, sorting out versions and addresses, and so on.

One possible working model for this product will be to have satellite audio engineering studios where people are processing the audio files and then going through an ISP like IUMA. Processed files will be uploaded to leased space provided by the server and then played by anyone who visits the site.

Downloading of CD-quality audio requires the use of the Dolby Digital compression standard to reduce the file sizes to something more manageable for Internet delivery. Using the Dolby Digital, depending on your compression settings, gains you 7:1 or 12:1 compression on the full CD quality. According to a number of observers, even at full bandwidth, the fidelity difference between a full linear 16-bit file and a Dolby Digital encoded file is fairly indiscernible. Because these compression technologies are based on perceptual coding, to encode the CD quality takes a lot longer than encoding the 14.4Kbps version. The software is analyzing the data and determining what harmonics are masked and what harmonics aren't. The compression algorithm basically extracts those portions of the audio content that you don't normally hear. Some audio professionals argue that the resulting sound files are definitely not what can be considered true CD quality, but others see the difference as imperceptible. Without compression, it is impractical to consider transferring entire CDs across the Internet since a single audio CD can contain up to 680Mb of data.

 A demonstration version of Liquifier Pro is included on the CD-ROM bundled with this book.

Server Setup for Liquid Audio

Much of the advice and the perspectives in this section came from conversations with Steve Ansell of Liquid Audio, who offered suggestions on preparing a server to use for Liquid Audio files. The requirements are no more demanding than for most Internet server setups. If someone is comfortable with setting up a typical Web server—Netscape's or Microsoft's server or the Apache (a free Web server)—then he or she should have no problem setting up a Liquid Audio server.

The server architecture is designed to scale from a small, single-machine setup to a server that can be distributed across multiple machines, including access to a database for a larger, more sophisticated site. An ambitious group of musicians with a bit of technical knowledge and some cash to invest should be able to leverage this architecture as a means to deliver their music on the Internet. To do so, they would need to have some knowledge of Web servers—at least the basic concepts of what it takes to set up a Web server and to know what an IP address is. They would also need to have their own machine on the Internet.

Hosting Capabilities

Liquid Audio is working on enhancements to the hosting capabilities in the newest version of their server software. This feature allows a company in the role of an Internet Service Provider (ISP) to set up a Liquid Audio server to host other musicians who lacked their own server.

A server equipped in this manner would be able to accept direct uploads from anyone with the appropriate account running the Liquifier Pro software. As can be seen in the Publish pane in Liquifier Pro, this function can be used to automatically send audio content to the server. This content gets processed following the upload on the server side so that it is ready to be streamed from a Web interface.

This feature allows anyone to publish audio material to an ISP equipped with the Liquid Audio software. To support this feature, the software has a function where you can set up individual accounts on the server and allocate the disk space to be available for each account. For example, you could make up an account and call it "Megadeth" and assign a password and an area on the server with 20Mb or so of disk space. Members of Megadeth could then use Liquifier Pro to connect to their area, type in their login and password, and perform file uploads. Each area shows up visually as a tree structure. You use drag-and-drop techniques to post files to the server.

One organization that caters to the professional broadcast community, EDnet, has been demonstrating the host capabilities of Liquid Audio at conferences such as the National Association of Broadcasters (NAB). EDnet uses this server architecture to host individuals who are previewing radio spots. They have a special version of the Liquid Audio software tailored to them called the SST Encoder and SST Decoder. The Encoder is actually a version of the Liquifier encoder.

The SST Encoder includes a few extra features to support EDnet's capabilities. Within this environment, they are hosting people who sell radio spots, such as ads and similar material. EDnet runs the server, and people use the Liquifier application to post files on the server for their customers to listen to the audio, demo it, and preview it. Customers can select the clip they like from the available selections.

This approach is very similar to a music environment, where a company like IUMA hosts independent labels or musicians who want to post their work. The host makes the Web page interface to the audio content and allows anyone to link to your area of the site and stream audio files.

Server Setup

At the moment, Liquid Audio server software runs only on Unix systems, Solaris and IRIX. Some portions of the application also run on BSDI. On a more sophisticated site, the architecture allows you to have the server software distributed across a number of different machines.

Basically, there are three components to Liquid Audio server. One piece, called the Content Manager, is the back-end piece that deals with all the files that handle the publishing capability. There is another piece that is called the Delivery Service, which is the front-end piece that actually does the streaming of music–the actual delivery of music. The Delivery Service can be scaled if you have a bigger network link and significant activity. The final piece—the CGI—works with the Web server; this is the component that has the Web interface.

To set up a Liquid Audio server, you install the server software on your selected hardware. The installation proceeds from a script that runs through a number of questions, asking questions about where to install individual components and where to create certain storage areas. For simplifying the configuration, there is an HTML-based application that brings up a Web page. Through this Web page, you can configure a server to your specific needs.

This procedure is generally followed by the server administrator to set up the server. As part of the process, you set up accounts for people to publish Liquid Audio files on the server. Once the server is up and running, someone using the Liquifier application would encode the music, enter all the copyright information and album-cover GIFs and so on, connect to the server, and publish directly from the Liquifier Publish pane. The next phase in this process is to actually integrate the links to the audio content into Web format; this involves constructing the Web page and embedding the correct URL in the page.

After you install the server, it becomes available for anyone to use through the publishing component of Liquid Audio. Once the music has been published to the site, the only thing left to do is to make the Web page to link to the content. The Liquid Audio server also supports interconnection with a database where information is stored at publish time directly into the database. Tools are available for a number of different databases that will dynamically generate Web pages from information that is stored in a database. In that case, you could have everything dynamically configured so that as soon as someone publishes audio, the newly created links become automatically available on the Web.

Database Interconnections

Although the product does not include its own database component, the Liquid Audio software can interface with two popular databases and export (publish) into these databases. Liquid Audio currently supports these databases:

- **MSQL:** A shareware database that you can download off the Net that is very popular for Web applications

- **Oracle:** An industrial-strength database for larger sites

You can also run the product without a database. In the simplest setup, you would install the software all on one machine, possibly even the same machine as your Web server, and in this configuration you would not have to employ a database. When you publish, the product uses what is called "Direct File Method." You publish and store the files on the server; then you create your Web pages to access the files. The files are stored on hard disk, but you can't pull the information out of the Liquifier files to put it on your Web page. The descriptive song information shows up in the Liquid Audio player window, but this information can't be shared for display on your Web pages.

The software architecture was designed to be extensible—to extend from a simple site with just one machine running the server components, without a database (so all you need is the software and a Web server), to complex, multiserver sites with distributed components.

All of the information that goes into Liquifier at publish time can be exported into a database. On the server side, you need to set up and define database tables. Beyond that, there are some extra database features that you can add to the product using your own tools. This can include timely information, purchase information, and details on how to link the information back to your Web page.

You can use the order button provided by the software to go back to your Web page and launch the order page. Or, optionally, you can perform dynamic HTML generation. If you want to take the data from Liquifier Pro that gets put into the database and then extract that data, you can use it to create Web pages automatically. You can also set up searches on music titles, categories, and similar items. Liquid Audio supports numerous advanced applications that may require external software. For example, while the product doesn't include an automatic Web-page generation tool, you can use a number of off-the-shelf applications in combination with Liquid Audio to accomplish dynamic page creation. Liquid Audio also works well with a number of freeware applications easily available on the Internet.

The most effective use of the Liquid Audio software involves dynamic link creation through the database interconnection. When this is set up on the server, as soon as something is published, you can click on the link that displays the list of songs in the database—immediately, the one you just published shows up there with all the information. You can click on the newly created link and stream it, listen to it, and so on, without having to do anything further. While this capability is certainly available, in a real-world case, you might want to have an intermediate step to satisfy the timing considerations of posting new publicly available files to the server. For example, when somebody first publishes an audio file, ideally you might want to have it transferred to a private area so that people can demo it. But, the process is much easier if you can extract key information from the database. In the optimum environment, you can share the information between the interface (what you see on the Web page) and the audio content (what you see in Liquid Audio player).

Network Interfacing

To support a Liquid Audio server properly, your system must be directly connected to the Internet. The server software expects to be positioned out on the Internet looking for connections—the same as a conventional Web server would be. Most sites that are running the Liquid Audio server should have a T1 link or a dedicated ISDN connection or something of that class.

The situation is much simpler for publishing Liquid Audio files. You can accomplish publishing over a dial-up connection. Keep in mind that if you're publishing large files, it's going to take awhile—perhaps several hours for the full contents of an album.

While it is feasible to send CD-quality music from a 28.8Kbps dial-up connection, you're probably not going to want to sit there at your computer waiting for it to finish. Because each Liquid Audio file is a composite file, it contains all the images for the different bandwidths that you want to support. This can result in a significantly large file if you include everything from 14.4K, 28.8K, ISDN-1, ISDN-2, all the way up to CD quality. For a single complete song, you may be dealing with tens of megabytes of audio data. An average file size on a Liquid Audio site for a full song is 10Mb or so. This will definitely take a while to download over a 28.8Kbps modem.

In the most common scenario, you want to complete all of your audio encoding and then save your file locally. Start the publish connection and let it proceed. The Liquifier Pro software lets the transfer take place in the background while you're still performing other tasks in the application—such as working on additional file encoding.

File transfers that consist of shorter segments—such as a series of 30-second clips in a few bandwidths—require much less time. Some Liquid Audio sites contain files that are smaller than 1Mb. Uploads in this case will require only a few minutes instead of hours.

If you're planning to set up a server to stream multiple lines, data demand issues will bear serious consideration. Just by the nature of the Internet, you will have to have a large conduit for the large amounts of data, and that single factor will probably represent your largest cost. For example, when you start looking at the cost of having a T1 line—which is not a huge data conduit—typical costs will be about a $1000 a month in many places. For many Liquid Audio users, the hosting model (where space is leased from a provider) will be the more cost-efficient approach.

Encoding Liquid Audio Files

This section presents tips that were shared by Jason Brownell, an audio engineer at Liquid Audio. Jason has worked in the digital audio field for a number of years. Like some other Liquid Audio staff members, he spent some time as an engineer at Studer EditTech and also worked for a time for the San Francisco Opera as an audio engineer. He worked with Phil Wiser to develop many of the audio presets used in the Liquid Audio encoder to achieve the optimal quality for streaming at both high and low bit rates.

Preparing for Encoding

The process of encoding files for Liquid Audio is much different from that for encoding files for RealAudio or StreamWorks because of the nature of the Liquid Audio software. For example, the RealAudio audio encoder is basically a batch encoding process—you direct a file in one end and get encoded audio out the other. The Liquifier is designed to be more of a mastering tool along the lines of existing computer-based audio tools. For this type of mastering, you bring in your source audio (either by recording it or bringing it in on the CD), view the waveform, perform the audio editing, and then preview all the compression options you might have. This approach lets you try out the processing on small sections of a song and then modify the processing parameters to improve the sound. Once you are satisfied with your results, you complete the process and create the encoded file.

In some ways, the Liquifier Pro application functions like a mini-digital audio workstation custom-tailored for encoding. Anyone who has worked with digital audio workstations should be immediately comfortable in the work environment.

In most cases, to prepare an audio file for encoding, you start with a source file consisting of the final stereo mix for the work and then bring it into the Edit pane in Liquifier. Within the Edit pane, you can perform simple clean-up of the file contents. If there are any stray audio artifacts at the beginning or end of the file, you can edit these problems out. By the time you're done working in the Edit pane, you should have the pristine master file that you want to use for encoding.

This is also the point in the program where you set marks for the clip. One of the unique features of Liquifier Pro is that it lets you work with a larger file, but mark a smaller clip. For example, you might start with a three-minute song that you want to make available for downloading. Assume that you want to make 30 seconds available for previewing. Rather than have two separate files stored on the server, Liquid Audio stores the whole song with markers that define a clip within it. When a person is streaming the clip, the software finds where the clip starts and ends within the larger audio file. For this reason, you don't need multiple copies of the same audio file stored on the site to support listening to a smaller section of the content. You can define a smaller clip within the larger file.

Also, the one single file that you create for a song contains versions at the different compression rates—you don't need multiple copies of files to support the different rates. Once again, all the audio content resides in one big file from which anyone can access whatever compressed version suits his or her requested delivery method.

The clip feature provides an additional set of options within the single file. In the Print pane, one program feature lets you encode just a clip, or a clip and the entire song—for each of the bit rates. For example, you could put in a clip and a song at the 28.8Kbps modem setting. Then when the file is stored on the server, the server can determine whether it will stream the whole song or just the clip at each bit rate. The server can look in the one file for the appropriate encoded version.

Processing effects added during encoding can optimize the audio file contents for each of the anticipated bit transfer rates. This is one of the primary features of the Liquid Audio preview function, which appears in the Liquifier Preview pane. You have a choice of each of the bit rates that the program currently supports with their names: 14.4 modem, 28.8 modem, ISDN. At each bit rate, the program supplies a list of factory presets. These are settings that the Liquid Audio engineers designed to sound best for different types of music at different bit rates. If you want to tweak the settings more, you can define a user preset. Liquid Audio offers an equalizer and dynamics processor for the user presets. You can also choose mono or stereo at each bit rate.

At low bit rates, from 28.8Kbps down, the mono setting is preferable because it allows higher-quality audio content to be generated for delivery. Sometimes mono is also the choice of preference for ISDN-1, if a file is being encoded for a single ISDN line and you want to achieve the best sound. Essentially, you have only so many bits to work with to maintain the streaming delivery—when you're dividing them up between two channels you start to compromise the audio quality just to get stereo. If you do your file processing in mono, you can have all those bits just for one channel. In most cases, what you lose by going from stereo to mono is worse than what you lose by trying to fit a lot of information into fewer bits.

Keep in mind, however, that notions of audio quality can be very subjective. Some people insist on stereo; without it, they don't think music sounds good. Technically, the file size of an encoded stereo size doesn't change—the bits per second are set at a particular bit rate. This ensures that the file size is a constant. But the difference is whether you are packing one channel or two into the same file size.

The transfer rates and file sizes are based on the low-performance end of what can be achieved for a particular connection. In other words, if an encoded file is set up for transfer at 28.8Kbps, it's really being designed for streaming at around 20Kbps. The program leaves a buffer to ensure consistent streaming; you can't expect to achieve the full bandwidth of the channel available to you. In the Liquid MusicPlayer, individual users can set preferences for determining how much buffering is going to be used, which helps compensate for different real-world transfer rates for a given modem connection. The buffer size can be increased to compensate for heavy Internet traffic. This creates a situation where the file initially takes longer to start playing back, but once it does start playing, the playback is smoother without breaks or gaps in the audio.

While you're encoding the file, there isn't anything you can really do to ensure that it will stream effectively. You're basically just creating a file of a certain size. The details of managing the streaming in a smooth manner are based on communication between the player and the server.

In general, the more you compress the file, the better luck you'll have with the streaming. However, if you start extracting more audio data from the file, while the streaming will work better, the file will sound worse. The way that the Liquifier is set up now, you choose the 28.8Kbps modem slot; that selection is basically a constant, pre-defined bit rate. The program doesn't give the user the ability to lower the bit rate at 28.8K. Instead, you can drop down to the 14.4Kbps slot. For example, as a user playing back audio files, even if you had a 28.8Kbps modem, you could elect to stream at 14.4Kbps (which you might want to do if your 28.8Kbps modem connection is bad).

The streaming is negotiated at the player end. For example, assume someone has an ISDN-1 line but it's being shared. If bandwidth is set down a notch to 28.8K, then the server will stream the 28.8Kbps version over the ISDN line. He or she will get much better performance, but lower sound quality.

Guidelines for High-Quality Encoding

The basic rule-of-thumb for achieving high-quality encoding results is: The higher the bandwidth, the less processing you should use. This notion may not be immediately obvious to those using the application for the first time. Because Liquifier Pro allows you to use different audio processing for each bandwidth, your equalization or compression settings can be stored as a user-defined preset at each bandwidth. The amount of processing used for a 14.4Kbps modem is going to be completely different from the processing used for a dual ISDN line.

Each preset contains settings for equalization and dynamics based on the Digital Dolby encoding preset at that bit rate. The parameters for the Dolby encoder, such as the number of bits per second and all the other specialized routines included in the AC3 algorithm, are predefined. The program doesn't easily give users access to those settings because users really need to know exactly what they are doing to work at that level. The average user or even a high-end audio person has sufficient control by setting the equalizer values and the dynamics at each bit rate.

The equalizer built into the program is a parametric equalizer. As you're working in the program, when you create a user preset, the program displays a box that shows a diagram of the signal flow. Within this diagram, there are pictures of the different processors available. If you click on the equalizer, Liquifier Pro displays a four-band parametric equalizer. You can choose low-shelf bandpass or a high-shelf for each band being processed. When you're in bandpass mode, you can choose the EQ and the width of the band. The program displays the curve for this setting.

If you select the dynamics processor. you have a choice of a compressor/expander and a limiter. Compression applied at the low bit rates can improve the overall sound quality of a selection. Typically, only light compression is required for near-CD quality and ISDN-2 channel quality. When possible, avoid doing a lot of processing at those levels. By definition, CD quality is supposed to be a copy that is indistinguishable from the original, so you want to minimize processing for signals at that level.

As you drop down to lower bit rates, the audio needs more help to sound good. Typically, a bit of compression improves. One technique that can be effective is to use the expander in reverse. An expander will take an audio level that is below a threshold and make it even lower (like a gate). A gate is the ultimate expander. Any audio information that falls below the threshold is cut off completely—which is infinity to one expander. What you can do is expand by either lowering the level below the threshold or raising it. Pick a threshold level and then take a low-level signal and raise it up a bit to achieve this effect. Then you can take the high-level peaks and compress them. All around, what this does is lower the dynamic range of the signal.

At the lower bit rates, if you lower the dynamic range of the signal, it helps the audio sound better when you compress it. This effect is similar, in a way, to radio. For AM radio broadcasts, engineers have to compress the sound in order to modulate the signal within the amount of frequency in the air waves that they have available. With FM radio, engineers have to compress the sound because they can get only so much dynamic range out of the little width of airspace that they have. Also, with the attenuated quality of FM radio or AM radio, the audio always sounds better if you compress it.

Some of this process is basically just an audio trick. On typical tiny computer speakers, sound reproduction is not handled very well, nor is dynamic range reproduced well. Processing the audio can compensate for these limitations.

As you're producing Liquid Audio files, it can be helpful to have different speakers for playback to simulate different environments of your users. For the highest-fidelity sound, use real monitor speakers. You can also connect inexpensive plastic computer speakers to your system to hear how the files will sound on a typical system. When compressing audio for a 28.8Kbps modem, assume that the person listening at the other end has a SoundBlaster card and similar speakers. Preview the selections through a SoundBlaster card and plastic speakers. In the Preview pane, before you encode, you can select a little section of the audio and then run your processing on it to see exactly what it will sound like. When you listen through the tiny speakers, you'll hear exactly what the user at home will hear.

When working with the Liquifier get the best possible sound, spend a lot of time exploring and using the Preview pane. Take advantage of the fact that you can go in and preview your compression options. The heart of Liquifier Pro is that you can preview what an audio file is going to sound like, without having to encode the entire file. As you gain more familiarity with Liquifier and its options, you can create user presets for different kinds of music—the types of music that you most frequently work with. You preview a collection of material and then create a user preset that you know works well with a particular type of music: jazz, for example, or hip hop. The same guidelines apply to rock, or classical, or folk, or spoken voice. Use your ears and your best audio judgments, and spend a lot of time using the Preview pane; your efforts will be rewarded with cleaner sounding Liquid Audio files.

Using the Presets

Presets that are included in Liquifier Pro handle a wide range of user requirements. The default presets that come up when you start the Liquifier at the 28.8Kbps modem setting are called Smooth Mono. The default for ISDN-1 is called Smooth Mono ISDN-1. If you don't have time to adjust the settings, these factory presets are the ones to use for the best overall results. For most people, the factory presets will handle a wide variety of music and sound types.

Once you get into tweaking the settings yourself, Liquifier Pro is designed to be a tool that allows people of varying knowledge to use it effectively. If you know nothing about audio, stick with the factory presets and you're probably fine. If you know more about audio and you're familiar, for example, with what a compressor can accomplish, you can go in and use it to make your individual selections sound better than they would using the factory presets. A lot of the kind of processing that you can do in Liquifier Pro is program dependent. The generic idea presented earlier for lowering the dynamic range of the signals for low bit rates—from ISDN-1 down—in general helps most music. Some rock tunes are already compressed so heavily that you don't gain anything by trying to compress them further. To achieve successful results, you do have to know more about what you're doing than when you use the user presets.

Digital Dolby Characteristics

The Digital Dolby method of compression removes data that isn't vital to the fidelity of the original sound source. During encoding, the algorithm goes through and analyzes the signal and at any point in time makes a determination of what frequency content is being masked by other frequencies. The algorithms are set up to make determinations such as "If someone were listening to this audio, they couldn't hear the energy in the signal at 1000Hz because there is energy at 1500Hz that is twice as loud. So the energy at 1000Hz is probably not essential—no one is going to hear it because there is energy near it that is much louder." This content that probably can't be heard is then discarded from the compressed file.

Certain types of music and sound compress better than other types. Sometimes the sounds that compress well and those that don't are counter-intuitive. The hardest thing to compress is white noise. White noise has energy at all frequencies that is equal all the time. It's random, so you can't find patterns during analysis. A single sine wave, a simple tone with no harmonics in it, is the easiest thing to compress. It consists of just one tone. You can throw away everything else from the audio content. It is just one single frequency, and you can represent it with very few bits.

Low frequencies take fewer bits per second to recreate than higher frequencies. Remember that our limitation is bits per second. If a sound wave has a frequency of 100Hz, which is 100 times per second, you don't need as many bits to represent that wave as you do if it is going 10,000 times per second. It takes 100 times as many bits to represent the 10,000Hz wave as it does to represent the 100Hz wave.

The implications of this are two-fold. Music with a lot of high-frequency content is hard to compress. Typically, classical music—even though within its frequency range is pretty dense—doesn't have very much high-frequency content compared to rock and roll, where you have cymbals crashing all the time. Classical music consists of primarily midrange frequencies in most cases. Even though it is dense in the midrange, classical music often compresses better than music that has lots of high-frequency content—like pop music or rock music. Jazz, where you have a cymbal going all the time, can be harder to compress as well. As a general rule, high-frequency content requires the most bits to represent.

The other implication is that as you are going down to lower bit rates, you lower your high-frequency response as well.

The factory presets for Liquifier Pro don't contain EQ settings. They do have a roll-off value, so that the audio rolls off the high frequencies as you go down in bit rates. The sample rate that the audio plays back in for the low bit rates is lower (it takes less data at 11KHz per second than at 44.1KHz per second). But, also, if a 28.8Kbps modem is at 11KHz, the upper frequency that can be reproduced is always at one-half the sample rate, so CD is 44.1KHz—you can go up to 22KHz in the audio range. When you're sampling at 11KHz, which is the 28.8Kbps modem, the highest frequency that you can reproduce is 5500Hz. There is some roll-off in the encoding algorithm to roll the frequencies up to 5500Hz, so that it doesn't alias the sample.

The Digital Dolby AC3 encoder includes an anti-aliasing filter. You can basically set the cut-off frequency so that it acts as a low-pass filter. When you set the cut-off frequency, you can prevent aliasing when you go down to a lower sample rate.

To compensate for the loss of high frequencies, you might want to boost these frequencies through equalization when going to lower bit rates. The factory presets do this to some degree. Knowing that the high end is being rolled off as you reduce bit rates, a generic EQ tip is to reduce the bassiness of the audio. Because the bass gets reproduced well at lower bit rates, and much of the high-frequency content is gone, the net, subjective perceptual result is that the audio sounds kind of bassy (even though the bass really hasn't been boosted). To compensate, you can roll off the low end when dealing with the low bit rates (ISDN and down). As always, you should do more processing the lower the bit rate. You can also put some of the high frequencies back in below the cut-off frequency. For example, if you are encoded for 28.8Kbps delivery, if the upper theoretical limit is 5000Hz, you can try to put in some boost at 3500 or 4000Hz. To give the selection the impression of having treble, you might do even more boost for 14.4Kbps delivery. A little bit of a bump at this range can improve sound for ISDN-1 delivery, but for ISDN-2 and above, you usually don't need to touch it.

Sample Sizes

For some other forms of compression, such as compression algorithms applied to WAV or AU files, you can further reduce file sizes by converting files from 16-bit samples to 8-bit samples. Using this technique for file-size reduction with Liquid Audio, however, doesn't make sense because the file gets saved in the Dolby AC3 format—which is not PCM encoding. You're working with a proprietary format that does not consist of straight sampling any more. The AC3 file has taken the audio information that it has been given, analyzed it, and extracted that into its own data format. It's no longer sampled at 8-bit or 16-bit.

An 8-bit file will sound different from a 16-bit file when run through the encoder. It will have different audio information in it. It doesn't matter what size your source file is because you're going to encode it based on a selected bit rate and length. The file is going to be the same size no matter what the source file size is.

Essentially, an 8-bit file at 22KHz still has the same frequency response, but it is just noisier. You're trying to encode more noise, which we know is bad for signal fidelity. Following this logic, there is no real advantage to using 8-bit files; the key point is that it doesn't affect the size of the encoded file at all. The encoded file is always the same size for the same length.

In general, you should always start from the highest sample rate and sample size you can. Most work should be done starting from regular CD quality audio:

44.1KHz, 16-bit. Because you can expect that many people will be using the Liquid Audio system to deliver high-quality audio, CD-quality audio is the logical starting point. Providing a high-quality downloadable version of a song is one of the strongest features of this product, in addition to its streaming capabilities.

Liquid Audio Tour

Most of the work involved in creating Liquid Audio files takes place in the Liquifier Pro application. A demonstration version of this product is included on the CD-ROM bundled with this book so that you can try it out yourself. The following tour highlights the tools and work environment that you will be using to produce Liquid Audio files.

Liquid MusicPlayer

The goal when working with the Liquifier is to create files that can be previewed through the Liquid MusicPlayer. Data created when creating Liquid Audio files can also be displayed in the Player window (for example, artist information and album cover graphics) and also used in conjunction with other applications to create Web pages on the fly.

 Liquid Audio's site (**www.liquidaudio.com**) includes links to numerous other sites that are using the technology, as well as their own set of samples. The Liquid Listening Pool, shown in Figure 7.8, lets you browse through a number of different musical selections and preview music in the Liquid MusicPlayer.

While at the Liquid Audio site, you can also download a free copy of the Liquid MusicPlayer. The player itself, shown in Figure 7.9, has a clean, streamlined design, with a row of buttons along the right side of the screen for displaying different types of content in the center panel, such as album notes and lyrics.

A click of the **Notes** button accesses descriptive information about the current selection, as shown in Figure 7.10. Notes data, lyrics, song information, album cover artwork, and so on are entered as a part of the music file as you are using Liquifier, and these items become an integral part of the single, stored file, along with the encoded music prepared for playback in one or more bandwidth settings.

Sites that specialize in offering independent musical works for preview and sale, such as IUMA (shown in Figure 7.11), are beginning to include Liquid Audio

Figure 7.8 Liquid Listening Pool.

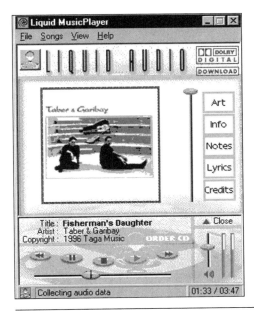

Figure 7.9 Liquid MusicPlayer.

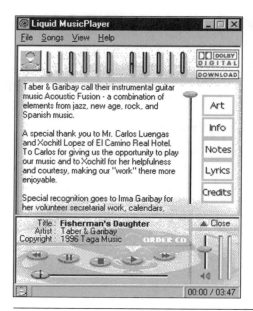

Figure 7.10 Notes displayed for a selection.

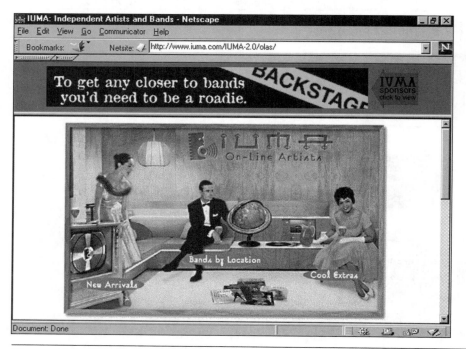

Figure 7.11 IUMA includes Liquid Audio for song previews.

samples among their RealAudio, MPEG, and AU offerings. In comparison to these other compression formats, the Liquid Audio previews seemed more fully dimensioned with a greater tonal range and better instrument separation. Whether this is a function of more carefully prepared files or the inherent superiority of the Dolby Digital compression algorithms is hard to say. Make your own comparisons at a site that offers these different formats and see what you think.

The Liquid MusicPlayer provides a consistent, well-organized window for previewing and extracting information about musical selections. Expect to see more examples of its use on the Web as more companies and individuals learn about the benefits of the technology and the high quality of the compressed sound files. The next section explains how you prepare files for use with the Liquid MusicPlayer.

Using Liquifier Pro

The Liquifier Pro application window, shown in Figure 7.12, includes a set of buttons along the left edge of the window that guide you through the basic functions of the program. You start by opening a file from one of several different formats:

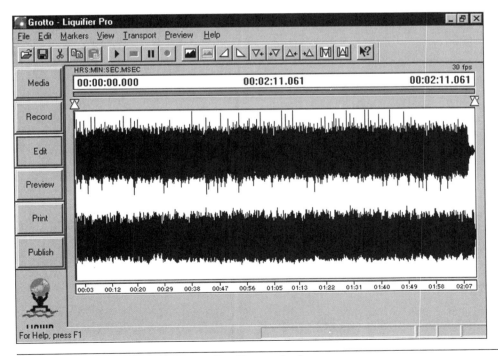

Figure 7.12 Liquifier Pro application window.

Windows PCM (*.wav), Streaming Audio (*.la1), and so on. As you import a sound file it appears in the central pane, as shown in Figure 7.12.

The **Media** button opens up a set of panels, shown in Figure 7.13, that lets you specify all the important information about a recording. You can enter song titles, names of the artists performing on the album, the recording studio and details about recording sessions, song lyrics, and album notes. All of this information becomes embedded in the song files, where it can be extracted to a database, used to supply data for the Liquid MusicPlayer, and—through third-party applications— used to construct dynamic Web pages describing the music content.

The Record window, shown in Figure 7.14, provides a means of importing music from a CD, retrieving digital data from a DAT recording, or recording directly through a digital sound board. Those methods that allow you to keep recorded music in digital format are the best ways to import. For example, if you have music recorded on DAT drive and you have a sound board that supports direct digital input (without performing an additional analog-to-digital conversion), this is an

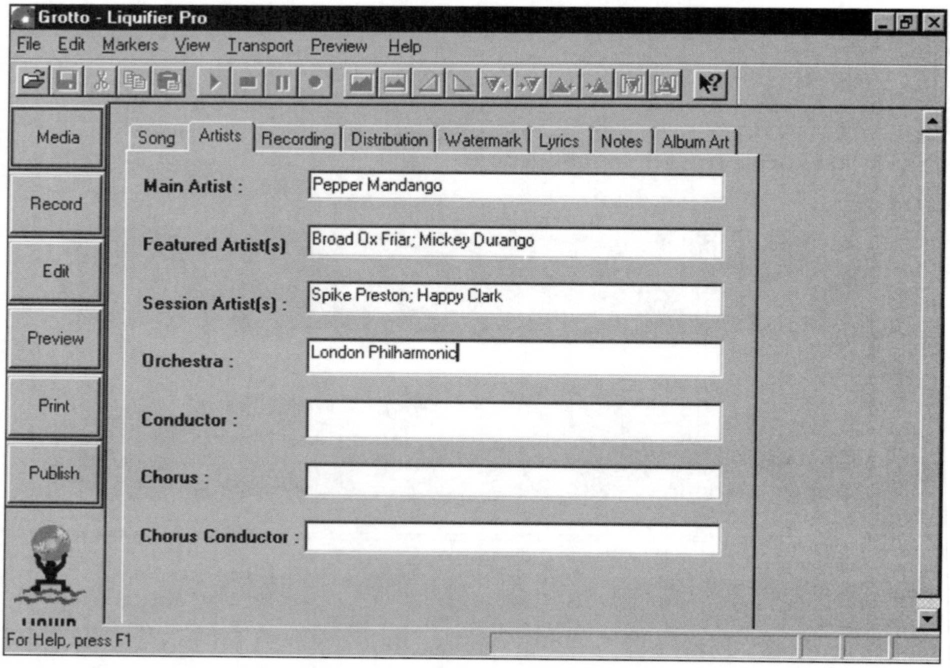

Figure 7.13 Media panels.

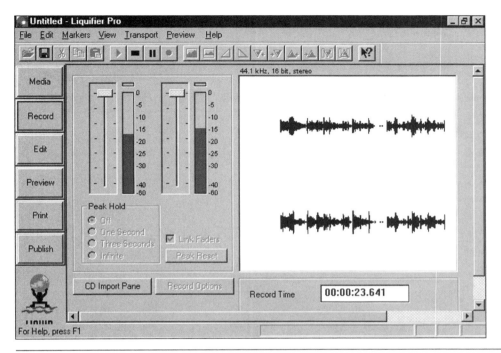

Figure 7.14 Record window.

effective means of retrieving the music data. If the song exists on a CD, and your computer's CD-ROM drive supports audio extraction, you can directly import the source file material from the CD.

Returning to the Edit window with an imported or recorded sound file, as shown in Figure 7.15, you can modify the existing waveform using crop, cut, delete, and paste functions. This window also lets you define a clip region so that a particular segment of a song identified as a clip can be played through the MusicPlayer without having to create a separate file. Fades can be applied to the clip within this window as well, or you can create fades that apply to the entire song file. Using the Zoom In and Out functions, you can select the precise positions within the waveform to work with.

Once you've trimmed and assembled the waveform contents to your liking, the Preview window (shown in Figure 7.16) lets you set up the encoding and listen to the differences between different encoding selections. This can be the most important task to the overall quality of your encoded material. The factory presets available at

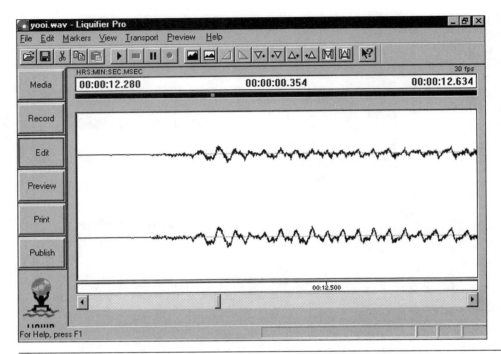

Figure 7.15 Zooming in on a waveform in the Edit window.

each of the bandwidth settings—14.4 Modem, 28.8 Modem, ISDN-1, ISDN-2, CD Quality—have been professionally constructed with equalization and dynamics settings that should work well for a large variety of music types. By selectively trying out the different factory presets and then listening to the results in the Preview window, you should be able to find a setting that works well for the selected music. If you don't like the sounds generated by the factory presets, you also have the option of going in and creating your own user presets and saving them for later use. The panel shown in Figure 7.17 leads you to each of the available options for user presets: Mono conversion, Sample Rate adjustment, an equalizer, dynamics, and Encoder settings. This panel can be carefully tailored to your preferences and then used in the Preview window to hear how the various processing effects will sound to your listeners. The individual selection can be set up to contain several different types of processing for each of the bandwidths; all of this information and encoding is stored in the final Liquid Audio file, where it is then ready for uploading to a server equipped with the Liquid Audio software.

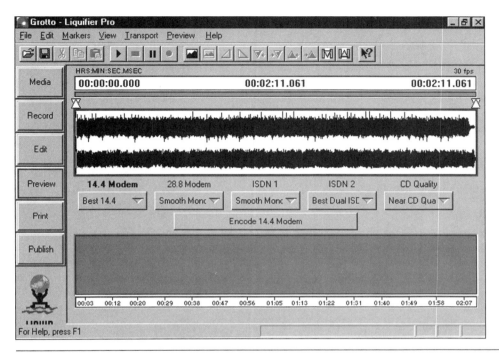

Figure 7.16 Preview window.

The Publish window, shown in Figure 7.18, is the final step in the music encoding and delivery process. From this window, you can create a list of Liquid Audio files for uploading to the designated server. This technique makes it a simple matter for independent musicians who are using an ISP equipped for Liquid Audio delivery to upload completed audio material to their storage space. The unique nature of the Liquid Audio server software can make music available through the server automatically from shortly after the time it is uploaded.

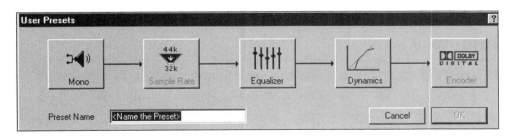

Figure 7.17 User preset options.

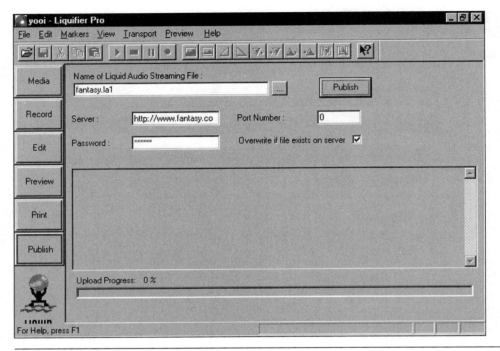

Figure 7.18 Publish window.

As you can see, Liquid Audio offers a fully self-contained method for encoding and distributing music on the Internet. The server software includes a variety of additional features that support online ordering, downloading of purchased software for playback or burning to recordable CD, and so on.

Liquid Audio's strengths are the quality of the Dolby Digital encoded audio and the fully integrated system for music previewing, purchasing, and distribution. Streaming audio files in Liquid Audio format will become more prevalent across the Internet as awareness of the format's advantages become apparent.

Summary

Streaming audio offers an immediacy and flexibility for delivering sound on the Internet that will favor its adoption by Webmasters working with audio for both music and voice applications. For certain kinds of applications–such as real-time Web broadcasting of live events–streaming audio is the only game in town.

8

MIDI on the Web

This chapter explains the techniques for distributing MIDI files on the Web and playing them back through a variety of MIDI plug-ins. The means by which MIDI music files can be integrated within HTML documents are covered, from the simplest playback of a MIDI file using a plug-in player to fully interactive music that generates unique patterns based on actions taking place as a document is being browsed. The different MIDI players and ActiveX controls are summarized, and examples are provided of how they can be used effectively on the Web.

The Web is finally emerging from the silent-movie era with more and more sites providing musical accompaniment to your browsing. If you've wandered into a site and were suddenly surprised to hear music streaming from your speakers, odds are that the music was contained within a MIDI file. The primary alternative to MIDI music on the Web, digital audio waveforms (stored in WAV, AU, or AIFF files), require 10 to 100 times as much file storage space. A new music format, however, called RMF combines all the other formats into a single compact storage form. MIDI is also used in derivative ways; for example, Microsoft's Interactive Music format uses combinational musical phrasing in conjunction with MIDI to generate original works in real time. Another similar product, KoanMusic, creates flowing and changing musical textures that are stored and played as MIDI notation and directed to a MIDI synthesizer for output. MIDI forms the basis for many different types of computer interaction involving music.

We start from the assumptions that you already have music in MIDI file format and that you're looking for the best ways to incorporate MIDI sound into your Web pages. For information on creating and editing MIDI files, Chapter 2 of this book provides an extensive description of the tools and techniques.

Underestimating MIDI

MIDI is a sadly misunderstood and often underestimated music composition and performance tool. Compared to all the other techniques for transferring musical data on the Internet, MIDI files deliver the greatest density of musical information in the smallest amount of storage space. Because MIDI is based on a notational system that precisely records and stores note events, note duration, and other characteristics of individual musical voices and sounds in a format that can be freely manipulated, MIDI can be adapted for musical training, compositional experimentation, and presentation of diverse musical styles. You can create complex rhythms using MIDI that would be difficult or impossible for a skilled drummer to perform. You can swap instrument voices to hear the difference in a melody line played on a clarinet as compared to a flute. You can modify the tempo, key, or character of a MIDI composition with a single command.

This flexibility of MIDI opens up incredible possibilities for Internet applications, particularly when combining the adaptability of this musical storage format with the scripting possibilities of JavaScript and VBScript. Companies such as Cakewalk Music Software are providing developers a head start in this area, providing an ActiveX developer's kit that uses wizard techniques for creating audio plug-ins for Internet use.

Why does MIDI keep struggling to earn some respect? Many still equate the technology with the early FM synthesizers and sound boards that did a less-than-awesome job of reproducing the voices of musical instruments. Others remember the early MIDI sequencers, such as standalone devices where you entered and edited drum patterns tapping a touch pad one beat at a time while viewing a tiny LED screen. Transported to the computer desktop, MIDI sequencing applications can perform all kinds of impressive feats, with multiple views of the music tracks, rhythm and chord composers, pushbutton transposition, conventional music notation displays, and on and on. Newer applications, products such as CakeWalk Professional and Voyetra Digital Orchestrator Plus, merge the benefits of MIDI sequencing with digital audio recording in full-featured multitrack software applications that can be run from the computer desktop. You can, for example, compose a complex MIDI orchestration using a dozen instrument voices and then add a synchronized vocal track recorded in digital audio. You can then go back and add a harmony line to the vocal track and mix the results down into a CD-quality stereo file. Desktop computer music recording and composition are flourishing in this digital renaissance.

In many ways, MIDI is the ideal medium for a composer to combine interactivity with computer-based events. This chapter demonstrates many ways in which this is possible.

To Plug or Not to Plug

One nice feature about distributing music in MIDI format is that the current versions of the major browsers—Microsoft Internet Explorer and Netscape Navigator—have built-in MIDI players. In other words, MIDI music is playable through built-in plug-ins or ActiveX controls, using your choice of MIDI playback devices available to your system, without having to download and install an additional plug-in. As a Web author, you can be assured that your MIDI files will reach an audience consisting of about 92 percent of all Internet websters—only a few text-oriented or early-generation browsers will be prevented from playing back MIDI files in real time. Even *those* users have the option of downloading MIDI files for later playback on their systems, using whatever MIDI equipment they have available.

Downloading and use of plug-ins and ActiveX controls has become much simpler with the release of Netscape's Communicator software suite, which includes Navigator 4, and Microsoft's evolving desktop Web environment centered around Internet Explorer 4. Despite this simplicity, however, many users will opt for the approach of least resistance—which is not downloading any plug-in at all. A number of special-purpose MIDI plug-ins do offer features that make them appealing to anyone hoping to gain the most from Internet MIDI music. This section looks at some of the available MIDI plug-ins and what they have to offer.

If the major browsers already have built-in MIDI playback capabilities, what's the point of downloading another type of MIDI player? Many of the MIDI plug-ins include enhanced features. Yamaha's MIDPLUG, for example, supports a subset of Yamaha's XG-MIDI standard. This includes support for General MIDI as well as additional support for many more instruments—540 in the full XG spec, extra voices—32 at last count, and extra data that captures and controls the expressiveness of different instruments (such as the breath control used with wind instruments). MIDPLUG also includes software synthesis, which offers wavetable-quality MIDI playback even if your sound board has only a cheap FM synthesizer built in. Other MIDI plug-ins offer a variety of other advantages over plain-vanilla MIDI playback, as will be discussed in this section. Most of these plug-ins also use a form of streaming playback, so that the MIDI file begins playing very quickly as the file contents are downloaded. Netscape's LiveAudio player, as it appears in version 3.0 of Navigator, waits until it has fully imported the file before it can begin—usually resulting in a pause of three or four seconds. Pauses can be slightly longer for larger files.

MIDI implementations are changing rapidly, as is everything else on the Web, and undoubtedly by the time you read this there will have been even more changes. The trend is toward incorporating MIDI playback with other audio formats, much in the same manner as audio processing applications have increasingly combined MIDI sequencers and digital audio tools. There is also a strong trend toward placing MIDI operations under the control of JavaScript or VBScript, allowing interactive elements to be added to an HTML page. For example, a page visitor might select a style of background music (Techno-Industrial or New-Age Dreamland) and then have a series of MIDI files in that genre play back in jukebox style. The following sections summarize the major MIDI plug-ins.

Interchangeable Players

To some degree, it doesn't matter what MIDI players your audience is using when they access HTML documents that contain MIDI files. Both Internet Explorer and Navigator are adept at recognizing and responding to MIDI files by MIME type, and a MIDI file will very likely play equally well through the Crescendo player as it will through Netscape's LiveAudio player as it will through Microsoft's built-in MIDI player. Unless you're using special features of a MIDI player, such as Beatnik's Groovoids or Yamaha's XG extensions, the differences in playback will be largely indiscernible. However, because console sizes vary widely, if you're using the <EMBED> tags to present MIDI files, make sure that the console dimensions are set to the largest player size (generally, a width of 200 and a height of 55) so that portions of the player don't get cut off in the display window.

LiveUpdate Crescendo

LiveUpdate's Crescendo MIDI music player for the Internet has been popular on the Web for a number of years, and LiveUpdate hasn't been standing still in their development. LiveUpdate, in partnership with Progressive Networks (the RealAudio folks), recently introduced a version of their product called Crescendo for RealMedia. This technology melds MIDI playback and streaming audio, allowing vocals or speech or additional instruments to be added to a set of MIDI tracks and delivered over the Web. The RealMedia architecture is designed to support streaming of a variety of media types with synchronization elements to coordinate the playback.

Other recent developments include a release of the MIDI plug-in that can run on most systems without any configuration of the MIME type at the server level, support for JavaScript and ActiveX controls, and release of an inexpensive set of tools that supports streaming MIDI playback from Web site servers without requiring extensive setup.

Crescendo StreamSite uses a key file that is resident on the server where the MIDI files are stored to enable streaming MIDI playback. The number of streams served is unlimited. The StreamSite product varies in price depending on the application, ranging from less than one-hundred dollars for personal use to several-hundred dollars for small commercial sites. For larger sites, LiveUpdate negotiates the licensing fee. StreamSite doesn't require any complex server configuration, making it a good choice for Web authors who are using ISPs for their Web storage space. The MIDI files streamed from the site can be heard by anyone with a free Crescendo player; music starts almost from the moment the MIDI file link is accessed, even over 14.4Kbps modem connections.

Using the Crescendo Plug-In with HTML

Both the free Crescendo plug-in and the inexpensive Crescendo Plus plug-in use the same attributes when embedded into an HTML file. The basic plug-in statement just lists the source file and the control-panel size, as follows:

```
<EMBED SRC="midisong.mid" WIDTH=200 HEIGHT=55>
```

As with many of the player plug-ins, Crescendo lets you alter the size of the embedded controls based on the attributes supplied for the height and width. The available players are as follows:

- **Full control panel with transport controls:** WIDTH=200 HEIGHT=55

- **Crescendo logo only:** WIDTH=82 HEIGHT=18

- **LiveUpdate logo only:** WIDTH=46 HEIGHT=50

- **Small note graphic:** WIDTH=16 HEIGHT=16

- **Hidden player:** WIDTH=0 HEIGHT=2

Crescendo has released version 2.3 of the Crescendo plug-in to operate without requiring that the server of the MIDI files be set up for a particular MIME type. The TYPE attribute within the <EMBED> tags serves notice as to the contents of the file. To implement the MIME-less approach, you can use the following <EMBED> statement:

```
<EMBED TYPE="music/crescendo" SONG="moonlite.mid" PLUGINSPAGE="http://www.
liveupdate.com/dl.html" WIDTH=200 HEIGHT=55>
```

The PLUGINSPAGE attribute points users who do not have the required version 2.3 plug-in to LiveUpdate's download site.

Other Crescendo Attributes

Other Crescendo attributes that you can use within <EMBED> entries include:

- **AUTOSTART="true":** Starts playback of the MIDI file immediately

- **NOSAVE="false":** Prevents MIDI files from being saved from within Crescendo

- **LOOP="true":** Recycles the selected MIDI tune over and over

- **BGCOLOR="#RRGGBB":** Sets the background color using hexadecimal values for the Red, Green, and Blue settings

- **TXTCOLOR="#RRGGBB":** Sets the color for the song counter that appears in the upper-right portion of the player using hexadecimal Red, Green, and Blue values

- **DELAY=*n*:** Delays the start of the streaming MIDI playback by the number of seconds specified by *n*

Add any of these entries within the <EMBED> tags in your HTML document to use the specialized attributes.

The full-size Crescendo console is shown in Figure 8.1.

Combining ActiveX and Plug-ins

A single <OBJECT> entry can be used in an HTML document to provide access both to Microsoft Internet Explorer users (who will be accessing MIDI files through the

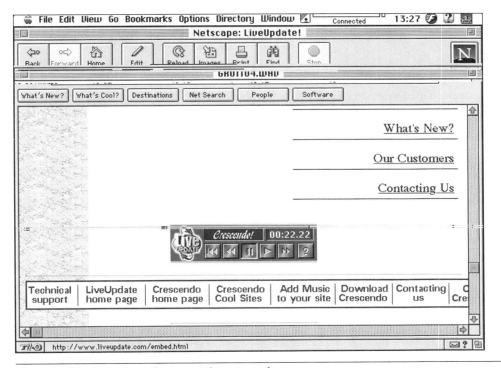

Figure 8.1 Full-size Crescendo console.

Crescendo ActiveX controls) and Netscape Navigator users (who require the plug-in version of the player). Navigator versions 3.0 and earlier do not recognize the <OBJECT> tag, but they can detect and interpret an <EMBED> entry sandwiched between an <OBJECT> entry. The dual-browser statement should read as follows:

```
<OBJECT ID=Crescendo

CLASSID="clsid:0FC6BF2B-E16A-11CF-AB2E-0080AD08A326"

HEIGHT=55

WIDTH=200>

<PARAM NAME="Song" VALUE="lullaby.mid">

<EMBED TYPE="music/crescendo" SONG="lullaby.mid"

PLUGINSPAGE="http://www.liveupdate.com/dl.html"

HEIGHT=55
```

```
WIDTH=200>

</OBJECT>
```

The JavaScript Approach

JavaScript provides an excellent means for sorting out differing browser requirements and for specifying the use of a particular player to be used for MIDI file playback (rather than relying on MIME types registered with the server). This approach
works for versions 3 of Netscape Navigator and Microsoft Internet Explorer, as well
as later versions. This technique detects the browser type reading the HTML file and
then writes the appropriate entries into the HTML document—an <EMBED> entry
for Navigator or an <OBJECT> entry for Explorer. The Navigator entry includes the
addition of a TYPE statement that, in this case, specifies the music file as being associated with the Crescendo player. The Explorer ActiveX component, of course, is
specified through the CLASSID identification. LiveUpdate suggests the following
script for accomplishing this.

```
<SCRIPT LANGUAGE="JavaScript">

<!--//Selects Crescendo as the MIDI player.



if (navigator.appName=="Netscape"){

    document.write("<EMBED TYPE='music/crescendo'")

    document.write("SONG='spamsong.mid'")

...document.write("PLUGINSPAGE='http://www.liveupdate.com/dl.html'")

...document.write("HEIGHT=55 WIDTH=200></EMBED>")}

else {if(navigator.appName=="Microsoft Internet Explorer")

...document.write("<OBJECT ID=Crescendo")

...document.write("CLASSID='clsid:0FC6BF2B-E16A-11CF-AB2E-0080AD08A326'")

...document.write("HEIGHT=55 WIDTH=200>")

...document.write("<PARAM NAME='Song' VALUE='spamsong.mid'></OBJECT>")

}

//--></SCRIPT>
```

The *if* clause is satisfied if the browser detected is Netscape Navigator, in which case the <EMBED> entry, complete with a Crescendo TYPE statement, is written to the HTML body. Otherwise, the *else* statement is performed, which checks for the presence of Microsoft Internet Explorer. If Explorer is detected, the <OBJECT> entry is written to the HTML body.

T I P LiveUpdate is working on their own software synthesizer module to be used in combination with the Crescendo plug-in. This will put them in solid competition with the software synthesizers available from Yamaha and Headspace.

 LiveUpdate offers downloadable plug-ins, ActiveX controls, and MIDI tips at their site:

www.liveupdate.com

Yamaha MIDPLUG

Not everyone has a stunning 32-voice wavetable sound board in his or her computer, and those websters who listen to MIDI files playing back through an FM synthesizer probably think that MIDI music doesn't have much to offer. They would probably much rather listen to vintage PacMan themes playing from local computer-game arcades. For those individuals, as well as anyone who has a full-fledged synthesizer connected to their computer, Yamaha offers the MIDPLUG—a combination software synthesizer and MIDI player that provides partial support for the XG-MIDI standard that Yamaha has been steadfastly promoting for a couple of years.

The Yamaha software synthesizer contains sets of instrument voices that are used for playback with the MIDPLUG player and, though the impact on the computer's processor can be jolting, the quality is remarkably good. The true effect of the XG format can best be appreciated by connecting an external synthesizer, such as the Yamaha VL70-m Virtual Acoustic Tone Generator or the MU80 Tone Generator. The VL70-m includes a set of extensions to the XG-MIDI standard to better support solo acoustic instruments, such as brass, woodwinds, and strings. The MU80 includes the full XG voice list, 537 individual instrument voices, as supported under the standard. This tone generator can also handle 64-note polyphony and has a capacity of 32-part multitimbral performance. The results are significantly more impressive than typical MIDI fare.

MIDPLUG is available for both Navigator and Internet Explorer users, but to use it you need either a Pentium or a Power Macintosh. The library of MIDI voices occupies a full 2 megabytes, so don't expect a compact, streamlined MIDI player along the lines of WebTracks by Wildcat Canyon. Those voices, however, are where the MIDPLUG earns its recognition. The quality of the instrument voices is particularly high, but—unlike Headspace's Beatnik—you can't extend the patch library with your own sampled sounds. If you're lucky enough to have a system containing a Pentium MMX processor, the new version of MIDPLUG that Yamaha has introduced for that model (the S-XG50C) runs much faster and doesn't consume processor cycles in the ravenous way that it does on standard Pentium machines (up to 50 percent of the processing power gets consumed by the software synthesis activities on a non-MMX computer).

Version 3 of the MIDPLUG now supports Netscape's LiveConnect, putting it within the controlling influence of JavaScript. As with all the LiveConnect options, this can be used in a number of interesting ways. Objects on the HTML page can be used to start or stop the playback of MIDI files through MIDPLUG. If you were feeling ambitious, you could design an image map that used MIDPLUG to play different songs for different areas clicked. One approach might be to use the image of an old-fashioned table-top jukebox with the song selections visible in the display. Clicking on an individual song selection could trigger MIDPLUG playback through LiveConnect.

Because MIDPLUG also exists as an ActiveX control for Explorer, a similar technique could be used for HTML viewing (and listening) from within Explorer. The same high-quality software synthesis could be enjoyed for anyone with the Yamaha MIDPLUG installed for their browser.

Embedding MIDPLUG into HTML Pages

The MIDPLUG follows the same conventions as most of the other MIDI players when it comes to inserting it into an HTML document. The player itself consists of a compact console (the normal size is HEIGHT=49, WIDTH=196) that features the usual assortment of controls. The console displays the name of the selection being played, and you can control the volume, start, stop, pause, rewind, and fast forward. To insert the basic MIDPLUG entry into an HTML page, with the attribute for starting playback automatically, you would enter:

```
<EMBED SRC="songname.mid" WIDTH=196 HEIGHT=49 AUTOSTART=TRUE>
```

To enter a selection so that it repeats continuously during playback, you add the REPEAT=TRUE attribute, as shown in the following line:

```
<EMBED SRC="songname.mid" WIDTH=196 HEIGHT=49 AUTOSTART=TRUE REPEAT=TRUE>
```

The full-sized player shows the song title in the console window, as shown in Figure 8.2, captured from UBIK's MIDI Music Bazzar.

 Visit UBIK's MIDI Music Bazzar for MIDI hints and tips at:

www.ubik.com

 For downloading the plug-in and additional instructions about using MIDPLUG, point your browser at:

www.ysba.com

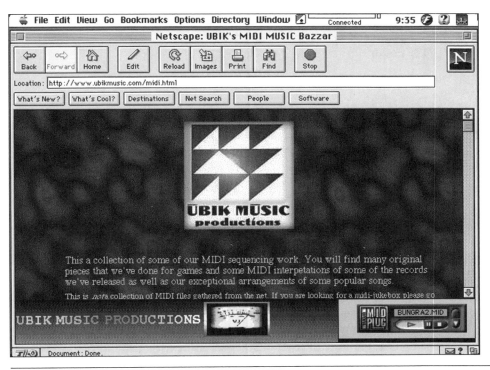

Figure 8.2 Embedded Yamaha MIDPLUG.

Wildcat Canyon WebTracks

WebTracks is a compact, speedy, reliable MIDI plug-in that works under all the major platforms, including the Mac and Windows versions of Navigator and Internet Explorer. The MIDI player uses its own file format, which is created in the Wildcat Canyon Internet Music Kit, but it can also play back standard MIDI files. The proprietary format requires a simple conversion from a standard MIDI file. This conversion can be accomplished using the Internet Music Kit, discussed in Chapter 2, which includes tools for generating your own original MIDI songs by combining phrases in different musical styles.

On the Macintosh side, WebTracks relies on the QuickTime Musical Instrument extension to generate synthesized sounds. For PCs, WebTracks is dependent on whatever equipment you have installed for MIDI playback; in many cases, this may be the sound board installed in the computer. You know the litany: If it's a wavetable board, it should sound great; if it's an FM synthesizer, not quite so great.

When a WebTracks file is detected (with the native .wtx format), the plug-in console appears on the Web page in a designated location. The recommended server setup requires the following MIME type additions:

MIME TYPE: audio

MIME SUB-TYPE: soundtrack

EXTENSION: wtx

The plug-in includes a set of options accessed by right-clicking the icon to fold down the menu, as shown in Figure 8.3. From these options you can adjust volume, set the output, or jump to the WebTracks WWW site.

More information on Wildcat Canyon products can be obtained from:

www.wildcat.com

Headspace Beatnik

One of the rising stars on the Internet music scene is Headspace, a California-based company founded by Thomas Dolby Robertson that has developed the Rich Music Format (RMF) and accompanying software to create and play back RMF files on the Web. The core technology of RMF merges several existing sound-file formats—including MIDI, WAV, AIFF, MOD, AU, and SDII—into a platform-independent

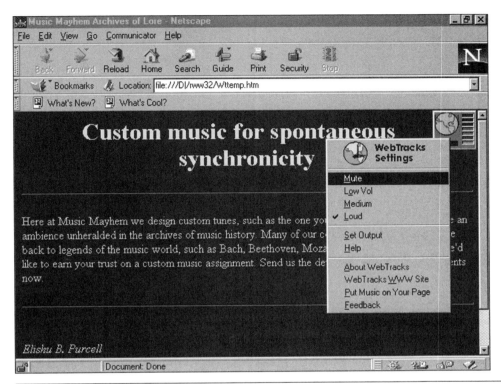

Figure 8.3 WebTracks plug-in options.

format that provides extremely compact file sizes. Sun Microsystems has licensed the Headspace-developed architecture to incorporate into the Java Virtual Machine for greatly improved audio capabilities within Java applications. RMF files created using Headspace's Beatnik Editor will be integrated into Java applications to provide music, sound effects, and voice through software synthesis. The sound quality is close to what can be obtained from expensive wavetable sound boards. The audio engine included in the Headspace architecture can also play back other industry standard file formats as well as its own native RMF format.

Internal Beatnik Functions

Beatnik excels in its built-in capabilities for interactivity. The player includes an extensive set of functions that can be accessed from within Java or JavaScript, allowing a Web content developer total integration of sound features from within an HTML document. One of the difficulties in creating interactive sound handling in HTML documents has been the download times associated with even relatively small waveform files. For sound effects and other interactivity sound cues, the Beatnik player includes a number of interesting internal sounds—referred to as Groovoids—that can be incorporated into events that occur in an HTML document. For example, the act of passing a mouse over an icon in a document can trigger the playback of a Groovoid, perhaps a sound effect of an opening door. Any of the normal onscreen events—loading a page, unloading a page, clicking a link, opening a window—can be connected with Groovoid playback. Sampled voices and other generated sounds can also be integrated into the Beatnik framework, allowing an expandable library of sounds to be built and used for many different types of Web interactions. User studies demonstrate that using sound as reinforcement for actions in a computer interface helps orient the user and provides valuable feedback during navigation and other actions. In the most fundamental ways, sound effects can confirm important actions—such as using the bell on a cash register to signify the completion of an online order. Without sound, many types of Web interactions can be quite ambiguous.

The range of interactive Groovoids includes sounds described as MouseOverDrone, Chimes, FunnyBeep, Magic, Sports Fanfare, InfoPulse, and CashRegister. The sounds are richer and more expressive than the typical beeps and boops used for desktop computer interactions, yet because they are built into the Beatnik player, they play back immediately when triggered. Figure 8.4 shows the Interactive Groovoid List currently enabled in Beatnik, which can be sampled by downloading the Beatnik player and clicking on any of the items. Headspace says they are working on additional Groovoids to expand the list.

Beatnik and JavaScript

Beatnik works especially well with JavaScript. JavaScript operations can involve almost every aspect of Beatnik playback. You even have the ability to go in and specify the playback of particular MIDI notes using selected instrument voices. Used in conjunction with an image map displayed on an HTML page, this feature allows you to play music as the mouse point passes over objects on the screen. This feature was used in an interesting application of Beatnik, illustrated in Figure 8.5, that uses an interactive magical harp to play back MIDI notes through the use of JavaScript.

Headspace's Web site is the first place to start exploring the capabilities of the fascinating new audio tool. First, of course, you need to install the Beatnik player (see Figure 8.6). It requires Navigator 3.0 or above and a Pentium or Power Macintosh class machine. Sorry, no Internet Explorer users. The JavaScript implementation

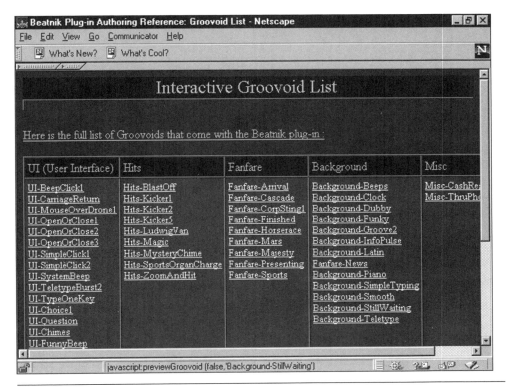

Figure 8.4 Interactive Groovoid List.

included by Microsoft in Internet Explorer 3.0 is not close enough to Netscape's to work effectively with the Beatnik player. Whether this situation will be improved by the version 4.0 release of Explorer is still unknown.

 Copies of the Beatnik plug-in for Macintosh and Windows Netscape users appear on the CD-ROM bundled with this book.

Once you've installed the plug-in, you can visit the Headspace site and take a walkthrough of Beatnik. Thomas Dolby himself conducts the tour, which highlights the various Beatnik features and gives you an eye-opening look at what this tool can accomplish. The tour progresses from simple demonstrations, such as being able to turn music on and off from an image icon embedded on a page, to a full-blown mixer that lets you dynamically control the playback of a multitrack piece of music by sliding levers and pushing controls. It's clear that this product was designed with full interactivity in mind.

Figure 8.5 Interactive Magic Harp.

An example of an elaborate Beatnik presentation implemented through JavaScript appears in Appendix D.

Headspace RMF Collections

Music in the RMF format can be created using the Beatnik Editor, which is available as a free download for Power Macintosh users during its beta release but will probably be only available by purchase by the time you read this. The Beatnik player doesn't have to work only with RMF files; you can configure Navigator to use Beatnik for playback of MIDI files, as well as other sound file formats. MIDI files in particular sound exceptionally fine through the software synthesis provided by Beatnik. The software synthesizer is designed to consume fewer processor cycles than equivalent plug-in products, such as Yamaha's MIDPLUG. Nonetheless, you're better off not running a lot of additional applications when Beatnik is busy turning MIDI files into music. You definitely can sense your system slowing down under the weight of the software synthesis while it is being performed.

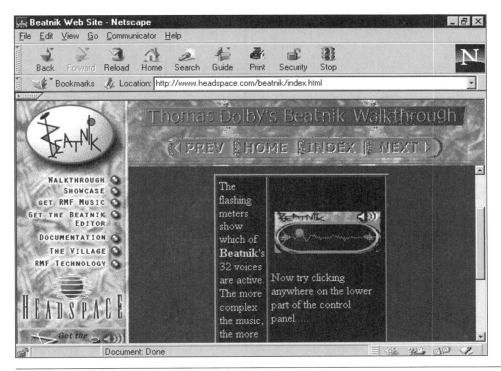

Figure 8.6 Beatnik player.

If you don't have the inclination to create your own RMF files, Headspace lets you purchase and license their collections for use on your site. If you're familiar with the music of Thomas Dolby, you have a sense of what to expect in these collections, although the samples available at the Headspace Web site cover a wide variety of styles and musical types. The prices on these collections seemed reasonable, with the range of $50 seemingly the average cost for several RMF files. Given the high quality of the music and the compactness of the RMF files, this could be an excellent way for anyone to introduce music to their Web site.

Copyright Control

Another important aspect of Rich Music Files is the ability to contain embedded and encrypted copyright information inside the file. This information travels with the file, making it difficult for software pirates to illegally sell or distribute works in RMF format. This also provides a mechanism to make it possible for anyone to contact the original author or composer of a musical work. Listeners can view the key information about a piece being played in the Beatnik player through a window in the player itself.

More examples of Beatnik interactions appear in Chapter 6 of this book. The fidelity and interactivity of Beatnik make it a strong candidate for wide numbers of uses on the World Wide Web. To really get a sense of the uniqueness and the flexibility of this product, you should visit the Headspace Web site and experience it firsthand. Most of the other music formats seem to pale in comparison.

 The Beatnik plug-in is included on the CD-ROM bundled with this book. Additional details about the Beatnik system can be obtained from the Headspace Web site at:

www.headspace.com

Different-Sized Consoles

An ongoing problem when using the <EMBED> entry for including MIDI players on your Web page is the varying size of the different player consoles. Unless you use a specific JavaScript or VBScript entry to test for the installed plug-in, if your <EMBED> entry includes WIDTH and HEIGHT console dimensions that don't quite match the MIME type configured for a user's particular MIDI player, you're going to most likely see only a portion of the player. In other words, if you're set up with an <EMBED> entry that supports the normal size of the Netscape LiveAudio player, it is going to cut the bottom portion of the Beatnik player off, if that's what the user has installed. Without the use of a script language to detect the plug-in type, there is no easy way around this problem—unless you pad the plug-in space for the largest possible console, which leads to some unsightly Web pages. However, a bit of extra padding can be a better approach in many cases; specifying the wrong console size can sometimes cause certain players to crash the browser display. Specifying a console size of WIDTH=280 and HEIGHT=180 usually prevents this problem because the dimensions are large enough to support all of the common MIDI player consoles. Another alternative is to hide the console using the HIDDEN=TRUE attribute with the <EMBED> entry.

QuickTime Software Synthesis

The Macintosh is, by nature, better equipped for MIDI file playback. Even if you are using only the built-in LiveAudio capabilities of Netscape Navigator on the Mac, you have access to the QuickTime Musical Instruments (QTMI) set—a collection of MIDI instrument voices based on the Roland Sound Canvas library. QuickTime version 2.5 is a significant improvement over the earlier version, well worth the upgrade.

The biggest disadvantage of using QuickTime's software synthesis is the burden it places on the Macintosh processor. This type of processing activity uses up a lot of cycles, and you may notice that other operations slow to a crawl when you're playing back MIDI files. As an alternative, you can use an external MIDI sound module.

 An easy way to couple an external MIDI sound module to your Macintosh is through the Open Music System, available as a system extension (free) from:

www.opcode.com/oms

If you feel the processor hit is too severe, external tone generators, even modestly expensive models, provide seriously enhanced MIDI playback. The Yamaha MU50 tone generator is compact and relatively inexpensive and includes the benefits of the XG-MIDI format. If you create your own MIDI sequences, you can also take advantage of the studio-quality effects processing that is built into this box.

QuickTime use is not limited to Macintosh users. Windows aficionados can now install QuickTime for Windows version 2.5, which will bring them in line with their Macintosh compatriots. QuickTime MIDI playback is not a bad way to go and will provide respectable MIDI playback on both platforms. You can also embed either MIDI or WAV audio sequences in QuickTime movies and use them in a variety of ways within HTML documents. Because this format is well supported throughout the Mac and Windows realms, it's a fairly portable means for moving sound around the Web.

The Downside of Software Synthesis

Software synthesis as implemented by the Headspace Beatnik player, Yamaha MID-PLUG, and QuickTime v2.5 can be an economical means of achieving wavetable-quality playback on a wide range of users' systems. Be forewarned, however, that this emerging technology is still capable of providing some pretty nasty surprises. Notes that unexpectedly sustain forever, weird pops and squeals, processor lockups, and other assorted audio frivolities are sometimes encountered, and there is no single easy cure for avoiding these kinds of problems. As software synthesis matures, it will become more stable. Until then, the price you pay for using it is to occasionally sacrifice reliability for rich, high-quality sound.

Server Preparation for MIDI Playback

It would be nice if the only thing that you had to do to place MIDI files out on the Web was to embed them in your HTML documents and have them available in the appropriate directories at your site. There is, however, one other important preparation that must take place at the server side to ensure that MIDI files are transferred over the Internet in accordance with their MIME type so that your browser can respond to them. Microsoft Internet Explorer functions without requiring an alert as to the MIME type, but for preparation for everyone else, you should ensure that the server is properly set up. Because most servers are set up in anticipation of working with MIDI because it is one of the most common file types on the Internet, in most cases, the server that you use through your local ISP will be properly set up already.

If not, however, or if you're configuring your own server to deliver MIDI files, the following entries should be made for the MIME.type information. For Unix servers, this often appears in a file called .HTACCESS.

MIME TYPE: audio

MIME SUB-TYPE: midi

EXTENSION: mid

TIP The Crescendo MIDI player uses a TYPE attribute in the <EMBED> statement, which supersedes the requirement for setting up the server's MIME type list to include MIDI. This is discussed earlier in this chapter in the Crescendo description.

Tips for Testing MIDI Play

By now you know that MIDI's strength is its compact size, but its weakness is the uncertainty of how the files will sound played back on different devices. If you want to really do your job as a Web author, you should test the playback of MIDI files to be included in your HTML documents on several different playback platforms. Start out using an inexpensive sound board with FM synthesis connected to a pair of cheap computer speakers. Try the playback through at least one higher-quality board, such as a Creative Labs AWE32 or Roland Sound Canvas. Also, try running the playback through a software synthesizer, such as the Headspace Beatnik player or Yamaha MIDPLUG. A properly prepared MIDI file should sound good even using FM synthesis for playback, and it should sound great on higher-quality playback equipment. This simple test will ensure more effective delivery of your MIDI songs—the way you intended them to sound—over the Internet.

Selecting a Specific Player in a Browser

Because many of the MIDI players have individual features that are unique, it can be difficult to settle on just one player to handle the MIDI requirements for all of your Web browsing. Maybe you prefer using the streamlined WebTracks player for quick journeys about the Net where you're not willing to slow your processor down with software synthesis, but when you want to seriously listen to some good MIDI music, you prefer to switch over to Yamaha MIDPLUG. Is there any easy way to select the plug-in of choice?

If you're running Netscape Navigator 3 under the Macintosh or Windows, you can use the General Preferences settings to determine what plug-in applies to the MIDI playback. As an example of how this works in version 3 of Netscape Navigator for the Mac, the General Preferences menu option brings up the panels shown in Figure 8.7. The Helpers panel offers a list of those plug-ins and helpers that will be used for the different MIME types recognized by Navigator. By default, the MIDI types—audio/midi and audio/x-midi—are assigned to Netscape's LiveAudio plug-in, which does a decent job if you have good MIDI synthesis available in your system, either through a wavetable-based sound board or Apple's QuickTime Musical Instruments.

If you want to change the assignment of a MIME type to correspond with a different plug-in, double-click on the item that you want to change. Navigator displays the Edit Type dialog box shown in Figure 8.8.

From within the Edit Type dialog box, you can reassign the MIME Type shown with the plug-in of your choice. In the case of the Macintosh, the Plug-Ins pull-down listbox displays all of the available items from the Navigator Plug-Ins folder. If you have added items since the last time Navigator was started up, you need to restart Navigator to display the full range of options. Select your choice for the indicated MIME type, and click **OK** to confirm your selection.

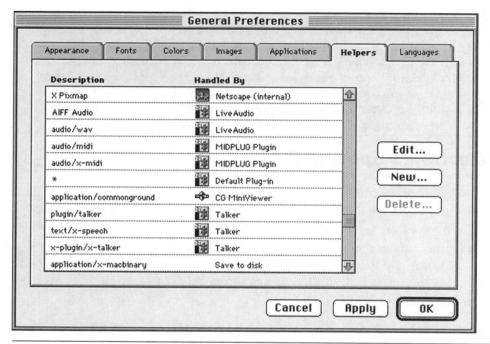

Figure 8.7 Helpers panel in Navigator.

You also have the option of setting the response to MIDI files to be keyed to the "Unknown: Prompt user" selection. If you have made that selection, Navigator prompts you each time it encounters a MIDI MIME type, and you can choose your plug-in at that time. The process is a bit cumbersome, however, and in most cases you will probably want to have the browser preset for a particular plug-in before you venture on line.

JavaScript and VBScript can be set to respond to the presence of plug-ins or ActiveX controls in the currently installed browser, but keeping up with the vast range of options available for MIDI players, in particular, is difficult. One possible use of the plug-in detection method would be to notify the page viewer if they did not have a particular plug-in type installed that you were relying on in your HTML document. You could then display an appropriate message and request that they download the suggested player from a link that is provided. Alternately, you could steer users away from a particular page, if you detected a necessary plug-in was not available, by dynamically writing the HTML links from the <HEAD> region of an HTML document. This extra complexity is one of the prices that you pay for getting involved with the more sophisticated features available through the high-end MIDI players.

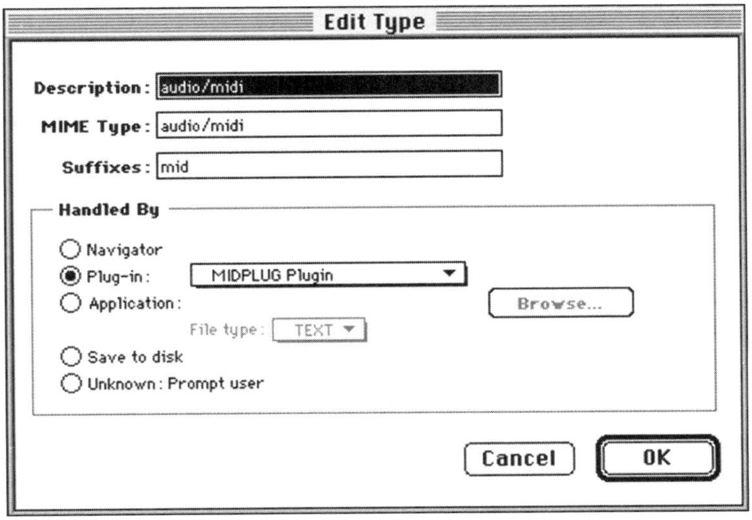

Figure 8.8 Edit Type dialog box.

Microsoft Interactive Music Control

Microsoft offers an Interactive Music control as an ActiveX component that provides the ability to create and play back music from HTML documents. This approach uses MIDI as its foundation, using either the Microsoft Synthesizer software for playback or the available MIDI synthesizer components installed in the user's system.

This product is unique in that it doesn't rely on actual MIDI files for the playback content, but generates MIDI music on-the-fly based on a number of factors that can be controlled by a Web author. If you read the section on Microsoft Music Producer in Chapter 2, you'll have an understanding of the environment in which music is composed. If music isn't embedded into Web pages as MIDI files, what does get embedded? The files that fuel the Interactive Music Control system consist of data describing the musical style in a .sty file and personality in a .per file. The styles and personalities mirror those used in the Microsoft Music Producer, with 110 preexisting styles and 27 personalities from which to choose. Before someone can hear this content, however, they must be running the necessary ActiveX control and synthesizer, available for download from Microsoft. Navigator users, of course, to be able to use the ActiveX control need to install the third-party plug-in that extends Netscape's browser for dealing with the Microsoft world. The song modules themselves, that is, the style and personality files, occupy anywhere from 5K to around 100K, certainly within a reasonable download range for anyone who wants to listen to music while browsing.

Music constructed using this approach changes a bit each time it is played. Even a particular selection using exactly the same style and personality will vary each iteration. The music can be precisely constructed to run for a particular length of time—if you've calculated that it takes two minutes and six seconds for somebody to download a particular graphic from your site, you can arrange a two-minute and six-second interlude consisting of music to keep them amused during the download.

A utility called the Interactive Music Express, included in the Authoring package, provides the basic audition tools for combining the styles, personalities, instrument selections, and other options for shaping the music. The output of this utility includes the supporting code—in either JavaScript or VBScript, according to your preference—to dynamically model the music you have specified. This code can be dropped into an HTML document where it becomes a dynamic, ever-changing music engine based on Microsoft's Interactive Music algorithms. Interactive Music Express can be run only from within Internet Explorer as it depends on Microsoft-specific HTML Layout Control. Netscape Navigator hasn't yet added supported for this HTML variation.

Is this really music? You'll have to listen for yourself to decide. Some of the composed pieces seem to be crafted by a real-time human composer with flashes of brilliance. Others have that dreary mechanical quality that plagues the worst computer-generated music. At the very least, it's a fascinating compositional tool that could have some interesting Web applications, given the compactness and uniqueness of its musical offerings. Keep in mind that the segments included within the Interactive Music Control were originally constructed by human composers. And, the technology offers some fairly interesting possibilities, such as music that alters in tempo as your mouse pointer passes over buttons or images on screen or smooth transitions from one mood to another as someone navigates from page to page at your site.

 More details on the Microsoft Interactive Music Controls can be obtained from:

www.microsoft.com/sitebuilder/features/imc.asp#synthesizer

The Zen of MIDI: Koan

Imagine someone being able to download a 7K file from your site and listen to up to eight hours of changing, cycling music. If you want the ultimate means of removing the bandwidth obstacle to music playback on the Web, Koan is the answer. Music is created in real time by the Koan player based on authored patterns that are composed and combined within the shifting framework provided by the software.

Koan once more emphasizes the fact that MIDI and Web applications work well together. The creator of this product, SSEYO, has come up with a unique system to freely generate MIDI music within author-selected parameters. After being produced using SSEYO's own application, Koan X Silver (free) or Koan Pro, these pieces are played back through the free Koan Web standalone player or the Koan plug-in.

The files composed for Koan use occupy even less space than typical MIDI files because they are basically a set of instructions as to how to play back a MIDI composition through the Koan software engine. More ethereal than the Microsoft approach to interactive music, the Koan pieces often resemble the ambient music compositions popularized by Brian Eno and similar artists. But these music composition tools also let you create hard-driving rockers and light jazz atmospheres, as well as the more moody New Age works. As such, Koan compositions often make suitable backdrops for Web environments and should be considered as another effective tool in the Web author's grab bag.

The free Koan Silver composition tool gives you a sense of the options you have available for creating music. As shown in Figure 8.9, you drag modules from a group of items to a mixer window. You have some control over the different aspects of the automatically composed pieces by varying the scale (for example, the Dorian scale is shown in the figure), the effects applied to the sound, the combinations of individual sound blocks, and other elements. Works in progress can be previewed through the transport controls in the upper-left portion of the window. About the time you start having fun with it, the music stops and a message appears encouraging you to purchase a real version of Koan Pro. You get five uninterrupted minutes of playback using the Silver version before you face this message and have to restart the playback.

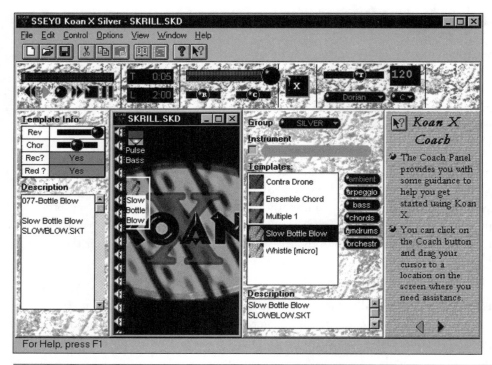

Figure 8.9 Koan X Silver composition in progress.

 The higher-end compositional tools offer much more control over the generative process. These are available for purchase or demo downloading from the SSEYO site at:

www.sseyo.com

SSEYO also offers freely downloadable Koan files that you can use on your Web site while you're learning how to use Koan Pro to make your own works.

Summary

MIDI, by its very nature, is the most interactive of the different music file formats. You can accomplish things using MIDI that are virtually impossible using WAV files or other similar formats. Products that extend the capabilities of MIDI to make it fully integrated with interactions within a browser include Headspace Beatnik and Microsoft Interactive Music Controls. Because of new technologies such as these, and MIDI's own inherent benefits of compactness and flexibility, we expect to see increased use of MIDI-based applications on the Internet.

Voice Synthesis, Recognition, and
Other Applications

This chapter explores the techniques for communicating with a computer through spoken commands and for using text-to-speech applications to listen to pages read by your computer. These two rapidly emerging technologies have a number of important Web applications, as explained in the following material. This chapter also covers encoders and decoders for delivering spoken voice over the Web.

Computers in the recent past have not excelled in providing a natural interface to humans. The most direct way to communicate with another person is by spoken words, preferably in a face-to-face situation where the nuances of body language, facial expressions, and eye contact convey more than the simple exchange of words. With a computer, the conventional interface has been a stunted compromise based on flawed conventions from the earliest days of the manual typewriters. Nearly everyone is familiar with the story behind the design of the typewriter keyboard layout, where the key configuration (QWERTY, as it is usually referred to) was set up to slow down typists so they wouldn't jam the keyboard mechanism by locking letters when typing too fast. Until recently, flat keyboard designs were also an additional stress, by forcing the fingers and wrists of typists into unnatural positions and causing numerous repetitive stress-related injuries, such as carpal tunnel syndrome. More recent contoured, ergonomic keyboard designs let hands and wrists curve in a more natural position, but most of these still use the clumsy QWERTY keyboard layout. As it has evolved, typing is a very cumbersome act, and it is still taught in most places the same way it was 100 years ago.

The conventional computer monitor also presents challenges; few people can tolerate extended periods of reading text on a computer monitor. The periodic scanning rate of the monitor's vacuum tube can be seen as a visible ripple traveling across the screen in many monitors, and this effect leads to eyestrain with continued use. As a conventional workaround, many people will print documents downloaded from the Web to read them later in a laser-printed format. This certainly helps eliminate the eyestrain problem, but it generates huge amounts of wasted paper.

DVORAK Keyboards

An alternative to the QWERTY keyboard has been available for a number of years but has only made limited penetration into the marketplace. The DVORAK keyboard offers a redesigned layout that places the most frequently used keys on the home row and organizes the other keys so that common combinations of letters will be easier to enter. Many computer users who begin experiencing symptoms of repetitive stress injury (tingling, numbness, and sharp pains in the hands and wrists) find that these symptoms disappear once they retrain themselves using the DVORAK method. Specialized computer applications available through companies such as Canon can remap the keys of conventional keyboards to use the DVORAK key organization.

 Additional information and free copies of the Dvorak International Newsletter can be obtained from:

www.dvorakint.org

For those with physical impairments that make it difficult to use a conventional computer system, the alternatives have generally been expensive custom systems that required specialized hardware and software, often costing tens of thousands of dollars. Blind or low-vision individuals have relied on text-to-speech synthesis and voice-control systems to listen to pages of text being read back to them or to guide the computer's actions. Those with physical limitations that prevented any use of the keyboard have relied on pointer systems or other types of entry devices to control the computer interaction, a workable but often slow and tedious approach.

The confluence of many different technologies now makes voice recognition and speech possible as a mainstream application set on many different platforms. The remarkable processing power in Pentium and PowerPC systems, combined with a new generation of Digital Signal Processing (DSP) ICs, brings many voice processing and recognition applications down from the mainframe to the desktop level. Improved sound boards, new algorithms for sound compression and speech synthesis, and a better understanding of audio signal processing have helped open new avenues for using voice rather than text in computer applications. You can now easily open up your Web pages to blind or low-vision users, using a combination of available plug-ins, helper applications, or native browser support tools. This chapter discusses techniques for integrating vocal elements within your Web pages and controlling your navigation with voice control.

Voice Tools and Applications

The importance of voice, both as a control mechanism and as a technique for communicating with Web users, has begun to be recognized, and a number of different applications are emerging. Some are available as plug-ins, others as helper applications. Features built into the latest generation of browsers, most notably Microsoft Internet Explorer and Netscape Navigator, are moving steadily toward robust support of different forms of audio optimized for voice. Unlike music, which requires a fairly wide dynamic range to sound convincing—which makes it more difficult to compress, audio content limited to voice can sound quite reasonable even when sampled at rates of 8KHz ps or 11KHz ps (16-bit resolution). Music, in comparison, starts sounding thin or "tinny" when sampled at rates under 22KHz ps. Because of this, certain applications and techniques have evolved that are tailored to voice applications, rather than general audio applications.

Current Voice Tools

The following list summarizes the approaches and currently available tools. Many of these tools are discussed in more detail later in this chapter.

- **Applications designed for speech compression and delivery:** Sometimes called speech coders, like EchoSpeech from Echo Speech Corporation and TrueSpeech from DSP Group, these programs are tailored to compressing speech while maintaining the quality, achieving compression ratios up to 18.5 to 1. Real-time playback of speech over the Web can be accomplished even using 14.4Kbps modems. While these are streaming audio applications (playback begins shortly after the file is requested, eliminating long download times), they are by nature best suited to voice applications. The compression algorithms and the sampling rates don't support the complexities of music very well.

- **Text-to-speech synthesis:** Tools available in this area include plug-ins and helper applications that can read back text in one of several, preselectable voices. While these types of voices generally have an amusing, mechanical lilt, the technology has improved to the point where word recognition is very good and the text that is read back is perfectly understandable. Macintosh users can take advantage of the Talker plug-in for Netscape Navigator, which reads back Web page contents using the System 7.0 (or later) English Text-to-Speech extension. Even though they are not specifically tailored for browsers, PC users can use products such as AT&T's WATSON Advanced Speech Application Platform V.20, DragonDictate's, text-to-speech plug-in, Berkeley System's outSPOKEN for Windows, the Productivity Works pwWebSpeak, and PC WholeWare's Clip&Talk 2.0.

- **Voice recognition products:** Products that employ voice recognition offer interesting possibilities for both entering text and controlling the computer while browsing the Web. Kurzweil's Voice and VoicePad, IBM's VoiceType, Dragon Systems' Dictate, and Articulate Systems' Power Secretary for the Mac fit in this category.

Using Voices within HTML Pages

The human voice carries messages within the tone and inflection of spoken words that expand the meaning beyond the words themselves. We're tuned to these nuances and subtleties from the time we are children, and this extra layer of communication can be put to work on a Web page. Certain kinds of communicated content—including humor, poetry, essays and personal opinion, irony, determination, and so on—can be skillfully expressed by voice. If you look at the kind of material on your Web site, you may find that some of the content lends itself well to live audio. For example, creative use of spoken voices within HTML documents lets you accomplish the following kinds of tasks:

- Design a page that uses the JavaScript onMouseOver event handler to announce the function of different navigational aids on the page with spoken descriptions. For example, after a five-second pause over a return arrow button, a spoken voice could announce, "Click here to return to the previous page."

- Greet users to your page with a spoken poem or a hearty verbal greeting. A human voice can often bridge the gap between the cold environs of the computer and the open-ended expanse of the virtual community.

- Let visitors hear text passages of original fiction or other dramatized works using speech synthesis techniques. The story-telling tradition runs deep in human history, and most people will stop anything they are doing to listen to a good story.

- Provide an alternate method of navigating through your site for vision-impaired users. Speech recognition can be used to control activities within the Web browser. Where possible, Web sites—like restaurants and public buildings—should be designed to accommodate the widest variety of visitors.

- Provide spoken training lessons that are enhanced by illustrations appearing on a Web page. For example, you could present a series of illustrations and narration explaining how to disassemble a 10-speed bicycle and replace certain parts on it.

- Give instructions on how to solve technical support problems for various types of mechanical products. Listeners can follow along with the instructions and perform the necessary procedures. Your site could show and explain how to open and change the blades on a food processor without slicing off your fingers.

- Dictate several pages of text into a word processor using a product such as Kurzweil Voice or IBM's VoiceType. Convert the page output to Web-ready Adobe Acrobat files by printing to the Acrobat driver. You can easily generate a variety of material for Web placement without having to keyboard the information.

- Provide pronunciation guides for foreign languages or spoken readings of locations on maps in an online travel guide.

The options are numerous and limited only by your imagination. This chapter provides several concrete examples of methods for placing speech on your Web pages.

Making Web Pages Accessible

While many organizations go to a great deal of effort to present information to the global Internet community, these same organizations often overlook the issues and considerations surrounding ensuring that Web-posted information is accessible to people with various disabilities. The flexibility now available in creating and structuring Web-based content should encourage designers to open up their pages for maximum accessibility. Audio, of course, is a big consideration, particularly when providing access for those who are visually impaired, but there are other issues as well. Consider the following guidelines for increasing the accessibility of Web pages by providing useful access systems for those with physical impairments.

- Blind users require a means of outputting documents in Braille format or hearing a readback of the contents of a page through speech synthesis. This can be provided by making a text-to-speech synthesizer available (through links or audio instructions) or by creating content areas that are maximized for Braille output (with text descriptions of any visual elements).

- Users who have low vision or who have dyslexia generally require over-sized text with generous spacing. Using the Cascading Style Sheet features now available in Internet Explorer or JavaScript-controlled style sheets in Navigator, you can make it possible for the user to bump the text to a comfortable reading size.

- When using audio to provide cues or orientation to events on the Web page, make sure that you provide a captioned equivalent for deaf users. Other audio content should also be examined for its accessibility to those with hearing impairments, and alternative content should be provided wherever possible.

- Keep in mind that some users with certain physical or mobility challenges may be unable to use a keyboard or mouse. Navigation paths that are simplified for someone using a mouth- or eye-controlled pointing device can be helpful in this regard.

Programming for Accessibility

With a clear understanding of the special challenges presented by different physical impairments, Microsoft programmer Peter Wong works in the Accessibility and Disabilities group helping to structure software so that it can be accessed by as wide a range of people as possible. Blind since the age of 14, Wong uses text-to-speech synthesis to read back screens on three of his office computers and uses a special keyboard for entry. He has worked on projects such as a fax machine with the ability to read back fax contents and a CD-ROM designed for deaf children that includes closed-captioning throughout its content. Other projects include a utility that converts a screen full of Chinese characters into notation that can be used to output to a Braille printer.

Extra Design Effort

The ease with which the computer can be adapted to present information in complementary, parallel ways makes it even more essential that Web designers and developers invest the time and energy to adapt HTML document for maximum accessibility. While this obviously increases design time, creative use of JavaScript, VBScript, and other tools can automate the accessibility of HTML documents, providing alternate paths for users at the click of a button. Style sheets can also make a big difference in providing large text layouts for anyone who has difficulty reading conventional font sizes on screen. Techniques that allow preferences to be turned on for document access can be used to turn on captioning, audio hints and tips, descriptive explanations of embedded video, text-to-speech output, and so on. This extra design effort can have a big impact in making the World Wide Web available to the widest possible audience.

Using TrueSpeech on the Web

TrueSpeech, a product of DSP Group, is a freeware audio compression application designed to offer voice-quality streaming audio over the World Wide Web. For Microsoft Internet Explorer 3.0 users, support is built into the browser, and you can begin reading and streaming files immediately. For Netscape Navigator 2.0 and later users, a plug-in is required.

 For details about this product and for downloadable players and convertors, point your browser to:

www.dspg.com/player/main.htm

After a short installation sequence, the TrueSpeech Player is installed with a link to your Navigator browser file. You can then use the TrueSpeech Player to access any file encoded in this compact format from the Web and embed audio files in this format within HTML documents. DSP also has a free batch conversion utility available as freeware that allows large groups of WAV files to be converted to TrueSpeech format in sequence.

TrueSpeech is optimized for use with sound files sampled at 8KHz, so it is clearly a format designed for voice-grade audio rather than music or anything other than simple sound effects. The advantage for Web developers is that the product is available for free, it can be run at the client level without requiring any kind of server setup, and support for creation of files in this format is built into Windows95. It works with standard Windows WAV files (PCM-encoded format) that can then be opened in the Windows95 Sound Recorder utility and saved in TrueSpeech format.

T I P TrueSpeech fits into a unique category between the streaming audio products, such as Liquid Audio and RealAudio, and the voice recognition and text-to-speech programs discussed in this chapter. It is a streaming audio application, but it's designed for streaming simple voice-quality audio at high speeds.

Sampling Rates for TrueSpeech Files

While you won't dazzle your listeners with the quality of speech supported with this application, you can achieve respectable playback of voice, and with some care you can create the necessary audio files without any tools more complex than a good-quality 16-bit sound board in your system and a decent microphone. While we recommend in many of our other audio applications throughout this book that you should initially record sound at the highest possible resolution and sampling rate and then downsample to the appropriate rate for Web delivery, if you're running under Windows 3.1, TrueSpeech insists on WAV files sampled at 8KHz, 16-bits. If you're running Windows95, you can convert WAV files sampled at different sample rates to TrueSpeech compressed formats (mono, 8KHz, 16-bits) by opening the WAV file in Sound Recorder (included with Windows95) and then saving the WAV file with the DSP Group TrueSpeech format selected. You won't gain much in this situation by using faster sampling rates and then converting, but you may want to experiment to see what achieves the best results on your system with your sound board. This technology is tailored more to handling audio input simply captured through your built-in sound board. The advantage of the TrueSpeech approach is in the ease and simplicity of file creation and the speed of playback over the Web.

Putting TrueSpeech Audio in an HTML Document

The first step in adding TrueSpeech to an HTML document is to create a TrueSpeech format file. If you're working with Windows95 or Windows NT, you can convert any existing WAV files to TrueSpeech format through the Sound

Recorder utility, or you can set the Sound Recorder to record at mono, 8KHz, 16-bits and record your narration directly through your system's sound board. If you're working in Windows 3.1, you can use the freeware TrueSpeech Converter utility to perform the file conversion, but you must start with a WAV file that is already stored in mono, 8KHz, 16-bit resolution.

Recording and Converting the Sound

The following example demonstrates the process in Windows95, assuming that you're creating a short introductory greeting to place at the beginning of an HTML document.

1. Open the Windows95 Sound Recorder utility. From the Start menu, select **Programs,** then **Accessories,** then **Multimedia** to find the Sound Recorder icon. The Sound Recorder window appears on the desktop, as shown in Figure 9.1.

2. Drop down the File menu from the Sound Recorder window and select **Properties.** The Properties for Sound dialog box appears, as shown in Figure 9.2.

3. If you want to record directly at the standard TrueSpeech sample rate, the displayed Audio Format should read PCM 8000Hz 16-bit, Mono. If you need to change this setting, under the Format Conversion box, select **Recording formats** from the drop-down listbox. Click the **Convert Now** button, and the Sound Selection dialog box appears, as shown in Figure 9.3. The standard qualities that appear under Windows95 do not include a named setting that includes the 8000Hz recording rate, so you can select the PCM format and choose the **Attributes** from the drop-down listbox to read 8000Hz, 16 Bit, Mono and save this setting using the **Save As** button and a name of your choice. Click **OK** to save the new settings and return to the Sound Recorder window.

Figure 9.1 Sound Recorder window.

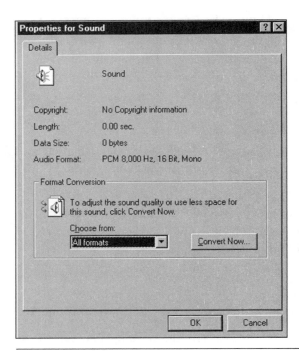

Figure 9.2 Properties for Sound dialog box.

4. Click on the **Record** button of Sound Recorder and record a narrative sequence into your system's microphone. (If you're at a loss for words, try this sequence from a Twilight Zone episode: "There are more things in heaven and earth and in the sky than can be dreamt of. And somewhere in between heaven, the sky, and earth lies the Twilight Zone.") My recording of this selection occupied 13.4 seconds. Even sampled at the low 8KHz sample rate, the resulting WAV file occupied 210Kb.

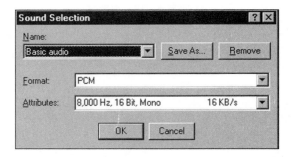

Figure 9.3 Sound Selection dialog box.

5. To convert this WAV file to TrueSpeech format, select the **Save As** option from the Sound Recorder File menu. When the Save As dialog box appears, click the **Change** button at the bottom of the box to bring up the Format options.

6. From the Format drop-down listbox, select the **DSP Group TrueSpeech**(TM) option, as shown in Figure 9.4. Note that you can save this selection under a name that you provide using the **Save As** button. This would let you save files directly to TrueSpeech format without a conversion. Click **OK** to save this setting.

Finding the TrueSpeech Option

If the **DSP Group TrueSpeech** option does not appear in your drop-down list of items, from the Windows95 Start menu choose **Settings** and then **Control Panel**. From the Control Panel selections, open the Multimedia panel and select the Advanced tab. Expand the list of Audio Compression Codecs, and you should see one called the DSP Group TrueSpeech(TM) Software CODEC. If it's near the bottom of the list, double-click the item and reset the priority in the General tab that appears (shown in Figure 9.5). The priority you select should be among the top six for this format to appear as a selectable format through Sound Recorder. Also, check to be sure that the option **Use this audio codec** is enabled.

---

7. When you return to the Sound Recorder window, click **Save** to convert the file to the new format. You can keep the WAV file extension and overwrite the earlier uncompressed file or rename the file. A progress bar appears to show you the state of the conversion. For this example, you can name the file twilight.wav.

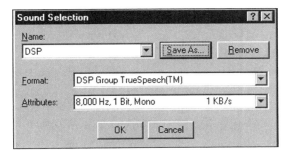

Figure 9.4 DSP Group TrueSpeech file format.

Figure 9.5 Changing the CODEC priority.

8. Note that the TrueSpeech version of the audio clip now occupies only 14Kb—a major improvement over the previous 210Kb. The file has been compressed by a factor of 15. These same compression rates can be achieved for most audio files. If you play the file back through Sound Recorder, you'll hear a slight modification of the sound quality as compared to the original uncompressed file, but the overall effect is not unpleasant.

You can use this same process to create any number of TrueSpeech format files that can then be embedded in an HTML document, as described in the following section. If you have a group of WAV files that you want to convert as a single operation, you can use the TrueSpeech DOS Batch Converter.

Putting TrueSpeech into an HTML Document

The process for embedding TrueSpeech audio into an HTML document varies depending on whether you are designing playback for Microsoft Internet Explorer or Netscape Navigator. Internet Explorer's native support for the format offers an additional option of playing sounds immediately upon loading the HTML document, as described in the following section. If you are going to use this approach, we recommend that you use JavaScript or another technique to detect the installed browser running the HTML document and branch to the appropriate introductory page.

> ## Normalizing Waveforms Before Compression
>
> When you're working with sound files that are downsampled to 8KHz sample rates, you need to pay particular attention to the quality of the overall sound if you want to produce usable sound output. One technique you might try is to take your original recorded WAV files, before compressing them in TrueSpeech, and run a normalization pass on them using any sound editor that offers this feature; for example, Sonic Foundry's Sound Forge or Macromedia's SoundEdit 16. When you normalize a sound file, you raise the volume of the stored waveform so that the highest-level sample in the file reaches a precise level (defined by you). This ensures that you're taking full advantage of the dynamic range that you have available for the sound file. If you are working with a set of files that will be played together, it is helpful to normalize them all to the same level so that perceptually they will play back at the same volume level. Small professional touches such as this can make a big difference in a sound-based Web presentation. Use all the tools at your disposal to produce the highest-quality sound.

Internet Explorer Native Support You can include TrueSpeech-formatted files that are designed for playback under Internet Explorer in a direct and simple manner, because Explorer has native support for this streaming audio format. Explorer v3.0 supports the HTML <BGSOUND> tag, so if you want the audio file to begin playing as soon as the page is loaded, add the following entry to the body of your HTML document:

```
<BGSOUND SRC="twilight.wav">
```

If you wanted the file to continue playing a number of times, you can add a loop statement indicating the number of times to loop. Looping can be made to continue indefinitely if you add the term "Infinite" to the loop statement, but this would not typically be appropriate for spoken voice segments, unless you wanted to drive your listeners berserk. Because the compression ratios of TrueSpeech are more suited to voice than music, you would normally not want to add a loop statement.

```
<BGSOUND SRC="annoy.wav" loop="Infinite">
```

You can also simply create a link to the file by name. When the user clicks on the link, a player pops up on screen in a window and streaming playback begins almost immediately. The player allows you to pause or replay any sections of the audio, and you can close the window when done.

T IP Netscape Navigator does not provide support for the <BGSOUND> tag. If you need immediate audio playback upon loading in Navigator you can use the onLoad event handler through JavaScript to place the sound player on a page and to start playback. See the example in the following section for more information.

Explorer also supports the <EMBED> tag for accessing TrueSpeech audio files. When Explorer detects the embedded TrueSpeech file, it places a simple player at the indicated location in the HTML document. The person viewing the page can then start and stop the audio through the player controls. The entry to accomplish this would be:

```
<EMBED SRC="twilight.wav" WIDTH=120 HEIGHT=24>
```

The WIDTH and HEIGHT entries create a space for the audio file player, which appears at that point in the HTML document where the <EMBED> tag is placed. The audio controls let you start, stop, pause, and change the volume of the playback.

Netscape Navigator TrueSpeech Playback Using Netscape Navigator, you need to provide a more circuitous route for providing access to TrueSpeech audio. This requires setting up an interim text file with a .tsp extension that contains a pointer to the actual TrueSpeech file to be played. Netscape Navigator 4.0 users running the Communicator release have an automated method of accessing and downloading the TrueSpeech plug-in for playback. Netscape Navigator 3.0 and later users can be given a link to the DSP site, attached to the TrueSpeech logo.

To provide access to a TrueSpeech file for Navigator users, follow these steps:

1. Open up Notepad or a similar simple text editor.

2. Create a file with a .tsp extension that contains both the URL of the Web site on which the files will be stored and any necessary directories. For example, to point to the twilight.wav file stored in the BIN directory of a Web site at www.zone.com, the file should contain this line:

```
TSIP>>www.zone.com/bin/twilight.wav
```

3. For this example, let's call the .tsp file zoner.tsp. Provide a link to this file through an HTML document. The link can be attached to any image or text phrase in your document. When someone accesses the link, if the TrueSpeech player is available on their system, a player appears in a window on the page, and audiostreaming of the .wav file referenced begins within seconds. Figure 9.6 shows the appearance of the TrueSpeech player.

> **WARNING** The reference to the URL that you include in the .tsp file should not contain the usual *http://* address preface. Simply list the Web site address by itself. For example, don't use: http://www.zone.com. Instead use: www.zone.com.

Whether the audio files are residing on a local server that you are administering or on a host system that you use through an Internet Service Provider, some server configuration details must also be taken care of.

Configuring the Server to Recognize TrueSpeech The MIME type for TrueSpeech files is application/dsptype.

The server may not recognize this MIME type unless you provide the necessary extension in the configuration file. For Unix servers, the MIME.TYPE configuration file should contain this entry:

```
application/dsptype              tsp
```

For a CERN HTTP server, enter a configuration line as follows:

```
AddType.tsp      application/dsptype        binary 1.0
```

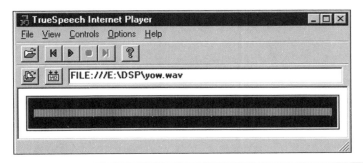

Figure 9.6 Spawned TrueSpeech player.

If your Internet access and home page are through an Internet Service Provider, contact your provider to make the changes shown to the configuration of their server.

Placing TrueSpeech Plug-Ins on a Page When tailoring playback to Navigator users, you can embed plug-ins directly on the Web page by using this variation of the previous example. Instead of spawning an instance of a full-sized player, this technique creates a compact set of controls that appears directly on the Web page, as shown in Figure 9.7.

1. Create a TrueSpeech file using the technique described previously.

2. Open Notepad or a similar simple text editor and create a file referencing the location of the audio file you want to play. Give the file a .tsi extension. For this example, we'll use the filename jude.tsi and reference an audio file from DSP's own Web site. The single line in jude.tsi should read:

```
TSIP>>www.dspg.com/samples/85/a5.wav
```

3. Add the plug-in to the page using an <EMBED> tag. To start the segment playing immediately, you could use a short JavaScript, as shown in the following example.

```
<HTML>

<HEAD><TITLE>Angry Man</TITLE>

<SCRIPT LANGUAGE ="JavaScript">

function zoner() {

document.write("<H1>Angry voice on the Web</H1><BR>")

document.write("<EMBED SRC="jude.tsi' WIDTH=200 HEIGHT=60 autostart=TRUE>")

}

</SCRIPT>

<BODY onLoad="zoner()">

</BODY>

</HTML>
```

The WIDTH and HEIGHT entries accommodate the plug-in on the Web page. The statement, autostart=TRUE, ensures that the audio file will start playing as

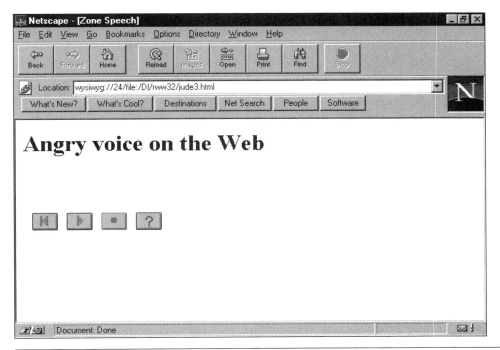

Figure 9.7 TrueSpeech plug-in as it appears embedded.

soon as the page loads. Because this script and the file jude.tsi are set up to access a server already configured for TrueSpeech playback (DSP's own site), you can try this example to get a sense of how TrueSpeech files play back in real time.

T I P To configure the server hosting your audio files to support plug-ins of this type, add the following entry to the MIME.TYPE file: audio/tsplayer tsi.

Music through TrueSpeech

Because TrueSpeech provides such a compact means of placing sound within an HTML document, you might want to experiment with creating WAV files containing simple musical passages and then converting these to TrueSpeech format. A one-minute segment of music can be stored in a 64Kb TrueSpeech file. The best results will be achieved using

> solo instruments played in a frequency range close to that of human speech. You might try recording banjo, piano, thumb piano, vibes, and similar instruments and then testing the sound by creating a TrueSpeech file and playing the file back through the TrueSpeech Internet Player. This method should prove suitable for providing background music to a Web page, offering musical cues while navigating, supporting simple sound effects, and similar applications.

EchoSpeech Options

EchoSpeech, a product of Echo Speech Corporation, is another alternative for placing compressed voice-quality speech within Web pages. This product is available in plug-in form supporting Internet Explorer 3.0 and Netscape Navigator 2.0 and later. Because EchoSpeech supports a higher sampling rate (11,025Hz versus the 8000Hz of TrueSpeech), the quality of playback is somewhat higher. Like TrueSpeech, EchoSpeech uses audiostreaming technology to begin playback shortly after file access begins. Unlike TrueSpeech, however, EchoSpeech requires a fee for use—currently $99 per Web site. This is fairly modest compared to some of the high-end approaches, such as setting up a server for Liquid Audio or RealAudio sound support. While commercial users must pay this fee, nonprofit organizations, educational institutions, and anyone using it for noncommercial applications are free to embed EchoSpeech files in their documents.

EchoSpeech, like TrueSpeech, is an audio solution that doesn't require extensive server setup to implement. The MIME.TYPE entry to configure a server for EchoSpeech is: audio/echospeech.es.

T I P Once the MIME type has been set up, EchoSpeech audio files can be inserted into an HTML document using the <EMBED> tag.

 Those users who are running browsers other than Explorer or Navigator can access EchoSpeech files using Helper Applications that Echo Speech Corporation has available on their Web site:

www.echospeech.com

Creating an EchoSpeech File

As raw source material, EchoSpeech uses monaural .wav files that have been sampled at 11KHz sample rates with 16-bit resolution. The EchoSpeech compression utility rejects files that haven't been created in this format. The compression utility has been designed to work with audio files containing speech, rather than music. While Echo Speech Corporation doesn't discourage people from trying to use the utility to compress and present music on the Web, they do say that the results can be unpredictable, depending on the type of music that is being compressed. The program is clearly intended for speech applications.

Follow these steps to create an EchoSpeech file:

1. Record a sound file with the sampling rates of the sound editing program set to 11KHz, 16-bits, Mono. Save the results as a .wav file. Optionally, if you have a sound file that you'd like to use that is in a different resolution, you can downsample using a conversion utility or a program like Sonic Foundry's Sound Forge. The Windows95 Sound Recorder utility can also perform this function.

2. Start the EchoSpeech Voice Coder program and select the source file. The Voice Coder program uses only a few basic controls, as shown in Figure 9.8.

3. Enter a name for the output file by clicking the **Select Output File** button. Voice Coder automatically supplies the .es extension.

4. Click the **Encode** button to start the compression process.

5. When the conversion is complete, Voice Coder lets you play back the newly created EchoSpeech file by clicking the **Transport** button under the output filename. You can compare the quality to the original file by clicking the **Transport** button under the source filename.

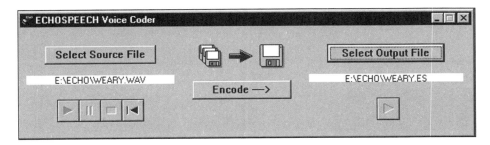

Figure 9.8 EchoSpeech Voice Coder.

Embedding EchoSpeech Audio

The familiar <EMBED> tag is used to incorporate EchoSpeech audio playback into an HTML document. The WIDTH and HEIGHT entries delineate a space for the EchoSpeech plug-in. The plug-in itself appears as a small rectangle with EchoSpeech 1.5, Voice of the Web, contained within it, as shown in Figure 9.9.

The <EMBED> statement for a file called weary.es should read:

```
<EMBED SRC="weary.es" WIDTH=120 HEIGHT=40>
```

The plug-in image also serves as a control for playback. If you click once on the image during playback, the EchoSpeech player halts until clicked a second time, causing it to resume. If the playback has completed, you can repeat the playing of the audio file by clicking the plug-in image again. You can also jump to the Echo Speech Corporation home page by clicking your right mouse button on the plug-in image.

The plug-in is designed to automatically begin playback as soon as an HTML document loads. You can cause an audio file to loop a specific number of times by

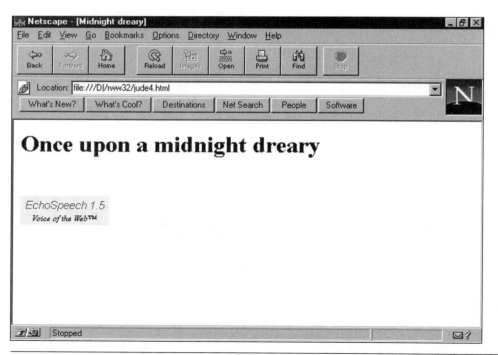

Figure 9.9 EchoSpeech plug-in as it appears in an HTML document.

placing a loop entry in the <EMBED> statement. For example, to loop the audio file six times, you would enter this statement:

```
<EMBED.SRC="weary.es" WIDTH=120 HEIGHT=40 LOOP=6>
```

Server Configuration

No server configuration is required other than the entry in the configuration file for the MIME type. The MIME type should be set to audio/echospeech .es.

As the Echo Speech Corporation points out, some Internet Service Providers can be resistant to the idea of adding any new MIME types to their configuration. In their Web site information, the company points out an alternative technique that you may want to try. You can post the audio files in compressed EchoSpeech format to a publicly accessible FTP site on which you have available storage space. The <EMBED> tag can then access the FTP directory, and streaming playback will take place as the files are retrieved from this FTP site. The only thing you need to modify to accomplish this is the SRC statement. For example, for an FTP site called ftp.audio_place.com you could retrieve a file named howl.es from the sound directory using this statement:

```
<EMBED SRC="ftp://ftp.audio_place.com/sound/howl.es" WIDTH=120 HEIGHT=40>
```

This technique is a useful workaround for situations where the service provider is unwilling to support the EchoSpeech MIME type. Access from an FTP site does not require any form of MIME type declaration.

Clean Recording for Low Noise

The EchoSpeech Voice Coder algorithms seem particularly susceptible to recorded noise and may actually bring it to the forefront of a sound file during coding. For example, if you create a voice recording using a microphone directly into your computer's sound board and there is a significant amount of computer fan noise in the source recording, that noise will be particularly noticeable in the EchoSpeech compressed version of the file. For this reason, you may want to create your source recordings in a quiet environment, recording directly to a cassette deck or a DAT recorder. You can then input the results, either digitally or through the sound board's A-to-D input, and compress the file using the Voice Coder. This creates significantly cleaner EchoSpeech files.

Echo Speech Corporation has also produced a streaming audio product called EchoCast that integrates DolbyNet software to provide a method for broadcasting high-quality music as well as speech over the Web. EchoCast is designed to eliminate elaborate server setup processes that are required for products such as RealAudio. It also can be used without having to pay per-stream charges as part of the license agreement. More details on EchoCast can be found through the EchoSpeech Corporation Web site.

Daily Words of Wisdom

Compressed streaming audio files created using applications such as TrueSpeech or EchoSpeech provide a simple means of placing audio on the Web without having to perform extensive server configuration. The following JavaScript example shows how you could use this technology to have your Web site present spoken words of wisdom that are different depending on the day of the week. The example uses EchoSpeech to perform the audio playback. The procedure first explains how to create the source files and then how to create an HTML document with the necessary JavaScript code.

Find a suitable source for some entries to use as the audio "wisdom" files. I picked a copy of *The Book of New England Wisdom*, published by Walnut Grove Press. While the book is, of course, copyrighted, the quotes within it exist in the public domain—many of them are more than 150 years old. Don't pick quotes out of any source to which you don't have rights.

Create a series of audio files using any convenient sound recording application with the format set to PCM (WAV) files, 11KHz sampling rate, 16-bits, Mono. As you record each quote, save the filenames starting with one.wav, then two.wav, and so on. For example, for the first selection, I picked a quote from Henry David Thoreau: "The man is richest whose pleasures are cheapest."

When you've finished recording all seven quotes, open the EchoSpeech Voice Coder. Start with the first WAV file, one.wav, and convert it to EchoSpeech format, letting the program maintain the same name but add the .es extension. Save the files in the same directory into which you plan to place the HTML file containing the JavaScript code.

Using your favorite HTML editor, enter the following HTML code and JavaScript.

```
<HTML>

<HEAD>
```

```
<SCRIPT LANGUAGE = "JavaScript">

wisdom = new Array(7)

wisdom[0] = "one.es"

wisdom[1] = "two.es"

wisdom[2] = "three.es"

wisdom[3] = "four.es"

wisdom[4] = "five.es"

wisdom[5] = "six.es"

wisdom[6] = "seven.es"

wisdom[7] = "eight.es"

var current_day = new Date()

wise_words = current_day.getDay()

document.write("<EMBED SRC+" + '"' + wisdom[wise_words] + '"' +

 "WIDTH=120 HEIGHT=40>")

</SCRIPT>

</HEAD>

<BODY>

<H1>Welcome to the arena of wisdom</H1>

</BODY>

</HTML>
```

Briefly, the script works as follows.

The first JavaScript entry (wisdom=new Array(7)) creates an Array object with eight elements (numbering begins at 0 and goes to 7). Each of the next eight entries populates the array, putting the names of the EchoSpeech files into positions 0 through 7. A variable is then created that consists of the JavaScript Date object. In the next statement, the getDay() method is used to find the number of the current day of the week for the Data object and assign that to a variable called wise_words.

The wise_words variable, which will be an integer representing the day of the week based on the day that the Navigator or Explorer browser detects when the HTML document is run, will be used to access one of the entries from the array (the name of the audio file to be played).

The document.write statement is then used to write an <EMBED> statement to the body of the HTML document. The statement consists of the source of the file to be used for the quotation—as represented by the wisdom [wise_words] entry. JavaScript substitutes the integer for day of the week for the wise_words variable, which in turn provides the position in the array from which the appropriate element can be retrieved. For example, on a Tuesday, the wise_words variable would be set to the value 2 when the getDay() method is run. The array statement would then be wisdom[2], which contains the entry "three.es". JavaScript substitutes the three.es in the <EMBED> statement so that the line written to the body of the HTML document will read:

```
<EMBED SRC="three.es" WIDTH=120 HEIGHT=40>
```

If the EchoSpeech plug-in has been properly installed for the browser, recognition of the .es extension will cause the EchoSpeech plug-in to be embedded into the HTML document, as shown in Figure 9.10.

For each day of the week, a different position in the array will be accessed and a different quote will be played back, in real time, when the page is initially loaded. You could adapt this script to play from a larger selection of quotes, or you could periodically just load a new set of EchoSpeech .es files into the directory (overwriting the old ones of the same name) and continue with an ongoing series of wise words.

Other Possibilities for Daily Messages

You don't have to be limited to providing a quotation on a daily basis, but you could use a similar technique to offer some type of audio greeting whenever a user views one of your Web pages. For example, you could include an audio message that points out where some new material has been added to the Web site or that announces some newsworthy item that would be of interest to those visiting your site ("A series of links to major CD-ROM title producers has been added to the Publishing area of this site" or "You can sample the latest songs from the Flaming Lizards album in the Just Released area."). Audio is an excellent means of drawing attention to points of interest, and it can be a very compelling means for guiding someone about your site.

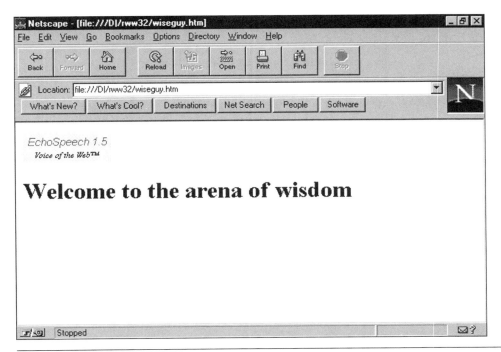

Figure 9.10 EchoSpeech plug-in for wise words.

Text-to-Speech through Talker

After six straight hours of reading text from your computer screen, have you ever wished you could just shut your eyes and have someone read the contents of a series of Web pages to you? With improvements in text-to-speech technology and an ingenious plug-in called Talker, you can use Netscape Navigator (v2.0 and later) as your personal Web page reader. The Talker plug-in runs on Macintosh and Power Macintosh systems that have Apple Computer's PlainTalk Speech Synthesis software enabled. This requires System 7.0 or a later version of the operating system. The necessary extension appears under the title Speech Manager in your Extensions folder, if it is installed. If it isn't, you can freely download a copy from Apple's Web site.

Speech synthesis requires far less bandwidth than other techniques of transferring audio across the Web and supports other interesting variations, such as the ability to read back pages in other languages.

A variety of Web pages enabled for playback through Talker can be found listed at the MVP Solutions site at:

www.mvpsolutions.com/PlugInSite/Talker.html

Other interesting or amusing sites set up to use Talker include:

- **Suspense Interactive:** Tales of mystery and espionage read to you, as shown in Figure 9.11, at www.suspense.com/interactive/.

- **Internet Webseum of Holography:** Uses both speech synthesis and speech recognition to showcase holographic techniques at www.holoworld.com.

- **Civil War Diary:** Provides an interesting online book that is read to you section by section at netnow.micron.net/~rparker/diary/index.html.

- **Three Toad Multimedia:** A site that both talks and listens at www.threetoad .com/main/9000.html.

- **Robert A. Heinlein quotes:** Provides a new quote each time you access the page at www.vitalnet.com/heinlein.

 For an example of a page synthesized for playback in Japanese, go to:

www.naotaka.com/talker/index.html

PlainTalk uses a variety of voices that you can select and change through a drop-down menu when the Extension is installed. Talker can use any of these same voices and can change from voice to voice while reading back text from the Web. You could create the equivalent to an online conversation between characters by switching back and forth between voices. The characters available in this speech synthesis model range from Trinoids (an alien-sounding voice) to Bruce (a surprisingly realistic male voice) to Princess (a young girl's voice).

Creating a Talking Web Page

The following steps explain how to create a talking Web page that relies on MVP Solutions' Talker plug-in. This, of course, creates a page where the talking portion is limited to Macintosh users, but other text and graphics can be viewed and navigated by users on other platforms.

1. Enter the text that you want read in a document ending in the extension .talk (for example, BLABBER.talk).

2. Place the file that you created in the same directory on the server where your other HTML documents reside.

3. Create an HTML document that contains the <EMBED> tag referencing the file that you want read. Also, include the path to the plug-in for users who don't have it installed. For example, the following <EMBED> statement accesses BLABBER.talk:

```
<EMBED SRC="BLABBER.TALK" WIDTH=10 HEIGHT=10
PLUGINSPAGE="http://www.mvpsolutions.com/PlugInSite/Talker.html">
```

This is all that is necessary to activate playback of Talker files for people browsing through your site who have the plug-in installed. Those who don't have the plug-in can follow the link provided to download it. You also need the MIME type properly defined at the server level, as described in the following section.

Figure 9.11 Suspense Interactive set up to read to you.

Configuring the Server for Talker

To work effectively with Talker files, you should configure your server to recognize the MIME type *text/x-speech* using the extension *.talk*. For those servers that include a configuration file titled MIME.TYPES (such as a Netscape Commerce Server), a single line can be entered reading:

```
text/x-speech        talk
```

If your server is administered through an Internet Service Provider, contact your provider and request that they provide support for the Talker plug-in, using a MIME type/subtype of *text/x-speech* and a file extension of *.talk*.

T **I P** An earlier version of Talker (1.0) used a different MIME type than version 2.0. This MIME type—plugin/talker—still works with Talker 2.0, but you would be better off to install the more current MIME type—*text/x-speech*.

Hints for Successful Talker Pages

The following hints can make Talker-enabled pages more accessible for those visiting your site.

- Place a note on your Web page informing visitors that the page can talk for those Macintosh users running Netscape Navigator 2.0 or later as long as they have Apple's English Text-to-Speech extension installed and the MVP Solution's Talker plug-in. You can provide your own additional information about how to equip their Macintoshes to access this feature or provide a dynamic link to the MVP Solutions' Talker page for further explanation.

 The best place to link in to the MVP Solutions' Talker page is at:

  www.mvpsolutions.com/PlugInSite/Talker.html

- Text included in the *.talk file that you reference does not appear on the Web page automatically. So that the viewer can read along with the speech synthesis if he or she wants, you should place the equivalent text on the Web page. This, of course, also provides a usable path for Windows and Unix users who cannot hear the pages talking.

- Point out somewhere in the beginning of your document that Talker pages can be stopped from talking by pressing the **ESC** key.

- You can make your Talker page more interesting by using embedded commands that alter different facets of the spoken voice. This includes having the ability to change the speaker, the pitch and rate of the spoken words, and the degree of emphasis put on words or phrases. Apple documents this in the "Speech Manager" chapter of the *Inside Macintosh* manuals.

Embedded Commands for Talker 2.0

A variety of commands can be inserted into the *.talk files that you create to guide the speech synthesizer. Some of the possibilities are:

- **Change the speaker:** Using the entry [[cmnt talkervoice=*speaker*]] indicates which of the several PlainTalk synthesized voices should be used for the following text. For example, you could alternate lines of dialog between Bruce and Victoria by prefacing blocks of dialog with the entries [[cmnt talkervoice=Bruce]] and [[cmnt talkervoice=Victoria]].

- **Time the talking to create complex interactions:** The [[cmnt talkerblock]] and [[cmnt talkergo]] commands can be used to pause talking while text continues to download [[cmnt talkerblock]] or resume talking at a particular point [[cmnt talkergo]]. These commands are most useful when used in conjunction with the embedded commands available to Speech Manager; for example, if you are producing complex text relying on custom phonemes or numerous pitch changes (such as when you simulate singing). A number of sites offer examples of this type of approach and the complexity that you can achieve using Talker on the Web. You can even make conversations overlap, for those users who have PowerPC Macintoshes and are able to play back the more complex synthesis.

The Browser That Talks: pwWebSpeak

With the computer market flooded with browsers of every shape and size, is there a need for still another browser? The Productivity Works thinks so. Their browser, pwWebSpeak, has a significant difference; it speaks. By interpreting the HTML code posted on Web sites, pwWebSpeak provides a speech synthesized narration of the contents, including identifying embedded graphics that are found within a document. pwWebSpeak also works in combination with RealAudio material, so that the browser provides integrated access to the wealth of streaming audio content across the Web that appears in RealAudio format. The Productivity Works has even released their latest version of their pwWebSpeak user's guide in RealAudio format, so the instructions can be played back in streaming mode. This browser provides an ideal nonvisual interface for the visually impaired or anyone who prefers to listen to Web pages rather than view them.

pwWebSpeak requires a supported speech synthesizer, either one of the two directly supported synthesizers or one of a long list that is indirectly supported through the Arkenstone SSIL Interface. The two directly supported synthesizers are:

- **TASSIST:** The Text Assist software from Creative Labs. This requires a Sound Blaster board.

- **SOFTVOICE:** Softvoice software also requires a SoundBlaster-compatible board.

In addition, pwWebSpeak can work through those speech synthesizers that include compatibility with an industry-standard interface, the Arkenstone SSIL interface, to provide the bridge between the pwWebSpeak software and the SSIL interface.

 The Productivity Works offers a collection of modules keyed to the individual synthesis packages that can be downloaded from their Web site at:

www.prodworks.com

The list of speech synthesizers supported through SSIL includes Apollo2, Artic 215, Audapter, DECtalk PC, Echo PC, Infovox version 3.5, Kurzweil Reading Edge, and a number of others.

Clearly, pwWebSpeak includes a fair amount of built-in intelligence to navigate the morass of text on Web pages and skip around the content that is unnecessary in conveying the meaning on the page. The program does well in handling text embedded in forms and tables— one of the stumbling blocks for other programs of this type. pwWebSpeak can interpret and handle headings, links, and similar page attributes; but it still has trouble with embedded JavaScript code. The Productivity Works is working on a fix for this problem.

Reading speeds can be dynamically adjusted, and the program offers the option of spelling out any terms that might be jumbled by the speech synthesizer.

pwWebSpeak also includes a specialized interface for using the AltaVista search engine and specifying topics to identify on the Web in a simplified manner.

The program also offers a large text option for low-vision users and a simplified graphical navigational display that can reduce navigation requirements to a few keystrokes. Progress is underway to couple the program to a voice-driven interface so that keyboard interaction will not be required at all.

Beyond the value of using speech synthesis to navigate the Web for the visually impaired, this method of extracting content from the Internet can also be rewarding for normally sighted users. Next time your eyes grow weary from scanning the flickering computer monitor, you might want to download an evaluation copy of pwWebSpeak and have Web pages read back to you. It may become your favorite method for touring the Web. For others whose vision impairments do not allow them to use a computer monitor, pwWebSpeak represents an essential communication tool that can open up the Internet for full exploration.

Working with Kurzweil VOICE

Kurzweil has for many years been one of the technology leaders in voice recognition technology. Their latest version of VOICE for Windows (version 2.5) offers a number of opportunities for Web developers who want to integrate spoken voice applications with their HTML document design, compose e-mail through dictation, or use the navigation functions available through this program to cruise the Web.

For example, if you are doing any serious Web development you undoubtedly spend a good deal of time keying in the text that will appear on the Web pages. VOICE provides a convenient means for driving that process through dictation. VOICE provides native support for the commands and menu options common to a number of different word processing applications and can also be trained to support just about any other kind of application imaginable, including HTML editors. Some setup and training may be required to get the program to do exactly what you want it to do, but once you've accomplished the setup process, you may find yourself giving up the keyboard completely. The technology has gotten that good— well, almost. Some operations will still be faster from the mouse or the keyboard, but you can combine dictation and voice commands with either mouse or keyboard activities, allowing you to get the best of both worlds.

To accomplish voice recognition successfully, VOICE adapts itself to your voice through a series of exercises in which you recite words from a displayed list into the specialized Andrea NC-50 noise-canceling microphone included with the product. After a period of operation, VOICE launches into a more elaborate exercise in which you "enroll," by repeating a sequence of words into the microphone for about 25 minutes and then turning your computer loose to process the voice patterns. The processing can take several hours—VOICE builds a library of these vocal patterns, referred to as a voice profile, and uses this library to improve the accuracy of recognition. VOICE can achieve accuracy rates of more than 97 percent at a dictation rate of 45 to 60 words per minute, equal to what a moderately skilled typist can achieve.

The training process is not essential to the operation of VOICE because the program uses algorithms that are independent of the speaker and based on a vocabulary of up to 60,000 words—right out of the box the recognition rate is fairly high. The built-in intelligence, however, can improve recognition over time as the program continually adapts itself to personal language patterns. As you are dictating, the program displays each word in a window and allows you to stop and make a correction if it has chosen the wrong word. Over time, the need for this type of correction becomes less and less. The recognition algorithms also have the capability of distinguishing between certain types of words based on their usage in a sentence—such as sorting out the multiple possibilities presented by "to," "two," and "too." If during dictation, you see an erroneous word entered, speaking the words "Correct-That" causes VOICE to display a selection window, as shown in Figure 9.12, that lists its top five choices for the word last spoken. From this list, you can either select the correct word (if displayed) or dictate the spelling of the word that was misinterpreted. VOICE stores the correction along with the voice samples for the current user and is likely to get the same word right the next time around.

If you need to spell a word to VOICE that is outside the range of its vocabulary, the program includes built-in recognition for the international phonetic alphabet—the same alphabet used by the aviation industry to clarify letters during radio communications between an aircraft and the control tower. "A" is dictated as "alpha," "B" as "bravo," "C" as "charlie," and so on. You can add new words to the vocabulary. This is an important feature for professionals working in an industry such as the computer industry, which is littered with jargon and specialized terms.

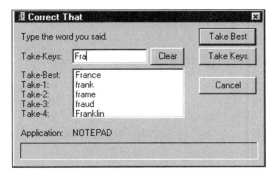

Figure 9.12 Correction window in VOICE.

The system actually works quite well—this paragraph was dictated using Voice. It mixed up a couple of words but managed to retain a fairly high recognition rate. It's actually kind of fun to enter text in this manner. Of course, if you are entering text into Microsoft Word you can then export your text directly into HTML format using the assistant application that is available from Microsoft. This could be a reasonably efficient way to deal with the bulk of your text entry and a nice way to avoid the threat of repetitive stress injuries from hammering on the keyboard.

While running VOICE, even while dictating you can issue voice commands that activate Windows menu functions or other commands. At any time you can display the Active Words list, as shown in Figure 9.13, allowing you to scan those words that are currently recognized as commands or simple text entries. As you can see, a number of common Windows menu options are available, and this list can be expanded to include your own custom commands.

The facility for being able to modify the existing command recognition lets you set up VOICE to use just about any Windows application, like that nifty HTML editor you purchased last week. There is already built-in support for the most common commands for a number of popular applications that are probably in the toolkits of most Webmasters, such as Netscape Navigator 3.0 and the Eudora mail program. Using VOICE, you can speak the vocal commands to log into the Internet, send your e-mail, search for topics or keywords, and sort through the current History list. The process for customizing VOICE to support additional applications is not difficult. It greatly expands the ability of this program to place your whole computer system under the control of your spoken words. Spending some time working with VOICE might permanently change the way you interact with a computer.

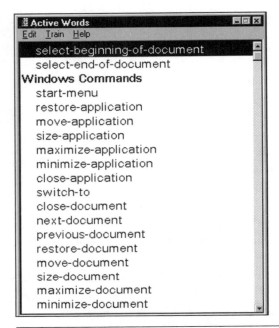

Figure 9.13 Active Words list.

Using DragonDictate

DragonDictate, from Dragon Systems in Newton, Massachusetts, is a capable, flexible voice recognition application that adapts well for a variety of Web uses. As is the case with Kurzweil VOICE, the program itself is speaker independent, but it can enhance its recognition capabilities by using training and an enrollment process. DragonDictate maintains a user list and retains profile information for individual users, so the more you work with the program the better it gets at responding to your voice commands and dictation.

Within a few moments of installing the program and enabling the microphone included with the package, you are running through a setup wizard that prompts you for a few of the most commonly used words in DragonDictate. The program then gives you the option to run a tutorial, which takes about 20 minutes to complete. The tutorial covers the basic principles of DragonDictate operation, explaining such topics as how to switch between Command Mode and Dictate Mode and how to correct mistakes made while dictating. Command Mode controls application functions and the operation of Windows. Dictate Mode controls the entry of text from spoken words. DragonDictate uses the international phonetic approach to spelling out words letter by letter (alpha, bravo, charlie, and so on).

DragonDictate also provides a mechanism for setting up applications to perform specific command operations that are based on your spoken words. This feature is accessed through the Vocabulary Manager portion of the program, as shown in Figure 9.14. As you can see, one of the natively supported applications is Netscape Navigator. You can configure DragonDictate to perform any of the navigation functions in Navigator, including the opening up of a particular Web location based on a spoken word, by training DragonDictate to recognize that word. With a bit of customization, you will be able to perform hands-free Web browsing. You can also set up the program to use the Composer component of the new Netscape Communicator software, allowing you to dictate HTML tags and text entry within the Composer window.

The Vocabulary Manager provides a graphical view of information stored within DragonDictate associated with vocabularies, groups, and words. Opening the window

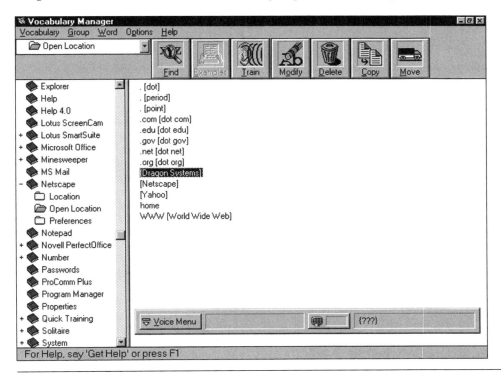

Figure 9.14 Vocabulary Manager.

in Vocabulary Manager titled "What Can I Say?" displays a list of terms that you can use at a particular point in an application. You can extend the terms to include your own. For example, while working with the item that represents Netscape Navigator, double-clicking on a displayed location brings up a window that lets you modify the entries and command operations associated with the location, as shown in Figure 9.15. Instead of typing a lengthy URL into your browser or scrolling through a long list of bookmarks to make a selection, you can simply speak a single word and activate the selection and access of a predetermined Web site. Other types of browser operations can be set up in a similar manner.

Mouse control can be accomplished by voice command using Dragon Systems' patented MouseGrid technology. Using this feature, the mouse pointer can be relocated to a specific point on the screen by speaking a few words.

A Text-to-Speech module installs in the same directory as the main DragonDictate application files and extends the program with the capability of performing speech synthesis from text displayed on screen. Whenever the voice recognition panel and microphone are active for DragonDictate, you can speak the command "Read That" to trigger the reading of the current onscreen text, if within a program that works with text. This feature also worked well with Netscape Navigator. You can open a Web page, use the Edit menu to **Select All** of

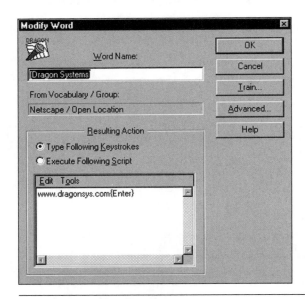

Figure 9.15 Modifying words.

the page contents, and then instruct DragonDictate to **Read That** by voice command. The speech synthesizer begins reading back the page contents from the beginning of the page. Several other **Read** options can be activated by voice command as well. Using this speech synthesizer in combination with the browser navigation commands described earlier lets you cruise through a series of Web sites and have the page contents read back to you through a nicely implemented speech synthesizer. Speech synthesis is improving rapidly, and this module included with DragonDictate does a fine job of interpreting punctuation marks in text, dealing with proper names that are encountered in a block of text, and adding inflections as part of reading back sentences. The technology is based on the TruVoice speech synthesizer developed by Centigram. An easy way to start the morning might be to have DragonDictate read your e-mail to you and then dictate your replies. The net effect is quite pleasant, and using the text-to-speech feature can be an effective technique for relieving eyestrain and obtaining content from the Web in a painless and relaxing manner.

Voice recognition is being extended for use in numerous other applications. For example, Dragon Systems has a product called PhoneQuery that is designed to allow telephone callers to make requests to a computerized service using natural speech. The product can be set up to handle incoming calls from the general public or used within a corporate structure to allow employees to call in to check messages or e-mail or even send faxes composed by voice control.

Dragon Systems also offers individual modules that are custom tailored to particular professions. For example, DragonTech is an extension of DragonDictate that includes terms more commonly encountered in the computer industry. An additional 60,000 computer-specific terms and phrases can be used within the 120,000-word dictionary. Other professions are also represented: DragonLaw supplies terminology best suited to legal professionals, while DragonMed provides a dictionary custom tailored to health care professionals. The legal and medical professions were among the first to adopt voice recognition systems to enable staff members to handle high-volume dictation requirements without the need for manual transcription or compiling written reports.

More information about Dragon Systems can be obtained from:

www.dragonsys.com

ListenUp Plug-In

If Star Trek commanders can talk to their computer consoles and tell them what to do, why can't you? Actually, you can—an interesting piece of software developed by Bill Noon allows Netscape Navigator to be configured to work in combination with Apple's PlainTalk Speech Recognition software on the Macintosh. By speaking phrases that are defined in a .ptlk file, you (and visitors to your site with the necessary plug-in installed) can navigate URLs and access local resources by spoken commands.

This plug-in requires each of the following items:

- A PowerPC-based Macintosh equipped with System 7.5 or later.

- Apple's PlainTalk Speech Recognition software; versions 1.4.1 and 1.5 both work.

- ListenUp PlugIn version matching PlainTalk Speech Recognition versions 1.4.1 or 1.5.

With the plug-in installed and the server configured to recognize the .ptlk extension to be associated with the MIME type plugin/listenup, you can create up to 100 spoken phrases that can direct Navigator to link to the specified URLs.

The <EMBED> statement is used to reference a .ptlk file in which you add the URLs to link to for the recognized phrases. For example, the following <EMBED> command can be used to reference the file speakup.ptlk.

```
<EMBED SRC="speakup.ptlk" WIDTH=40 HEIGHT=40>
```

The contents of the .ptlk file should contain the spoken phrase to be recognized, followed by the Web site URL to which you want to jump. For example, the phrase "Fast Eddy" could be used to link to a (fictional) Web site as follows:

```
"Fast Eddy"=http://www.poolcue.com/great_games/archives.html
```

 The ListenUp plug-in can be downloaded from Bill Noon's Web site at:

snow.cit.cornell.edu/noon/ListenUp.html

Summary

The spoken word is a powerful means for communicating emotion, nuance of expression, and subtleties of human communication that are not always conveyed by print communication. As you have seen in this chapter, there are a number of ways that you can use spoken words to guide, inform, entertain, and amuse your Web page visitors. The choice of an approach for placing speech on a page should be made based on bandwidth considerations—the amount of speech to be presented should help determine the best way to provide it. Speech synthesis can be used where large volumes of text are meant to be read. Shorter segments are amenable to compression techniques accessible through TrueSpeech and EchoSpeech. As in all Web endeavors, keep your imagination active and try to find new ways to express ideas and to communicate with spoken words.

Live Conversations
on the Internet

This chapter examines the tools and techniques for voice communication across the Internet, including Internet telephones, conferencing utilities, and electronic voice mail. Procedures for setting up and using many of the major applications in this area are provided.

Packets hopping from server to server through the Web can contain anything expressible in digital form: images, animation, audio, encrypted phone numbers of Hollywood stars, or digitized voice communications relayed by satellite from other star systems. This capability has made it possible to create programs that enable real-time conversations to be carried on over the Internet. While the audio quality isn't up to the startling clarity of optical-fiber transmissions, you can converse with anyone around the globe for essentially the price of a local telephone call (equivalent to your Internet access contact charge). If you've priced international phone rates lately (or even domestic rates during prime business hours), you'll realize that this feature is an incredible hidden benefit of the Internet that could save anyone who makes a lot of phone calls hundreds of dollars a year. Netscape Navigator 3.0 and beyond includes a companion Windows product called CoolTalk, which is essentially a digital telephone for Web use. Two-way audio communications of this sort are referred to as Internet telephony. This approach relies on the built-in sound handling capabilities of a computer or an add-on sound board, which digitizes the outgoing words as they are spoken into a microphone and plays back the spoken responses through speakers attached to the computer's sound port or a headset attached to the audio output.

Other similar Internet phone products abound, in the form of Navigator and Explorer plug-ins and standalone applications. The market leader at press time was VocalTec's Internet Phone product, followed by Quarterdeck's Web Talk and Netspeak's Web Phone. Depending on the capabilities of the computer's sound board or built-in sound, conversations are either half-duplex (where only one side or the other can talk at a time—sound is either being transmitted or received at any given moment) or full-duplex (where the transmission and reception can be handled simultaneously—voices overlap, just as in face-to-face conversation). There are also a host of related features, including virtual whiteboards, which allow graphic images to be transferred from one station to the next, and real-time messaging via typed-in strings.

Mutually Compatible Web Phones

Although standards have existed for some time now, the notion of interoperability still hasn't caught on with Web phone producers. For this reason, you can't talk to someone who is using different Internet phone software. If you're using CoolTalk software, the person you contact must also be using CoolTalk. If you're using IPhone, the party called must also be using IPhone. This, clearly, represents a fairly significant impediment to the widespread use of Internet telephony. Think of what the situation would be if you tried to call someone from an AT&T telephone, but couldn't speak with them because their phone was manufactured by General Electric. Support for the existing telephony standards will hopefully overcome these barriers to interoperability.

Telephone companies, not surprisingly, view Internet telephony as a serious threat to their conventional communication channels (and profit streams) and have repeatedly petitioned the FCC to establish regulations restricting this use of the Internet, so far without success. In the public responses to date, the FCC has essentially taken the position that this form of voice communication will encourage healthy competition and they do not have plans to regulate it. As with all things in the administrative and regulatory domain of the communications industry, however, this could change in an instant. Companies and investors behind Internet telephony have been impatiently testing the wind, not quite ready to launch their vessels should the direction of the gusts suddenly change. A strong statement of intention from the FCC might help stabilize this industry—which is obviously still in its infancy—and open the door to further product development and investment.

Variations on the Telephony Theme

Not everyone has a Web site, but nearly everyone uses the telephone. Internet telephony has sprung up on a playing field fractiously occupied by many national and local telephone companies, most of whom view this new upstart with distrust and disdain. Different models for real-time and deferred voice communication are being explored, and the approaches being developed are often unique and very innovative—as they must be to accommodate the basic structure of data transfer on the Internet. Survival and acceptance of this new voice communication medium are not guaranteed, but the tools being developed show an increasing degree of sophistication, and the public generally looks with favor at the opportunity to escape the stiff long-distance fees that characterize most of the nation.

Within the technological cauldron, in spite of the political discussions, product development goes on. New products are popping up in the market almost weekly. These products range from the simplest of shareware Web phones to sophisticated audio conferencing tools that make workgroup collaboration possible on a global scale. The characteristic that all these approaches share is that they use the Internet as the medium for transmitting the packets containing the digitized replicas of human speech. Unlike the phone switching networks (PBX), which establish a finite uninterrupted path between two speakers linked by phone, and like everything else on the Internet, the packets bearing spoken words find their own route from source to destination, welding a path from server to server, dodging obstacles and impediments along the way. If the transmission goes smoothly, the digitized pieces of spoken words can be seamlessly extracted from the packets, decoded, and played back in real time without even a hint of delay. If the transmission gets bogged down or the routing becomes too circuitous, the words may begin to drop out or crackle or become garbled.

In practical use, at least for communications within the boundaries of the United States, the level of quality and responsiveness of most Web phones is quite high. Some of these products offer a selection of CODECs so that you can perform digitizing and compression at different quality levels using different algorithms. Many of the CODECs have their own characteristic sound; to gain an extra measure of compression, you may end up with a voice that comes out sounding slightly metallic, like a robot with a head cold, or you may hear peculiar ringing associated with the voice, as if the speaker is talking from inside a hyperbaric decompression chamber on a swaying Coast Guard vessel. Selecting different CODECs lets you tailor the Web phone voice quality to suit the capabilities of your system, sound board, and Internet connection. As with most things, the higher-quality settings work best with the fastest processors, fastest Internet links, and the most capable sound boards. However, many of the Web phone products work fairly well even using 14.4Kbps Internet interconnections. Using internal intranets or WANs relying on T1 and better connections, the overall responsiveness and quality jump appreciably. Corporations, in particular, that have their international branches linked with reliable, high-speed network channels should experience a high degree of reliability and responsiveness for applications such as audioconferencing. However, if you are trying to set up a conference situation through dial-up links to reach parties in the Australian outback, or a rural Chinese province, or a small village in Costa Rica, the inconsistencies in the international telephone links will probably contribute to your downfall.

The following subsections highlight some of the different approaches to telephony.

When Long Distance Becomes Local

Probably the most familiar form of Internet telephony, Web phones or Internet phones, bypass conventional telephone switching networks and relay communications between two or more people through server-to-server TCP/IP routing. In some cases, this is accomplished solely through the interfaces provided by the computer. As you're sitting in front of your machine with your microphone plugged into your sound card and poised before your lips, you identify someone you want to call—either from a directory provided by a service or by directly calling the party's Internet address—and, if they happen to be logged on and running the equivalent Web phone, they hear the incoming call signaled, and you can begin talking. As you can see, there are a lot of "ifs" in this scenario. The party you are calling may have to be registered through a specialized directory offered through the service providing the Web phone access. They have to have their computer turned on, and they must be logged into the Internet with the appropriate software running. The appropriate software, of course, is the same version of a Web phone product that you are using. This technique is not as simple as picking up a phone and dialing someone's number—at least not yet.

However, some hybrid approaches combine the inexpensive packet-switching abilities of the Internet with the convenience of the telephone, so the scenario is somewhat different. You're sitting at your computer and you want to call Melvin Cobler, an Amish dairy farmer who doesn't have a computer—in fact, he only has a telephone to be able to occasionally talk to his daughter in Pasadena, who gave up the faith to try her hand at acting in Hollywood. You enter Melvin's number in your Web phone, the number is relayed through a gateway service that carries most of the communication through the Internet until it reaches a relay point in Melvin's home town, where the Internet gateway switches over to the standard telephone PSTN switching. Melvin's phone rings, he answers, and your conversation is carried out primarily over the Internet with a brief (probably local) journey through the PSTN.

You can even take this approach one step further and leave the computer out of the mix for the caller. Both parties can use standard telephones, and the call itself can be routed through the Internet gateway. Because the Internet transmission replaces the conventional long-distance communication, this type of phone call can be processed at a rate equivalent to the Internet connection charges (and whatever Public Switched Telephone Network or PBX charges might apply).

Internet Telephony Gateways

Internet telephony gateway services provide a bridge between the fully connected telephone switching networks that reach telephones all over the world and the packet-switching world of the Internet. As with other types of gateways that match dissimilar kinds of data and data protocols, the telephony gateway can link two geographically separated telephones, provide computer-to-telephone links, or provide a connection to the phone network from directly within a Web browser. The gateway itself consists of hardware and software that provide the interface between the telephone switching network and the Internet. Most products of this type include various voice mail options, call monitoring and tracking, billing modules, and so on. The basic scenarios for gateway use are as follows.

Suppose your multinational company has a branch office in Denver, Colorado, and a main headquarters in Reston, Virginia. Lots of phone calls go between these two locations on a daily basis, so you install one Internet gateway in Denver and another in Reston. This gives you a basic telephone interconnectivity scheme, as shown in Figure 10.1.

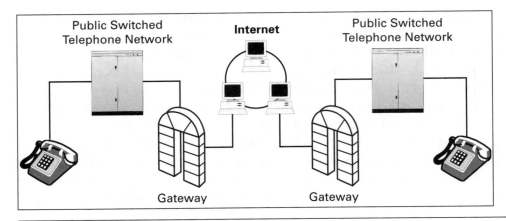

Figure 10.1 Telephone-to-telephone communication.

Note that with this approach, telephone calls from your Denver branch connect locally with the gateway, which then shoots the compressed voice communications through the Internet to the gateway in Reston. The gateway in Reston decompresses the voice communication, reconnects the call to the PSTN, and the listener on the other phone hears the original speaker. Depending on the quality of the audio compression scheme chosen and the behavior of the Internet on that particular day, audio quality of the phone call should be fairly good, though not as crisp as what we've come to expect from conventional telephone service.

You can also call someone using an Internet phone (on the computer) from a standard phone. To do this, the caller originates a call to the PC, which travels through to the nearest gateway. The gateway supports an interactive voice attendant that provides instructions for connecting to the person at the appropriate PC using tones tapped into the caller's telephone keypad. The gateway then routes the call directly to the user's computer, and the conversation can begin (if the person happens to be nearby and can respond to his or her Web phone). This type of scenario is shown in Figure 10.2.

The next possible scenario involves a computer-to-telephone link. In this case, shown in Figure 10.3, a person originates the call from an Internet phone on a PC. The call is routed across the Internet until it emerges at the gateway that is closest to the destination of the telephone being called. The call skips from the Internet back onto the PSTN and rings the phone at its final destination. To the person receiving the call, it appears no different than if someone had called using a standard telephone (except for whatever audio artifacts color the voices from the compression/decompression process).

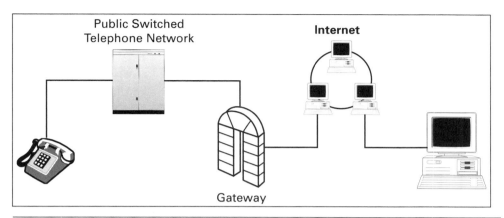

Figure 10.2 Telephone-to-computer communication.

A final—and extremely interesting—possibility is to originate the call from a Web browser plug-in, as shown in Figure 10.4. The call still travels over the Internet, gets put back onto the PSTN through the gateway, and rings a phone at the other end, but the difference in this case is that the browser manages the call origination. In other words, from inside a Web browser, with a properly equipped computer configured for Internet telephony, you could click a button and initiate a phone call to a company's customer support line, order processing line, or other kind of information service. Companies that pay thousands of dollars to maintain toll-free 800 lines could field incoming calls through the gateway at local rates. Customers calling the service would have the convenience of generating the call right from the browser while looking at merchandise they want to buy or while running a program in a separate window that

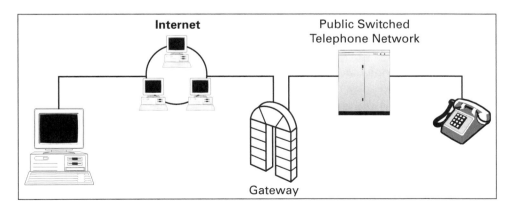

Figure 10.3 Computer-to-telephone communication.

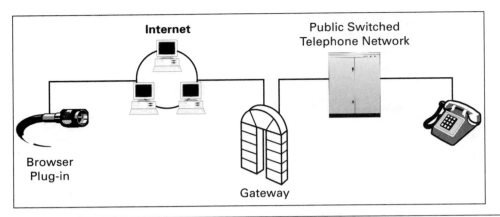

Figure 10.4 Browser plug-in-to-telephone communication.

they want to discuss with the technical support folks. This final scenario may provide one that becomes increasingly popular as companies seek ways to increase service to customers while reducing costs.

Some significant hardware and software setup is required to set up a gateway and get it running smoothly. Companies such as VocalTec and NetiPhone (described in the next section) are wholeheartedly embracing this approach with a range of products and custom setup services.

Despite political rumblings from mainstream telephone companies, many different vendors are getting into the Internet telephony ring with gateway products. One of the key companies engaged in pursuing this approach to long-distance communication—with a number of different products—is a Northvale, New Jersey company named VocalTec. VocalTec is the same company that produces the popular Internet Phone and a number of other Internet telephony products handling things such as voice mail attachments to mail messages (see the next section) and audio conferencing tools (Internet Conference Professional).

 You can visit VocalTec's Web site at:

www.vocaltec.com

Another contender in the Internet telephony arena with a marked interest in gateways is NetiPhone, one of the more recent entrants in the field. NetiPhone relies on the gateway technique for bridging the distance between caller and the person being called; however, NetiPhone runs exclusively on the PC. While you can reach someone else who has only a telephone (not a computer), you can't originate calls on your telephone and route them through a gateway. NetiPhone offers free evaluation software for Windows95 and Windows NT users to let you try out their approach.

You can visit NetiPhone's Web site at:

www.netiphone.com

Internet Phone Products

Choosing a Web phone isn't like picking up a telephone at your local Staples or Office Depot. The first thing you have to consider in your selection is who out there is also using the same type of Internet phone (or has access to the software). If you try to use one of the less popular Internet phones, and if you can't persuade any of your colleagues or friends to download and install the necessary software at their end, you may have no one to talk to, unless you wander through the Web phone equivalents of chat rooms in search of strangers to converse with. For this reason, there are fairly compelling reasons for selecting and using the more popular Web phone products. The sheer likelihood of finding someone to talk with becomes far greater. The Web phones described in the following subsections are ranked in terms of popularity based on a December 1996 survey conducted over Voice of the Net. The rankings could easily have changed by this time, but it is fairly likely that the leaders will still be somewhere near the top of the heap.

VocalTec Internet Phone 4.0 One of the earliest pioneers in the Internet phone market, VocalTec has had time to refine and improve its software to the point that it has won the lion's share of the market and it continues to win popularity and design awards. Fully maximized, the control panel occupies a reasonably small portion of screen real estate, and it can be progressively reduced in size by two more levels, shrinking down to a very inconspicuous fraction of its original size.

To locate other Internet Phone users over the vast uncharted wastelands of the Internet, VocalTec provides a server that tracks and connects users, chat style, through listings in public rooms that display potential chatters by categories of interests. VocalTec's site tends to be lively compared to some of the newer Internet phone services that haven't had time yet to accrue a loyal base of customers. Besides selecting users that you want to converse with from these listings, you can also initiate Internet phone calls by the recipient's special Internet Phone address or e-mail address. The software also lets you create a personal directory that simplifies connecting with the people that you most often need to contact. This newest version also lets you connect to other users by entering their IP addresses, a feature that was not available in the previous release of the product.

The Chat Room facility included with Internet Phone and supported by VocalTec's servers is a major draw of this product for many people. You have the option of creating private chat rooms that you can use to communicate with friends, family, or business associates. Someone else can only get into the chat room if they know the exact (unlisted) name of it. If you're feeling more gregarious, you can create a new chat room that does appear in the chat room listings and then wait for equally amiable souls to enter into it for conversation. And, of course, you can also cruise from chat room to chat room seeking like-minded conversationalists to discuss any conceivable topics or simply engage in idle banter. Why not? You're only paying for a local phone connection. You can also establish a favorite chat rooms list to use whenever you want to revisit a chat room that you found enjoyable or stimulating.

Speaking of stimulating, be prepared to encounter legions of public chat rooms that revolve around the hormonal energies of their participants. While looking for the Philatelists Chat Room of Wisconsin, you'll no doubt blunder past steamy chat rooms with names like Androgynous Seniors Seeking Viscid Contact, Flaming Hot Women in Peru Want You!!!, and the always subtle !SEX!SEX!SEX!SEX!SEX!. We were afraid to venture into any of these chat rooms to see what people were actually talking about, but you'll quickly learn to steer a course around them if you're looking for shared topics on a more metaphysical plane.

When you open the Online Directory, as shown in Figure 10.5, the Internet Phone software scans through the lists of current public chat rooms and builds a directory. When you select a chat room to join, a list of the current participants in that chat room appears. You can right-click on the name of anyone on the list to display the information about that person (as they entered it when they configured Internet Phone). By highlighting the name of the person you want to talk with and clicking the **Call** button (or simply double-clicking the name), you can initiate a conversation. Click **Hang Up** to end the call.

Incoming calls can be signaled by one of several means. Internet Phone can be set to simulate the ringing of a telephone. Optionally, you can set up the program so that an Animated Assistant taps on the inside of your computer monitor and alerts

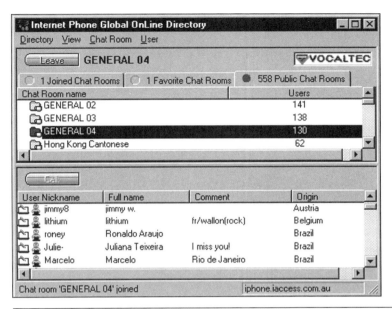

Figure 10.5 Online Directory display for Internet Phone.

you. You can also detect a call through a red blinking **Answer** button, a "ringing" status appearing in the message line, the caller's name and nickname popping up in the User Information field of the panel, or a ringing telephone symbol appearing in the session list.

You can add your own photograph to the Internet Phone control panel, shown in Figure 10.6, or simply use the more anonymous cartoon character, the ubiquitous Animated Assistant that plays a major role in the program, popping up in key situations to provide feedback and comments. To answer the Internet Phone, you click the **Answer** button or drop down the Phone menu and select the **Answer** option. At that point, you can start talking with the caller. As with other products of this type, you have a number of audio options that you can use to choose the level of voice quality—a factor that depends on the type of and degree of compression employed.

Internet Phone also allows you to send voice mail to other users—even those who are not Internet Phone users. The catch is that nonusers have to download a special player, available for free through the VocalTec Web site. Recorded messages can be up to one minute in length, recorded through a special panel that pops up for your use. Messages received by other Internet Phone users can just be opened as

Figure 10.6 Internet Phone control panel with sleeping assistant.

attachments and automatically played through the built-in voice mail player that is included with Internet Phone.

The ease of use and simple configuration for this product should make it appealing to a wide audience. The audio configuration panel, shown in Figure 10.7, appears automatically the first time you run the software and guides you through the process of setting levels and preparing the Internet Phone for use. Basically, you click the **Start Test** button and record a short audio segment. When you stop speaking, Internet Phone plays back your recorded voice at the equivalent level that someone else will hear it during a conversation. If you don't like the automatic settings, you can choose a manual setting, or—with some sound boards—activate an Automatic Gain Control (AGC) feature that will boost the volume if your voice drops below a certain threshold.

If you're running a high-performance computer, Internet Phone gives you the option of going in and selecting the CODEC to use for compressing your audio output. Because CODECs differ quite a bit in terms of quality and vocal characteristics, you may want to experiment with the different settings until you find one that suits your voice and preferences. Whatever CODEC you are using, Internet

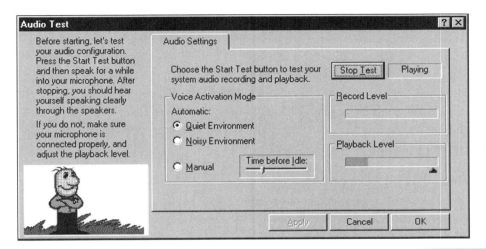

Figure 10.7 Audio configuration for Internet Phone.

Phone uses the same CODEC when it decompresses the audio data on the computer of the person that you called.

Hypertext links can be embedded into HTML documents to allow users (who also need to have Internet Phone installed on their systems) to call you by clicking on the link. If you have a fixed IP address, you can reference the link to this address. If you subscribe to VocalTec's Addressing Service, which maintains a directory of users by a variety of information, you can attach the link to your e-mail address or your assigned Internet Phone address. To add a link to your Internet Phone account, use the following statement:

```
<A HREF=iphone:your_name@address.com>You can talk to me through an Internet
Phone by clicking this link.</A><P>
```

Substitute your e-mail address for your_name@address.com, if you are registered with VocalTec's Addressing Service, or use your IP address, if it is a fixed address. Note that most IP addresses as assigned by Internet Service Providers are dynamic—that is, a new temporary IP address is assigned to you each time you log on to the service and that address lasts only the length of the session. This feature offers an interesting method for providing some live interaction with humans on the Web, although you are obviously limited to that subset of the universe equipped with the necessary Internet Phone. As the RTP standard becomes more prevalent, this type of feature should be widely available on the Web regardless of the type of Web phone in use.

A whiteboard comes with the product, allowing ideas to be discussed and described in graphic terms, even among a group of collaborating team members. For example, a sketch placed on the whiteboard by one workgroup member could be annotated by other members in real time. Changes made to the image on the whiteboard are circulated to all the other connected workgroup users, so that everyone sees the same basic display. The whiteboard can be easily popped up in the middle of a conversation by clicking an icon on the Internet Phone control panel (shown in Figure 10.6).

More details on VocalTec can be found in Appendix C.

Voxware TeleVox Voxware's TeleVox rates among the top audio quality of the current crop of Internet phones, which isn't too surprising since the company specializes in audio voice-compression technology. TeleVox installs in Windows95 or Windows NT systems. Versions for other platforms, including the Macintosh, are under development.

 TeleVox is available as a free evaluation version on Voxware's Web site at:

www.voxware.com

TeleVox is simpler than some of the other competing products, which can either be a boon or a disadvantage, depending on your outlook. It uses a wizard-like approach for setting up and configuring the product, and it will automatically link to its communication server at the end of the configuration process if your system is set up for the interconnection. The interface for this product is correspondingly simple, as shown in Figure 10.8.

Voxware uses a unique technology that they call MetaVoice to model the characteristics of the human voice. Rather than using the actual waveform of a speaker's voice, the MetaVoice software creates a mathematical representation of the words spoken, which can then be replicated as a waveform when reproduced at the destination. Using this technology, TeleVox offers you the option of selecting some non-human sounding entities in place of your own voice for talking with others. Voxware calls this option VoiceFonts. The MetaVoice technology is noteworthy for its extremely high compression levels—it typically can deliver very high-quality speech in approximately one-third the bandwidth of other competing CODECs. This degree of compression also enables TeleVox to work at much slower data transfer rates—as low as 2400bps for voice communication.

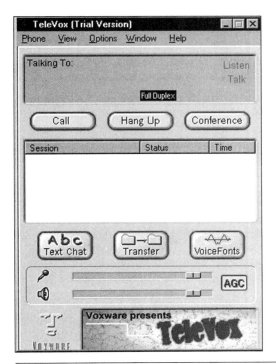

Figure 10.8 Interface for Voxware TeleVox.

The feature list of TeleVox isn't as extensive as some of the competing products, but it does include multiuser conferencing facilities, text-based chat, a caller ID feature, call blocking, full-duplex operation, and the ability to transfer files. Incoming calls can be picked up automatically. The most distinctive feature of TeleVox is the efficiency of its audio compression and the surprisingly clean vocal qualities reproduced by its mathematically modeled playback. If you enjoy presenting yourself as a star-tripping denizen of a world populated by silicon-based life forms, you'll probably also take full advantage of the VoiceFonts option.

Voxware also produces a plug-in called ToolVox that enables playback of speech over the Web. ToolVox is also based on the MetaVoice technology. Additional information about Voxware products can be found in Appendix C.

Netscape CoolTalk Netscape's CoolTalk offers Windows, Macintosh, and Unix users a simple way to converse, send voice messages, and collaborate in real time using a shared graphical workspace called the whiteboard. The whiteboard is a result of work completed by a small company called Insoft that was acquired by

Netscape in early 1996. The audioconferencing capabilities of CoolTalk are significantly more extensive than those available through other software, thanks to Apple's collaboration with Netscape to add the Apple QuickTime Conferencing (QTC) technology to the Macintosh client software. Audioconferences using CoolTalk can be simultaneously carried out by workgroup members on diverse platforms, including Macintosh, Windows, and Unix systems. The features available to developers through the Netscape ONE development platform allow real-time audio and videostreaming through distributed plug-ins. Both Apple and Netscape have been active participants in the evolving H.323 international standard that provides an interoperability framework for computers that need to share audio or video data across the Internet or over intranets. Since Netscape's initial release of CoolTalk, other conferencing utilities with whiteboard products have reached the market, but CoolTalk is still impressive in its implementation.

The whiteboard essentially gives you and the other parties that you are conferencing with a graphical work area that is accessible and viewable to everyone in real time. You can share any ideas that can be sketched onto the paint-style tablet, as shown in Figure 10.9, as fast as you can enter them and up to the limits of your graphic abilities. Design ideas that used to be born over plates of pasta in Silicon Valley restaurants, sketched on napkins, can now be formulated over the Internet by collaborators in five different countries. The graphics generated in this fashion can be saved to an image file, complete with all the annotations from the full range of collaborators.

CoolTalk can be run by itself, or you can access its features from within Netscape Navigator 3.0. Netscape also supports a directory site that makes it easy to identify other CoolTalk users, either from an alphabetical listing or other means. There are also a host of useful features built into the program, such as the ability to set up an answering machine that offers a greeting when other CoolTalk users try to contact you and can record their incoming messages for later access. You can screen incoming calls by viewing an information screen describing the caller before you actually answer the call.

Netscape includes CoolTalk as a part of Navigator 3 and beyond; earlier Navigator users can download a free version of CoolTalk from the Netscape Web site. Because the universe of Navigator users is larger than that for many of the other products discussed in this section of the book, your odds of contacting other CoolTalk users and initiating conversations will be much greater. You still have to convince someone that you want to converse with to install and set up CoolTalk for

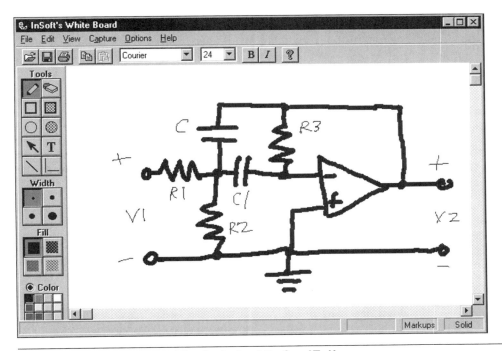

Figure 10.9 Whiteboard included with CoolTalk.

use, but because recent Navigator users already have the software, this should be much less work than if someone has to download an additional 4Mb program. The setup sequence for CoolTalk is described later in this chapter.

See Appendix C for more information about CoolTalk.

Encrypted Conversations Unless you're under surveillance by the FBI or speaking on a cellular phone, you have reasonable assurance when using a public telephone that no one is listening to your calls. Telephone calls placed over the Internet don't always have the same degree of protection; anyone who is able to hack his or her way into a stream of packets and intercept your audio communication could be privy to the details of a personal or proprietary phone conversation.

Encryption provides a means for protecting nascent Internet callers from the perils of malicious snooping. One such product is PGPFone—PGP stands for Pretty Good Privacy. This phone is based on work by Phil Zimmerman, who devised encryption standards for e-mail several years ago. He has recently incorporated his company under the title Pretty Good Privacy, Inc. in San Mateo,

California, with a suite of products intended to secure all forms of digital communication, including e-mail, fax transmissions, images, video, and telephony communications. Another interesting product offered by Pretty Good Privacy, Inc. is called PGPcookie.cutter, which is software that lets you selectively prevent the use of cookies by sites that you contact while you are browsing the Web. Cookies are used by some organizations to track data about where you've been and what you've done while navigating the Web—clearly a breach of privacy if you would prefer not to give out this information. PGPcookie.cutter intercedes by monitoring the HTML stream, noting where cookies are specified, and then implementing the level of blockage that you select.

 PGPFone is available in Macintosh and Window95 versions, as freeware from MIT's Web site at:

> **web.mit.edu/network/pgpfone**

You can also visit Pretty Good Privacy, Inc. at:

> **www.pgp.com**

PGPFone employs speech compression and solid cryptography protocols to provide telephony connections through modems, including connections made over the Internet. Designer Phil Zimmerman has been an active voice in campaigning for many computer-related personal privacy issues and is an outspoken advocate of publicly available encryption standards.

Another Internet phone product called Speak Freely offers both cryptographic and non-cryptographic versions. The non-cryptographic version is to assuage any parties that want to place versions of Speak Freely on their Internet site or public bulletin board that they won't be antagonizing any government agencies that discourage encrypted conversations. A Windows95 and Windows NT version is available, and this new Release 6.1 phone can communicate with earlier 16-bit Windows 3.X versions, as well as the Speak Freely for Unix version. As with many phones of this type, a communication server provides a means of locating and contacting other phone users through a phone book directory. You can also test the setup and operation of Speak Freely through remote echo servers that will return any words that you speak through the phone in a few seconds, a handy way to explore the effects of different levels of compression and different modes of operation.

Speak Freely takes advantage of an advanced compression algorithm called LPC-10, providing sound compression at factors up to 26 to 1 while still maintaining good fidelity. Sound packets can be transmitted with internal identification numbers so that the receiver can discard any packets that are out of sequence or that duplicate other packets. This option is a function of the robust transmission option available through LPC-10, and it is particularly useful in environments where traffic-laden networks make real-time communication difficult or impossible. Speak Freely can communicate flawlessly without pauses and breaks in the received sound packets even in difficult network situations.

 Speak Freely can be downloaded from:

www.fourmilab.ch/netfone/windows/speak_freely.html

This program was also designed using the Internet RTP protocol, so it can communicate with other products designed around the protocol. So far, acceptance of the RTP protocol has not been universal, but more and more companies seem to be gravitating toward its support, so interoperability should improve in future products of this type.

Voice Mail over the Web Mail attachments can consist of many different elements (the full range of MIME types), and one of the increasingly important file types in this category has become voice mail attachments. Internet telephony products that make it possible to exchange an encapsulated voice mail message that arrives in someone's Internet mailbox have reached the market and extended the range of human communication in one more way.

The limitations of printed e-mail have long been known—humor, levity, or sarcasm in a message sometimes does not come across as such to a reader, and this misinterpretation can cause embarrassment, anger, or wounded feelings. A whole vocabulary of special character-based symbols—the family of emoticons—has been developed to help get across some of the nuances of speech that don't transfer well in print. ;>) (wink, wink, nudge, nudge). But even emoticons cover only a narrow range of human expressiveness, far less than can be conveyed in a live audio message.

With products such as VocalTec's Internet Voice Mail, you can send voice mail messages (with or without text or other attachments) to anyone with an Internet e-mail account. The process is simple: you enter the recipient's e-mail address, you record the message, you send it. A voice mail player can be embedded with the message so that anyone who doesn't have VocalTec's Internet Voice Mail software installed on their system can hear the message. Versions are available for Windows95, Windows NT, Windows 3.X, Windows for Workgroups, Power Macintosh, and 68000-series Macintoshes. You're out of luck if your intended recipient is on a Unix machine; otherwise, you have a fairly large audience that you can confidently reach.

 If you want to try this product, you can download an evaluation version of the software from:

www.vocaltec.com

While you're on site, you might also want to retrieve VocalTec's popular Internet Phone Release 4, which can also be obtained in evaluation form. Internet Phone Release 4 has a feature that lets you leave voice mail for other Internet Phone users, one more option in a growing array of Internet communication possibilities.

The Voice of the Net

Certain sites on the Web seem to become energy magnets, where hot topics, political views, emerging trends, and industry news coalesce in a steaming jambalaya serving a common interest. Jeff Pulver's site is such a site, with a self-proclaimed interest in advancing the technologies of Internet telephony and extending the benefits of low-cost telephone communication through the Internet to people throughout the world. As vainglorious as this goal might seem, the perspective appears to be sincere, and the insights and industry news provided make it worth a serious visit and a permanent bookmark within your browser. Pulver is generally credited with coining the term VON (voice/video on the Net), which has percolated through the popular press and has now become the common term for referring to this area of Internet activity.

This site also provides links to numerous other audio-related sites, expanding far beyond the boundaries of telephony to include streaming audio, audio teleconferencing, and similar technologies. The site reverberates with political undertones—there is definitely a point of view and one that is frequently expressed very strongly. The content is authoritative, and Pulver seems comfortable in the role of telephone company gadfly, spotlighting the efforts by many telephone companies to shut down Internet telephony or to impose strict regulations on it through the FCC. If you want to know what the latest story is on the Internet telephony front, this is a worthwhile place to visit. Jeff Pulver is the author of *Internet Telephony*, also published by John Wiley & Sons.

 You can visit Jeff Pulver's site at:

www.pulver.com

Multi-Vendor Integration Protocol (MVIP)

Rapidly evolving fields, such as Internet telephony, need standards to drive the technological evolution and keep hardware and software developers moving in some kind of reasonably coordinated direction. The Multi-Vendor Integration Protocol, established in 1990, tries to do just that for companies involved in Internet telephony. Although to date many of the vendors in this field continue to embellish products in nonstandard ways and to sprout features and enhancements that violate established protocols, there appears to be strong movement toward adoption of a number of telephony standards. Because of the fierce independence of many software producers, the interoperability of various Web phones and conferencing utilities has been extremely low.

In a number of significant areas, however, MVIP has made it possible to build the hardware and software framework within which telephony technology can establish a foothold. Some of the areas where strong progress has been shown include the development of physical interfaces for switching and routing equipment, network protocols for telephony, standards for CODECs and digital signal processing, and similar kinds of *de facto* standards. *De facto* standards are significant in that they are generally developed and agreed upon voluntarily by a large number of manufacturers and organizations before being more formally submitted for approval by a standards organization, such as ANSI, ISO, or IEEE. *De facto* standards provide guidance and direction for manufacturers during formative stages of a new technology and allow the technology to progress prior to the standards being formalized.

Manufacturers realize that market survival depends on a large, established base of customers who look for products that are portable, flexible, and dependable under a wide variety of circumstances. This encourages a certain spirit of cooperation among competing vendors who realize that without standards, a developing market may be stillborn. MVIP serves as a neutral arbiter to help sort out the differences between manufacturers and also to bring together the diverse factions of the telephone and computer communities, two separate cultures that previously have had little interaction in their technological pursuits.

MVIP provides a solid means for melding PC technology with proprietary PBXs, opening up a tremendous range of potential computer telephony applications. The idea is to make it possible to directly connect any standard variety desktop computer to the public switched telephone network and then to be able to manipulate the telephone calls through software control. The scope of MVIP goes well beyond the basic concerns of Web phone developers seeking commonality of products for an expanded market, but many of the issues addressed by MVIP can lead to an improved environment for telephony applications on the computer.

Configuring CoolTalk for Use

Netscape's CoolTalk uses a wizard approach to simplify software configuration, during which it tests key components of your system, provides sampling of your voice through a microphone at different sampling rates (allowing you to hear the maximum quality that your system is capable of), and confirms that your system is set up and ready for two-way telephony. This wizard, shown in Figure 10.10, is automatically run when you first access CoolTalk, and you can later reconfigure any parts of the program.

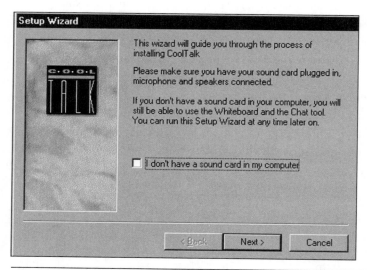

Figure 10.10 Starting the Setup Wizard.

If you're starting the Setup Wizard through Windows95 and using the **AutoDial** option for Web access, don't be disconcerted when the dialog box appears to connect to your Internet Service Provider. You don't need to be online to set up CoolTalk; just click the **Cancel** button to continue.

Once you click **Next** from the initial Setup Wizard screen, a dialog box appears that lets you configure CoolTalk for the maximum data transfer rate of the modem you have installed in your system, as shown in Figure 10.11. The highest rate, 28,800bps or LAN, applies to systems that either have a high-speed modem installed or have a direct connection to a local area network, which often provides the best performance for CoolTalk. Select the option that most closely corresponds with your system and then click **Next** to continue.

The next dialog box announces that the wizard is going to check your system for an installed sound board. This may generate a conflict or problem if you have another application active that uses the sound board, so you are advised to shut down any other applications before continuing. Once you click **Next** to initiate the test, the wizard takes a few seconds to examine your system and then displays a dialog box, shown in Figure 10.12, with its testing conclusions. If you have a board installed in your system that emulates another type of sound board, such as a board with SoundBlaster compatibility, the wizard may determine that you have two sound boards. This isn't a problem, though you may want to select the option for

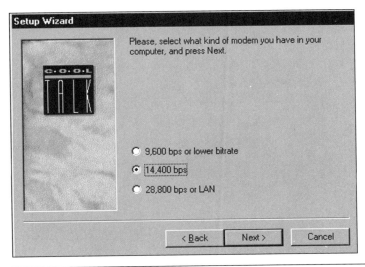

Figure 10.11 Selecting a modem data transfer rate.

Record and Playback, using the drop-down listboxes, that best suits the audio features that you want to access (for example, selecting the option that enables you to gain Full Duplex communication).

When you click the **Next** button again, if your sound board is active with the speakers turned on, the wizard vocally welcomes you to CoolTalk. At this point, you've won the major battle, and the rest of the setup should be effortless. If you don't hear the audio greeting, the wizard coaches you through rechecking your sound board installation and getting it re-established. Once you hear the audio greeting, you can click **Next** to move on to the sampling rate tests that let you decide the appropriate tradeoff between voice quality and performance. If you elect to listen to the sample by clicking **Next,** the dialog box shown in Figure 10.13 appears. If you don't want to waste your time with Lo-Fi sound, you can check the box to skip 8KHz testing.

Again, the wizard prompts you for your perceptions of the sound (or the absence of sound) and provides some coaching depending on your responses. You then get to hear the 5KHz sampling rate, if you so choose, but be forewarned: The poor woman's voice sounds as if she has been dropped into an aquarium filled with gelatin. In most cases, you will want to avoid using 5KHz playback unless you are running a very low-performance system and you have no other choice.

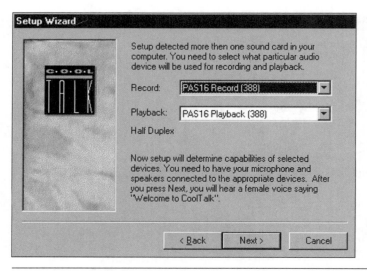

Figure 10.12 Confirming the installed sound board.

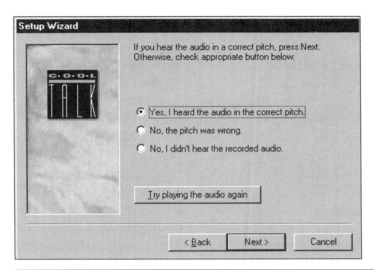

Figure 10.13 Sampling rate at 8KHz.

At this point, a couple more clicks of the **Next** button brings you to the portion of the setup that lets you test the recording quality of your system. Plug in a microphone to the audio input jack of your sound board and follow the test instructions. Extremely cheap microphones clearly won't give you any kind of an audio edge and may add some unflattering qualities to your voice, so if you have access to a professional or semiprofessional microphone, make use of it. You may need an adapter to go from a standard microphone's phone plug to the mini-jack input of your sound board, but these are easily obtainable through Radio Shack or a similar electronics outlet.

Once connected, click the **Next** button to begin recording and click **Next** again when done. CoolTalk plays back your recorded voice. This will be the approximate quality that listeners will hear when you are audioconferencing. Pay particular attention to the volume level of the sound. You can adjust the record level of your sound board, if necessary, or choose a different microphone, in some situations, to improve recording. Sometimes the impedance of a particular microphone will not be suitable for use with a given sound board. After playback, you can respond to the quality of voice on the screen.

If you're happy with the audio test results, CoolTalk launches a performance test of your system, marked by a progress bar, as it analyzes the CPU power of your system and provides a result as a percentage of the amount of power available (for example, if the screen tells you that you have 200 percent of the power required to run CoolTalk, you can rest easy).

Now you're into the portion of the setup where you get to fill in a series of forms. This information will become available through the directory server, if you choose to use Netscape's IS411 directory, so be prudent when listing any information that you might not want to be public. For example, if your business has an 800 number, and you don't want inquisitive CoolTalk users calling you up on your 800 line, you might not want to provide the listing. The fields in the business card are pretty much self-explanatory, as shown in Figure 10.14. If you have a scanned photo of yourself more recent than your high-school yearbook photo, you might want to include a photograph to accompany your business card. Click the button to the right of the Photo field to navigate to the directory holding the image that you want to use. This will be presented to someone who seeks information about you through the phone directory or when you make contact with another CoolTalk user. If you're not so wild about having your face posted around the Internet, you could use another image, such as your business logo, a cartoon caricature, or a Celtic symbol harkening back to your early ancestors.

Once you've got your business card set up, CoolTalk displays one final confirmation screen, congratulations to you on your successful configuration, and then launches the compact CoolTalk conference window, as shown in Figure 10.15.

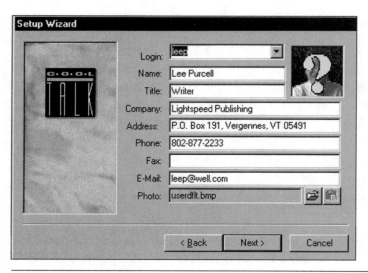

Figure 10.14 Filling out the business card.

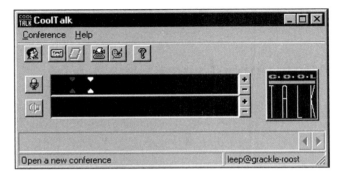

Figure 10.15 CoolTalk conference window.

From this window, you can initiate conversations with other CoolTalk users, launch the whiteboard to emphasize your words with graphics, or set up the answering machine to field incoming calls for those times you don't want to respond to the ringing CoolTalk phone.

At this point, you're ready to initiate calls to other users, which can be done using the domain addresses of users (user@domain.com) or an IP address in numeric format (such as 123.141.111.121). The other user must be online using CoolTalk (or have their CoolTalk Watchdog installed, which is software that monitors calls and pops up the application when someone tries to reach you). They must be accessible through a fixed IP address or a dynamic address that can be relayed through their ISP. Another somewhat easier option may be to access users through the CoolTalk IS411 directory operated by Netscape (or another IS411 directory), where you can scan listings of anyone registered with the service and click their name to initiate contact. Note that when you were installing the CoolTalk software, the program asked you if you wanted to register; if you select **Yes** to this option, your personal information will be transferred to the server directory the first time you access it. If you want to check this option, select the **Options** item from the Conference menu to bring up the Conference tab. The option—Make me available through server—determines whether your personal information will be posted when you access the directory server. If you don't want to be publicly listed, uncheck this box.

There is a whole social world springing up around the community of Internet phone users, something that you may or may not want to get involved in. CoolTalk makes sense for both business and personal users, and it's hard to discredit a technology that lets you easily make international phone calls for the price of your local

Internet connection. With the specter of the FCC regulating this form of communication a possible threat, enjoy the access while it is available.

Moving Audio Fast Enough to Hear

Many of the products and technologies in this book depend on real-time transfer of audio information at a rate that is fast enough to avoid breaks or drop-outs in the audio playback. If you're talking with someone on a Web phone and every third sentence drops out, it's going to be difficult to have any kind of reasonable conversation without everyone getting very irritated. When you're listening to a RealAudio broadcast on the Internet, your tolerance for drop-outs or pauses in a piece of music or news broadcast may wear thin if this irritating event happens too often. A $15 transistor radio doesn't have any trouble playing back audio in a fairly continuous sequence. Why is this so difficult to do over the Internet?

We've discussed some of the techniques that software producers use to ensure fast and continuous delivery of audio files over the Internet, such as buffering the arriving audio file and starting playback from the buffer, but we haven't really talked about why it's so difficult to achieve real-time audio playback on the Internet. The reason is thoroughly ingrained in the infrastructure of TCP/IP, the protocol that determines the transport techniques used to move data between cooperating computers. TCP/IP includes both a connection-oriented protocol (the TCP part), which enables processes on different computers to exchange information, and a connectionless protocol (the IP part), which specifies the services by which data is moved between computers. Fundamentally, TCP/IP moves data by means of packets.

Transmission Control Protocol/Internet Protocol (TCP/IP) uses a transfer model that takes individual chunks of data—whether a portion of an audio file, a text file, or e-mail message—and encapsulates this data into a series of packets. Hundreds of packets may be required to move a five-minute segment of compressed audio across the Internet. Each packet is marked with its destination and contents, but the routing is determined on-the-fly. The flexibility of TCP/IP allows individual packets to find their own route to the destination, moving from server to server in a series of hops determined by the availability of current network resources. Two packets may leave at the same time, move to the destination over different routes, and arrive out of sequence. TCP/IP just reassembles the order of the packets at the destination.

Internet routers clearly play an important role in this process by determining the best route to follow to a given destination. To some degree, routers carry a representative model of the topology of the Internet, through both their own internal routing tables and information that is exchanged with other routers. Even if a router doesn't know the exact location of a specified destination address, it knows the correct router (that will have this information) to send the packet to next. In this cooperative manner, routers can precisely locate and direct a packet to a specific computer host—one host among millions that exist on the Internet.

Following Packets on the Internet

If you're curious about the routing that a group of packets follows, if you're on a Unix machine you can use the **traceroute** command to follow their progress across the Internet. For example, if you were going to issue a request to access the Web site at www.headspace.com, you can enter the command as follows: traceroute www.headspace.com. The utility then presents a series of lines, each line showing a single node that the packet encountered during its travels toward the indicated site. Typically, at each one of the indicated nodes, a router made a decision as to which way to route the packet next. A given packet might traverse dozens or even hundreds of nodes to reach its final destination. For a visual depiction of Internet routing and network statistics, to gain a view of what traffic demands exist on the Internet at a single point in time, visit:

 www.ra.net

If obstacles are encountered over the network and the network traffic becomes too thick, TCP/IP may start throwing away packets to make more room. The protocol then issues a request for the originator to resend the dropped packet or packets. Ideally, if the rate of these requests reaches above a certain threshold, the transmitting station can decrease its transfer rate to avoid exceeding the available bandwidth. The self-adjusting feature is useful for moderating the available bandwidth of the Web at a given point in time, but packets containing real-time information (such as audio or video) are at a disadvantage under this scheme.

When packets are dropped in this manner, it takes a certain amount of time to issue the retry request and another delay as the transmitting station reissues the requested packet. If the contents of the packets are simply segments in a text file, these delays don't create any time-critical problems. If the contents of the packets are the first three sentences out of the mouth of an announcer multicasting the first play of the Super Bowl, the process doesn't work. The delays result in chopped or distorted speech. For this reason, software producers have worked to find ways around the inherent limitations of the basic TCP/IP transfer approach.

To avoid the inherent delays in the TCP/IP resend method, technologies that rely on streaming data transfers can use the User Datagram Protocol (UDP) on top of TCP/IP. This protocol eliminates the resend requests by sacrificing the reliability of the data transmission. Instead of being resent, many dropped packets are simply lost. There are a couple of approaches to dealing with lost packets to lessen their noticeability in a stream of information, particularly audio information. In some situations, error correction codes are used to attempt to replace bits that are missing within a portion of the data stream, but this approach does not work very well for data loss at the packet level—usually, the packet either is there or it isn't, and if it isn't, error correction schemes can't fill in the entire missing packet contents.

Another approach is called error mitigation, and this approach is more effective for the types of streaming data encountered on the Internet. Using error mitigation, software creates a substitute for the lost data—basically, some "filler" that lessens the intensity of the missing data. Error mitigation involving audio material frequently employs white noise (a random pattern of audio waves that audibly sounds like that hiss you hear when your television is tuned to a channel with no signal) as a replacement for blank data. Blanking the missing audio segment or holding the previous audio sample until the next piece of data usually results in audible artifacts, such as snaps and ticks, whereas white noise tends to blend in with the rest of the audio material. Obviously, error mitigation of this sort works only for very brief passages—large groups of dropped packets would result in objectionable blasts of noise.

Other protocols are under consideration to help alleviate the infrastructure issues that make it difficult to transfer real-time material on the Internet. The Real-Time Streaming Protocol (RTSP), backed by Netscape and Progressive Networks, provides higher-level control features that can still operate on top of the existing infrastructure. Another protocol that has been endorsed by the IETF is referred to as the Real-Time Transport Protocol (RTP). This approach offers synchronization between the transmitting station and the receiver and additional features for managing lost packets. Delays of real-time material between source and destination would be greatly reduced by the techniques offered under RTP. As audio content becomes more prominent on the Internet, it is vital that the Internet infrastructure be extended with the necessary protocols to better manage the flow of this data.

Collaborative Computing

As the tools improve and more companies realize the potential of linking work-group members around the globe inexpensively through Internet telephony, this technology's role in advancing collaborative computing is steadily advancing. The same tools that serve to link dial-up users communicating through modems at 28.8Kbps can be used on a company's internal network, usually at much higher speeds and with better results. Although audioconferencing features serve as the core of this technology, sometimes with the addition of a whiteboard for collaborative graphic exchanges, a number of products, such as Microsoft NetMeeting, are extending the metaphor further to include videoconferencing over the Internet and similar extensions.

The push is also on to expand the potential of audioconferencing using the Internet as the communication medium. The following subsections offer a couple of examples of products designed to support long-distance collaboration.

Microsoft NetMeeting

Microsoft's NetMeeting software, now in its version 2.0 release, includes audio-conferencing, as well as a number of extended features to support videoconferencing, data exchange via the familiar whiteboard model, and numerous other features to diminish the barriers encountered by geographically separated team members collaborating on projects. Microsoft has designed this product around a set of standards and offers NetMeeting as a platform around which other vendors can build complementary products that take advantage of real-time communication using Internet telephony.

Like Netscape's CoolTalk, Microsoft NetMeeting is based on the ITU H.323 standard, which provides interoperability guidelines for products that use streaming audio or video data. The video portion of NetMeeting was developed in conjunction with Intel. To increase the level of standards support in the product, Microsoft has also made NetMeeting compliant with the Internet Engineering Task Force Lightweight Directory Access Protocol (LDAP), which includes definitions for IP directory extensions. This support will enable NetMeeting to obtain current directory information from servers that are set up under LDAP. Microsoft's own Internet Locator Server fits this description.

Microsoft has also made available a resource kit designed to simplify the setup and use of NetMeeting. Network administrators, IS organizations, and third-party developers will receive details on how to set up and configure Net Meeting and how to design firewalls to increase security when the product is being used. If you don't want clever hackers listening in on your proprietary discussions of new Java-enabled computer engines, the firewall approach will undoubtedly be high on your list of priorities.

At the heart of the product is an Internet phone, including full support for audio-conferencing, but Microsoft is quick to point out the features of NetMeeting that separate it from other Internet phones on the market. The standards-based approach encourages interoperability. Users can locate other NetMeeting users either from directly within the program or from a Web page, making it possible to quickly locate and join appropriate conferences. Microsoft operates a User Location Server (ULS) to simplify the process of finding and identifying other users who are actively running NetMeeting. The product also supports Multipoint Data Conferencing, Microsoft's term for describing the ability to demonstrate a program running on a computer with others participating in a conference. Actions can be demonstrated—scrolling through an application, opening up menus, activating pro-gram features—while the audio conferencing allows a running commentary of the interactions on screen.

A shared clipboard incorporated in the tool provides an easy way for conference members to cut and paste items from a document between their respective loca-tions. NetMeeting also supports wholesale file transfer.. Files can be transferred to a single member or to everyone in a conference. The audioconferencing portion of the product can be supplemented with a text-based chat feature—offering a simple means of recording decisions or key points of discussion from an online conference.

NetMeeting can also be integrated into an HTML document by providing a link on a Web page. This provides an easy means to allow fellow NetMeeting users to contact each other. This approach could also be adapted to a customer support envi-ronment, where a company's Web page could allow callers to converse with support personnel by clicking a link and then using the NetMeeting phone to communicate in real time. For Internet Explorer users, NetMeeting also has ActiveX controls that facilitate creating or joining conferences from within a Web page.

 For more details about NetMeeting, contact Microsoft at:

www.microsoft.com

VocalTec Internet Conference

VocalTec's Internet Conference Professional software offers the ability to conduct an audioconference online, allowing conference members to discuss the contents of documents displayed within a browser or actual Web sites. For example, conference members can browse a series of Web sites, with each participant viewing the same screen, and actually mark up the image on screen to point out a particular feature of someone else's site or to highlight any item. This capability also extends to OLE documents, making collaboration within any OLE-compliant applications a simple matter for conference members. VocalTec is pitching the product as a real-time multimedia collaboration tool, and in many ways this is a description that is quite apt.

For example, imagine that you have a technical White Paper that you have developed discussing audio on the Internet and you want to discuss the paper with colleagues and get some feedback. Using Internet Conference, you make arrangements for your fellow collaborators to meet online at a specified time. Using the whiteboard, you display the Microsoft Word document containing your White Paper and place the program in Edit mode, allowing others to make changes to the contents of the original Word file. Sarah, the company's premier wordsmith in the Boca Raton office, performs some quick edits on your introductory paragraph—other team members can see the edits as they are made. Then Lou, the technical wizard of the team, currently on the road in San Jose, California, working from a portable computer, corrects a paragraph where you are describing data transfer protocols on the Internet. Finally, Elizabeth—the marketing manager—makes some changes to the copy despite the fact that she is at home in Boston, Massachusetts, recovering from a ski injury that sprained her ankle. The completed and fully edited Word document can be saved in its new form by each of the team members. Other applications that are compliant with OLE 2.0 can be edited online in this manner, including Microsoft PowerPoint and Excel.

If your trust in your colleague's editing abilities isn't quite as forthright, you can also place a document in the whiteboard space in Review mode, which allows anyone to view the contents, but only you can make the edits and changes. There is also a Presentation mode that enables you to display a series of pages from a document, each page pasted into the whiteboard workspace as a bitmapped image. A single-button **File Transfer** feature lets you immediately send any selected document to anyone currently logged into the active conference.

VocalTec has designed the product to interact with applications other than Microsoft's OLE-compliant tools. Using a macro development facility, you can integrate other products into this whiteboard presentation model and make them available for conference discussion as well.

Conference members meet through a server logon procedure. A conference room is established, and then members enter the established room. This is similar to the approach used in VocalTec's Internet Phone conferencing, except that the rooms are called Chat Rooms in Internet Phone parlance. Address books can be established that contain the names and contact information for specific workgroup members, perhaps the various committees that exist in your particular organization. Members can then be summoned as a group to join a conference. A moderator is assigned in each conference, whose role is to synchronize the various onscreen events, including directing attention to any particular area of the whiteboard. Because the whiteboard accommodates a possible size of 2000×1500 pixels, there is a lot of screen real estate to scroll through and a moderator may need to focus conference members' attention on a particular detail being displayed. VocalTec gives a number of examples of different groups using Internet Conference Professional, including doctors discussing x-rays, journalists collaborating on articles, teachers planning curriculum, engineers completing logic designs, and so on. Perhaps the age of the virtual office is finally at hand. Earlier attempts to accomplish similar virtual workgroup environments using video teleconferencing over public telephone lines achieved tepid acceptance, largely due to the expensive equipment and telephone line costs. The Internet offers a lower-cost alternative that also provides the additional advantages of being able to move the actual files being discussed from site to site at the click of a button.

As with VocalTec's other products, you can try Internet Conference, both the Personal and Professional editions, by downloading evaluation copies from their Web site. Online conferencing is a tool that has finally come of age, and its benefits are just beginning to be fully realized.

See Appendix C for more information on VocalTec.

Summary

As you can see, tools relying on Internet telephony have reached mainstream status, and many companies and individuals are realizing that geographic boundaries can be greatly reduced using Internet phones and audioconferencing facilities. For high-tech brainstorming, casual conversation, business negotiations, social contacts, and general communication, the Internet is offering a serious challenge to Ma Bell and all of her offspring.

11

Push Technology:
The Promise of
Things to Come

This chapter provides an overview of the directions that push technology is taking the Web, including those areas where audio is being integrated into the content distributed through various channels. A directory of the major products and players involved in the push technology marketplace is also provided in Appendix C. Savvy Web authors may want to take the knowledge acquired in the book and apply it to innovative uses of audio.

No matter how you manage to deliver audio over the Internet, you still have to attract users to your Web site and keep them coming back. You might build an outstanding site with RealAudio and the latest-and-greatest technology, but if users can't find it among the millions of sites clogging the Internet, you're not going to draw a large audience.

A new phenomena that is spreading through the Internet promises to be the solution to this problem. And that is what is loosely called "push technology." This refers to a mechanism where Web site content is delivered to users who subscribe to such services, rather than their having to go hunting for the content. Most of all, it allows Webmasters to track their subscribers and give demographic reports to advertisers.

The Origins of Push

Push technology made its first appearance in February 1996 with the arrival of PointCast. It has since spawned a major industry, with a wide variety of specialized companies and services. And this is only the beginning. According to a market research report from The Yankee Group, by the year 2000, 30 percent of Internet revenues, or $5.7 billion, will derive from push technology. That's up from $10 million made in 1996. The largest portion of that figure (some $3.3 billion) is expected to come from retail purchases, according to the Yankee Group report.

It has certainly generated a great deal of press attention. Some magazines have said push technology heralds the evolution of the Internet into a brand new type of medium. *The Wall Street Journal* said in a December 13, 1996 story: "Web broadcasting brings a fundamental shift that promises to spur the development of electronic commerce and reshape the balance of power in the technology and media industries." *Business Week* said that Webcasting will "save the Internet from collapsing under its own weight."

Wired magazine's March 1997 issue front cover read: "Push!: Kiss your browser good-bye" Inside the front section, the editors exclaimed: "The outlines of a new type of media are visible ... Push media's most revolutionary advance may be the creation of a whole universe of broadcast networks."

What the Fuss Is All About

What does push technology really mean, and how does it work?

Push refers to the delivery of content directly to the user, rather than the user needing to seek it out (or "pull") it off the Internet. It's also known as "Webcasting" because it is akin to a television or radio broadcast. Push technology companies even refer to their programs as "channels." But Webcasting stands out from traditional broadcasting because users can select and customize the content being delivered and choose when and how they'd like to receive it. The content also generally has links that lead the user back to the Web, and the selections can range from text, music broadcasts, Java applications, and even software updates. The content can be as personalized as desired, down to the user's specific tastes and interests.

Push technology differs fundamentally from "pull" technology because the client asks the server to send any new information automatically. And this new information can be downloaded to users (or "subscribers") even when they're offline. How the content is delivered on screen depends on the push vendor—some provide it as screen savers; others as wallpaper, news flashes, or headlines. The user can decide when and at what intervals he or she would like the new content delivered.

What this means is that it makes Net surfing more automatic—users specify what "channels" of content they're interested in—and special software delivers the material from the Internet to their computers at predesignated intervals.

Collecting Demographic Data

Push technology also provides advertisers with the quantifiable demographic data they demand about Web site traffic. Many push vendors can generate reports on the demographics and numbers of users or subscribers to each channel. Plus the ever-elusive "clickthrough" rates can actually be measured by Webmasters. Many products ask users to register for information, which gives the content provider the equivalent of a subscriber base—a set of users who will automatically receive and view its information. Hence, the Web development business model changes from a "build it and hope they come" with pull technology to "attract users, keep them, and attract new ones" with push technology.

Webmasters can also receive feedback on exactly how many people received, viewed, and interacted with its broadcast content. They are even given the opportunity to select any content delivery model they want, including advertising sponsorship, subscription fees, online/electronic commerce, and direct marketing. And many vendors allow companies to deliver not just Web site content, but any type of company information or file type.

Moreover, push services allow corporations like General Motors, US West, and Citibank to set up their own "channels," providing company information to employees over their intranets.

The Players

The push technology market is comprised of a broad spectrum of companies, from those that serve as "content broadcasters," to those that provide technology to content providers, allowing them to directly bring (or "broadcast") their content to the user. Content delivery methods are many-varied, including everything from screen savers, e-mail, to news flashes and links to related Web sites. And they span varying degrees of difficulty for Webmasters to use and maintain—from the turnkey solutions to the program-your-own variety. Push solutions are being used to deliver audio broadcasts and announcements, including music samples.

Let's take a look at some of the major players. We must say this market is changing so quickly that some companies might close while others will emerge by the time this book is published.

PointCast

PointCast was the first company to come out with a push delivery system in February 1996. Today, its product line is directed toward corporate users who need to get the latest stock information, news headlines, sports and weather reports, or who use PointCast on their intranet server. It now prides itself as being an "Internet broadcast network," serving 1.2 million users.

All PointCast channels are displayed in the same interface, just with text and graphics. They do not support audio delivery because the company believes audio is "too disruptive in an office environment." However, a company spokesperson claims they are looking into adding audio capabilities in the future.

Content providers include such heavy-weights in the publishing field as the *Los Angeles Times*, the *Chicago Tribune*, and *The Boston Globe*. The content runs as a screen saver or as a standalone application.

PointCast just recently came out with PointCast Connections, which allows anyone to broadcast their own channel. It's meant to be used by intranet users to keep up to date on company announcements. The Connections channel will run alongside other PointCast channels, as well as alongside internal company news broadcasts via a corporate intranet with PointCast I-Server. I-Server clients include large corporate intranets, special-interest groups, and even Microsoft.

Because it downloads complete files, users need to have a healthy amount of hard disk space available, as well as a fast modem. The company recommends T1 lines, but says 28.8 modems are adequate.

As shown in Figure 11.1, viewers can customize a scrolling stock ticker or access charts with six weeks of stock prices, volume data, and more provided by Standard and Poor's Comstock. Viewers can also access SEC filings from EDGAR Online or news from Newsbytes News Network, PR Newswire, and Business Wire for the companies that interest them.

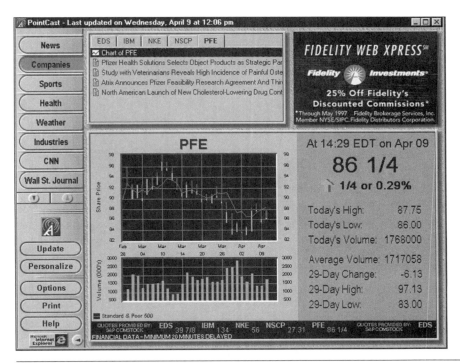

Figure 11.1 Financial information through PointCast.

Full-color, up-to-the-minute weather maps are available, as shown in Figure 11.2, that can be expanded to fit the screen display.

In keeping with the broadcast model, PointCast also serves up animated advertisements with its channels. The ads can never be turned off by the user.

BackWeb

Developed by the Israeli company BRM Technologies, with offices in San Jose, California, BackWeb provides both a server and customized content for a turnkey solution. The company licenses servers to companies and organizations so they can build their own broadcast channels. They do not develop or license content. Customers can use the server to broadcast any content, not just from a Web site, including multimedia files.

BackWeb also provides an authoring program, the BALI Editor—similar to Macromedia's Lingo program—which creates "Flashes." The developer can use BALI if desired, or let BackWeb handle the programming. These Flashes notify

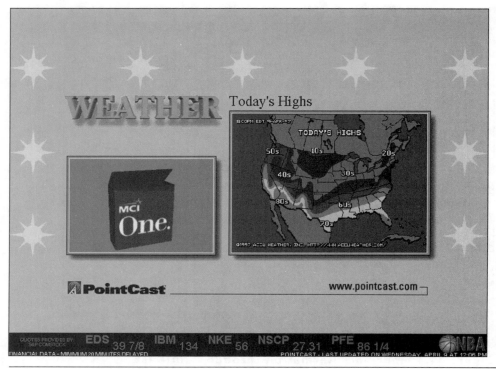

Figure 11.2 Weather map displayed in PointCast.

users of new messages that have been sent to their computer, which they can view if they'd like. If the user doesn't respond, the message will then disappear. The user can also access more information on a linked Web site if he or she so chooses. Flashes can also contain audio files, which the user can keep on or off.

The BackWeb content is downloaded from the server, when the keyboard is idle or whenever the user stalls on the Internet. The downloads are progressive, picking up where they left off each time.

What this means for audio transfer is that rather than making the user endure a long download time, large files are sent incrementally to the user's computer via the selected channel whenever the user is offline. Once the entire file is downloaded, the user is notified.

The BackWeb server's "polite downloading technology" breaks large files down into small packets and sends them when the user's browser connection is not actively in use. When the user clicks on a link, the transmission is interrupted until the line is released, and the transmission of packets then continues from where it last left off.

Because of this download technique, Jesse Albert, operating manager of the Web development agency Media Revolution in Santa Monica, California, says he plans on using BackWeb to send audio files over the Internet, without regard to file size. "To Media Revolution, the ability to send large files in a nonintrusive manner and in such a way where there is no degradation to the user's bandwidth is a huge value, especially in the entertainment community, which most of our clients are. This is a perfect solution for sending large clips and trailers." Albert says he also appreciates the fact that his clients retain ownership of their channels' branding and look, and that no advertising is required, unless it is their own.

Push technology like BackWeb allows Media Revolution to "truly target the end user and deliver much richer files and content in a more controlled environment," Albert adds. "We like the proactive nature of the relationship, rather than waiting for the user to visit our sites. And we like the ability to entice and reward our visitors."

On the client side, the BackWeb server keeps track of user download and interaction data and gives a report to channel managers. The server can track how may users received the information (which BackWeb calls an "InfoPak"), how many times the InfoPak's notification played on the user's screen, how many times the user interacted with the content in any way, and advertising click-through rates when users click from a Flash to a sponsor's Web site.

BackWeb server clients can also specify how the content should be delivered, including which platforms, which screen resolution, which plug-ins would be required for the content (including RealAudio), and whether to deliver to clients without audio capability.

BackWeb allows any company to build their own channel. The developer can send any type of file through the Internet to BackWeb. BackWeb then turns the files into a screen saver or wallpaper, which are activated whenever there is a lull in the user's Internet connection. Companies can also send "InfoFlashes" or announcements (including audio). Volvo, for instance, uses an audio flash to post announcements.

BackWeb user Michele Andolina, Information Services Manager with NetMediaUSA, uses BackWeb to advertise his company's CDs. He delivers wave files to BackWeb, which then takes care of posting the files on their server.

Andolina says the real challenge lies in reducing the file size and not losing audio quality. (See the sidebar for tips on how to prepare audio files.)

Internet marketing consultant Peggy Miles uses BackWeb for her American Singles Web site. BackWeb helps her to deliver selective matchmaking, she says, and gives the user instant gratification of information. It also helps make the user's screening process simpler, she says. BackWeb is far more appealing than e-mail notices because of the graphic presentation they're able to use, Miles adds.

Audio Delivery and BackWeb: Q&A with Rob Otto, Director of Channel Sales at BackWeb

Q: How does BackWeb provide high performance and high quality for audio delivery?

A: Because BackWeb downloads transparently in the background, you do not have any file size limitations. Therefore, BackWeb can send the audio clips in whatever file format the end user wants. In addition, you can segment the delivery so that those users with low bandwidth can get a reduced file size, while those on a T1 line can get the highest audio "resolution" available.

Q: How does one prepare audio files for delivery via BackWeb?

A: No special preparation is necessary. You just tell BackWeb where the files are located and post them to the server. BackWeb does the rest.

Q: Can the user listen to audio channels from BackWeb without being on the Internet?

A: That is the true power of BackWeb. We download files transparently to the users' hard drives using idle time on their Internet connection. Once the file has been downloaded, BackWeb lets them know with a Flash. After that, they can play back the files any time—whether they are online or off.

Q: What types of audio files are supported by BackWeb?

A: Because we are just a delivery and notification mechanism, we can deliver any type of audio files you choose.

> Q: How does the playback quality of BackWeb compare to streaming audio (such as RealAudio)?
>
> A: Because we download the files before playing back, the quality can be as high as CD-ROM or better! The quality of playback is limited only by the system that is playing the file.

Marimba

Marimba was founded by former Java programmers at Sun Microsystems in May 1996. Four months later, they released Castanet, a Java-based program to build and deliver push channels. Although channels are automatically distributed and installed like applets, they appear to users more like applications. Channel user interfaces are not constrained by Web page or browser limitations, and they can deliver multimedia files.

Marimba provides its technology to channel developers. In the Marimba model, channels are delivered by "transmitters" to "tuners" residing in your system. You use the Tuner to tune in whatever channels you desire. Anyone can run a Transmitter. In other words, it works something like cable television.

Using Castanet's Tuner interface, you subscribe to channels provided by the Castanet Transmitter, which sends applications and updates to your system. The channels are saved on your hard drive and can be viewed at any time, even when you're not connected. When you are connected, the channels automatically begin updating by contacting the Transmitter, so you're always using the newest version of the software and reading the latest content. Castanet downloads only new files to the computer. And each channel can have its own look and feel rather than fitting into a preexisting template. Channels are downloaded through Marimba's Web site, or through the Castanet transmitter.

Castanet has the ability to tune in everything from business applications to games. The advantage to publishers is the flexibility and customization; the downside is the Java programming work involved. The Marimba tuner license can be scaled to reach 100 customers or can be obtained for an unlimited amount of users.

A Castanet channel can consist of anything that can be created in Java. Channels enabled by Castanet include multimedia entertainment, customer service, and productivity applications. Content providers who use Castanet include the Children's Television Workshop, Sony Picture's Columbia TriStar Interactive division, which features Shockwave games, CNN Investment Channel, HotWired, ZDNet, and

Yahoo!. Several large corporations also use it for distributing information and software to customers, agents, and employees.

Marimba is not currently developing elaborate delivery solutions for audio; however, this may change within the next year, according to a company spokesperson. For the time being, Castanet can be used to deliver brief radio broadcasts and audio clips.

Castanet's main advantage to content providers is the creative control they get in developing their own channels with Marimba's technology. Webmasters can also update their channels automatically.

Intermind

Seattle, Washington-based Intermind calls itself a "communications company," with a mission to allow "every individual or organization to create and control their own personal channels of information exchange." The company wants to help anyone distribute content, whether they have a Web site or not. Along those lines, they offer a simple solution for the masses that doesn't require programming or major expense. The company also serves as a service bureau, since it helps small businesses and individuals that don't own their own servers or have the resources to build new content delivery systems. With simple page code, a site can be converted into channels.

Intermind Communicator, released in October 1996, allows anyone to publish and subscribe to an unlimited number of customizable Web channels. Communicator works through the user's Web browser. It does not download files directly to the user's computer, and Communicator will work only with Web sites that have signed up as partners.

Intermind has partnered with Times Mirror Magazines to deliver customized news, features, and other information over the Web through the Communicator program. Other companies that use Intermind for channel delivery are HotWired, Discovery Channel Online, Virtual Vineyards, CBS News, and PBS Online. The software is free to individuals, students, and noncommercial sites. Internet Publisher charges no fees to companies with fewer than 500 subscribers. A server fee of several thousand dollars applies to uses with more than 500 subscribers.

No additional server software is required. Anyone with access to a Web server can offer updates to subscribers, ranging from small text files to rich multimedia content, including RealAudio or Shockwave files. Subscribers can subscribe or unsubscribe at any time within their browser and remain completely anonymous if they choose.

Publishers can also get this type of feedback about subscribers: number of total subscribers to each channel published; reports on channel activity (number of subscribers per channel and per topic); reports on clickthroughs within channels; which channels and topics they read or deleted; direct text feedback from subscribers on a specific channel. All feedback and reports are anonymous, as they track group subscriber activity, not individual activity.

Intermind claims to offer the best of both worlds, allowing publishers to create their own channels and be able to "broadcast" from their own site, while the Intermind software installed on users' computers collects stats that are periodically forwarded to the Intermind Web site.

When the user is online, a little box will pop up in the right-hand corner of the computer screen, like an icon, alerting the user to new content. If the user clicks on it, the Internet browser will appear, which will then link the user to Intermind's Web site where it will have a list of new items among the subscribed channels to choose from. Because everything is displayed on the Intermind Web site it eases the bandwidth load. Intermind users range from home users to large corporations. Intermind plans to branch into the intranet arena.

Setting up a channel does not require programming or scripting. Using Intermind's "Publishing Wizard" form, you type in the channel topic, a brief description of the channel, your Web site's URL, the polling frequency (i.e., monthly or bimonthly newsletter), and that's the extent of the setup process. Figure 11.3 shows the channel directory screen in Intermind.

RealAudio and Shockwave files can also be delivered because they run off the Intermind Web site. Intermind claims to deliver "light channels" to reduce bandwidth constraints.

The user has to have an Internet connection to pull the subscribed content, but the browser doesn't have to be online. Communicator will pull in the background; a dialog box or icon will indicate updates, which can be viewed in the browser. Nothing is pre-downloaded.

Addicted to Noise uses Intermind to promote new album reviews. It sends out small sound clips in their channel updates. When the subscriber is updating the channel, a headline alerts them to the latest album review and points to the user to the RealAudio sample.

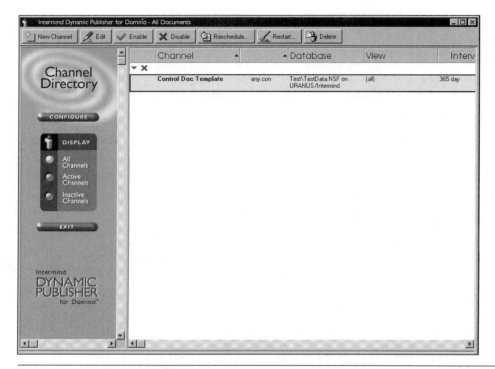

Figure 11.3 Channel directory in Intermind.

Figure 11.4 shows a typical screen from the Personal Edition page generated by Intermind.

Other Players

The push marketplace is quickly filling up with other players who provide specialized push delivery services. Just like their predecessors, they range from the low-end variety for home users to sophisticated systems for corporate intranets.

For instance, Astound's WebCast lets users port existing HTML pages into a channel format and automatically send their new pages to a server for channel creation. Diffusion, Inc. offers a service called IntraExpress that helps information distributors select the people with whom they'd like to communicate. It also lets users decide what kind of information they want and how and when they'd like to receive it—whether by e-mail message, fax, or pager message. Wayfarer Communications' Incisa client/server software is an "intranet Webcasting solution"

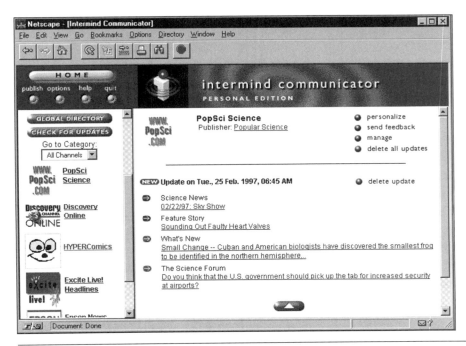

Figure 11.4 Intermind Personal Edition page.

that delivers headlines of company information to employees, and the information is personalized to each individual, such as 401(K) plan information.

Downtown from inCommon is an open-platform software product that allows publishers to create their own channels. It learns a user's browsing patterns and "looks ahead" to the next page or object the user would like, then brings it to the user.

InContext Corporation's InContext FlashSite product allows for offline browsing of the Web, with flexible scheduling options and the ability to run multiple downloads simultaneously.

Caravelle's Transceive uses a "smart-pull" technique to deliver relevant content to desktops from any Web site available on the Internet or an intranet. No server software or subscriptions are required.

Cyber Vista's Data Grabber Maximizer System allows a user to extract information from any type of digital file, including HTML, audio, and video files, and deliver it to a predesignated location. The recipient can then specify where he or she would like that information delivered, including a Web page, fax, spreadsheet, or other application.

Individual Inc.'s Freeloader automatically pushes Web site content during the middle of the night to subscribers, which can be viewed offline. It's a cross between an offline browser, which gathers news on the Web during off-peak hours and stores it on the hard drive as HTML documents, and a push information delivery service. HeadLiner from Lanacom displays news headlines in four ways: as a screen saver, in ticker-tape fashion, on a Web browser, or in a "NewsTitle viewer," which is displayed in the title bar of any active application. First Floor Inc. provides both "Smart Bookmarks" for cataloging and monitoring Web sites, as well as a "Smart Delivery" client/server suite of tools that helps MIS administrators organize and distribute documents, Web pages, data, and catalog information via intranet servers. As a matter of fact, AOL's Driveway product uses FirstFloor's change notification and offline viewing technology, enabling AOL members to automatically retrieve customized and updated content from AOL and the Web, to view at any time. Members will be able to automatically subscribe to their favorite content areas and Web sites and be notified of new content in these sites.

The CDF Standard: Push for Everyone

While these and other companies are offering their own varieties of push services, Microsoft has spearheaded the availability of "push for everyone."

Microsoft legitimized push technology by developing the channel definition format (CDF) standard. At the Internet World show in March 1997, Microsoft announced this standard for push technology to the World Wide Web Consortium (W3C). CDF is an open format for the publishing of Web-standard channels that will allow Web publishers to optimize the broadcast of their content to Internet users. CDF is based on technology developed by PointCast. PointCast plans to license the software needed to create content channels free of charge to any content publishers on the Web.

Microsoft's new Internet Explorer 4.0 will turn any Web site into a Web "broadcaster," with the use of CDF. At the same time, Microsoft announced that its next version of Internet Explorer browser, version 4.0, would automatically enable any Web developer to be a Web broadcaster by supporting CDF.

The CDF format has the benefit of being able to support any existing HTML content. In other words, any of the techniques described in this book for incorporating audio into HTML documents can be used within the push framework. This provides a high degree of flexibility for Webmasters who want to take advantage of both the most advanced audio capabilities now available on the Web as well as to utilize push technology for channeling information and sound content to subscribers.

Microsoft also entered into strategic relationships with three Internet broadcast technology developers—AirMedia, BackWeb, and FirstFloor Software—to integrate their technology with Internet Explorer 4.0.

CDF offers developers these features:

- **Open format**: Any company can author content to take advantage of CDF, any server can run Web sites that are enhanced by CDF, and any broadcast-enabled client software can access channels available on Web sites using CDF.

- **Low cost**: The CDF specification will save content development costs by allowing Web content developers easy access to a market of millions of compatible clients, using readily available software.

- **Use of compelling Internet technologies**: CDF enables sites to publish channels utilizing either HTML or specialized broadcast technologies.

The channel definition format will eliminate the need for multiple browsers and plug-ins that have been necessary to receive "broadcasts" from push delivery vendors. CDF creates a single format so that any channel can be viewed, rather than needing specialized viewers to receive channels from different vendors. With CDF, a Webmaster can define the look, feel, and content of his or her push channels. And with a CDF-enabled browser, such as Internet Explorer 4.0, the user can seamlessly establish a subscription channel.

In other words, CDF will allow a user to receive content from any push provider, no matter what service it came from. Without this kind of standard, someone using PointCast can't receive content sent using BackWeb's language, and vice versa.

Industry analyst Vin Crosbie says, "It's like the pre-Web days. Everyone who had content had to cut a deal with the proprietary online services, such as AOL, CompuServe, and Prodigy, and the consumer had to have a subscription to all these different services to read the publications they wanted. We're in the same kind of situation right now with 'push,' where it is primarily available only through services like BackWeb, PointCast, and Intermind, and that doesn't make sense. The CDF format will open it up to everyone because you won't need proprietary clients anymore." Crosbie believes the CDF standard could eventually supplant HTML.

Many of the major push vendors have given their support of the CDF specification, as well as Internet publishers, including America Online, CompuServe, Geocities, Hearst New Media, HotWired, Infoseek, Excite, and Ziff-Davis. America Online announced that its new Driveway product will support CDF, enabling any Web publisher to broadcast content to AOL's 8 million members.

The CDF standard addresses text, animated ad banners, and primitive video ads. In other words, everything you can find on PointCast. Nothing fancy. No razzle-dazzle multimedia presentations.

Meanwhile, Microsoft's rival Netscape Communications Corp. has announced plans to submit its own standard for Internet broadcasting to the World Wide Web Consortium (W3C) that will rival Microsoft's CDF standard. In the meantime, Netscape is embedding push functionality into its new Constellation browser that will be very similar to CDF, only more Java-based. It is tentatively named Channel Profile File Object (CPFO). Based on HTML, Java, and HTTP, it will allow users to easily develop push information channels. Rather than having to choose between these two standards, push vendors may adopt both to reach both Netscape and Microsoft audiences.

Netscape recently signed a deal with Marimba to bundle the Castanet tuner with Constellation. (Ironically enough, Marimba is also writing an ActiveX version of the Castanet tuner for use with Internet Explorer 4.0.) Netscape also plans to include PointCast as well as elemedia's Media Plus technology in future browser releases. Media Plus components will enable Netscape customers to receive a higher quality of voice, music, and video over the Internet.

The battle between the browser giants should foster only more push technology improvements.

Audio and Push Technology

Outside of brief audio clips and links to audio files on Web sites, push is not currently being heavily used to deliver audio on the Internet. This is largely due to bandwidth constraints. Most of the audio is being delivered by on-demand, where users are linked to the Web site, or by simulcasting.

Before audio becomes more suitable for push delivery, the bandwidth hurdle needs to be overcome. Large audio files, especially music selections, are bandwidth hogs and take far too long to download in the existing infrastructure, even with T1, T3, and ISDN lines. Improving compression techniques—including MPEG and Dolby Digital AC3—should continue to lessen the bandwidth problems, but for the near future, audio will remain a luxury for many of those subscribing to push channels.

The content that is being delivered by push systems appears to be putting a strain on corporate networks. A study conducted last year by market research firm Optimal Networks revealed that almost a fifth of corporate network traffic stems from push delivery methods. And yet push technology is used only by 12 percent of users, the study reported. The data traffic from 4000 users at six Fortune 500 companies was studied during four months in 1996. The PointCast Network topped the list of largest number of bytes sent, generating 17 percent of all traffic for 12 percent of users. By contrast, Netscape's home page was accessed by 70 percent of users, and yet accounted for just 12 percent of all network traffic. PointCast maintains that their new I-Server should help reduce bandwidth strain.

Within the next five years, industry observers expect the bandwidth problem to be solved. The race is currently on between telephone, cable, and even electric companies to provide cable wiring in homes and businesses. Some cities, such as Boston, are already set up with Internet-ready cable. The general consensus in the industry is that the bandwidth issues will be worked out within the next few years.

Satellite delivery systems are quickly becoming a reality. At the last Milia conference in France, a Zurich-based company called Fantastic Corp. announced its use of satellites and cable television to broadcast data to computers. According to the company president, this method can deliver data 1400 times faster than a standard modem, or 1000 times faster than the only operating satellite delivery system, DirectPV, which sends data 14 times faster than a 28.8 modem. Low earth-orbiting satellites can also send data once customers install antennas on their computers.

A new technology invented by TIBCO of Palo Alto, California, allows subscribers to fetch information at the middleware level without putting demands on the server, thus saving time and bandwidth. Other companies are also working on solutions that use new streaming protocols to deliver content more efficiently.

Besides the bandwidth obstacle, push is not practical for a majority of home users because most computers in the United States only have 8 megabytes of RAM or less, according to the market research firm Computer Intelligence. Multimedia-rich content, including audio files, is too much for these home computers to handle.

How to Prepare Audio Files for Push Delivery

Steve Liminoff, audio engineer at Music Annex in San Francisco, explains how he prepares audio (voice and music) files for push delivery (or what he calls the "conversion process"):

1. Get the cleanest audio possible. If it's a voice-over, make sure you record it in a room with low frequency, low-noise floor, a really clean environment with a clean microphone—the mike has a lot to do with how good it will sound way down the road. Most push is delivered at 8-bit because the technology does not allow for full bandwidth audio.

2. Record to DAT tape format or into a digital workstation at 44.1KHz. Most people work off of multiples of 44KHz for a sampling frequency. Then cut to desired length. A recipe for quality is to record the signal as loud as possible, up to digital full scale, without distorting.

3. To even out the peaks and valleys, I use the ProTools' Ultra Maximizer—it looks at the highest and lowest peaks and makes sure they don't go over zero, and pulls the audio up to the peak levels, whether semicompressed and expanded or limited. The volume frequency is increased so when the audio is coming in through a shielded speaker, it comes in at the same volume so you can hear it clearly.

4. Then we find out from the client what word length he or she wants—8-bit or 16-bit 44.1KHz, 22.050, or 11.025—to truncate the sampling frequency. All audio on the Internet, except RealAudio files, should be at 11.025 or 22.050 because of the loading time. It is possible to deliver a 16-bit file at 44.1KHz through RealAudio, depending on the modem speed (28.8 or faster).

5. After you've downsampled and cut the files and saved them as 8-bit or 16-bit, then put them on a storage device like a Syquest or a Zip drive and hand them over to the programmer.

"It's unfortunate that the technology has come about so fast that it's unable to keep up the demands of quality that we've placed on it," says Liminoff. "As music engineers we demand the highest quality possible. But anything associated with the Internet and with push is a compromise, period."

Future Outlook

While push technology is currently being used to provide brief music broadcasts and audio announcements, it is only a matter of time until technological obstacles will be surmounted and channels will deploy longer streams of audio.

For the time being, you may think of push technology as a way to draw attention to the Web sites you've created with all the whiz-bang audio technology described in this book.

HTML 3.2 Primer

The lingua franca of Web browsers is still HTML and the latest version to gain official sanction is HTML version 3.2. While HTML is not the only way to place content on the Web, some HTML is required even if you intend to use other means for placing most of your content. For example, a new crop of Java applet construction tools, including Coda by RandomNoise, makes it possible to build an entire Web site in the form of a Java applet, effectively bypassing the vagaries of various browser interpretations of nonstandard HTML tags. The Java applet containing the Web page content, however, still must be embedded in a rudimentary HTML document.

Another technique that allows you to escape the differences of Microsoft and Netscape browser interpretation is portable document format files (.pdf), such as Adobe Acrobat. Both Microsoft Internet Explorer v3.0 plus and Netscape Navigator 3.0 plus provide native support for Acrobat files. This enables a Web author to enclose content in a .pdf file, including virtually any content that can be created in a word processor or document publication tool, and reference the Acrobat files from within an HTML document, or dynamically reference the files using JavaScript. Portable document files can include links to other HTML documents or livelier content (including audio), such as QuickTime movies. A similar tool that uses the term "digital paper" rather than "portable document format" is Common Ground, a product of Hummingbird Communications. Common Ground, however, does not have native support in the Internet Explorer and Navigator browsers—a plug-in must be downloaded for viewing these files from the Web. Both of these techniques support the display of pages by means of a form of streaming, similar to streaming audio files, where an accessed page can be displayed without having to download the entire file containing the page.

With the browser wars continuing to stir controversies and many nonstandard tags and implementations running loose over the Web, the World Wide Web Consortium (W3C) has managed to achieve a measure of stability with the passage of the HTML 3.2 standard. HTML 3.2 doesn't contain any radically new features, but rather standardizes a host of popular features that have been in use for some time on the Web without any form of official sanction or approval by a standards organization. Industry infighting sabotaged the release of HTML v3.0, so the approval of version 3.2—supported by all of the major industry players—provides a solid development bedrock for HTML authoring. This appendix summarizes the features that are available through HTML v3.2, particularly for those of our readers who are coming to this book from more of a musician background—in other words, people who have done little or no Web authoring. Obviously, there are entire books written about HTML, so an appendix can provide only a brief overview and the mention of a few other references that might prove helpful. If you like the Sourcebook approach, we recommend the *HTML Sourcebook* by Ian S. Graham (also published by John Wiley & Sons). HTML is a big topic and deserves some room for proper discussion. This primer, at least, should put you on the right track.

Quick Vocabulary Lesson

If you're not familiar with the HyperText Markup Language, the first barrier to understanding is the terminology associated with HTML. This section provides a quick introduction to the vocabulary surrounding HTML; these are terms that will be frequently encountered throughout this appendix. If you have a clear understanding of each of these terms, the rest of this primer will be much easier to follow. As is typical of computer terminology, many of the terms are shortened to acronyms (for example, Document Type Definition is usually seen as DTD). If you already have some familiarity with HTML, you might want to skip over this section.

Anchor: Used in two ways, an anchor is both a reference to a hypertext link that is contained in an HTML document and a fixed location within a document. An anchor entry within a document can specify a link that is a destination to be jumped to by clicking on a graphic or highlighted text area—this is done through a HREF tag (Hypertext Reference). When used in this manner, an anchor is usually called a *link*. An anchor can also indicate the start of a fixed location in a document that can be linked to. In this usage, it is usually called an *anchor*.

ASCII (American Standard Code for Information Interchange): ASCII is a defined set of 128 characters represented in the form of 7-bit character codes. This is the basic character set used to present text within an HTML document. The ASCII character set also includes a number of nonprintable control characters used for communication.

Browser: A browser is a software application designed to view HTML documents and navigate links on the World Wide Web.

DTD (Document Type Definition): Any of a number of formal specifications that define markup languages within the larger framework of SGML. HTML is one kind of DTD.

Element: An element is an object or item in an HTML document. Most elements are identified by tags that indicate the start and stop points of an element (such as <BODY>Text goes here. </BODY>). The term *container* is often applied to elements that have contents. Other elements can be empty.

FTP (File Transfer Protocol): FTP is a protocol for exchanging files between computers connected via the Internet. A computer set up to act as a server for FTP transfers is called an FTP site. Any computer running the necessary client software can connect to the FTP site and access file upload and download areas (subject to those permissions and passwords determined by the individual FTP site). If you are creating HTML documents that you want to make available through an Internet Service Provider (ISP), typically you will use FTP to upload these files to the directories provided to you by the ISP so that they can be made publicly available through the Internet.

Home page: A home page is the initial page, composed as an HTML document, that serves as an entrance to a World Wide Web site. Both individuals and organizations use the home page as entry point to the full site contents.

HTML (Hypertext Markup Language): A set of conventions for constructing and presenting platform-independent information on the World Wide Web. HTML documents consist of a combination of text entries and special-purpose tags that control page elements. HTML is a Document Type Definition of SGML.

ISP (Internet Service Provider): An organization that offers Internet access and sometimes server space to customers. If you don't maintain your own Internet server, you can often provide a home page through an ISP by posting your HTML files to a directory area offered by the ISP for your use. If you create HTML documents that contain elements that must be processed by a server (such as server-side image maps or forms that require server-side processing), you must either have your own server or make arrangements with your ISP to provide the equivalent functionality on their server for you.

SGML (Standard Generalized Markup Language): A high-level standard that defines and describes a framework for markup languages. SGML includes HTML (which is one of the simpler markup languages). Some of the more complex applications of SGML are employed by the government and large-scale corporations to distribute platform-independent documents on a variety of media.

Features of HTML 3.2

As previously mentioned, many of the features of HTML v3.2 have been in wide use already on the Web without official sanction. Other features that are also already in wide use on the Web, such as Netscape's implementation of multiple frames in an HTML document, did not make it into the standard, although most observers think that frames will be included in the very next update. Perhaps the most important single addition to the structure of HTML that was included in version 3.2 was the definition of cascading style sheets. Style sheets provide a means for different aspects of page formatting—such as font sizes and colors, margins, graphic positioning, and so on—to be defined by an external style sheet file. These same elements can also be controlled by means of JavaScript, so that an onscreen button can be used to change the page display in a number of ways or the display can be altered by reference to an external JavaScript linked from within an HTML document. Style sheets allow Web authors to achieve control of the elements presented in a typical HTML document with far more precision and flexibility than has been available previously (some might argue that there was no precision or flexibility previously).

HTML 3.2 maintains full backwards compatibility with HTML 2.0, which is fortunate considering the hundreds of thousands of HTML documents already posted around the Web designed to this earlier standard. The new 3.2 standard addresses such items as text flow around images, applet embedding, multimedia embedding, tables, and style sheets. A brief summary of the new features follows:

- Support for client-side image maps. Image maps are areas in an HTML document that show one or more graphics that contain links to other locations. While HTML 2.0 supports image maps, they have to be processed on the server side, which often is not possible if your Web page space is provided by an Internet Service Provider. Client-side image maps can be embedded in an HTML document and processed effectively by the browser reading the file. The <AREA> tag references the image map contents.

- Addition of an applet tag (<APPLET>) that allows you to access Java applets from within an HTML document.

- A formalized model for presenting tables in HTML documents. Table support has been previously implemented in a variety of ways within different browsers.

- A number of improvements to text and paragraph alignment, for more control over page layout in an HTML document.

- Support for various numbering options when presenting ordered lists, including Arabic numbers, lowercase letters, uppercase letters, lowercase roman, and uppercase roman.

- Extensions to the image tag <IMG> to improve display and positioning of graphic images on the Web page.

- The addition of a <SCRIPT> tag to allow the use of scripting languages inside an HTML document.

- Numerous formatting options for controlling many different aspects of a page presentation. Many of these options can be controlled through use of external style sheets, JavaScript, or VBScript.

These features may not be particularly startling because many of them have already been in widespread use. However, HTML 3.2 standardizes them so that all companies producing browsers can uniformly incorporate these features, and browser interactions should become more predictable.

Basic HTML

HTML documents contain a variety of information that is read and interpreted by Web browsers, including:

- Text for display on the screen as blocks, lists, or tables.

- Links, which are connections to other HTML documents. A link can be represented by an image or a line of text highlighted in some manner. Click on the link and the Web browser seeks out and downloads the HTML document referenced by the link. Jumping from link to link, following a trail of documents, is what some people refer to (ad nauseam) as Web surfing.

- Images that can be displayed or suppressed, depending on the current settings of the Web browser that encounters them (sometimes people turn off the image display feature of their browsers for faster loading and access of the page content).

- Embedded items, such as Java applets or multimedia elements. Some of these elements can be handled in the native environment of the Web browser—that is, the Web browser already contains the ability to process and present them (for example, MIDI music files). Other elements require a plug-in or extension to the browser to be accessible, such as some of the Virtual Reality Markup Language (VRML) elements.

Tags are used to distinguish these different elements. Each tag is contained within a pair of angle brackets, such as <BODY>. Many tags also include a starting tag <BODY> and an ending tag </BODY> to identify a particular type of content enclosed between the tags. For example, the <BODY> tag identifies body text, the simplest form of text in an HTML document. If you wanted to add a line of body text to a Web page greeting new viewers, the line would be contained between the starting and ending tags, as follows:

```
<BODY>

Welcome to the stimulating Web page of Willie Moroni! I'm happy to see you made
```

```
it here.<BR>
```

```
</BODY>
```

Other tags use this opening and closing tag format, such as:

```
<TITLE>Customer Support Page for Yelsin Electronics</TITLE>
```

which becomes the title that appears at the top of the browser window. Another example is:

```
<HTML>
```

```
....content....
```

```
</HTML>
```

which identifies the complete contents of an HTML document.

T I P Most HTML tags are not case-sensitive. In other words, the browsers don't pay any attention to the capitalization that you use within a tag. If you enter <BODY> as a tag, it will be interpreted the same way if you enter <body> or even <bOdY>. If, however, you include JavaScripts within an HTML document, the JavaScript language *is* case-sensitive and you need to follow the proper conventions in order for the browser to interpret the script properly.

HTML documents can be constructed either in some type of text editor that produces ASCII text (a simple example is the Microsoft Window's NotePad utility or the Macintosh program BBEdit) or in some type of special-purpose HTML editor that adds the tags for you and helps with the document construction (such as Adobe's Page Mill). It's sometimes helpful when you're first learning HTML to work in a text editor at the lowest level so that you can get a good idea of the basic requirements of creating HTML documents. Once you gain some experience, you can use specialized HTML editors more effectively to streamline the production of Web pages.

Creating HTML Files with a Word Processor

You can use a conventional word processor for producing HTML files (such as Microsoft Word or Nisus Writer), but you must remember to save your documents as plain ASCII files. Most word processors have an option to save a file as "text only with line breaks." This is the option you should choose for any files that are intended for use as HTML documents. The additional formatting information that is added to a file saved in the native word processing format will render your document unusable as HTML files. Also remember to add the .htm or .html extension to the file (overriding any file extensions that the word processor normally adds to files that it saves—such as .doc).

HTML documents should be stored as ASCII text using a file extension of .htm or .html (for example, page_one.htm or main.html). One or more of these documents is stored on a server or at a location specified by your Internet Service Provider. The server site determines the Universal Resource Locator address (URL) that is used to access the documents. For example, if you have a document called enigmas.htm that is located on the server located at www.mysteries.com in a directory called yow, the URL to that document would be:

```
http://www.mysteries.com/yow/enigmas.htm
```

The http:// preceding the rest of the address identifies the protocol in use for exchanging the data contained in the referenced document. The protocol referenced here, http://, of course, refers to the protocol used for Web transfers, the common means for moving HTML data across the Internet. Most Web browsers can now infer the protocol from the address, so that when you're specifying the URL, you can leave the http:// out of the address (for example, just specifying www.mysteries .com). To maintain formality or to ensure clarity, you may want to routinely include the http:// portion of the URL.

Viewing HTML Documents

Some people mistakenly believe that you have to be logged on to the Internet if you want to view an HTML file. In truth, you can open and view any HTML file from your computer desktop without being on the Internet at all. Simply launch your Web browser and when the Connect dialog box (or equivalent) appears to prompt you to start the Internet login process, select Cancel to defer logging on. The browser then completes its loading and you can access an HTML file by selecting the **Open File** (or equivalent) option, usually located in the browser File menu. Navigate to the location of the HTML file that you want to view (on one of your local hard disk drives) and select the file. Any links contained within HTML documents that are local (either in the file you are viewing or another HTML file that is accessible on your hard disk drive) can be followed—in many ways, HTML can be used as a generalized method of creating hypertext documents that can be used locally, from diskette, from CD-ROM, or from other media. Some companies use HTML documents to provide customer support information or marketing literature on diskette or CD-ROM. Your use of HTML does not have to be limited to the Internet. You can also test HTML files that you create from any of the examples in this appendix by starting up your browser and opening the appropriate file.

Sibling of SGML

HyperText Markup Language is a vastly simplified subset of Standard Generalized Markup Language (SGML), which is codified in International Standard ISO 8879. SGML is a complex and ambitious language that seeks to create a common exchange medium for large documents distributed on multiple platforms. SGML has won favor with many institutions and organizations, such as the U.S. Government and corporations, seeking to disseminate complicated documents in a form that can be easily updated and distributed to many different platforms. You don't have to know anything more than this to work effectively in HTML. Simply being aware of the parentage of the language is enough. This will help explain the first tag that must appear in an HTML document meeting the 3.2 standard:

```
<!DOCTYPE HTML PUBLIC "-//W3C// DTD HTML 3.2 Final//EN">
```

This cryptic-looking tag merely identifies the following document contents as belonging to version 3.2 of HTML for browsers that encounter the files.

Bare Bones HTML Document

An HTML 3.2 document in its most rudimentary form requires only an identifier for the document type and a title, as expressed in the following entry:

```
<!DOCTYPE HTML PUBLIC "-//W3C// DTD HTML 3.2 Final//EN">

<TITLE>A Place for Trading Zinc Futures</TITLE>
```

The <!DOCTYPE> declaration alerts all browsers that the following contents include elements of the HTML 3.2 standard.

The <TITLE> becomes the name of the document as displayed in the browser title bar or other prominent location.

Using Descriptive Titles

Choosing a descriptive title for an HTML document is very important in two ways. First, the title provided will be used whenever someone creates a bookmark while viewing a document. If you title a page "Items for Sale," it will make less sense as a bookmark title than if you use a more descriptive title, such as "Poe's First Edition Books for Sale." Second, the title chosen is used during a WAIS search of a server's contents, so the more descriptive the title, the better chance that a search will appropriately identify the key contents of the document to someone looking for a particular topic.

A more realistic HTML document would include some additional elements, as in the following example:

```
<!DOCTYPE HTML PUBLIC "-//W3C// DTD HTML 3.2 Final//EN">

<HTML>

<HEAD>

<TITLE>A Place for Trading Zinc Futures</TITLE>

...other elements for the HEAD, including JavaScripts...

</HEAD>

<BODY>

...main contents of the HTML document, including text and images...

You've come to a place where you can earn a fortune doing futures trading in

zinc. Please read on...

</BODY>

</HTML>
```

Within this basic framework, elaborate and intricate Web pages can be constructed. The <HTML>, <HEAD>, and <BODY> start tags are no longer required because any Web browser compliant with the HTML 3.2 standard can infer these contents automatically. The tags can still be routinely included in an HTML document, particularly if you have gotten in the habit of using them for previous versions of HTML.

Tags Included in the HEAD

The <HEAD> area of the document can include several additional tags, including:

<TITLE>: Identifies the title of the HTML document. *This element is always required.*

<ISINDEX>: Supports simple keyword searches by a variety of search engines. *Optional.*

<BASE>: Identifies a base-level URL for helping resolve address references using relative URLs. *Optional.*

<SCRIPT>: Defines the scripting language in use in the following series of entries, such as JavaScript or VBScript. *Optional.*

<STYLE>: Reserved for style sheet references in future implementation of HTML. *Optional.*

<META>: Designed to present certain name and value pairs; for example, the name of the author of a document. *Optional.*

<LINK>: Defines a relationship with another HTML document or external resource. *Optional.*

Of these tags, <TITLE> and <SCRIPT> are the two that you might be expected to use as novice Web authors. The others are primarily of interest if you are doing more formal or elaborate Web authoring projects.

SCRIPT Tag

Script languages for use within Web browsers have become increasingly popular, with JavaScript and VBScript leading the pack. Scripts consist of a series of statements that are interpreted by the browser (not compiled before use, as are Java applets).

The <SCRIPT> tag identifies the type of script immediately following the tag. A closing tag </SCRIPT> must be used to distinguish the end of the script statements. JavaScripts can be placed either inside the <HEAD> area of an HTML document or within the <BODY> area. Scripts in the <HEAD> area, however, are executed before the body contents load, which is necessary for some kinds of script execution.

For example, a simple script to create a function for submitting a form to the server would be included in the head as follows:

```
<SCRIPT LANGUAGE="JavaScript">

function submitForm()   {

        document.forms[0].submit();

}

</SCRIPT>
```

If this script appeared within the <HEAD> of an HTML document, it could then be called from the body as part of a link to trigger the submit form function. The link statement to trigger it would appear as follows:

```
<A HREF="JavaScript:submitForm()">Click once to submit the form entries</A>
```

This example assumes that you've also created an HTML form on the page. The first form appearing in a document is referenced by JavaScript as:

```
 document.forms[0].
```

If the language being used in the script was VBScript, you would change the initial <SCRIPT> entry to read as follows:

```
<SCRIPT LANGUAGE="VBScript">
```

This tag may be also used in the future for other scripting languages that are developed for use with HTML documents.

Style Tag

The style tag provides a means of defining and controlling the attributes of an HTML document, including such characteristics as margins, heading sizes and font colors, and page background colors. The <STYLE> tag is reserved in HTML 3.2, but closely tied to the work being done by the W3C group in standardizing the CSS1 (Cascading Style Sheets Level 1) specification for general release. JavaScript and VBScript can be used to control the elements defined by a style sheet in more dynamic form.

The <STYLE> tag, for example, can be used to specify the characteristics of any of the elements that JavaScript can interact with. In the following example, the level-one heading (H1) in an HTML document is defined as being displayed in red:

```
<STYLE TYPE="text/Javascript">

tags.h1.color="red"

</STYLE>
```

The use of cascading style sheets will provide a whole new spectrum of opportunities for Web authors to control the display of different aspects of an HTML document and allow the appearance of entire documents to be modified by simply making a reference to a different style sheet.

You can also use the <LINK> tag to connect with a style sheet that is external to the HTML document being constructed. For example, the following line would import the characteristics of the style sheet indicated at the specified URL:

```
<LINK REL=STYLESHEET TYPE="text/Javascript"
HREF=http://www.styles.com/neat_styles" TITLE="Formal">
```

Upon being opened, the HTML document would indicate to the browser to retrieve and apply the styles from the style sheet stored in neat_styles. Styles for elements not included in the style sheet would remain the same as the standard styles even after the style sheet was imported.

Body Content

The body of an HTML document contains most of those elements that we're used to seeing when we are viewing someone's Web page. Links to other sites, images, tables, and basic text content appear within the body of a document. Any text that is simply entered into an HTML document without any other tag is considered to be body text. The standard font, color, and size attributes are applied unless some other information is provided to change these characteristics.

You do, however, have to provide some instructions to the browser as to how to separate blocks of body text. Browsers will merge text together as one continuous block unless you indicate the extent of individual paragraphs by using the paragraph <P> tag. The <P> tag indicates the start of a block of text to appear in a paragraph and, optionally, an end tag </P> to specify the end of the paragraph. If you don't specify the end, browsers capable of presenting HTML 3.2 documents can determine from the context in the file where the end of the paragraph is.

For example, the following simple HTML document contains a level-one heading and two individual paragraphs:

```
<HTML>

<HEAD>

<TITLE>Solar Power Primer</TITLE>

</HEAD>

<BODY>

<H1>Alternative Energy Through Solar Power</H1>

<P>Improvements to solar-cell technology have made it possible to construct a

home, even in the most northern states in the U.S., without having to depend on

power being sent to your home by a power utility. Pioneering individuals who

adopt this approach are said to be "off the grid."</P>

<P>It only takes a bit of research and some calculation to determine the equip-

ment that is necessary to support a house of a particular size at a particular

latitude. You may need to factor in your basic living requirements to perform

these calculations, including the type of appliances that you regularly use

(refrigerators, televisions, stereo equipment, and so on), the exposure of your

home site to the sun, and the storage capabilities of the batteries used to

supply energy when the sun isn't shining. This site helps you determine these

factors. </P>

</BODY>

<HTML>
```

When displayed in a typical Web browser, this HTML document appears as shown in Figure A.1.

Most of HTML tags function in a similar fashion, using start and end tags to determine where the bracketed element should appear on a page.

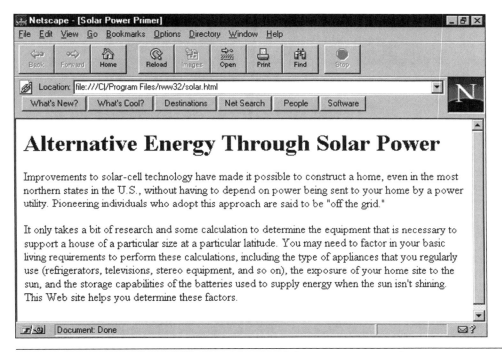

Figure A.1 A simple HTML document with two paragraphs.

WYSIWYG HTML Editing

To avoid the trial-and-error approach for determining how an HTML document will be displayed when it appears in the browser, use an HTML editor that provides two windows: one for entering the HTML code and another for viewing the results as they appear in the browser. There are many fine editors that fit this description. A shareware product called ReVol Web Worker is a good example of a tool that offers this dual-view approach to editing. Figure A.2 shows the previous two-paragraph HTML document example as it would appear during editing in Web Worker.

Although many of the HTML editing tools can remove the need for memorizing the individual tags and learning the syntax for applying them, it is usually helpful to initially try constructing documents just using a simple text editor. Such an approach will give you a foundation in how a basic HTML document is constructed, knowledge that can be valuable even when you accelerate the HTML construction process using a special-purpose editor.

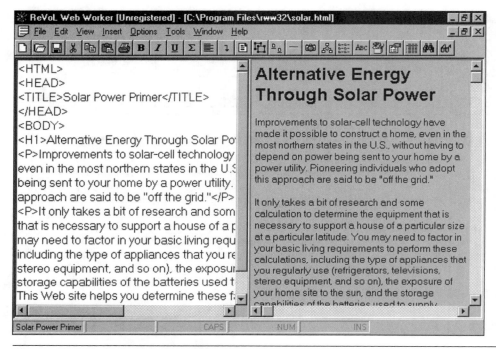

Figure A.2 ReVol Web Worker dual view.

Body text is one of the elements that can be manipulated by means of a cascading style sheet. For example, if you consistently use dark backgrounds on your Web pages, you might want to universally ensure that the body text always appears in white. You could do this by adding a style statement that specifies the body text as white, as shown in the following example:

```
<STYLE LANGUAGE=Text/Javascript>

body.color = "white"

</STYLE>
```

Blank Lines and Spaces

Web browsers ignore blank spaces and empty lines that appear in an HTML document. Even though you might separate a block of text in the source HTML document with three or four empty lines, the browser will ignore them all. Only a paragraph tag will keep a number of text blocks from merging together into one continuous chunk of text. Browsers also ignore indentations of text, so even if you want the first sentence in a paragraph to be indented several characters, you can't accomplish this by adding spaces or tabs at the beginning of the paragraph. This is where an HTML editor that provides an easy way to view the browser's interpretation of the document format can be especially valuable.

Headings

You might have noticed in the previous section that the Heading of the sample document was assigned using the tag <H1>. HTML 3.2 supports five additional levels of headings: <H2> through <H6>. Top-level headings are represented using a large display font and bolder text than underlying headings. Just as in a reference book, headings help orient the reader to the structure of the material being presented and the relative importance of each topic in the document.

WARNING   To maintain the hierarchical structure of your documents, avoid skipping headings. In other words, always follow a level-one heading <H1> with a level-two heading <H2>, not a level three or four (<H3> or <H4>). You should also use the level-one heading first in a document (don't start with level two or three). Following this convention ensures that all browsers will be able to identify and display the appropriate hierarchy of the headings in a document.

Heading tags are containers; in other words, they have both a beginning and ending tag, as shown in the following example:

```
<H5>Some thoughts on crossing the Atlantic in a kayak</H5>
```

Anchors and Links

Web surfing and other high-speed navigation through sites depends on anchors and links. Anchors represent mileposts—fixed locations within an HTML document to which a link can be attached. Links provide the physical means for jumping to an indicated topic. To the person viewing the Web page, a link appears as a highlighted item that usually indicates the destination of the link. Clicking on the link instructs the Web browser to load the HTML document indicated as the URL or, optionally, to jump to an indicated anchor in a document that is already loaded. Links don't have to be constructed as text; a link can be attached to an image so that clicking on the image will cause the browser to jump to the destination that is specified. This particular feature of HTML is tremendously important—it allows

Web pages all over the entire Internet to be referenced and accessed by the simple act of creating a link. Through this feature, the World Wide Web becomes an enormous hypertext document with the ability to cross-reference topics within any available documents.

TIP Formally, an entry using the <A> tag is referred to as an anchor, whether it identifies a fixed location in a document (through a NAME) or designates a destination for a link (through an HREF). Informally, however, you may want to distinguish between the two types of <A> tag statements by thinking of fixed locations as *anchors* and hypertext jumps as *links*.

The <A> tag is used to designate anchors and links. When the <A> tag is used with a NAME statement, the entry determines the milepost that can be referenced by name and accessed from another location. For example, the following statement specifies an anchor named "rodent_warren."

```
<A NAME="rodent_warren">This is where rodents gather.</A>
```

The text following the bracketed name statement is optional. A link also appears as part of the <A> tag, but it includes an HREF entry that points to another location (either inside the current document or in another external document). The link entry must also include text or an image to give the user something to click on to access the link. An example of a typical link entry follows:

```
<A HREF="http://www.space_college.net/index.html">Go to space college!</A>
```

In this case, clicking on the link causes the Web browser to locate and access the file called index.html from the URL indicated: http://www.space_college.net.

If the link is designed to jump to a specified anchor in the document (rather than an external document), the HREF entry should include a # symbol to properly designate it. For example, if the link was intended to bring the viewer to the previously created anchor named "rodent_warren," the reference should be expressed as follows:

```
<A HREF="#rodent_warren">Visit the local rodent warren today.</A>
```

You can combine the link to the named anchor with an external reference, specifying both the URL and the anchor name in the same HREF entry, as shown in the following example:

```
<A HREF="www.rats.com/warrens/#rodent_warren">Visit the remote rodent warren
today.</A>
```

Together, anchors and links provide a means of navigating with the browser to a variety of destinations. You are not limited to Web sites (URLs with an http:// reference), but you can also reference FTP sites, gopher sites, telnet sites, or even files located on your server's hard disk drive. Files stored locally in a subdirectory beneath the current directory can be referenced using a relative pathname—rather than providing the entire pathname for the file, it is necessary only to provide the subdirectory and filename. For example, to link to a file called "aussies.html" in a subdirectory called "Australia," the entry could be expressed as follows:

```
<A HREF="Australia/aussies.html">Aussie archives</A>
```

Images and Color

If Web pages contained only black-and-white text, they would be very dreary places to visit. Fortunately, there are a number of tags that make it possible to add images to an HTML document and apply color to different elements, such as the background of the page or individual fonts.

The basic image <IMG> tag simply indicates where in a document to place the image and the location and name of the image file to use. Valid graphic file types for use in an HTML document include JPEG, GIF, and X Bitmap (XBM) format files. Many Web browsers are also now providing support for a new graphic file format called the Portable Network Graphic (PNG) format. Large graphic images can take a long time to download, so prudent Web authors reduce their size by either scaling the image size or reducing the file dimensions by running the graphic through some type of utility that reduces the color palette and otherwise compresses the file size. Such techniques can greatly reduce the time required to download graphics and, thus, the annoyance encountered by those visiting the Web page.

The simplest form of an image statement just provides the source of the graphic to be placed in the indicated position on the page. The following example identifies the source of the image as the file named FELIX.gif:

```
<IMG SRC="FELIX.GIF">
```

If the image to be used is located somewhere other than the local directory where the HTML document resides, a URL reference can be used. The URL follows the same format as that used by HREF entries described earlier, as shown in the following example:

```
<IMG SRC="www.felines.com/headquarters/felix.gif">
```

By default an image will be positioned on the left margin of the page. The following example uses the <P> tag to locate the image within its own paragraph.

```
<HTML>

<HEAD><TITLE>In Pursuit of Wisdom</TITLE>

</HEAD>

<BODY>

<H1>The Wisdom Institute</H1><P>

<HR>

<P>The wisdom of cats is known to a large part of the world's population. Our

president, shown below, reflects on that fact.<P><HR>

<IMG SRC="felix.gif">

</BODY>

</HTML>
```

When displayed in a Web browser, the HTML document in the previous example presents the image as shown in Figure A.3.

T I P Note that the <HR> tags—which stand for horizontal rule— place rules within the displayed text. Rules offer a distinct—if somewhat overused—means for isolating text and image areas displayed on a page.

An image doesn't have to be isolated from text; it can be placed directly beside a text entry. Alignment tags and sizing tags are used to define how much space the

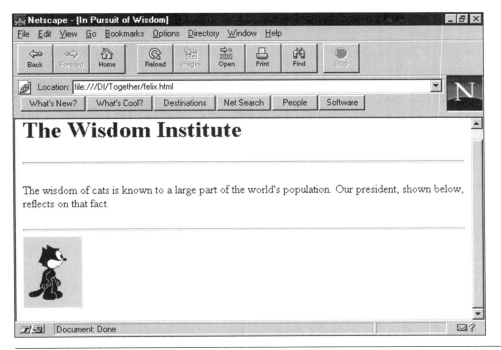

Figure A.3 Image placed in an HTML document.

image occupies and where on the page it will go in relation to the other elements. The following section describes these tags.

Image Alignment The <IMG> tag can include attributes that specify the size in pixels of the image. Image size is presented in terms of height and width. For example, the following image entry indicates that the browser should designate a region 140 pixels high and 50 pixels wide for the image stored in the file GERONIMO.jpg.

```
<IMG SRC="GERONIMO.JPG" HEIGHT=140 WIDTH=50>
```

To accommodate browsers that can't handle graphic display, you can include an ALT entry. ALT signifies that the following text string should be displayed in place of the image for those browsers that do not have graphics capabilities or whenever the person viewing the Web page has the automatic graphics downloading option of his or her browser turned off.

An ALT entry is inserted within the <IMG> tag as shown in the following example:

```
<IMG SRC="lizard.gif" ALT="Large, snarling lizard" HEIGHT=80 WIDTH=120>
```

T I P While the HEIGHT and WIDTH statements are not absolutely required, they help ensure that the browser will properly position and size the graphics. These two statements also help ensure that JavaScript can properly handle the manipulation of any specified images; you should always include a HEIGHT and WIDTH entry when you're using JavaScript on a Web page that contains images.

If text and a graphic both appear on the same line, by default the browser will align the bottom of the image with the text that follows. However, you can override this default and display the graphic centered or at the top of the paragraph. To do this, use the ALIGN entry. For example, to align a graphic with the top of the paragraph, use an entry similar to the following:

```
<IMG SRC="big_top.jpg" ALIGN=TOP>
```

To center a graphic within its own paragraph, use the <P> tags in combination with the <IMG> tag, as shown in the following example:

```
<P ALIGN=CENTER>

<IMG SRC="STAR_LOGO.GIF">

</P>
```

One of the additions for HTML 3.2 was a pair of attributes—hspace and vspace—that let you place space around the perimeters of an image. As you might suspect, vspace adds vertical space, specified in pixels, around the image, and hspace adds horizontal space, also in pixels. Without this specification, most browsers use a default of a pixel or two to separate images from surrounding text. If you'd like to add, for example, 40 pixels of space, you can use hspace and vspace, as shown in the following example:

```
<IMG SRC="big_sky.gif" HSPACE=40 VSPACE=40>
```

An image can also be used as the item that is clicked to follow a link. The following section describes how to accomplish this.

Images as Links An image can be identified as the object that when clicked will launch the browser toward a new destination. An image constructed for this purpose can optionally include a corresponding text description that describes the link. In many cases, though, such as in the case of an image that displays the logo of an organization that the link references, the additional text may be extraneous.

To embed a link within an image, bracket the link between <A> tags, as shown in the following example:

```
<A HREF="http://www.freestuff.com/giant_bin"><IMG SRC="freebies.gif"></A>
```

The image represented by freebies.gif will be identified by a border. Click within the image boundaries and the browser will access the Web site indicated by the URL.

If you don't think the image itself is fully explanatory as to where the link goes, you can include text to describe the link destination, as shown in the example:

```
<A HREF="http://www.freestuff.com/giant_bin>Want free stuff?<IMG
SRC="freebies.gif></A>
```

In this case, the text line (Want free stuff?) appears directly before the image. You could also place the text entry after the image simply by making the entry for the image source followed by the text that you want to appear after it.

One additional image-related attribute is the border. By default, images that appear within an <A> tag are displayed with a border by browsers. Those images that appear outside the <A> tag typically don't have a border. The border attribute not only indicates that an image has a border, but it lets you specify the thickness in pixels of the border. This could confuse viewers, who typically associate the border with a clickable image that contains a link, but the option is available to you. To add a 6-pixel border to an image outside of a pair of <A> tags, make the entry as follows:

```
<IMG SRC="fungus.jpg" BORDER=6>
```

To remove a border from an image that appears between <A> tags, you could use an entry similar to the following:

```
<A HREF="pictures/bin"><IMG SRC="fungus.jpg" BORDER=0></A>
```

The BORDER=0 entry removes the border from the image.

Image Maps HTML 3.2 adds the ability to create image maps that execute from the client side. In other words, a single image can be placed on a page with specific areas designated within it so that when you click on a region, you go to the corresponding

URL. The server doesn't need to get involved with figuring out how to handle the map links; everything happens on the client side, making the process far simpler to execute.

The <MAP> tag serves to identify the areas within an image that are active links. The coordinates, specified using the <AREA> tag, are given in pixels, so you need to use an image processing program that lets you identify coordinates in terms of pixels in order to calculate the correct values to insert. The <MAP> entry also lets you assign a name to the image map that you are creating. When the image representing the map is embedded in the HTML document using the SRC entry, the USEMAP entry connects the mapped coordinates by name to the image—which activates the links that you have created.

A SHAPE attribute used as part of the <AREA> tag lets you determine a shape, including RECT for rectangle, CIRCLE, POLY for polygon, and DEFAULT, to define the region that activates the link.

The coordinates for a rectangle are based on establishing an x/y reference in pixels and then defining another point to determine the opposite corner of the rectangle. For example, if the first coordinate was 0, 0 and the second was 40, 40, the 0, 0 identifies the upper-left corner of the rectangle and the 40, 40 identifies the lower-right corner. These two points are all that is necessary to map the dimensions of the rectangle.

The process of creating and embedding an image map requires two separate tasks: (1) using the <IMG> tag to place the graphic for the image map in the document and to identify the name of the map where the coordinates are given and (2) creating the map itself with the <AREA> tags defining the coordinates and their links. The following example shows how a typical map would be set up:

```
<IMG SRC="flyer.gif" USEMAP= "skymap">

<MAP NAME="skymap">

<AREA SHAPE=RECT COORDS="0, 0, 25, 25" HREF="stratosphere.html">

<AREA SHAPE=RECT COORDS="25, 0, 50, 25" HREF="ionosphere.html">

<AREA SHAPE=RECT COORDS="50, 0, 75, 25" HREF="troposphere.html">

<AREA SHAPE=RECT COORDS="75, 0, 100, 25" HREF="ground.html">

</MAP>
```

Clearly, the dimensions of the bitmap used for the image map (in this case, flyer.gif) must precisely match the dimensions and the coordinates defined by the four areas created in the <MAP> entry. Different shapes use a different coordinate system. For example, the CIRCLE shape requires an x/y coordinate to indicate the center of the circle and then another coordinate to specify the radius in pixels. The following entry would create an area shape with the center of the circle at 20, 20 and a radius of 30 pixels:

```
<AREA SHAPE=CIRCLE COORDS="20, 20, 30" HREF="back.html">
```

If a created image map is designed to be handled on the server side rather than the client side, the ISMAP entry is used to reference the map, rather than the USEMAP entry.

Background Color The color that applies to the background of an HTML document is white by default, but you can specify a different color to use, either by using a color name (which may not be recognized by all browsers—Navigator recognizes a large set of color names) or by indicating the Red-Green-Blue values (RGB) in hexadecimal notation. There are 16 color names that are defined under HTML 3.2; they are listed in Table A.1 with the equivalent RGB value.

When specifying a color for any use—whether it is to be used as a background color, link color, or the color of a font—you can use either the hexadecimal RGB value or the color name. For example, the following two entries for specifying the background color of a page both generate a background color of Aqua:

```
<BODY BGCOLOR="#00FFFF">
```

```
<BODY BGCOLOR="aqua">
```

Links also can be assigned color values. If you change your background color in an HTML document, you might also have to change the color of the links as they appear on the page to make sure that they are visible. For example, to change the VLINK color to Teal, you would enter this as:

```
<BODY VLINK="teal">
```

The VLINK entry refers to those links that have already been visited. Browsers also recognize a LINK, which is a new link on a page, and an ALINK, which is a link that is currently active. Colors of any of these items can be modified in the same way.

Table A.1 Color Names Defined under HTML 3.2

Color Name	RGB Value
Black	#000000
Silver	#C0C0C0
Gray	#808080
White	#FFFFFF
Maroon	#800000
Red	#FF0000
Purple	#800080
Fuchsia	#FF00FF
Green	#008000
Lime	#00FF00
Olive	#808000
Yellow	#FFFF00
Navy	#000080
Blue	#0000FF
Teal	#008080
Aqua	#00FFFF

Background Pattern You've probably seen Web pages that show a graphic image, rather than a solid color, as the background. This can be an attractive effect if done with care and if done in a way to ensure that the text on the page remains legible. Background patterns can be compact by using a feature called tiling, which is a small part of an image repeated over and over until it fills the entire browser window. You don't need to specify any particular attribute to cause tiling to occur—browsers perform this automatic pattern fill based on the image referred to in the BACKGROUND statement. For example, if you have a textured graphic of a piece of rough paper stored in a file named ruf_papr.gif, you could add it as a background pattern using the statement:

```
<BODY BACKGROUND="ruf_papr.gif">
```

Always test your backgrounds thoroughly after you have changed them to make sure that you haven't made links or text completely unreadable. Also keep in mind that large background patterns increase the download time for the page on which they appear—a factor that can be very annoying to visitors to your Web page. Keep your background patterns simple and compact for best results.

Linking to External Files

If references to images, sound files, movie files, and so on are included in line—that is, as part of an HTML document—they are downloaded with the contents of the page and displayed, played, or activated under control of the current preferences set within the browser. This obviously results in longer download times and reduces the user's control over those images, sounds, or movies that he or she might actually want to access. An alternative is to provide a link to an external source containing the file (such as an image, movie, or sound). Unless the link is clicked, the external file is not accessed.

You can provide external links to many different types of external files. The file extension determines how the browser will respond to the linked file. If a plug-in is available for accessing the file, the browser will use it automatically if the extension is recognized, or prompt to download the appropriate plug-in for playback. If native support for the file format is available, the appropriate action will be initiated. For example, if the link pointed to a MIDI file (.mid extension), both Netscape Navigator and Microsoft Internet Explorer will initiate MIDI playback.

Other file types and their extensions include graphics (.gif for a GIF image, .tiff for a TIFF image, .jpg or .jpeg for a JPEG image), sound (.aiff for an AIFF sound file, .wav for a WAV sound file, .au for an AU sound file), and movies (.mov for a QuickTime movie, .mpeg or .mpg for an MPEG movie).

To provide a link to an external file, you use the standard HREF entry but substitute the filename (and path, if necessary) for accessing the resource. For example, to access a sound file called "singing.wav," you would enter:

```
<A HREF="singing.wav">A chorus of happy children</A>
```

Clicking on this link would download and play the file in a computer equipped for sound playback.

You can also use this technique to provide a link to a large graphic that is downloaded when a smaller, thumbnail image is clicked. The statement to accomplish this might be as follows:

```
<A HREF="Chugundo.gif"><IMG SRC="Tiny.gif"></A>
```

This approach gives the user the opportunity to decide whether to view the larger image.

Embedding Special-Purpose Files

The <EMBED> tag allows files with particular kinds of extensions to be referenced as source data in an HTML document and then activated or played based on parameter settings. This is a common technique for referencing files that require a browser plug-in for playback.

Different types of plug-ins use different parameters, so you should check the manufacturer's documentation for what parameters apply. A typical <EMBED> entry for playing back a MIDI file might be as follows:

```
<EMBED SRC="hot_song.mid" WIDTH=100 HEIGHT=30 AUTOSTART=TRUE REPEAT=TRUE>
```

This <EMBED> entry specifies that the browser should play the MIDI file titled hot_song.mid. It also indicates the dimensions for the MIDI player that will appear on screen. The AUTOSTART and REPEAT settings specify that the song should be played as soon as it is loaded and then repeated at the conclusion.

The <EMBED> tag is particularly valuable for placing audio content within an HTML document. A number of specific techniques for accomplishing this are provided in Chapters 4 and 5.

Embedding Java Applets

The <APPLET> tag is a new addition for HTML 3.2. This tag allows all Java-enabled browsers to run a referenced applet from within an HTML document. A set of parameters enclosed within the tag identifies the code and the basic operating environment for the applet. An alternative text entry can be provided for those browsers that do not support Java or those that have disabled Java in the browser preferences.

A simple applet insertion would be as follows:

```
<APPLET CODE="HiThere" width=25 height=15>

<PARAM NAME=snd value="greeting.au">
```

```
A spoken greeting and song played from a Java applet.
```

```
</APPLET>
```

Not everyone keeps the Java function of their browser enabled, so if you depend on the material contained in a Java applet on your Web page, you might want to include an alternative routing for non-Java browsing. You can also use JavaScript to detect whether Java is currently enabled on the viewer's browser and select the appropriate routing to an HTML page based on that setting.

More HTML

If you understand the fundamentals of HTML, as described in this primer up to this point, it is fairly easy to incorporate additional elements into a page. Many of the additional elements deal with methods for placing certain kinds of information, such as material in formatted tables or ordered lists, onto the page while maintaining careful control of the presentation. These types of tags can be very useful, but they are not essential to a basic HTML document. We recommend that if you want to explore the possibilities of HTML further, you should investigate one of the references or Web sites that offer in-depth discussion of HTML.

As a place to start, you might try one of the following links:

- http://www.asianet.net/resources.html

- http://members.aol.com/kirrak9/cyberbase.html

- http://union.ncsa.uiuc.edu/HyperNews/get/www/html/lang.html

- http://WWW.Stars.com/Authoring/HTML/

- http://kingdom.inter.net/PSIWeb/webtools/

- http://www.cris.com/~raydaly/htmljive.html

Viewing HTML Source Files

Learning the techniques to effectively place different kinds of material within an HTML document (and have those elements display in the same manner that you intend them to) takes a bit of practice and continued exposure to the conventions. One good approach for learning HTML design is to view the source files for other people's pages. You can do this from directly within your browser. For example, from within

Netscape Navigator, while a document is being displayed, drop down the View menu and **select Document Source**. A window appears with the full source contents of the document currently in your browser window. By studying the ways that others embed graphics and audio material, create tables, present lists, and so on, you can quickly pick up the fundamental knowledge you need to construct your own Web pages. This technique has long been used by programmers, who study the program code of skilled programmers to learn how to efficiently perform various functions and accomplish tasks. HTML documents that you are viewing can also be saved as a file and then examined and used as a template for different functions that you might be trying to accomplish. Studying the way that someone else accomplishes a difficult task could save you hours in trying to accomplish the same thing.

B

Glossary

The terminology in this book covers a broad range of technologies and disciplines—from audio esoterica to Internet jargon to programming terminology associated with Java and JavaScript. We've provided this glossary to offer some help in bridging the interdisciplinary boundaries, but, clearly, the limitations of space make it impossible to be completely comprehensive. Several additional references are listed in Appendix C, *Audio and Internet Resources,* which should help provide more in-depth coverage of some of the specialized topics.

A-Law A compression scheme for voice-grade signals. As defined by the G.711 recommendation (the Geneva Recommendations), A-Law describes the technique for encoding 16-bit PCM waveforms as 8-bit nonlinear data. The algorithm used is similar to the telecommunications standard commonly in use in the United States.

Acoustics The term *acoustics* refers to the science of sound. It can also be used in reference to those characteristics of a particular environment—such as a room or performance hall—that influence the perceptual qualities of sound occurring within it. An entire discipline is devoted to design techniques for creating theaters, studios, and auditoriums where the sound characteristics will be favorable for performances or recording.

Adaptive Delta Pulse Code Modulation Abbreviated as ADPCM; an audio data compression scheme. Several variations of ADPCM exist—the different varieties are not generally compatible. Microsoft Windows95 includes two variations selectable from within the operating system: Microsoft IMA ADPCM CODEC and Microsoft ADPCM CODEC. This type of compression is usually employed to compress voice recordings.

AGC Automatic Gain Control. An electronic circuit, often used in recording input devices, that dynamically adjusts the recording level by varying the gain of an input amplifier. Amplification is turned up for soft sounds and turned down for louder sounds. The goal is to achieve the optimum recording level without any signal distortion.

Aliasing A form of distortion that results if a high-frequency sound is recorded digitally at too low a sample rate. Aliasing can be heard as a low-frequency rumble in the sound recording. Many digital audio sound processing applications include an anti-aliasing filter that can be used to strip out the high frequencies before the sampling takes place. If aliasing occurs during a recording, it is difficult or impossible to remove without significantly modifying the contents of the recording.

Alligator Clip A connecting device that resembles the jaws of an alligator, used to make temporary cable connections, such as grounding the chassis of a recording device to a stable ground. The spring-loaded jaws can be clipped to a variety of objects, such as protruding screws, terminal studs, or battery cases.

Alternating Current AC. The worldwide standard used by utility companies for delivering electrical power to homes and businesses. The current regularly reverses the direction of flow in periodic cycles that can be represented as a sine wave. Many electronic devices use transformers or adapters to convert alternating current to direct current (which flows only in one direction) for use in their circuits.

Ambience The atmosphere that surrounds one in a given environment. Audio ambience deals with the representative sounds of a particular place, such as the sounds of a crowded tavern, the sounds of the marshlands on a summer night, or the sounds of a subway station at rush hour. Ambience can be used to establish a particular mood or locale through audio cues.

American Standard Code for Information Interchange Abbreviated as ASCII; a character set that is in common use by many of the computers around the world. The ASCII character set is limited and is often extended to support additional symbols, foreign alphabets, and diacriticals.

Ampere A fundamental unit of electric current. An ampere is the amount of steady current that generates a force of 2×10^{-7} newtons between two parallel wires separated by a distance of one meter. Current flow in computers and electronic devices is commonly measured in milliamperes, units of one-thousandth of an ampere.

Amplify To raise the amplitude of a signal. Compare to *attenuate*, which means to diminish the amplitude of a signal.

Amplitude The relative intensity of a sound wave. The term *amplitude* is also applied to electrical signals.

Amplitude Modulation A process by which the amplitude of a waveform is varied over a specific length of time. If the amplitude is varied relatively slowly, we hear the modulation as a tremolo effect (a wavering tone). If the amplitude is varied more rapidly, the effect changes the timbre of the waveform by creating large numbers of side frequencies.

Analog-to-Digital Conversion The technique by which continuously varying input, such as a sound wave, is converted into a discrete series of digital values representing the magnitude of the data at each point in time that a sample was taken. The greater the number of samples collected, the more accurate the representation of the original data will be. Sampling rates for CD-quality audio are 44,100 samples per second.

Asynchronous Transfer Mode Abbreviated to ATM; a connection-oriented technique for handling network transfers. ATM uses small, fixed-size cells to deliver data from point to point across networks. The technology offers promise for real-time transfer of voice, audio, and video, as well as conventional data transfers.

Attachment Some form of data file that can be transferred with an e-mail message. Attachments are supported by many of the major e-mail applications.

Attack Time The ramp representing the start of a sound. Certain sounds have a fast attack time, such as the crack of a snare drum or the spoken letter "K." Other sounds have a slow attack time, such as a low note on a pipe organ or the spoken letter "O." Many analog synthesizers provide the ability to adjust the attack time of a generated sound. Digital sound processing applications also often provide a means of varying the attack time when filtering or processing sounds.

Attenuate To diminish the amplitude of a signal. Compare to *amplify*, which means to increase the amplitude of a signal.

Audio Compression Manager Abbreviated as ACM; a compression standard and interface developed by Microsoft for .wav file manipulation. The ACM works from within Windows to compress and decompress .wav file data and to manipulate audio data using Digital Signal Processing techniques.

Audio Console A device for combining and processing the signals produced by a number of other pieces of audio equipment, including microphones, synthesizers, tape recorders, guitar amplifiers, and tone generators. Also called a *mixing board*, *mixing console*, or, simply, *board*.

Audio Range The range of frequencies audible to the human ear. Most people can hear frequencies between 16Hz to 20KHz. The term *audio spectrum* is sometimes used to mean the same thing.

Axis The line that bisects the area representing a microphone's pickup pattern. Voices or instruments directly in front of this line are said to be *on-axis*; voices or instruments to the side of this line are said to be *off-axis*.

Backbone Network A network that serves as a central interconnect for large-scale internetworking.

Baffle A sound-cushioning apparatus, generally portable, that can be used to dampen or alter the acoustic characteristics of a room or recording studio.

Balanced Connection A type of audio connection consisting of two signal carrying wires and a ground wire. A transformer or equivalent device is used on one end of the connection to eliminate unwanted signals from being induced into the line, such as the hum generated by power lines. Most professional-quality audio equipment uses balanced input and output connections.

Bandwidth The sum total of data that can be transferred through a given communications channel in a set amount of time. For example, the nature of audio and video data requires a higher bandwidth to support transfer of the information, which is why the source files are often compressed for transfer.

Baud The number of signal transitions per second on a transmission line. This can be the same as the bit-per-second data transfer rate, or it can be different, depending on whether di-bits or tri-bits are used as part of the transmission scheme.

Bias Tone A tone outside the audible range added to a recorded tape by the recording head. The bias tone causes the tape to respond more consistently to the full range of frequencies being recorded. A typical bias tone is between 50KHz and 150KHz, well above the hearing range of the human ear.

Bidirectional Microphone A type of microphone in which the pickup pattern extends to both sides—the resulting pattern resembles a figure-8. Noise rejection on the axis perpendicular to the figure-8 is enhanced.

Binary File A file containing bit-level information, rather than simple text. Binary files may consist of audio information or images. They generally must be reproduced bit-for-bit to avoid corruption of the content.

Bit Depth The number of bits that are used as part of a sample to recreate a sound wave. The two most common bit depths are 8-bit and 16-bit. Some high-end digital audio sound processing tools use a 24-bit digital sample internally when processing sound files. The higher the bit depth, the greater the fidelity of the sampled sound. The term "sample size" is sometimes used to refer to the bit depth.

Bridge A computer that forwards packets between two or more interconnected networks. Bridges can store and forward complete packets, unlike repeaters, which simply forward the sum total of all electrical signals. A bridge is also different from a router, because it works using physical addresses, unlike a router, which uses IP addresses.

Buzz Noise induced into an audio circuit, generally from power current at 60Hz cycles being inducted into the signal because of ineffective grounding or unshielded signal lines.

Calibrate To set an audio device level to correspond with a fixed standard. This is often done with VU meters to establish a reference sound level for recording or mixing applications. Digital sound processing software also generally includes an option to set the incoming sound level through the sound board to correspond with an onscreen representation of a VU meter.

Cannon Connector The most common connector for professional microphones, consisting of three pins and a snap-on latch. This type of connector supports balanced signal transfers. Also called an XLR connector.

Cardioid A common pickup pattern associated with unidirectional microphones. The cardioid pattern resembles a "heart."

Capstan The part of a tape recorder transport that consists of a metal cylinder driven by a motor that advances the tape past the recording and playback heads at a precise speed.

Center Frequency A term used during equalization to refer to the center frequency within a band of frequencies that are being equalized. Equalization refers to the process of boosting or attenuating certain frequency bands while processing a given sound.

Channel A signal path followed by an audio signal. For example, most mixing consoles have auxiliary SEND and RECEIVE channels. Stereo devices have a left and right channel.

Chorus An audio effect that simulates a single sound source coming from several different sources. This effect is accomplished by taking a signal, creating a copy of it, and merging the delayed, modulated copy with the original signal. The Chorus effect is supported by many digital audio sound processing applications.

Client-Server A method used in distributed systems based on interactions between a client program and a server program. The client issues requests to the server; the server responds with the appropriate data or other information.

Clipping A form of distortion that occurs when sound peaks exceed the maximum input level that is supported by a recording device. Digital clipping results in the sound peaks being recorded at the maximum high-end value. Extreme examples of digital clipping are difficult to correct in a recorded file, but most digital audio sound processing applications have routines that can reduce the audio impact of less extensive forms of clipping.

Close Miking Situating a microphone within several inches of the source of the sound.

CODEC Abbreviated form of Coder/Decoder. A CODEC is a type of compression standard, usually applied to audio or video data compression. MPEG,

ADPCM, and A-law are examples of CODECs. The greater the compression rate, the more signal loss generally occurs when the compressed data is decoded. For this reason, some CODECs, such as ADPCM, are more suited to compression of voice data, rather than music or complex sounds. Some compression standards, such as MPEG, work best when they have dedicated hardware support, such as an IC or circuit board that performs the compression and decompression at high speeds.

Complex Sound Any sound consisting of more than one frequency. Most naturally occurring sounds fit in this category.

Compressor An electronic device that reduces the difference between the sound levels in the loudest and softest passages of a piece of music. This makes it possible to make the relative amplitude of the softer passages greater while preventing the louder segments from distorting during recording or playback. This effect is also available in many digital sound processing software packages. It is also often used when recording instruments that produce sharp amplitude peaks, such as bass drums and bass guitars, to allow a fuller, richer sound without peak distortion.

Condenser Microphone A microphone that employs a capacitor (also called a condenser) to capture sound waves by varying the electrical relationship between two plates. Condenser microphones require either an internal power source, such as a battery, or an external power supply in order to produce an output.

Conductor Any substance that allows free passage of electrical current. For example, the cables connecting a stereo amplifier to a pair of speakers generally use copper wire as the conductor.

Connectionless Service A technique that applies to packet delivery as implemented through the Internet Protocol. Each packet or datagram is handled independently, as an individual unit that has both a source address and a destination address.

Crosstalk The undesired contamination of signals from one audio circuit bleeding into another. An example of crosstalk is the signal on one track of a multi-track tape affecting the signal on the adjacent track.

Cycle The full transition of a wave through its positive and negative extremes and back to the starting point. Both sound waves and electrical waveforms exhibit measurable cycles.

Crossfade A mixing technique that fades in one audio segment while another is fading out so that the two overlap for a brief time. Many digital audio sound processing applications support this effect.

Crossover Network An electronic circuit that splits an audio signal into two or more components, sending each component to a separate set of speakers. For example, high-frequency sounds are directed to speakers designed for high-frequency playback; low-frequency sounds are directed to sub-woofers.

Cut An abrupt transition from one audio segment to another (without fading).

Dead Environment An environment designed to suppress echo and reverberation so that sounds occurring within it remain uncolored. Cushions, baffles, and similar types of sound-absorbing materials are used to create a dead environment. Most recording studios are set up to be dead environments.

Decay The period of time that a sound diminishes before becoming inaudible.

Decibel A sound measurement unit that is based on a logarithmic scale. A decibel reading of 60 represents a 10-times greater relative level of sound than a decibel reading of 50. This scale covers an extremely wide range of relative sound volumes. A soft whisper is approximately 10 decibels. The sound of typical traffic on a city street is somewhere around 70 decibels. A Boeing 747 during takeoff generates about 100 decibels of sound. This unit of measurement is abbreviated as "dB." Decibels appear as the common unit of measurement in many types of sound recording input devices, such as the standard VU meter found on tape recorders.

Degausser A device containing an electromagnetic used to eliminate magnetic fields or magnetic patterns. For example, a bulk eraser is a form of degausser used to erase a reel or cartridge of magnetic tape. Degaussers are also used to demagnetize the recording heads of tape recorders.

Diaphragm A thin, flexible material used to reproduce sound waves. A microphone converts sounds waves to electrical signals by means of a diaphragm. A speaker converts electrical signals representing sound waves to the air movement patterns that we perceive as sound.

Direct Box An interface that contains impedance matching circuitry used to split the signal from an electric guitar, microphone, or other device, and direct it to two or more inputs. For example, an electronic synthesizer output might be sent to both a mixing board and an amplifier.

Direct Current A single directional flow of current that is incorporated in many types of computer and logic board circuits, as well as audio equipment.

Directional Characteristics The pickup pattern associated with a microphone. Each type of microphone is sensitive to sound waves in a characteristic pattern and also tends to reject sound waves from certain locations. The directional characteristics of a microphone determine its optimal uses. For example, a uni-directional cardioid pattern is frequently used for vocal work in rock bands because the microphone picks up the voice clearly but tends to reject other sounds from off-axis directions.

Discoloration The alteration of a reproduced sound by undesired sound arti-facts, poor frequency response in certain frequency bands, or other forms of sound degradation.

Distant Miking A technique that places the microphones further away from the sound source to obtain more of the ambient atmosphere of a room or perfor-mance hall.

Distortion Generation of inaccuracies in a sound being recorded or played back that are generally viewed as unfavorable to the sound quality. The exception is the distortion that is produced as electric guitar feedback or saturation that is used expressively as part of the music.

Dithering A technique for masking quantization noise by injecting noise into a signal.

Domain Name System Abbreviated as DNS; a system that maps names into the equivalent IP addresses as represented in dotted decimal notation. This system is built around a distributed database that is circulated among participating servers. A hierarchical structure is maintained, with servers at higher positions in the hierarchy keeping information about the range of servers in lower posi-tions. This system provides considerable flexibility to allow site managers inde-pendence in assigning machine names and addresses.

Dotted Decimal Notation A convention for depicting IP addresses by means of four 8-bit numbers constructed in base 10, each individual number separated by a dot (period). A large number of TCP/IP applications can handle this nota-tion, rather than requiring individual machine names for destinations.

Downsampling A technique by which a digitally recorded sound is reduced to a more compact storage format by changing the bit depth and/or the sampling rate. Downsampling is frequently employed to reduce the size of sound files for transfer to Web applications, games, or other media where the file size must be minimized. Depending on the quality of the software tools used for downsampling, the fidelity of the downsampled sound file can still be maintained to high standards. Inadequate tools result in a seriously degraded sound.

Dropout Signal loss resulting from imperfections in magnetic tape (when performing analog recording) or sampling losses (when performing digital recording). Dropout can also apply to streaming audio playback when packets are lost during the audio data transfer across the Internet; white noise is sometimes substituted to mask signal glitches of this type.

Dynamic Microphone A type of microphone that relies on a flexible diaphragm connected to a magnet with a coil. The diaphragm vibrates in response to sound waves and converts the waves to a signal as the coil vibrates within the magnetic field. Dynamic microphones do not typically require a battery or external power source.

Dynamic Range The variation in relative volume between a very soft sound and very loud sound, particularly as this variation occurs in a recorded or performed musical sequence. The dynamic range must be taken into account when recording a musical source to ensure that both the soft and the loud passages will be accurately recorded. An electronic device known as a compressor is used to reduce the amplitude of the loudest portions of music to allow the relative volume of the softer passages to be more prominent. Many digital sound processing applications support effects that make it possible to enhance the dynamic range of a piece of digitally recorded sound.

Encryption A technique for scrambling the information in a transmitted file or voice communication so that the information can be transmitted with full privacy. To be accessed, the person receiving the information must have the corresponding encryption key.

Epoch Date An arbitrary baseline date used as a reference point for measuring time. The TCP/IP convention is to use January 1, 1990 (Universal Standard Time) as the baseline. Time is always expressed between communicating TCP/IP applications as the number of seconds that have passed since the epoch date.

Equalization Enhancing or suppressing certain frequency ranges in a complex sound wave to achieve specific effects. Many digital audio processing applications provide tools for manipulating the equalization (EQ) of a recorded sound.

Fade The slow ramp-up or ramp-down of the amplitude of an audio segment. A fade-in is considered the gradual increase in volume from 0 to a predetermined level. A fade-out is considered a gradual decrease from the current level of sound down to 0.

Fader A type of volume control found on many different types of mixers that uses a sliding lever to adjust the volume.

Feedback An audio event characterized by part of the output of a signal feeding back into the input. This results in a wailing or howling sound that can increase in volume and damage speakers or ears if not curtailed. Controlled feedback is sometimes used in rock performances as one of the elements of expression.

File Format A specific defined method for storing particular types of data on the computer. Many different file formats exist for audio data. In the Windows environment, .wav files are the most common. On the Macintosh, the .aiff format is prevalent. Unix users often use the .au format for storing audio information. Digital audio sound processing applications generally provide tools for converting one type of sound file format into another.

File Transfer Protocol Abbreviated as FTP; a high-level protocol that is considered the standard under TCP/IP for transmitting and receiving files between two communicating computers.

Filter An electronic device, either active or passive, that is used to attenuate a certain range of frequencies. Sophisticated digital filters are employed in some digital audio sound processing applications to eliminate very specific types of sound artifacts, such as the pops and clicks that occur on very old vinyl recordings. Filtering is one form of equalization.

Firewall A security system constructed of routers and networks that separates an organization's internal network resources from the connections to the external Internet.

Flanging An audio effect characterized by a cycling "swooshing" kind of sound that can generally be set to certain frequencies. An external sound box used by many electric guitarists called a Flanger is used to apply this effect to the sound of a guitar.

Flat Response Uniform, consistent reproduction of the entire range of frequencies directed into an audio processing device. For example, if a microphone has a flat response, it accurately reproduces all frequencies equally, without boosting low-range sound waves or attenuating high-range signals. Audio equipment that delivers a flat response is generally prized for recording and playback applications.

Flutter An audible variation in the speed of a tape recording device caused by irregularities in the speed of the transport mechanism. Higher-quality tape recording devices have transports designed to minimize flutter.

Frequency Response The characteristics of an audio device for reproducing the frequencies of the various signals that are fed to it without unduly emphasizing or diminishing any particular range of frequencies. The frequency response of devices such as microphones is sometimes expressed as a graph showing the relative levels at which different frequencies are reproduced by the mic. Generally, a flat frequency response is favored for most types of recording.

Frequency Spectrum The full range of frequencies contained in a particular signal. The range of frequencies associated with audio are from 20Hz to 20,000Hz. Many digital audio applications provide tools for analyzing the frequency spectrum of a recorded waveform. Equalization effects can be applied to improve the sound of recorded waveforms by boosting or diminishing certain frequency bandwidths to achieve balance and separation. For example, extra clarity can often be added to a recording of rock music by slightly boosting the high frequencies (8000Hz to 12000Hz) and low frequencies (20Hz to 200Hz) and slightly reducing the midrange frequencies.

FX Abbreviation for sound effects.

Gain The level of amplification provided by a device expressed in decibels. The higher the value, the more amplification can be achieved.

Gateway A means of interconnection between two different types of computers that use different protocols. A gateway can be used, for example, to transfer electronic mail between systems running incompatible network protocols.

Gooseneck A flexible metal attachment that mounts a microphone to a microphone stand. The gooseneck portion of the attachment can be curved and repositioned to locate the microphone at a precise point in space.

Graphic Equalizer An equalization device, or the software equivalent, that provides independent faders that control discrete frequency bands. A complex sound wave can be precisely shaped by amplifying or attenuating the various frequency bands, usually depicting graphically from low-end frequencies to high-end. For example, a five-band graphic equalizer provides a set of five faders that control the relative amplitude of five distinct frequency bands.

Ground A common reference point for an electrical circuit. Earth ground is usually considered the ultimate grounding point because it has a zero potential. In a complex studio environment, if a common ground is not used for all the equipment being used, this will frequently result in line noise or hum because different levels of ground can affect the integrity of the data signals.

Hard Wiring A soldered circuit connection where electrical points are wired together, as compared to circuits that can be modified through the use of jacks and plugs.

Harmonics The multiples of a given fundamental frequency. Harmonics influence the character and perception of a sound. Most complex sounds include a full range of harmonics in addition to the fundamental frequency.

Head The recording and playback element of a tape recorder that comes in direct contact with the magnetic tape. Some recorders use separate record and playback heads. Over time, the recording head tends to become magnetized by the passage of magnetic fields across its surface and it must be degaussed to remove the accumulated residual magnetism.

Hertz The basic unit for measuring frequency. A single Hertz represents one cycle of a wave, through its full positive and negative transition. A KiloHertz is 1000 cycles.

High Cut Filter A type of filter that diminishes sound waves occurring above a selected frequency threshold.

High Output Tape A variety of audio recording tape that can hold a much "hotter" signal than ordinary magnetic tape. This allows higher amplitude signals to be recorded without inducing distortion.

Hiss A constant noise characteristic of most types of analog recording. Hiss consists of a persistent, complex, high-frequency noise that becomes more prominent during pauses or silences in a piece of music. The nature of analog recording equipment makes it difficult to eliminate hiss, although Dolby and other noise reduction techniques can reduce it substantially. Digital recording techniques make it possible to effectively eliminate hiss as a recording problem, even in the quietest passages of a piece of music.

Hop Count A means of describing the distance between two locations on the Internet. The hop count expresses the total number of routers that separate the source and destination.

Host A computer system connected to a network. A host computer can be any system capable of being interconnected to a network—from the most humble personal computer to the most powerful mainframe.

Hypertext Markup Language Abbreviated as HTML; a subset of SGML that enables platform-independent pages to be transferred and interpreted by different browsers all over the Web. The current version of HTML is 3.2, as approved and ratified by the World Wide Web Consortium (W3C). HTML contains both text and links, enabling viewers to follow a trail of URLs to other Web pages.

Hypertext Transfer Protocol Abbreviated as HTTP; the protocol used on the Web to allow linking between various Web sites.

Impedance The sum total of opposition to current flow in an alternating current circuit. Impedance consists of both the resistance of the circuit plus the reactance, which is a factor of the inductance and capacitance. Impedance matching is an important factor in maximizing the level of a signal being channeled from one point to another. By making the impedance of a load correspond closely to the impedance of the source of power, the most efficient transfer takes place. For example, an impedance-matching transformer is an electronic device that can connect two audio devices that do not have equivalent impedances. This results in a higher-quality signal transfer.

Inches Per Second The common means of measuring the speed of an analog tape recording device, expressed as the number of inches of tape that pass by the capstan in one second. Usually abbreviated as IPS. High-quality recorders generally support 15 IPS recording speeds or better.

Input The circuit (and connector) into which an audio signal is directed for audio recording or processing. For example, mixer boards have several inputs to handle incoming audio signals, which are then processed and directed to one or more audio outputs.

Integrated Services Digital Network Abbreviated as ISDN; a form of digital network service available through telephone companies in most areas of the country. ISDN connections can achieve three or four times the maximum data transfer rates of conventional telephone lines carrying data in analog form.

Internet A global network consisting of more than 4 million computers linked through routers and other networks that rely on the TCP/IP protocol to route data and exchange information.

Internet Phone A method for voice communication over the Internet that exchanges digitized vocal exchanges in real time between two or more users who are equipped with sound boards, microphones, and the appropriate software. Internet phones are becoming popular because they can provide long-distance communications at local telephone rates. Through the use of gateway services, Internet phones can also be used to place calls to individuals who have only conventional telephones.

Internet Service Provider Abbreviated as ISP; a company that provides access to the Internet, as well as a range of services. Many ISPs provide server storage space to allow you to construct your own home page or operate a business. If you plan to deliver audio files through an Internet Service Provider, you must often request that they add support to their server for the MIME file types that you intend to distribute through your Web pages.

IP Address A 32-bit address identifying a host computer interconnected to the Internet. Each address consists of a network identification and a host identification in order to simplify routing of data.

IP Datagram The fundamental unit of information exchange on the Internet. An IP datagram consists of a bundle of data identified with a source address and a destination address.

Jack A type of receptacle designed to accept a plug. For example, most guitar amplifier inputs consist of quarter-inch phone jacks that accept the phone plugs of a standard guitar cord.

Line Level The most common signal level supported by a wide range of audio devices. Line-level signals, such as the output from a CD player, are higher than microphone-level signals. The highest signal level is speaker-level. Many sound boards accept both line-level and microphone-level signal inputs. If, however, a microphone-level signal is directed to a sound board that supports only line-level inputs, the signal will not be strong enough to accurately reproduce, unless it is boosted first through a mixer board.

Loop A section of tape containing audio that can be played over and over because the end of the tape is spliced to the beginning.

Low Cut Filter A form of equalization that filters out frequencies below an established low-frequency threshold.

Mail Gateway A computer linking two disparate electronic mail systems, performing any reformatting necessary to ensure proper delivery on the destination system.

Media Control Interface Abbreviated as MCI. The Media Control Interface is used by Microsoft Windows to facilitate communication with multimedia devices, such as sound boards, laser disc players, and CD-ROM drives. Devices that include MCI drives can be placed under program control by most software using multimedia elements.

Mic Level A low-level signal generated from a microphone. Mic-level signals typically have to be amplified to line-level signals for use by an audio device. A mixing board is one common way of boosting mic-level signals to line-level signals.

Mic Splitting A technique by which the signals coming from one or more microphones are split and redirected to two or more mixing boards. This allows two independent mixes to be controlled. For example, one mix might direct the microphone signals to the PA system for a stage performance and the other to a broadcast channel for a live feed.

Midrange Frequencies Generally considered those frequencies occurring between 400 and 3000 Hertz.

Musical Instrument Device Interface Abbreviated as MIDI. The MIDI standard provides a means for musical equipment communication and for storing or creating music in an editable notation. MIDI consists of control, timing, and data information transferred serially between devices at 31.25Kbps transfer rates.

MIDI information communicated over the Web is a compact means of providing music to Web site viewers while minimizing bandwidth concerns.

MIDI Time Code Abbreviated as MTC; a means for synchronizing MIDI-enabled programs through absolute time clocking. Provides a MIDI equivalent to the SMPTE time code.

Mini Connector A common type of connector found on many cassette recording devices. Sometimes referred to as a *Miniphone Connector*.

µ-Law Pronounced mu-Law; a compression algorithm defined within the Geneva Recommendations. This method of compression encodes PCM signals at 16-bit depths into 8-bit nonlinear storage formats. This means of compression is employed frequently in telecommunications applications in both Europe and Asia. In the United States, a similar standard, A-law, is more commonly encountered.

Multicast A technique that can create copies of a single packet and route the copies to a number of different destinations. An Intercast multicast feature is supported by IP and can be applied to multicasts of audio material, such as live performances or newscasts.

Multipurpose Internet Mail Extensions Abbreviated as MIME; a protocol that provides support through e-mail applications and browsers for a variety of file types, each devoted to a particular type of data. For example, there are MIME types, generally identified through the file extension, for supporting MIDI (.mid), audio (.wav), and other types of data.

Multitimbral The ability to play back more than a single instrument sound at a time. Each sound is considered a timbre. Midrange synthesizers are able to simultaneously play back 16 timbres at once.

Multitrack Tape Recorder A type of tape recorder that has more than two separate channels for recording and playback. Separate channels can be used to record individual instruments or voices, such as recording the bass on Track 1, the vocals on Track 2, and the guitar on Track 3. Channels can then be recombined or rearranged through a mixing board. The current generation of multitrack recording devices are digital devices, such as DATs and ADATs, which use helical scan recording heads similar to those used for video recording equipment.

Mute To suppress the sound of an audio recording or playback device. Many computer MIDI applications and multitrack digital sound processing programs provide a means to mute individual channels of music to hear what certain instruments sound like alone or in combination with others.

Name Resolution A system for determining the name that corresponds with a given address. As implemented under the domain name system (used on the Internet), remote name servers are used to identify the IP address that corresponds with a specified machine name.

Newbie Someone only recently acquainted with the World Wide Web.

Noise-shaping A technique to diminish quantization noise by shifting its frequency spectrum. Audio quantization noise that occurs when sampling at 44,100Hz can be reduced by shifting the noise to a frequency of 22,050Hz.

Nondestructive Editing A method for manipulating digital sound information without altering the original source recording. Software that supports nondestructive editing lets you insert markers into a sound file that specify what effects are to be applied to the selected region. The effects are dynamically applied during playback, but the original file remains intact and unchanged. Nondestructive editing can be a valuable tool for trying out different digital effects while still maintaining your original data.

Normalization A technique for uniformly raising the sound volume of a file to a specified level. When performed digitally, normalization ensures that the full dynamic range of the recorded sounds will be utilized. This effect also strongly influences the perceptual sense of the volume level of the music when played back. For example, if you were creating several files for downloading from the Web, you would want to normalize all of them to the same level so that they sound similar when played back.

Nyquist Frequency One half of the digital sample rate. The Nyquist Frequency represents the highest frequency that can be recorded without injecting aliasing distortion into the sound sample. A digital recording performed at a sample rate of 44,100Hz can accurately capture wave forms with a frequency as high as 22,050Hz (the maximum level of human hearing) without aliasing distortion. For recordings performed at lower sampling rates, an anti-aliasing filter is necessary to avoid distortion of frequencies above the Nyquist Frequency.

Off-Axis A point that is outside the optimal pickup pattern of a microphone. Sound waves occurring in proximity to the off-axis will not be reproduced.

Omnidirectional A pickup pattern of a microphone designed to capture and reproduce sounds from all directions. Omnidirectional microphones perform most consistently with frequencies below 5000Hz.

On-Axis A point that is within the optimal pickup pattern of a microphone. Sound waves occurring in proximity to the on-axis are uniformly reproduced (per the frequency response characteristics of the microphone).

Output In audio terms, the circuit and connector that direct a signal to another device.

Overdub The process of recording additional tracks while synchronized to (and playing back) previously recorded tracks. For example, a single musician could create a piece of music with several different parts by overdubbing the instruments one after another to a multitrack recording device.

Overmodulating Directing a signal to an audio device at too high a level for processing. This results in a form of distortion.

Packet A small block of data that is transmitted across a network that supports packet switching (such as the Internet).

Pad A resistor used to damp a signal in order to avoid overloading an input device. Sometimes a resistive pad is used to prevent a microphone signal from over-saturating a preamplifier circuit.

Pan A gradual movement of a sound between channels. Most mixers and many software applications designed for multitrack recording and mixing provide a pan control that lets this function be controlled with a knob or slider.

Parametric Equalizer A type of equalizer that controls three separate elements of equalization: the bandwidth to be amplified or attenuated, the center frequency for each frequency band being processed, and the degree of attenuation or amplification. Many digital sound processing applications include support for parametric equalization.

Patch Bay A collection of jacks usually placed in an accessible location in a recording studio that allow interconnection of devices by patch cords. Instead of having to recable an entire equipment configuration, cables can be rerouted and reconfigured through the patch bay. This device is sometimes called a *patch panel*.

Peak The loudest point in an audio segment. Usually determines the highest level of recording that can be achieved, unless compression and/or limiting are used to prevent distortion of the peak signals.

Peak Program Meter A type of meter that displays only the peak volumes of an audio segment, rather than the fluctuating levels as displayed by a VU meter. Many digital audio sound processing applications include a graphic display that performs the same function as the peak program meter, helping to detect and prevent recordings that have signal clipping from exceeding the peak allowable signal level.

Phone Connector Sometimes called a quarter-inch phone connector, these types of plugs and jacks are used with a number of different audio devices, including electric guitars and amplifiers. Two-conductor mono versions are available (sometimes called *"tip-sleeve"*) as well as three-conductor stereo versions (also called *"tip-ring-sleeve"*). Few computer sound boards directly support inputs of these types, but adapters are available to convert Phone connectors to the small RCA connectors found on most sound boards.

Pickup Pattern A proscribed area, or field, within which a microphone can capture sound waves with accurate frequency response and fidelity. A variety of pickup patterns are possible, include figure-8 patterns and cardioid patterns. The type of musical or voice recording application determines what type of pickup pattern is most suitable.

Pinch Roller A rubber cylinder that applies pressure to magnetic recording tape, forcing it against the capstan. The pinch roller ensures uniform contact as the tape is passing through the recording area.

Playback Head That part of a tape recording device that interprets the magnetic signals recorded to tape and translates them into electrical signals.

Plosive The burst of air generated vocally when certain syllables are spoken, such as words beginning with "b" or "p." Plosives can cause a popping sound through a microphone unless the microphone is somehow filtered with a noise cushion or the vocalist remains a certain distance away from the microphone head. This is one of the most common problems when recording speech or singing.

Polar Pattern The field representing through a diagram the relative areas of sensitivity that a microphone has to pick up sounds from different axis points. Sometimes called a *field pattern*.

Polyphony The sum total of pitches or instrument voices that can be simultaneously played. Typical digital workstations support from 16- to 32-note polyphony. Even though your fingers might be able to press only 10 keys at a time, MIDI sequences constructed on the workstation can contain up to the number of voices or notes supported by the workstation—32-note polyphony provides a very full, rich sound.

Pop Filter A foam windscreen or similar device that shields the microphone. Designed to prevent plosive sounds from being recorded.

Pop Server A mail server that supports the Post-Office Protocol, a common means of exchanging e-mail messages over the Internet.

Post-Production The audio work that is done after the initial recording has been completed. Post-production work includes all of the sound processing, including editing, mixing, equalization, normalization, and so on, that is performed in order to create a well-balanced and finalized audio segment.

Potentiometer A resistor that serves as a volume control by varying the amount of voltage available in a signal.

Presence An audio characteristic that provides the illusion that the voice or instrument being played is right next to the listener. Boosting signal frequencies slightly in the 2KHz to 8KHz range can increase the presence of the audio.

Proximity Effect A characteristic of many microphones that causes the bass frequencies to be emphasized when the microphone is placed very close to the sound source. This effect is most pronounced with microphones that have a cardioid pickup pattern.

Punch-In A technique used to drop in a new piece of recorded material within a specified region of a sound recording. Recording is limited to the indicated region so that recorded material before and after the punch-in area will not be affected.

Quantization The representation of a continuously variable signal, such as a sound wave, as a series of discrete amplitude values stored in a digital format.

The accuracy of quantization is a factor of how many bits are used to pinpoint the amplitude level at each sampling instant. Using 8-bit analog-to-digital conversion, you can distinguish up to 256 levels. Amplitudes above or below the 256 defined levels are rounded off. Using 16-bit analog-to-digital conversion, you can distinguish up to 65,536 values. This is also referred to as the *resolution of quantization*.

Quantization Noise An undesirable characteristic of performing quantization at low bit depths that results in audible noise in the waveform. Quantization noise is present to some degree in all sampled digital material, but it is audibly most noticeable when playing back low-resolution samples with 8-bit depths. The noise can be heard as a "shushing" sound in the recorded material.

Rack A cabinet constructed of metal or wood designed to hold a bank of audio devices. Professional racks are constructed to handle audio equipment designed to uniform widths of 19 inches. A typical equipment rack might contain a DAT recorder, a parametric equalizer, a reverb unit, a mixing board, and a compressor/limiter. Some computer-based sound recording environments contain the equivalent to all of this equipment, requiring nothing more than a professional-grade sound board and the appropriate software.

RCA Connector A common, monaural plug and jack configuration, found on many kinds of home stereo equipment. Sometimes called a *phono connector*, this type of connector is frequently found on computer sound boards, cassette players, and similar devices.

Recording Level The volume of a signal about to be recorded, either to tape or to a digital storage medium. For the best recording quality in both analog and digital frameworks, the level of the recording should be as high as possible without causing distortion or clipping. A peak meter can be used to ensure that the recording level does not exceed the capacity of the input device.

Release Time A finite length of time during which a compressor reduces its output signal to the level that existed before compression was applied.

Resample Changing the sampling rate of digitally recorded material. The sampling rate can be adjusted downward (causing frequency loss) or upward (where missing data points are interpolated). When resampling downward, anti-aliasing must be performed to avoid aliasing distortion in the sound file.

When resampling upward, although the sampled sound has a greater resolution, the overall quality will not be improved from the original sound file. For some purposes, though (for example, recorded Red Book audio data to a recordable CD), a specified sampling rate must be followed (44,100Hz for Red Book recording).

Ribbon Microphone A type of microphone that employs a thin strip of ribbon fashioned from metal that is suspended within a magnetic field. Sound vibrations transferred to the ribbon cause electrical signals to be generated within the magnetic field. The ribbon serves as a conductor and as the equivalent to a diaphragm in a conventional microphone. Ribbon microphones are often used for vocal work and for broadcasting when optimal quality is desired.

Root Mean Square Abbreviated as RMS; a measure of sound intensity over time. The RMS value of sound data relates to the user's perception of the relative amplitude of the sound volume during defined intervals of time.

Router A computer-controlled device designed to connect two or more networks. Packets are forwarded from network to network based on address tables that are maintained and updated by the routers. Each router has the ability to determine the optimal next-hop address to send a packet to, based on the destination address of the packet, and the routing tables that are currently in effect.

Sample Rate The number of samples per second that are captured when digitally recording a sound. The greater the number of samples taken, the higher the accuracy of the digitally recorded material. The CD-quality standard is 44,100Hz sampling rate, but many DAT recorders and digital sound boards sample at 48,000Hz. Lower sampling rates, such as 11,025Hz are often used for recording voices digitally, where it's not as important to capture a wide frequency range.

Saturation A form of distortion that results when a signal is recorded at too high a volume. The fidelity of the sound is marred by a muddy, indistinct quality.

Sibilance An undesirable over-emphasis of certain sounds, such as the "s" and "ch" sounds, that occurs sometimes when a microphone is placed directly in front of a singer's or speaker's mouth. Placing the microphone off to the side can often eliminate the additional high-frequency emphasis.

Signal A sound as represented in a magnetic, electrical, or digital storage format.

Signal-to-Noise Ratio The comparative value between the average audio level and the level of noise that exists in a broadcast or recording. A signal-to-noise ratio is usually presented using decibels as the unit of measurement. Signal-to-noise ratios of broadcast material and analog recordings are significantly less than can be achieved with digital recording techniques. For example, a signal-to-noise ratio of approximately 50dB is considered acceptable for broadcast and analog recording. Most high-quality digital sound boards are capable of signal-to-noise ratios in excess of 90dB.

Site An Internet host system that may support a variety of protocols. For example, an FTP site accommodates the uploading and downloading of files using the File Transfer Protocol. A Web site uses the HTTP protocol to support linking and accessing to other Web sites. Sites must be specifically set up to support a particular protocol before someone can access the site with the necessary tools.

Society of Motion Picture and Television Engineers Abbreviated as SMPTE. Most commonly referred to as a time code used to synchronize device playback. The time code expresses intervals in divisions of hours, minutes, seconds, and frames. Frame rates for SMPTE synchronization range from 24 to 30 frames per second. SMPTE is sometimes used to synchronize audio events and playback of multimedia material in computer applications.

Sound Check A pre-performance assessment of sound recording or reproduction equipment to eliminate any problems with the current configuration, sound levels, or microphone positioning. Mixing levels are often finalized during the sound check to establish the best quality sound for the performance or recording.

Stereo Miking The use of two or more microphones to achieve a contextual perspective of the sound being recorded, so that different instruments and voices appear to exist in a set spatial relationship. This effect can be simulated to some degree by the use of pan controls during a mixdown.

Splitter Box An apparatus that takes the signals from one or more microphones and sends them to two or more destinations. Sometimes called a *stage box*.

Synthesis The modeling of sound waveforms by electronic means. Synthesis can be performed by both computer sound boards and external synthesizer devices.

Tempo The number of beats per minute in a piece of music. The tempo determines the rhythmic quality of the music.

Threshold of Compression A preset signal level used with a compressor to determine when the compression effect should be applied. At the threshold of compression, the compressor is activated; when the signal recedes below the threshold, the compressor returns to the prior level setting after a specified release time.

Transducer Any device capable of converting one form of energy into a different form. For example, a microphone is an example of a transducer, as is an audio speaker. A piezo-electric pickup on a guitar is another form of a transducer.

Transformer A type of electrical circuit that converts the impedance and level of an incoming signal without altering the frequency. Impedance-matching transformers are often used to optimize the signal levels of different audio devices during recording.

Transient Response The ability of a device to quickly reproduce short-lived signals, as measured in units of time.

Transmission Control Protocol/Internet Protocol Abbreviated as TCP/IP; the dominant means of transferring data over the Internet by means of packets that encapsulate the data and send it off from server to server to reach a specified destination.

Unbalanced Connection A two-conductor connection between audio devices. One wire serves to carry the signal and the other serves as the ground reference. An unbalanced connection is more susceptible to noise and electromagnetic interference. This method for connecting audio devices is not generally used for professional applications.

Unidirectional A microphone that is optimized for response to sounds primarily from an on-axis position while rejecting sounds from off-axis positions. Most cardioid microphones are unidirectional. This type of microphone is particularly effective for close-miking situations where it may be necessary to block out sounds on either side of the sound source.

Uniform Resource Locator Abbreviated as URL; a systemized means of specifying Web addresses and files. Each URL contains a protocol reference (such as FTP or HTTP), the name of the requested host (such as www.smarky.com), a port reference (optional), one or more directories, and a filename. For example, a typical URL might be: http://www.smarky.com/lo_noise/sounds.htm

Upload The act of transferring a file over a modem to a remote computer. For example, if you receive your Internet access through an Internet Service Provider, you need to upload the files containing the data for your Web home page to a designated location on the ISP's server.

User Datagram Protocol Abbreviated as UDP; a method by which one application can send a datagram to another application. UDP is a TCP/IP standard protocol that includes techniques for verifying data delivery through a checksum and allowing the sending program to identify a specific application running on a remote machine. UDP is used in some streaming audio and video applications to ensure that packets aren't lost and data transmissions do not become confused.

Unix shell account A form of Internet account that lets you enter commands via a Unix command line.

Velocity In MIDI terms, the relative strength at which a note is played or released by the MIDI controller. MIDI keyboards that have velocity sensitive keys are able to detect and notate the velocity of each played note.

Voice-over An audio narration that is presented generally accompanying other material, such as background music or sound effects. A voice-over segment may be composed and mixed into the foreground during post-production after the other audio or video material has been completed.

Volume Unit Meter VU Meter. An indicator that displays the volume level of complex sounds expressed in terms of decibels. One volume unit is equivalent to a one-decibel change in volume. The VU meter is a standard component of both mixing consoles and many digital audio sound processing applications that run on the computer, offering a clear indication of the "average" level of the sound so that volume adjustments can be easily made. Some computer-based VU meters also include a peak display that holds the highest peak detected during the last few seconds and displays a flag if the level gets high enough to cause signal clipping.

Waveform The graphical representation of any phenomena that exist in the form of waves, such as sound waves. The waveform displays both the frequency and the amplitude of the pressure variations that represent the sound wave. Most digital audio sound processing applications let you display a visual image of the shape of a sound file waveform on screen and let you manipulate the shape—and, consequently, the sound—using various editing tools.

Wavetable A set of digitally recorded sound that can be manipulated and accessed for playback. Wavetable sound boards contain digital samples of various instruments, captured at high resolutions, and are able to use these samples through General MIDI to provide very realistic music playback. Wavetable synthesis can also be performed as a software application, although this places significant demands on the computer's processor.

Web server An application that lets you make HTML documents available through your computer system. If you have the hardware or resources to operate your own Web server, you can generally use server space through an Internet Service Provider (which is using its own Web server applications to operate its site).

Woofer A type of speaker designed for handling low frequencies. A cross-over network can be used to direct only the low-frequency bandwidth to a woofer.

Yahoo! One of the most popular search services available on the Web. Accessible at: www.yahoo.com

Zero VU The baseline reading on a VU meter that is used to provide comparative readings of various audio signals. Most VU meters provide some form of calibration to set this baseline value against a standard reference.

Audio and Internet
Resources

The convergence of audio and computer technologies brings together individuals from many different pursuits and career areas. This appendix provides a collection of resources that should help anyone needing to find a means of expanding their knowledge in a given area.

Digital Audio References

For more in-depth material on specialized audio topics, consider the following resources.

Audio Files for WWW

From Schools OnLine comes this Web page called Making Internet Audio Files for the Apple Macintosh computer. A glossary of technical terms and a link to Sound Recording Utilities is given.

 www.ultralab.anglia.ac.uk/pages/Schools_OnLine/
Using_Audio/#top

Digital Sound

The Digital Sound page has sound editor and software synthesis links, sampling utilities, sample FTP and WWW site links, manufacturer contacts, and even some MIDI information. Patches, samples, pictures, and information on an enormous list of synthesizers can be found here.

www.xs4all.nl/~rexbo/index.htm

Doctor Audio Links

An extensive compilation of links to pro audio and MIDI manufacturers home-pages, WWW audio resources, MIDI related Web sites, music related resources, and online music and audio publications can be found here.

www.doctoraudio.com/links.html

MIDI Resources

MIDI Technical Fanatics Brainwashing Center contains excellent technical documents, tutorials, specifications, and MIDI programming tips. There are also links to MIDI files, software, company contacts, relevant news, and some humor to spice the pot.

www.servtech.com/public/jglatt/

MIDI (Musical Instrument Digital Interface) is another Web site with a good introduction to MIDI and the MIDI specification. From here you can go to some of the better MIDI links on the Web, find more MIDI files to download, and peruse more MIDI related software sites.

www.rsa.lib.il.us/%7Ewbeckner/midi/midi.html

KeyKit is a free software offering, a MIDI programming language with graphical user interface for both algorithmic and real-time musical experimentation. The source code (and executables for Win95) can be downloaded after a simple registration procedure.

www.nosuch.com/keykit/

The Sound2MIDI info page presents, Sound2MIDI, a real-time audio to MIDI conversion software package that can take any vocal or monotonic (single note at a time) musical instrument signal from mic or line input and translate it into MIDI events

www.audioworks.com/s2m.htm

MOD

The MOD page has an introduction to MOD and tutorials on what MOD is. Download links for MOD players and lots of information are included here for the inquisitive.

www.teleport.com/~smithtl/modpage/modpage.htm

Here's a list if of other MOD related Web sites:

- MAZ Home:
  www.th-zwickau.de/~maz/

- Module Links:
  red.muskoka.com/~joe/mods.html

- Drew's XM Music page:
  www.pnc.com.au/~drew/index.html

- Impulse Tracker:
  www.citenet.net/noise/it/

- What is a MOD?:
  http://www.armory.com/~greebo/whatis.html

- Binary Beats:
  intranet.ca/~mdeabreu/binbeat.html

- MOD Files:
  drum.csv.warwick.ac.uk/music/drum/mods.html

- MOD Related Links:
  www.rz.tu-ilmenau.de/~cstiller/links.htm

- Mod4Win:
  www.mod4win.com/

Principles of Digital Audio

Principles of Digital Audio, Third Edition, Ken C. Pohlmann, McGraw-Hill, 1995.

Ken C. Pohlmann's *Principles of Digital Audio* has matured and evolved through three editions, gaining a following along the way, until now it is considered the landmark reference in this field. Pohlmann is the president of Hammer Laboratories, a research and testing firm that specializes in audio technologies, and a professor of the music engineering programs at the University of Miami in Coral Gables, Florida.

This book covers the full range of digital audio topics, including digital recording techniques, theories and principles behind digital sampling and storage, digital storage devices, compression techniques, and so on. This is a very technical work, but well-written and thoroughly readable.

Principles of Digital Audio is available through:

www.amazon.com

Sound Glossary

A complete glossary of sound terminology is yours at this Web site. Nicely hyperlinked by alphabetic indexing, this should prove useful and may be one you want to bookmark.

pantheon.yale.edu/~harada/sound/howsdef.html

Music Enhancements and Specialties

This section is kind of a catch-all for interesting and specialized applications and products that may peak your interest or lead you into some worthwhile exploration.

Csound

Csound is a software synthesis and signal processing program that supports almost any type of synthesis, sampling, and signal processing. It is popular in many of the university music labs and among numerous composers. The program has been ported to almost every computer platform. If you are new to Csound check out the on-line Csound manual to get an idea of its capabilities and processing power. Documents, tutorials, links, binaries and sources, scores and orchestra files, tools, etc. are all available from Songlab's Csound page.

www.snafu.de/~rubo/songlab/midi2cs/csound
.html#DOCUMENTS

DIY Hardware

The Hardware Web is a site containing circuit schematics and info for the Do It Yourself (DIY) constructor. Schematics for MIDI interfaces and a copy bit deleter that sets the copy bit in digital audio signals (allowing you to copy digital recording more than once) are given at this site.

homepage.cistron.nl/~nctnico/index.htm

Electronic and Computer Music

This Web site links you to numerous university computer music labs, contains MIDI related links, including a MIDI primer, and has links to an assortment of software offerings and some interesting miscellaneous links to information on Theremin, fractal music, genetically programmed music, and more.

www.rsa.lib.il.us/%7Ewbeckner/midi/midi.html

The Computer Music Software page intelligently points you to a number of computer sound software packages and has an extensive resources list of links and houses some uncommon leads.

capella.dur.ac.uk/doug/software.html

Fractal Music

Fractal music is one of the most exciting things happening in new music research. Generated by a recursive process, an algorithm is applied multiple times to process its previous output. Perhaps you have enjoyed the fractal images and movie files that can be found on the Web. Here are two URLs that contain good tutorials on fractal music, along with very impressive collections of links to additional fractal music theory, software, music examples, and more.

Fractal Music Project:
www-ks.rus.uni-stuttgart.de/people/schulz/fmusic/

Fractal Music Lab:
members.aol.com/strohbeen/fmlsw.html

Interfacing Microphones to Sound Cards

Shure Product Support has an excellent technical bulletin Web page that can help you properly connect and use a quality microphone with your computer sound card. Signal levels, mic polar patterns, impedance matching, and cabling considerations are all discussed here intelligently, yet in layman's terms. Illustrations show how to wire a mic cable that allows a balanced-line mic to be plugged into your sound card. How to adapt condenser mics to operate on a voltage from your sound card is discussed, as well as other microphone issues. Several pages of special information for especially for Macintosh users showing how to connect any microphone to your Macintosh is given. If you use your mic for voice recognition, some helpful recording tips are listed here too.

www.shure.com/app-soundcard.html

Intellectual Property Issues

Read how the intellectual property law now applies to cyberspace. Links to concerned activity groups and organization providing information are given here.

sunsite.unc.edu:80/id/negativland/intprop.htm

The Fraunhofer Institute fur Integrierte Schaltungen has devised a technique for distribution of digital multimedia that manages copyright overhead. Multimedia Protection Protocol (MMP) can store and transmit additional information like International Standard Record Code ISRC, composer, artist, duration information, etc. MMP is especially able to protect compressed multimedia data like ISO/MPEG Layer-3 audio.

www.iis.fhg.de/departs/amm/layer3/mmp/

IUMA

IUMA is Web site that helps alternative musicians to market songs and videos. The help pages of IUMA are a good place to start if you need a guided tour or want to examine the lists of most frequently asked questions. Having trouble with a Web audio plug-in? Useful information is included here that may answer your questions.

www.iuma.com/IUMA/help/

Microtonal Music

John Starrett's Microtonal Music page is a gold mine of information. It provides links to notes on microtonal music, acoustics, psychoacoustics, instruments, software, musical examples, resources; shows respect to the pioneers of microtonal music; lists current microtonal composers; links you to the microtonal journals; and more.

www-math.cudenver.edu/~jstarret/microtone.html

Chas Stoddard has a wonderful Web site for those of you with GS synthesizers, GS compatible sound cards, or modules. The page begins with a well-written history and theory of microtonality and scale temperament. Zipped archives containing standard MIDI files containing SysEx messages for 75 different musical temperaments can be downloaded from this site. The files are empty (no music); they simply contain the SysEx string to evoke the musical temperament. Use the files as tuning templates. This is a great resource if your equipment is GS compatible.

www.interlog.com/~stilpaul/scug/help/temper.html

Multimedia File Formats for the Internet

This is a beginner's introduction to Internet file formats and is directed to the PC user. However, it is a well-organized site with lots of useful information even for the not-so-newbie.

rodent.lib.rochester.edu/multimed/tablef.htm

Pitch Palette by Justonic Tuning

Justonic Tuning, Inc., of Vancouver, British Columbia, has developed a MIDI-based software tool that allows *just intonation* principles to be applied to music composition and playback. Just intonation is a technique for creating pure musical intervals based on exact frequency divisions, rather than the approximations that are used for our traditional equal-tempered scale. The resulting music has a brightness and purity that must be heard to be appreciated. You can apply this sonic purity to your music by installing Pitch Palette from Justonics. A number of different MIDI synthesizers are on the list of supported devices and new ones are being added on a regular basis.

You may contact Justonics at:

E-mail: info@justonic.com
www.justonic.com

Speech Coding

Here is an information resource on speech production and perception, sampling, quantization, vocoding, waveform coding, and hybrid coding. It offers useful technical information if you work with speech on the computer or on the World Wide Web.

wwwdsp.ucd.ie/speech/tutorial/speech_coding/speech_tut.html

Stomper

Stomper is a drum sound synthesizer program for PC that's available for download from Zap's place. The free software is MusicWare; if you use it send him a copy of your music (for listening only; you retain all rights). It can save the drum sound samples you create as .wav files. Also check out his suggestions for putting music on the Web, using RealAudio, his interactive RADio Zap (Internet radio), and the other interesting things available here.

www.lysator.liu.se/~zap/main.html

Webmonkey

This is a Web site by developers for Web-site developers. This resource contains lots of clearly stated tips and insights on Web page construction. No matter what level of design you have presently mastered, there is undoubtedly something here that will stimulate your creative juices. A good site to bookmark, new information is always blossoming from this lively Web site.

www.webmonkey.com

WRN

The World Radio Network (WRN) is now providing international radio broadcasts on demand over the Internet. A variety of broadcasts from news to arts and culture are available here in RealAudio and StreamWorks format. Tune in to your short-wave alternative, Internet radio.

www.wrn.org/index1.html

Organizations

The following organizations may prove useful in your audio education.

Just Intonation Network

The official Web site of the Just Intonation Network provides a primer on Just Intonation, information on 1/1, the journal of the network, listings of upcoming events, and access to the Just Intonation store where recordings and books can be purchased. A good list of links to other tuning related Web sites is also here. Announcements of music events, releases of recorded or published material, or info on other alternate-tuning related sites for their hyperlink list can be e-mailed to: JINetwk@DNAI.COM.

More information can be obtained from:

www.dnai.com/~jinetwk/

MMA (MIDI Manufacturers Association)

Among the many roles this organization plays in furthering the standardization and acceptance of MIDI in the computer and music communities, the MMA has been active in promoting copyright protections for MIDI sequences and recorded MIDI music. The U.S. Copyright Office now accepts filings for copyrights on original music in Standard MIDI File (SMF) format.

Details can be obtained from the MMA site:

home.earthlink.net/~mma/smf_usco.htm

Listings

This section includes contact information for a number of the companies that appeared in this book.

Acadia Software
1300 Massachusetts Avenue, Suite 220
Boxborough, MA 01719-2203
508-264-4881
www.acadians.com

AudioWorks, Ltd.
P.O. Box 9099
London, N20 9BG UK
www.audioworks.com/s2m.htm

Justonic Tuning, Inc.
1650 Alberni Street
Vancouver, B.C. Canada V6G 1A6
604-682-3456
www.justonic.com

Metsan Corporation
P.O. Box 681272
Schaumburg, IL 60168-1272
847-301-8536

Musician's Friend
P.O. Box 4520
Medford, OR 97501
800-776-5173
www.musiciansfriend.com

Musitek
410 Bryant Circle, Suite K
Ojai, CA 93020
805-646-8051
Fax: 805-646-8099
www.musitek.com

Netscape Communications
Corporation
415-937-3777
E-mail: info@netscape.com
home.netscape.com

NoteWorthy ArtWare, Inc.
209 South Fuquay Avenue, Suite 120
Fuquay-Varina, NC 27526-2254
919-557-5794
Fax: 919-557-6157
www.ntworthy.com

PG Music, Inc.
111-266 Elmwood Avenue
Buffalo, NY 14222
250-475-2874
Fax: 250-658-8444

QCCS Productions
1350 Chambers Street
Eugene, OR 97402
503-345-8117

VocalTec
35 Industrial Parkway
Northvale, NJ 07647
201-768-9400
Fax: 201-768-8893
www.vocaltec.com

Voxware
305 College Road East
Princeton, NJ 08540
609-514-4100
Fax: 609-514-4101
www.voxware.com

Voyetra Technologies
5 Odell Plaza
Yonkers, NY 10701-1406
www.voyetra.com

Wildcat Canyon Software
1563 Solano Avenue, #264
Berkeley, CA 94707
510-527-5155
Fax: 510-527-8425

Zefiro Acoustics
P.O. Box 50021
Irvine, CA 92619-0021
www.zefiro.com

Push Technologies Companies

Astound Incorporated
www.astound.com
415-845-6200 (United States)
905-602-4000 (Canada only)

BackWeb Technologies
www.backweb.com
800-863-0100

Caravelle Inc.
www.caravelle.com
800-363-5292 (United States and Canada)
613-225-1172 (International calls)

Cyber Vista
www.cybervista.com
415-372-0800

FirstFloor, Inc.
www.firstfloor.com
800-639-6387
415-968-1101

inCommon, LLC
www.incommon.com
415-345-5432

inContext Corporation
www.incontext.com
416-922-0087

Individual, Inc.
www.individual.com
617-273-6000

Intermind Corporation
www.intermind.com
800-625-6150
206-812-8408

Lanacom, Inc.
www.lanacom.com
800-962-7499
416-490-7744

Marimba, Inc.
www.marimba.com
415-328-JAVA

Microsoft Corporation
www.microsoft.com
206-452-5400

Netscape Communications
Corporation
www.netscape.com
415-937-2555

PointCast, Inc.
www.pointcast.com
408-253-0894

Wayfarer Communications
www.wayfarer.com
800-300-8559
415-903-1720

JavaScript Example
Using Beatnik

JavaScript and Beatnik provide a potent combination for enhancing Web pages with sound. JavaScript excels at managing the interactivity, and Beatnik contributes the readily accessible sound elements through the Headspace audio engine and the LiveConnect-compatible interface (see Chapter 6 for details). The following script example takes the viewer on a journey into a cave on a lagoon. Music and sound effects are merged, and the audio content changes in response to viewer interaction, including movement from page to page and the proximity of the mouse pointer to areas defined in an image map. The script was developed by Paul Sebastien, Director of Production at Headspace. Paul is also a professional musician with a platinum record to his credit earned by his group, Psykosonik, which specializes in electronic musical fare.

 The HTML files, RMF music files (the native Beatnik format), and graphic images for Sebastien's Musical Cave Adventure on the Lagoon appear in the folder called *cave* on the CD-ROM included with this book. Both Macintosh and Windows versions of the Beatnik plug-in are also included on the CD-ROM.

One of the chief advantages of the approach used in this script is the simplicity of performing elaborate musical interactions with a minimum of scripting. The largest portion of code appears in the persist.html file and most of the code there is the JavaScript music-object, a pre-defined library of functions that provide a bridge between the JavaScript and HTML elements in the document and the capabilities of the Beatnik plug-in. Although in this case the music-object library was included within an HTML file accessed by the script, the library, represented by the file music-object.js, can also be accessed through an external JavaScript reference. The music-object.js file is also included on the CD-ROM for use by JavaScript developers.

By running the HTML files in the cave directory on the CD-ROM (starting with caveindex.html) and examining the JavaScript code, HTML, and music-object.js contents, you can gain a great deal of insight into how to accomplish impressive audio interactivity in your own Web development projects.

The MYST-like presentation guides the viewer into a cave as ambient music swells and changes in response to mouse actions and sound effects, such as lapping water and electronic effects, accompany the journey. The first scene, as shown in Figure D.1, appears at the outer entrance to the cave. As Paul cautions viewers, you should let all of the HTML elements load before clicking on anything in this scene. As the RMF files load and begin playing, you hear background music, and the final sound element to load is the lapping water sound effect. At this point, clicking in the middle of the cave entrance propels the script forward to the next scene.

A series of scenes unfolds, guiding by the user's clicks, until you reach the interactive musical tub, shown in Figure D.2. Moving the mouse pointer over the polygons in the tub and the two ears suspended in the background causes different musical pitches and effects to play. These functions are controlled by JavaScript actions tied to an image map. The <AREA> tag for the image is used to define hotspot regions, and those hot spots are ties to the appropriate JavaScript functions. The functions communicate directly with the Beatnik music object, which in turn drives the Beatnik plug-in. Actions such as playing notes and starting and stopping RMF file playback are done in this manner.

You can view the interactions that take place to initiate the music by viewing the caveap3.html file, later in this section. Note that the areas designated for playback

Figure D.1 Entrance to the interactive cave.

of sound consist of complex polygons composed of numerous points. Some type of graphic utility for creating the point coordinates for the image map would definitely be an asset because these complex shapes would be difficult to map out manually.

Study the following series of .html files to see how the basic ingredients of the musical cave were constructed and how the musical interactions were accomplished through the music-object library.

caveindex.html

```
<HTML>
<HEAD>
  <META NAME=" GENERATOR"  CONTENT=" Mozilla/4.0b3 [en] (Win95; I) [Netscape]" >
  <TITLE>Sebastien's Musical Cave Adventure on the Lagoon</TITLE>
</HEAD>
<FRAMESET ROWS=" *,0"  BORDER=0>
<FRAME SRC=" DOCS/cavestart.html"  NAME=" content"  MARGINHEIGHT=0 MARGINWIDTH=0
```

```
SCROLLING=NO</HEAD>
<FRAMESET ROWS=" *,0"  BORDER=0>
<FRAME SRC=" DOCS/cavestart.html"  NAME=" content"  MARGINHEIGHT=0 MARGINWIDTH=0
SC<BODY>



</BODY>
</HTML>
```

cavestart.html

```
<HTML>
<HEAD> <TITLE> Approach the Mysterious Cave! </TITLE> </HEAD><BODY BGCOLOR=BLACK
TEXT=CCCCCC LINK=FFFFCC VLINK=FFFFCC>
<P><BR>
<MAP NAME=" navMap" >
<AREA SHAPE=" circle"  COORDS=" 199,43,515,359"  HREF=" caveap2.html" >
</MAP>
```

Figure D.2. Playing the interactive tub.

```
<DIV ALIGN=CENTER>
<IMG SRC=" caveap1.jpg"  USEMAP=" #navMap" ><P><B>
'Mysterious Cave on the Lagoon'</B> <P> Graphics,Music,Interactivity (c) 1997
<A HREF=" mailto:pauls@headspace.com" > Paul Sebastien </A><BR>
</DIV>
</BODY>
</HTML>
```

caveap2.html

```
<HTML>
<HEAD> <TITLE> Keep going... </TITLE> </HEAD><BODY BGCOLOR=BLACK>
<P><BR>
<SCRIPT>
function gotoScene (sceneName) {
        window.location = sceneName;
}
</SCRIPT>
<MAP NAME=" navMap" >
        <AREA SHAPE=" rect"  COORDS=" 0,386,637,476"  HREF=" cavestart.html" >
        <AREA SHAPE=" rect"  COORDS=" 199,43,515,359"  HREF="
javascript:parent.persist_frame.water.stop (true);
parent.persist_frame.dripping.play (); gotoScene ('caveap3.html')" >
        </MAP>
<DIV ALIGN=CENTER>
<IMG SRC=" caveap2.jpg"  USEMAP=" #navMap" >
</DIV>
</BODY>
</HTML>
```

caveap3.html

```
<HTML>
<HEAD> <TITLE> Still closer... </TITLE> </HEAD><BODY BGCOLOR=BLACK>
<P><BR>
<SCRIPT>
function gotoScene (sceneName) {
   window.location = sceneName;
}
</SCRIPT>
```

```
<MAP NAME=" navMap" >
        <AREA SHAPE=" rect"  COORDS=" 0,386,637,476"  HREF="
↳javascript:parent.persist_frame.water.play (true);
parent.persist_frame.dripping.stop (true);
gotoScene ('caveap2.html')" >
        <AREA SHAPE=" rect"  COORDS=" 199,43,515,359"  HREF=" tubshot.html" >
        </MAP>
<DIV ALIGN=CENTER>
<IMG SRC=" caveap3.jpg"  USEMAP=" #navMap" >
</DIV>
</BODY>
</HTML>


<HEAD> <TITLE> Play Sebastien's Interactive Tub! </TITLE> </HEAD><BODY BGCOLOR="
↳BLACK"  ONLOAD=" parent.persist_frame.spooky.stop (true)" >
<SCRIPT>
function gotoScene (sceneName) {
    window.location = sceneName;
}
</SCRIPT>
<map name=" navMap" >
<area shape=" rect"  coords=" 0,386,637,476"  href="
↳javascript:parent.persist_frame.spooky.play (true);
parent.persist_frame.dripping.play (true);
parent.persist_frame.polebeat.stop (true);
gotoScene ('caveap3.html')" >
<area shape=" circle"  coords=" 229,119,50"  HREF=" javascript:with (parent
↳.persist_frame.earleft) {playNote (14,1,31,getNoteNumber ('A3'),100,900)}"
↳ONMOUSEOVER=" with (parent.persist_frame.earleft) {play ()}" >
<area shape=" circle"  coords=" 476,117,55"  HREF=" javascript:with (parent
↳.persist_frame.earright) {playNote (15,1,31,getNoteNumber ('C4'),100,900)}"
↳ONMOUSEOVER=" with (parent.persist_frame.earright) {play ()}" >
<area shape=" polygon"  coords="
↳282,163,288,211,285,232,281,240,280,253,272,267,275,275,314,280,339,271,331,
↳255,318,231,314,215,313,194,317,162,316,153,282,156,281,156,283,165,284,165,
↳284,165,282,165,282,162,282,162"  HREF=" javascript:with
```

```
↵(parent.persist_frame.polebeat) {if (isPlaying ()) {stop ()} else {play
↵(true)}}; parent.persist_frame.dripping.stop (true)" >
<area shape=" circle"  coords=" 269,310,24"  HREF=" javascript:with
↵(parent.persist_frame.notes) {playNote (13,1,10,getNoteNumber ('G4'),70,900)}"
↵ONMOUSEOVER=" with (parent.persist_frame.notes) {playNote
↵(13,0,97,getNoteNumber ('G3'),115,100)}"  ONMOUSEOUT=" with
↵(parent.persist_frame.notes) {setController (13,10,0)}" >
<area shape=" circle"  coords=" 190,295,21"  HREF=" javascript:with
↵(parent.persist_frame.notes) {playNote (14,1,96,getNoteNumber ('A4'),70,900)}"
↵ONMOUSEOVER=" with (parent.persist_frame.notes) {playNote
↵(14,0,97,getNoteNumber ('A3'),115,100)}"  ONMOUSEOUT=" with
↵(parent.persist_frame.notes) {setController (14,10,20)}" >
<area shape=" circle"  coords=" 174,255,20"  HREF=" javascript:with
↵(parent.persist_frame.notes) {playNote (15,1,10,getNoteNumber ('C4'),70,900)}"
↵ONMOUSEOVER=" with (parent.persist_frame.notes) {playNote
↵(15,0,97,getNoteNumber ('C4'),115,100)}"  ONMOUSEOUT=" with
↵(parent.persist_frame.notes) {setController (15,10,40)}" >
<area shape=" circle"  coords=" 250,240,19"  HREF=" javascript:with
↵(parent.persist_frame.notes) {playNote (13,1,96,getNoteNumber ('B4'),70,900)}"
↵ONMOUSEOVER=" with (parent.persist_frame.notes) {playNote
↵(13,0,97,getNoteNumber ('E4'),115,100)}"  ONMOUSEOUT=" with
↵(parent.persist_frame.notes) {setController (13,10,60)}" >
<area shape=" circle"  coords=" 400,238,19"  HREF=" javascript:with
↵(parent.persist_frame.notes) {playNote (14,1,10,getNoteNumber ('G4'),70,900)}"
↵ONMOUSEOVER=" with (parent.persist_frame.notes) {playNote
↵(14,0,97,getNoteNumber ('G4'),115,100)}"  ONMOUSEOUT=" with
↵(parent.persist_frame.notes) {setController (14,10,85)}" >
<area shape=" circle"  coords=" 417,276,20"  HREF=" javascript:with
↵(parent.persist_frame.notes) {playNote (15,1,96,getNoteNumber ('C5'),70,900)}"
↵ONMOUSEOVER=" with (parent.persist_frame.notes) {playNote
↵(15,0,97,getNoteNumber ('A4'),115,100)}"  ONMOUSEOUT=" with
↵(parent.persist_frame.notes) {setController (15,10,105)}" >
<area shape=" circle"  coords=" 372,304,22"  HREF=" javascript:with
↵(parent.persist_frame.notes) {playNote (16,1,10,getNoteNumber ('C5'),70,900)}"
↵ONMOUSEOVER=" with (parent.persist_frame.notes) {playNote
↵(16,0,97,getNoteNumber ('C5'),115,100)}"  ONMOUSEOUT=" with
↵(parent.persist_frame.notes) {setController (16,10,127)}" >
```

```
<area shape=" polygon"  coords="
⌐123,256,86,271,67,284,57,300,54,315,67,327,98,342,131,353,151,356,187,362,218,
⌐366,247,366,251,352,248,329,204,324,164,318,143,309,141,293,148,280,148,268,
⌐142,255,130,253"  HREF=" javascript:with (parent.persist_frame.waterleft) {play
⌐()}"  ONMOUSEOVER=" with (parent.persist_frame.waterleft) {play ()}" >
<area shape=" polygon"  coords="
⌐345,369,387,367,427,360,450,356,488,348,512,339,535,327,552,313,551,285,534,
⌐273,512,261,484,253,466,247,448,244,440,251,448,274,446,291,438,296,421,310,
⌐407,322,375,333,339,347,335,358"  HREF=" javascript:with
⌐(parent.persist_frame.waterright) {play ()}"  ONMOUSEOVER=" with
⌐(parent.persist_frame.waterright) {play ()}" >
<area shape=" polygon"  coords="
⌐262,11,295,98,312,133,335,171,385,196,432,198,420,152,411,92,455,49,511,42,546,
⌐86,552,156,523,194,519,221,561,243,600,250,630,230,636,59,634,15,612,7"  HREF="
⌐javascript:with (parent.persist_frame.yeah) {play ()}" >
</map>
<DIV ALIGN=" CENTER" >
<IMG SRC=" tubshot.jpg"  USEMAP=" #navMap" >
</DIV>
</BODY>
</HTML>
```

persist.html

```
<HTML>
<HEAD> <TITLE> persist </TITLE> </HEAD><BODY BGCOLOR=BLACK>
<!--****************************** FIXED CODE ******************************-->
<SCRIPT LANGUAGE=JavaScript>
function mo_play (param1,param2) {
    if (this.ready) {
        clearTimeout (this.fadeTimeout);
        if ((typeof (param1) == "boolean"  || typeof (param1) == "number" ) &&
⌐typeof (param2) == "string" ) {
            document [this.pluginName].play (param1,param2);
        } else if (typeof (param1) == "string"  || typeof (param1) == "boolean"
⌐|| typeof (param1) == "number" ) {
            document [this.pluginName].play (param1);
        } else {
            document [this.pluginName].play ();
```

```
        }
    }
}

function mo_playGroovoid (param1,param2) {
    this.play (param1," groovoid://"  + param2);
}

function mo_stop (fade) {
    with (this) {
        if (ready) {
            clearTimeout (fadeTimeout);
            if (typeof (fade) != "boolean" ) {
                document [pluginName].stop ();
            } else {
                document [pluginName].stop (fade);
            }
        }
    }
}

function mo_pauseAtZero () {
    with (this) {
        if (ready) {
            if (getVolume () == 0) {
                pause ();
                clearTimeout (fadeTimeout);
            } else {
                pauseTimeout = setTimeout (name + '.pauseAtZero ()',500);
            }
        }
    }
}

function mo_pause (fade) {
    with (this) {
        if (ready) {
```

```
            if (typeof (fade) != "boolean" ) {
                clearTimeout (fadeTimeout);
                document [pluginName].pause ();
            } else if (fade) {
                fadeFromTo (getVolume (),0);
                pauseAtZero ();
            } else {
                clearTimeout (fadeTimeout);
                document [pluginName].pause ();
            }
        }
    }
}

function mo_setLoop (state) {
    if (this.ready) {document [this.pluginName].setLoop (state)}
}

function mo_setAutostart (state) {
    if (this.ready) {document [this.pluginName].setAutostart (state)}
}

function mo_fadeTo (toValue) {
    if (this.ready) {document [this.pluginName].fade_to (toValue)}
}

function mo_fadeFromTo (fromValue,toValue) {
    if (this.ready) {document [this.pluginName].fade_from_to
(fromValue,toValue)}
}

function mo_setReady () {
    with (this) {
        if (document [pluginName] != null) {
            ready = true;
        } else {
            setTimeout (name + '.setReady ()',500);
```

```
            }
        }
}

function mo_setMonophonic (channelNo,state) {
    with (this) {
        if (channelNo == 0) {
            for (var channelCount = 1; channelCount <= 16; channelCount++) {
                monophonic [channelCount-1] = state;
            }
        } else {
            monophonic [channelNo-1] = state;
        }
    }
}

function mo_getMonophonic (channelNo) {
    with (this) {
        if (channelNo >= 1 && channelNo <= 16) {
            return monophonic [channelNo-1];
        } else {
            return false;
        }
    }
}

function mo_noteOn (channelNo,param2,param3,param4,param5) {
    with (this) {
        if (ready) {
            if (monophonic [channelNo-1]) {
                noteOff (channelNo,notesOn [channelNo],127);
            }
            if (param4 != null && param5 != null) {
                notesOn [channelNo] = param4;
                document [pluginName].noteOn
 (channelNo,param2,param3,param4,param5);
            } else {
```

```
                    notesOn [channelNo] = param2;
                    document [pluginName].noteOn (channelNo,param2,param3);
                }
            }
        }
    }


    function mo_noteOff (channelNo,noteNo) {
        with (this) {
            if (ready) {
                notesOn [channelNo] = 0;
                document [pluginName].noteOff (channelNo,noteNo,127)
            }
        }
    }


    function mo_playNote (channelNo,param2,param3,param4,param5,param6) {
        with (this) {
            if (ready) {
                if (monophonic [channelNo-1]) {
                    noteOff (channelNo,notesOn [channelNo],127);
                }
                if (param5 != null & param6 != null) {
                    notesOn [channelNo] = param4;
                    setProgram (channelNo,param2,param3);
                    document [this.pluginName].playNote
(channelNo,param4,param5,param6);
                } else {
                    notesOn [channelNo] = param2;
                    document [this.pluginName].playNote
(channelNo,param2,param3,param4);
                }
            }
        }
    }


    function mo_playSample (sampleName,pan,volume) {
```

```
    if (this.ready) {document [this.pluginName].playSample
↳(sampleName,pan,volume)}
}

function mo_setGlobalMute (muteState) {
    if (this.ready) {document [this.pluginName].setGlobalMute (muteState)}
}

function mo_setPanelDisplay (displayType) {
    if (this.ready) {document [this.pluginName].setPanelDisplay (displayType)}
}

function mo_setPanelMode (panelMode) {
    if (this.ready) {document [this.pluginName].setPanelMode (displayMode)}
}

function mo_setVolume (volume) {
    if (this.ready) {document [this.pluginName].setVolume (volume)}
}

function mo_setTranspose (transpose) {
    if (this.ready) {document [this.pluginName].setTranspose (transpose)}
}

function mo_setTempo (tempo) {
    if (this.ready) {document [this.pluginName].setTempo (tempo)}
}

function mo_setReverbType (reverbType) {
    if (this.ready) {document [this.pluginName].setReverbType (reverbType)}
}

function mo_setController (channelNo,controllerNo,controllerValue) {
    if (this.ready) {document [this.pluginName].setController
↳(channelNo,controllerNo,controllerValue)}
}
```

```
function mo_setProgram (channelNo,param2,param3) {
    if (this.ready) {
        with (this) {
            if (param3 != null) {
                document [this.pluginName].setProgram (channelNo,param2,
param3);
            } else {
                document [this.pluginName].setProgram (channelNo,param2);
            }
        }
    }
}

function mo_setTrackMute (trackNo,state) {
    if (this.ready) {document [this.pluginName].setTrackMute (trackNo,state)}
}

function mo_setChannelMute (channelNo,state) {
    if (this.ready) {document [this.pluginName].setChannelMute
(channelNo,state)}
}

function mo_setTrackSolo (trackNo,state) {
    if (this.ready) {document [this.pluginName].setTrackSolo (trackNo,state)}
}

function mo_setChannelSolo (channelNo,state) {
    if (this.ready) {document [this.pluginName].setChannelSolo
(channelNo,state)}
}

function mo_getPanelDisplay () {
    if (this.ready) {return document [this.pluginName].getPanelDisplay ()} else
{return "" }
}

function mo_getPanelMode (panelMode) {
```

```
      if (this.ready) {return document [this.pluginName].getPanelMode ()} else
⌐{return "" }
}

function mo_getVolume () {
      if (this.ready) {return document [this.pluginName].GetVolume ()} else
⌐{return 100}
}

function mo_getAutostart () {
      if (this.ready) {return document [this.pluginName].getAutostart ()} else
⌐{return false}
}

function mo_getLoop () {
      if (this.ready) {return document [this.pluginName].getLoop ()} else {return
⌐false}
}

function mo_getReverbType () {
      if (this.ready) {return document [this.pluginName].getReverbType ()} else
⌐{return 0}
}

function mo_getTempo () {
      if (this.ready) {return document [this.pluginName].getTempo ()} else {return
⌐120}
}

function mo_getTranspose () {
      if (this.ready) {return document [this.pluginName].getTranspose ()} else
⌐{return 0}
}

function mo_getController (channelNo,controllerNo) {
      if (this.ready) {return document [this.pluginName].getController
⌐(channelNo,controllerNo)} else {return 0}
```

```
}

function mo_getProgram (channelNo) {
    if (this.ready) {return document [this.pluginName].getProgram (channelNo)}
    else {return 0}
}

function mo_getTrackMute (trackNo) {
    if (this.ready) {return document [this.pluginName].getTrackMute (trackNo)}
    else {return false}
}

function mo_getChannelMute (channelNo) {
    if (this.ready) {return document [this.pluginName].getChannelMute
    (channelNo)} else {return false}
}

function mo_getTrackSolo (trackNo) {
    if (this.ready) {return document [this.pluginName].getTrackSolo (trackNo)}
    else {return false}
}

function mo_getChannelSolo (channelNo) {
    if (this.ready) {return document [this.pluginName].getChannelSolo
    (channelNo)} else {return false}
}

function mo_isPaused () {
    if (this.ready) {return document [this.pluginName].IsPaused ()} else {return
    false}
}

function mo_isPlaying () {
    if (this.ready) {return document [this.pluginName].IsPlaying ()} else
    {return false}
}
```

```javascript
function mo_isReady () {
    return this.ready;
}

function mo_getNoteNumber (noteName) {
    noteOffset = this.noteNumbers [noteName.substring (0,1).toLowerCase ()];
    if (noteOffset == null) {
        return 0;
    } else {
        sharpFlatOffset = 0;
        sharpFlatPos = noteName.indexOf ('b',1);
        if (sharpFlatPos == -1) {
            sharpFlatPos = noteName.indexOf ('#',1);
            if (sharpFlatPos == -1) {
                sharpFlatPos = 0;
            } else {
                sharpFlatOffset = 1;
            }
        } else {
            sharpFlatOffset = -1;
        }
        octaveNo = noteName.substring (sharpFlatPos+1,noteName.length) - 0;
        return 12 + octaveNo * 12 + noteOffset + sharpFlatOffset;
    }
}

function mo_getNoteName (noteNumber) {
    return this.noteNames [noteNumber % 12] + (Math.floor (noteNumber / 12) -
1) + "" ;
}

function mo_getVersion () {
    return ('1.1');
}

function mo_getPlatform () {
    return (Navigator.userAgent);
```

```
}

function musicObject (name) {
    this.fadeTimeout = setTimeout ('//',0);
    this.name = name;
    this.pluginName = name + "Plugin" ;
    this.ready = false;

    // *********** reflected plug-in functions ***********
    this.play = mo_play;
    this.playGroovoid = mo_playGroovoid;
    this.stop = mo_stop;

        //**WORKAROUND** stop (true) overload uses a workaround
    this.pause = mo_pause;
        //**EXTENDED** pause (true) overload allows a fade until pause
    this.setLoop = mo_setLoop;
    this.fadeTo = mo_fadeTo;
    this.fade_to = mo_fadeTo;
        //**DUPLICATED** for LiveAudio compatibility
    this.fadeFromTo = mo_fadeFromTo;
    this.fade_from_to = mo_fadeFromTo;
        //**DUPLICATED** for LiveAudio compatibility
    this.setAutostart = mo_setAutostart;
    this.playNote = mo_playNote;
    this.noteOn = mo_noteOn;
    this.noteOff = mo_noteOff;
    this.playSample = mo_playSample;
    this.setPanelDisplay = mo_setPanelDisplay;
    this.setPanelMode = mo_setPanelMode;
    this.setGlobalMute = mo_setGlobalMute;
    this.setVolume = mo_setVolume;
    this.setTranspose = mo_setTranspose;
    this.setController = mo_setController;
    this.setProgram = mo_setProgram;
        //**EXTENDED** new overloaded version which accepts channelNo, bankNo,
and prgramNo parameters
```

```
this.setTempo = mo_setTempo;
this.setReverbType = mo_setReverbType;
this.setTrackMute = mo_setTrackMute;
this.setChannelMute = mo_setChannelMute;
this.setTrackSolo = mo_setTrackSolo;
this.setChannelSolo = mo_setChannelSolo;
this.getPanelDisplay = mo_getPanelDisplay;
this.getPanelMode = mo_getPanelMode;
this.getVolume = mo_getVolume;
this.GetVolume = mo_getVolume;
    //**DUPLICATED** for LiveAudio compatibility
this.getAutostart = mo_getAutostart;
this.getLoop = mo_getLoop;
this.getReverbType = mo_getReverbType;
this.getTempo = mo_getTempo;
this.getTranspose = mo_getTranspose;
this.getController = mo_getController;
this.getProgram = mo_getProgram;
this.getTrackMute = mo_getTrackMute;
this.getChannelMute = mo_getChannelMute;
this.getTrackSolo = mo_getTrackSolo;
this.getChannelSolo = mo_getChannelSolo;
this.isPaused = mo_isPaused;
this.IsPaused = mo_isPaused;
    //**DUPLICATED** for LiveAudio compatibility
this.isPlaying = mo_isPlaying;
this.IsPlaying = mo_isPlaying;
    //**DUPLICATED** for LiveAudio compatibility
this.isReady = mo_isReady;
this.IsReady = mo_isReady;
    //**DUPLICATED** for LiveAudio compatibility

// ******** extended authoring API functions *********
this.setReady = mo_setReady;
this.setMonophonic = mo_setMonophonic;
this.getMonophonic = mo_getMonophonic;
this.playNotePlus = mo_playNote;
```

```
      this.pauseAtZero = mo_pauseAtZero;
      this.getNoteNumber = mo_getNoteNumber;
      this.getNoteName = mo_getNoteName;
      this.getVersion = mo_getVersion;
      this.getPlatform = mo_getPlatform;

      // ****************************************************
      this.monophonic = new Array
(false,false,false,false,false,false,false,false,false,false,false,false,false,
⌇false,false);
      this.notesOn = new Array (0,0,0,0,0,0,0,0,0,0,0,0,0,0,0,0);
      this.noteNumbers = new Array ();
      this.noteNumbers ['c'] = 0;
      this.noteNumbers ['d'] = 2;
      this.noteNumbers ['e'] = 4;
      this.noteNumbers ['f'] = 5;
      this.noteNumbers ['g'] = 7;
      this.noteNumbers ['a'] = 9;
      this.noteNumbers ['b'] = 11;

      this.noteNames = new Array ("C" ," C#" ," D" ," D#" ," E" ," F" ," F#" ,
⌇" G" ," G#" ," A" ," A#" ," B" );
}

//---------------------------------------------------------------------------

//                              SONIFICATION LIBRARY CODE

//---------------------------------------------------------------------------

function xFrame (functionName,functionParameters) {
    if (top.persist_frame != null) {
        if (top.persist_frame [functionName] != null) {
            eval ('top.persist_frame.' + functionName + '(' +
⌇functionParameters + ')');
        }
    }
```

```
}

function randomFromList (prefix,suffix) {
    total_items = randomFromList.arguments.length - 1;
    if (total_items == 0) {
        return prefix + suffix;
    } else {
        with (Math) {random_itemno = round (random () * (total_items - 1)) + 1}
        return prefix + randomFromList.arguments [random_itemno] + suffix;
    }
}

</SCRIPT>
<SCRIPT LANGUAGE=JavaScript><!-- //

polebeat = new musicObject ("polebeat" );
waterleft = new musicObject ("waterleft" );
waterright = new musicObject ("waterright" );
notes = new musicObject ("notes" );
earleft = new musicObject ("earleft" );
earright = new musicObject ("earright" );
yeah = new musicObject ("yeah" );
water = new musicObject ("water" );
dripping = new musicObject ("dripping" );
spooky = new musicObject ("spooky" );

// --></SCRIPT>

<EMBED SRC=" polebeat02.rmf"  TYPE=" audio/rmf"  PLUGINSPAGE="
http://www.headspace.com/beatnik/plug-in/index.html"  HIDDEN WIDTH=2 HEIGHT=2
AUTOSTART=FALSE LOOP=TRUE VOLUME=100 NAME=" polebeatPlugin"  ONREADY="
polebeat.setReady ()" >
<EMBED SRC=" water-left03.rmf"  TYPE=" audio/rmf"  PLUGINSPAGE="
http://www.headspace.com/beatnik/plug-in/index.html"  HIDDEN WIDTH=2 HEIGHT=2
AUTOSTART=FALSE LOOP=FALSE VOLUME=72 NAME=" waterleftPlugin"  ONREADY="
waterleft.setReady ()" >
<EMBED SRC=" water-right03.rmf"  TYPE=" audio/rmf"  PLUGINSPAGE="
http://www.headspace.com/beatnik/plug-in/index.html"  HIDDEN WIDTH=2 HEIGHT=2
```

```
⌐AUTOSTART=FALSE LOOP=FALSE VOLUME=72 NAME=" waterrightPlugin"  ONREADY="
⌐waterright.setReady ()" >
<EMBED SRC=" stub.rmf"  TYPE=" audio/rmf"  PLUGINSPAGE="
⌐http://www.headspace.com/beatnik/plug-in/index.html"  HIDDEN WIDTH=2 HEIGHT=2
⌐AUTOSTART=FALSE LOOP=FALSE VOLUME=100 NAME=" notesPlugin"  ONREADY="
⌐notes.setReady ()" >
<EMBED SRC=" left-ear04.rmf"  TYPE=" audio/rmf"  PLUGINSPAGE="
⌐http://www.headspace.com/beatnik/plug-in/index.html"  HIDDEN WIDTH=2 HEIGHT=2
⌐AUTOSTART=FALSE LOOP=FALSE VOLUME=80 NAME=" earleftPlugin"  ONREADY="
⌐earleft.setReady ()" >
<EMBED SRC=" right-ear04.rmf"  TYPE=" audio/rmf"  PLUGINSPAGE="
⌐http://www.headspace.com/beatnik/plug-in/index.html"  HIDDEN WIDTH=2 HEIGHT=2
⌐AUTOSTART=FALSE LOOP=FALSE VOLUME=80 NAME=" earrightPlugin"  ONREADY="
⌐earright.setReady ()" >
<EMBED SRC=" newyeah-8.wav"  TYPE=" audio/wav"  PLUGINSPAGE="
⌐http://www.headspace.com/beatnik/plug-in/index.html"  HIDDEN WIDTH=2 HEIGHT=2
⌐AUTOSTART=FALSE LOOP=FALSE VOLUME=25 NAME=" yeahPlugin"  ONREADY="
⌐yeah.setReady ()" >
<EMBED SRC=" water.rmf"  TYPE=" audio/rmf"  PLUGINSPAGE="
⌐http://www.headspace.com/beatnik/plug-in/index.html"  HIDDEN WIDTH=2 HEIGHT=2
⌐AUTOSTART=TRUE LOOP=TRUE VOLUME=100"  NAME=" waterPlugin"  ONREADY="
⌐water.setReady ()" >
<EMBED SRC=" drips.rmf"  TYPE=" audio/rmf"  PLUGINSPAGE="
⌐http://www.headspace.com/beatnik/plug-in/index.html"  HIDDEN WIDTH=2 HEIGHT=2
⌐AUTOSTART=FALSE LOOP=TRUE VOLUME=100"  NAME=" drippingPlugin"  ONREADY="
⌐dripping.setReady ()" >
<EMBED SRC=" spookytrack.rmf"  TYPE=" audio/rmf"  PLUGINSPAGE="
⌐http://www.headspace.com/beatnik/plug-in/index.html"  HIDDEN WIDTH=2 HEIGHT=2
⌐AUTOSTART=TRUE LOOP=TRUE VOLUME=100"  NAME=" spookyPlugin"  ONREADY="
⌐spooky.setReady ()" >
</BODY>
</HTML>
```

Beatnik's Future

As this simple introduction to the power of Beatnik might suggest, there is a wealth of understated power in this plug-in that can be tapped by savvy Web designers interested in maximizing their musical output in the most efficient way. With Sun's licensing of the Headspace audio engine for the next iteration of Java, this audio technology is sure to enjoy a long and prosperous future.

In the meantime, JavaScript provides the best way to get at the low-level components of the music engine. A wide variety of actions are supported, such as playing individual notes through MIDI, defining original sound samples for MIDI playback, transposing a musical passage to a different key, choosing files for playback, and so on. You could also design a technique for random note generation within the boundaries of JavaScript. Using JavaScript, you can attach musical or sonic results to most of the activities associated with an HTML document, such as clicking a link or submitting a form. Audio feedback can provide important cues for page viewers.

Headspace is working on more elegant means for handling the use of custom samples played through the audio engine, but at the moment an approach they refer to as the "pseudo-bank" works nicely. This technique allows an RMF file containing sound samples (of your choice—anything from short mouse clicks and beeps to nature sounds like the crash of thunder) that are designed to be used on a particular Web site. You can then load the file on the Web page as if you were playing the file, which makes the samples available for playback through JavaScript. Once the pseudo-bank is present, you can use the **playNote** command to play the samples using mouseOver of mouseDown actions. Optionally, you could use these extended sounds as part of another MIDI file or RMF file. If you use this approach in a frameset, you can have the sound playback persist across an entire Web site. This allows you to construct ambient background music or sound effects (wind and waves, for example) to enhance the visitor's experience while touring the site.

The Beatnik player also supports nine different types of MOD files. MOD files have percolated about the Web in various formats for some time and Beatnik provides a solid platform for playback, which may help increase the popularity of this format. The RMF format in many ways supplants the need for using MOD (since it can accomplish many of the same musical techniques in a less hackish manner), but some very interesting musical works exist already in MOD format, so having this support in the audio engine is a plus.

We asked Paul Sebastien what advice he would give developers interested in using Beatnik to its best potential. He replied that a basic background in either JavaScript programming or another scripting language is an important prerequisite. While JavaScript is not as intuitive as Lingo (Macromedia Director's scripting language), the learning curve is not as steep as full programming languages, such as C++ or Java. If you can master JavaScript and learn the structures, it will be much easier to work with Beatnik and to construct useful scripts.

Authoring tools are under development that will provide access to Beatnik's audio functions at a much higher level, so you won't need to execute the low-level functions manually under JavaScript control. The future of Beatnik looks bright and this suggests a bright future for audio on the Internet as well.

CD-ROM Contents

This appendix describes the contents of the CD-ROM and the installation procedure for each item. You can find additional details about the software within the individual folders on the CD-ROM; most packages include a readme file with technical details about the software and its use.

Equipping Your PC for Digital Audio

Most PC systems sold today include some form of digital audio sound processing in the form of a sound board or integrated circuit on the system's motherboard. You'll need sound capabilities in your system to run many of the audio applications provided on the CD-ROM. Those applications that utilize MIDI playback require a sound synthesizer accessible to your system, either an external tone generator or keyboard synthesizer. Internal sound synthesizer support can be provided by a MIDI wavetable or FM synthesis included on your sound board.

Most Macintosh users already have the basic sound support built into their system; consult the individual details of each software package for specific requirements.

Your browser also contains some built-in audio capabilities, whether you're using Internet Explorer or Netscape Navigator. You can extend the capabilities of your browser with various plug-ins and ActiveX components, as discussed throughout this book. Two of the most important Web audio tools recently developed—the Headspace Beatnik plug-in and the Liquid MusicPlayer from Liquid Audio—are included on the CD-ROM. By installing these components, you can access files from the Web that have been designed for these players.

PC Trial Version Software

The following sections briefly describe each of the software items included on the CD-ROM specifically designed for PC users. We suspect that many PC users will also have Macs running the MacOS at home or in the office, so be sure to investigate the software packages and demos included on the Macintosh portion of the CD-ROM as well.

Acadia Software Infuse

Infuse, as discussed in Chapter 6, is a well-designed JavaScript and HTML editor. Newcomers to JavaScript will appreciate the extensive online documentation and intuitive organization of the scripting tools. JavaScript pros will enjoy the time-saving features and streamlined interface.

To run the Windows95 trial version of Infuse, locate the **infuse** folder inside the **acadia** folder on the CD-ROM. Double-click the **Setup** icon and follow the onscreen instructions. The trial version provides full access to all program features and it is operable for 30 days following the installation.

 For more information about Acadia Software products, point your browser to:

> **www.acadians.com**

Aimtech Jamba

Jamba lets you construct Java applets without programming. As covered in Chapter 6, you can easily add audio-enhanced applets to your Web pages using Jamba. If you're not a programmer and you want to learn Java, this is an easy way to get started.

To run the Windows95 trial version of Jamba, locate the **jamba** folder inside the **aimtech** folder on the CD-ROM. Double-click the **Jambatrl** icon and follow the onscreen instructions. A readme file in the **jamba** folder provides additional information about the trial version and its use. The trial version is fully functional for 30 days or 100 uses.

Visit **www.aimtech.com** for additional information.

Cakewalk Pro Audio 6.0

Cakewalk Pro Audio 6.0, from Cakewalk Music Software, provides integrated multitrack MIDI and digital audio recording for Windows95 users. This professional-grade software handles every aspect of music creation and editing directly from the desktop.

To install the demonstration version of Pro Audio, double-click the **Setup** icon inside the **Cakewalk** folder. Follow the onscreen instructions to complete the installation. The demonstration version of Cakewalk Pro Audio lets you record, edit, and play back music on the PC, but you cannot print or save your music.

For more information about digital audio applications and tools, point your browser to:

www.cakewalk.com

Headspace Beatnik plug-in

Headspace, Inc. has introduced a set of musical tools and an audio engine that promises to revolutionize the use of sound on the Web. The Beatnik browser plug-in includes its own sound synthesizer so that MIDI files played back through it on any platform will sound equivalent, maintaining high quality regardless of the type of sound synthesizer included in the computer. The Beatnik plug-in uses software synthesis; in other words, your computer's processor does much of the work to converting the music data into sound. This requires a fairly fast processor, which typically requires a Pentium-level computer. The plug-in provided is for Windows95. Beatnik, once installed, can play back MIDI, WAV, RMF, and MOD file types. You can create your own RMF files using the Headspace Beatnik editor, available through the Headspace Web site. To install the Beatnik plug-in, you must be using Netscape Navigator version 3.0 or later. The Microsoft Internet Explorer browser will not work with this plug-in since it does not support Netscape's LiveConnect environment.

Double-click the **Beatnik** icon in the **headspac** folder on the CD-ROM. Follow the instructions that appear onscreen to complete the installation. The **library** folder inside the **headspac** folder contains the music object library, constructed in JavaScript, which serves as a dynamic interface to the Beatnik audio engine functions. The music-object.js file can be embedded in your own scripts or accessed externally through JavaScript. For an example of the Beatnik audio engine in action, once you have installed the Beatnik plug-in, open the caveindex.html file in the **cave** folder. Let the entire first page load before clicking anything on the page. The text content of these HTML files appears in *Appendix D* of this book.

 More information on Headspace RMF file creation and samples of music and sound effects can be obtained by visiting:

www.headspace.com

Hohner-Midia Samplitude Studio

Samplitude Studio, from Hohner-Midia, is a high-caliber multitrack recorder and digital sound processing application. It turns a desktop computer and sound board into a sophisticated recording studio capable of producing professional quality sound output. It handles an unlimited number of tracks—up to the capacity of your computer to process the output.

To install Samplitude Studio, open the **sampstud** folder and double-click the **Setup** icon. Follow the instructions that appear onscreen to complete the installation. The demonstration version of Samplitude Studio allows only 1 minute of recording and the Save option is disabled. Total effects processing is also limited to less than 1 minute.

 More information about other Hohner-Midia digital audio products can be obtained from their Web site at:

www.hohnermidia.com

Liquid MusicPlayer and Liquifier Pro

The Liquid MusicPlayer, from Liquid Audio, Inc., provides access to files that have been encoded using the Liquid Audio format. This enhanced version of the Dolby Digital encoding scheme offers some of the cleanest compressed music available anywhere on the Web. The Liquid Audio approach also supports a full commerce model for the transfer, sale, and exchange of music files across the Internet. Files are watermarked with copyright information for the protection of musicians and publishers. The encoded file format also includes data about the artist, recording details, copyright information, and the equivalent to digital liner notes. Liquid Audio files have become popular for previewing music clips prior to purchase on sites such as IUMA and Music Blvd.

To install the Liquid MusicPlayer, double-click the **lmp-setup** icon in the **liqaudio** folder on the CD-ROM. You can also install the Liquifier Pro evaluation software by double-clicking the icon titled **evlq120D** in the same folder. The Liquifier Pro software guides you through the process of creating Liquid Audio files that can be played back through the Liquid MusicPlayer and distributed on the Web. The evaluation software limits the length of a sound file that can be processed and supports only 14.4Kbps and 28.8Kbps compression options. Information on how to use Liquifier Pro appears in Chapter 7.

 Once you've installed the Liquid MusicPlayer, you can sample a number of songs encoded for playback in this format by visiting the Liquid Audio Web site at:

> www.liquidaudio.com

Metsan MidiText

MidiText, from Metsan Corporation, is a DOS-based tool that allows the full range of MIDI capabilities to be accessed through text commands. The program requires an MPU-401 interface for MIDI playback, a common feature on many MIDI-equipped sound boards and external synthesizer units. Optionally, you can enable MPU-401 emulation on your sound board or save the output from the MidiText demo to a standard MIDI file, where it can be played through any MIDI application or through your browser.

The MidiText demo is located in the **metsan** folder on the CD-ROM, including several demo files that were created to show the capabilities of this program. For instructions on program use, refer to the Read file located in the folder. For more information about Metsan MidiText, you can contact: Metsan Corporation, P.O. Box 681272, Schaumburg, Illinois 60168. Their telephone number is: (847) 301-8536.

Musicator Audio

Musicator Audio is another bright star in the digital audio revolution—a well-designed music composition tool that simplifies sequencing, scoring, and digital audio sound recording and processing. The demo version included on the CD-ROM is designed for Windows95 use.

To install Musicator Audio, open the **musicato** folder and run the program musauddm.exe. Follow the onscreen instructions to complete the installation. The demonstration version of this product has limited print and save capabilities. The Readme file in the **musicator** folder includes additional information about the product.

 For more information on the latest version of Musicator Audio, visit:

www.musicator.com

Musitek MIDIscan v2.5

MIDIscan, from Musitek, is a program that converts scanned sheet music into MIDI files. As discussed in Chapter 2, MIDIscan can handle multiple staves and adapts itself well to a wide variety of printed music content. The program includes a simple, streamlined sequencer that lets you playback and process the MIDI files generated. To install MIDIscan, double-click the **MIDIscan** icon in the **musitek** folder and follow the onscreen instructions to complete the installation. The demonstration version of MIDIscan allows 10 complete MIDI conversion sequences. Playback is limited to two channels.

 Further information about Musitek products can be obtained from their Web site:

www.musitek.com

Samples and Clips

The samples folder contains an assortment of sound effects and short song sequences, many of them incorporating interesting digital audio effects, merging the real world with the digital world. The short sound effects clips are available for your use, to be used in any multimedia projects or as samples in a MIDI application. The song files (mankey.wav, gdtir&r.wav, boiler.wav, and frogie.wav) are copyrighted (1997) by Jordan Hemphill. Play them, process them using the sound applications included on the CD-ROM, and enjoy them, but remember that they are protected by copyright. Some brief insights into the WAV file collection follow.

The song file, frogie.wav, is a short novelty piece that includes samples of frog croaks that are paste mixed onto a stereo recording of guitar and vocal.

The song file gdtir&r.wav, is a stereo guitar and vocal piece with electronically generated samples that are paste mixed between phrases. Samples of taxi horns and bicycle bells from India are used. A section of vocal wave is reversed and repeated three times. Also, a short processed sample of tabla is included near the end of the piece.

The song file, mankey.wav, is a stereo recording that features acoustic guitar and vocal. Percussive samples from ceramic bottles and other objects are paste mixed into the recording. One instrument passage was segmented at zero crossings and randomly rearranged with some segments reversed.

The song file, boiler.wav, is a stereo recording of acoustic guitar and vocal. Steam sound samples were made from a cappuccino steamer. A sample of a woodpecker is used as a drum roll. The shattering sound near the end is the sound of a piece of dry cedar being split with an axe. Also, a Hawaiian guitar sample and sounds of squeaky water faucets are mixed into the piece.

The shorter WAV files in this folder can usually be recognized by their sound, maybe with a hint from the filename. Feel free to use these in any of your own works.

 For more examples of audio experimentation and tinkering, visit the Web site of Jordan Hemphill at:

www.jps.net/jordanh

Slow Boat

The **slowboat** folder includes three original songs by David Purcell in pre-release versions. Final release versions of these songs will be included on the upcoming album Slow Boat to San Francisco. The WAV files in this folder can be opened and played in most sound applications. All of this material is copyrighted by David Purcell (1997), so feel free to listen and experiment with these pieces, but be aware that copyright restrictions prevail. Don't duplicate or distribute these songs.

This music doesn't fit into any particular genre, but draws on elements from several different sources. Like the phenomenally successful Women in Technology by White Town, these songs demonstrate how much can be accomplished in a simple home studio with a multitrack recorder and some honest talent. Give a listen and see what you think.

David is also a multimedia developer with a talent for working with Macromedia Director. A sample of his recent work, the quixotic and awe-inspiring Digital Museum, can be viewed at his Web site:

www.sirius.com/purcell/dm.html

Sonic Foundry Sound Forge

Sound Forge, from Sonic Foundry, has been the pre-eminent digital audio application on the PC since its introduction several years ago. The latest version, 4.0, includes a number of features that make it ideally suited to process files for Web applications, including built-in encoders for producing RealAudio files. Demo versions of Sound Forge (both Windows 3.1 and Windows95) are included, as well as three of the most popular plug-ins: the batch converter (for processing groups of sound files), the spectrum analyzer (for viewing the sound characteristics of sound files graphically), and the noise reduction plug-in (for industrial-strength processing of noisy material, such as vinyl records being transferred to digital format). In the **sonic** folder, you'll find four additional folders: Forge.40 (for Sound Forge), Batchcon.40 (for the batch converter), Noisered.40 (the noise-reduction plug-in), and Spectrum.40 (the spectrum analyzer). Each of these folders includes a pair of folders: Win16 for the Windows 3.1 version of the product and X86 for the Windows95 version. Open the folder that is appropriate for your platform (Win16 or X86) and run the Setup program from the **Disk1** folder inside.

The demos are fully functional versions of each product, but they contain restrictions on file saving, cutting and pasting to other applications, and other minor restrictions as described in the readme file included in the folder. Also, in its demo form, Sound Forge can only be run for 15 minutes each session.

 The full collection of tutorial files and other sound-related information can be obtained from the Sonic Foundry Web site:

www.sfoundry.com

Symantec Visual Café

Visual Café by Symantec is a visual design tool that creates Java applets. As discussed in Chapter 6, Visual Café is well equipped to handle the integration of audio content into a Java applet. Besides being a visual design tool, this application also provides a well-designed coding environment that allows seasoned programmers to work on a line-by-line basis or flip back and forth between the graphic and code views. The Windows95 trial version of Visual Café is a fully functioning application that times out 15 days after installation. To install the program, double-click the **vctrial1** icon inside the **symantec** folder on the CD-ROM. Follow the instructions that appear onscreen.

 More information about Symantec products can be obtained from:

www.symantec.com

Voyetra Digital Orchestrator Plus

Voyetra has always excelled at packing a large number of high-end sound-processing features in a moderately priced package. Digital Orchestrator Plus (DOP) is a fine example of a capable, professional quality digital sound application with many cutting-edge features. You can compose and playback both MIDI and digital audio tracks with a wide range of processing effects and editing options available.

To install the Digital Orchestrator Plus demo, open the **Dopdemo** folder and run Setup. Separate installations are performed depending on whether you are running a Windows 3.1 or Windows95 machine. Follow the instructions that appear onscreen to complete the installation. The complete set of video tutorials for the product is included in the **Tutorial** folder to give you the opportunity to evaluate the product features in detail.

 More information on Voyetra Technologies products can be found at:

www.voyetra.com

Macintosh Trial Version Software

The following sections briefly describe each of the software items included on the CD-ROM specifically designed for Macintosh users. We suspect that many Mac users will also have PCs running Windows at home or in the office, so be sure to investigate the software packages and demos included on the Windows portion of the CD-ROM as well.

Beatnik plug-in

Headspace, Inc. has introduced a set of musical tools and an audio engine that promises to revolutionize the use of sound on the Web. The Beatnik browser plug-in includes its own sound synthesizer so that MIDI files played back through it on any platform will sound equivalent, maintaining high quality regardless of the type of sound synthesizer included in the computer.

The Beatnik plug-in uses software synthesis; in other words, your computer's processor does much of the work to converting the music data into sound. This requires a fairly fast processor, which excludes very early Macintosh equipment from the mix. Beatnik, once installed, can play back MIDI, WAV, RMF, and MOD file types. You can create your own RMF files using the Headspace Beatnik editor, available through the Headspace Web site. To install the Beatnik plug-in, you must be using Netscape Navigator version 3.0 or later. The Microsoft Internet Explorer browser will not work with this plug-in since it does not support Netscape's LiveConnect environment.

Double-click the **Beatnik Plug-in Installer.1** icon in the **Beatnik** folder on the CD-ROM. Follow the instructions that appear onscreen.

 More information on Headspace RMF file creation and samples of music and sound effects can be obtained by visiting:

www.headspace.com

Liquid MusicPlayer

The Liquid MusicPlayer, from Liquid Audio, Inc., provides access to files that have been encoded using the Liquid Audio format. This enhanced version of the Dolby Digital encoding scheme offers some of the cleanest compressed music available anywhere on the Web. The Liquid Audio approach also supports a full commerce model for the transfer, sale, and exchange of music files across the Internet. Files are watermarked with copyright information for the protection of musicians and publishers. The encoded file format also includes data about the artist, recording details, copyright information, and the equivalent to digital liner notes. Liquid Audio files have become popular for previewing music clips prior to purchase on sites such as IUMA and Music Blvd.

To install the Liquid MusicPlayer, open the application, Double click to finish install, in the **LAPlayer** Folder on the CD-ROM. This application will walk you through installing the helper application in your browser and setting up your preferences. It will also search the disk for older versions of LA MusicPlayer and ask you to delete them.

Once you've installed the Liquid MusicPlayer, you can sample a number of songs encoded for playback in this format by visiting:

www.liquidaudio.com

Rarefaction demo

The sound library of Rarefaction includes the work of a number of noted sound sculptors; the title may sound pretentious until you listen to their work and realize that the audio emanating from your speakers may have never before existed in nature. Like plutonium, this audio work is the product of human tinkering with simpler base elements. The wonders of digital sound editing become apparent in this edgy, sometimes brilliant collection. The sound clips are sometimes used as samples in MIDI or MOD work or incorporated into multimedia presentations, film, or video works. Noted contributors, such as Thomas Demuzio, Charles Maynes, Gerry Basserman, Snow Cone, Ron MacLeod, and others, have their work represented here.

The Macromedia Director demo includes clips from a number of different CDs, including the well-known *A Poke in the Ear with a Sharp Stick*. The demo file, Rarefaction Demo, appears in the **Rarefaction** folder under **Rf demo**. You can run the Director demo directly from the CD-ROM on a reasonably fast system. If you have difficulty during playback, try copying the **Rarefaction** folder to your hard disk and running the demo from your hard disk drive. The **Sounds** folder contains the audio clips that you can incorporate into your own work.

 For news updates on recent releases from Rarefaction, visit:

www.rarefaction.com

Symantec Visual Café

Visual Café by Symantec is a visual design tool that creates Java applets. As discussed in Chapter 6, Visual Café is well equipped to handle the integration of audio content into a Java applet. Besides being a visual design tool, this application also provides a well-designed coding environment that allows seasoned programmers to work on a line-by-line basis or flip back and forth between the graphic and code views. The trial version of Visual Café is a fully functioning application that times out 30 days after installation.

To install the program, open the **Visual Café** folder inside the **Symantec** folder on the CD-ROM. Double-click the **Visual Café 1.0.1 Trial** icon and follow the instructions that appear onscreen.

 More information about Symantec products can be obtained from:

www.symantec.com

Symantec Visual Page

Visual Page by Symantec is an HTML editor that fully supports WYSIWYG page construction. Working from a library of templates and basic visual components, you can quickly build HTML documents that appear exactly as they will when viewed in a browser. Links can be connected using drag-and-drop techniques. Visual Page also handles the integration of other components on an HTML page, including Java applets, plug-ins, and JavaScripts.

The trial version of Visual Page is a fully functioning application that times out 30 days after installation. To install the program, open the **Visual Page** folder inside the **Symantec** folder on the CD-ROM. Double-click the **Visual Page Trial 1.0.1** icon and follow the instructions that appear onscreen.

 More information about Symantec products can be obtained from:

www.symantec.com

User Assistance and Information

The software accompanying this book is being provided as is without warranty or support of any kind. Should you require basic installation assistance, or if your media is defective, please call our product support number at (212) 850-6194 weekdays between 9 am and 4 pm Eastern Standard Time. Or, we can be reached via e-mail at: wprtusw@wiley.com.

To place additional orders or to request information about other Wiley products, please call (800) 879-4539.

Index

A

<A> tag, 452–453
AC outlets, 118
Acadia Software, 232–235, 243
accessibility, programming for, 344
Acrobat, 59, 191–204
ActiveX controls, 57, 203, 222, 275–276, 312–313, 316–317, 332–334
ADAT (A Alesis Digital Audio Tape), 100, 106, 110
Adobe Systems
    Acrobat, 59, 191–204
    PDF (Portable Document File) format, 48, 58–59, 192–200
Adobe Web site, 204
ADPCM compression standard, 136, 199, 471
AES/EBU (Audio Engineering Society/European Broadcast Union) standard, 108, 111
aftertouch, 35
AGC (Automatic Gain Control), 390, 466
AIFF file format, 19, 192
Aimtech, 236
Albert, Jesse, 421
aleotoric music, 91–92
alias distortion, 120
anchors, 451–453
Ancient Future Web site, 27
Andolini, Michele, 421–422

antique instruments, 66
AOL (America Online), 428–430
<APPLET> tag, 236, 462–463
applets
    creating, in Jamba, 237–243
    sound embedded in, 235–237
<AREA> tag, 458
Arkenstone SSIL Interface, 367–369
arrangements, 43–44, 82–85
Astound, 426
AT&T (American Telephone & Telegraph), 380
attributes (listed by name)
    AUTOSTART attribute, 316
    BGCOLOR attribute, 316
    DELAY attribute, 316
    HEIGHT attribute, 209, 218–219, 328, 352, 354, 358, 456
    HREF attribute, 201, 452–453
    LOOP attribute, 225, 316
    NAME attribute, 231
    NOSAVE attribute, 316
    SRC attribute, 231
    TXTCOLOR attribute, 316
    TYPE attribute, 250
    WIDTH attribute, 209, 218–219, 328, 352, 354, 358, 456
AU file format, 19, 136, 235, 305
Authorware (Macromedia), 215
AUTOPLAY parameter, 121, 122
AutoScore, 78–81
AUTOSTART attribute, 316
AWAVE, 141–142

Using the Software

This software contains files to help you utilize the models described in the accompanying book. By opening the package, you are agreeing to be bound by the following agreement: